Post-Ality
|
Marxism
and
Postmodernism

Post-Ality: Marxism and Postmodernism

edited by
Mas'ud Zavarzadeh
Teresa L. Ebert
Donald Morton

1

Transformation
Marxist Boundary Work in Theory, Economics, Politics, and Culture

Maisonneuve Press, Spring 1995

Post-Ality: Marxism and Postmodernism

© Copyright 1995, Maisonneuve Press
P.O. Box 2980, Washington, DC 20013-2980

All rights reserved. Brief quotations used in articles and reviews are encouraged provided clear acknowledgment to this book is given. For any other reproduction, please contact the publisher.

Maisonneuve Press is a division of the Institute for Advanced Cultural Studies, a non-profit organization devoted to social change through cultural analysis.

Printed in the U.S. by BookCrafters, Fredricksburg, VA.

Library of Congress Cataloging-in-Publication data
Post-Ality: Marxism and postmodernism / edited by Mas'ud Zavarzadeh, Teresa L. Ebert, Donald Morton.
   p. cm. -- (Transformation -- Marxist boundary work in theory, economics, politics, and culture : vol. 1)
       Includes bibliographical references.
       1. Communism. 2. Post-communism. 3. Postmodernism--Social aspects.
       4.Marxist school of sociology. I. Zavarzadeh, Mas'ud, 1938-
       II. Ebert, Teresa L., 1951-   . III. Morton, Donald E. IV. Series.
HX44.5.P67   95-20353
335.43-dc20   CIP

ISBN 0-944624-27-8 quality paperback

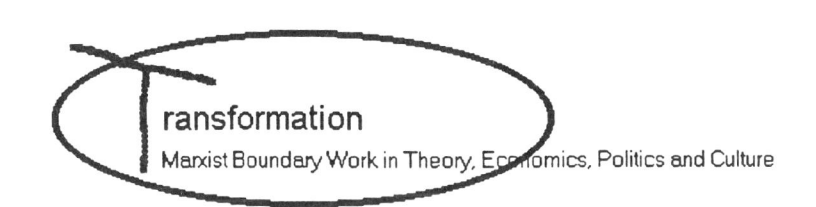

Transformation
Marxist Boundary Work in Theory, Economics, Politics and Culture

1. *Post-Ality: Marxism and Postmodernism*

Post-Ality: The (Dis)Simulations of Cybercapitalism	Mas'ud Zavarzadeh	1
The De(con)struction of Marx's *Capital*	Robert Albritton	76
Wonders Taken for Signs: Homi Bhabha's Postcolonialism	Alex Callinicos	98
(Untimely) Critiques for a *Red Feminism*	Teresa L. Ebert	113
A Marxist Critique of Post-Structuralist Notions of the Subject	Greg Dawes	150
Queerity and Ludic Sado-Masochism: Compulsory Consumption and the Emerging Post-al Queer	Donald Morton	189
The Politics of Hegemony: Democracy, Class, and Social Movements	Alan Sears and Colin Mooers	216
Narrative as Meta-Narrative: Post-Modern Tension and the Effacement of the Political	Colin Hay	243
Labor Theory of Language: Postmodernism and a Marxist Science of Language	Bob Hodge	252
Identity, the Other, and Postmodernism	Jorge Larrain	271
Culture, Identity, Class Struggle: Practical Critique of the Discourse on Post-Marxism	Paul Le Blanc	290
"Left" Journals After the "Post" and the Construction of the Political "Everyday"	Jennifer Cotter	302
Books and Periodicals Received		317
Announcements		319
Notes to Contributors		331
Notes on Contributors		334

On Transformation Now

These are not friendly times for starting a new Marxist journal, and yet these are exactly the times in which a new Marxist journal is urgently needed to provide transformative knowledges for social change. *Transformation: Marxist Boundary Work in Theory, Economics, Politics and Culture* is a response to the crisis of revolutionary theory and praxis. The (post)modern "left" has abandoned the project of revolution in favor of bourgeois democracy, marginalized problems of labor, class and exploitation, and elided the centrality of "need." More to the point, "left" theory has deserted economic and labor issues at a time of increasing class differences between North and South, the poor and the rich the world over, a time when the workers of the world are increasingly subjected to exploitation by ever more innovative technologies and subtle forms of management to keep the rate of profit high for transnational cartels.

Transformation is a biquarterly of historical materialist analyses of international modern and (post)modern economic, political and cultural practices, their history and consequences. The goal of *Transformation* is to produce effective knowledges for understanding the world in order to change it.

There are, of course, many journals publishing texts on the contemporary situation from neo-marxist, postmarxist, social democratic, feminist, postcolonialist, anti-racist, lesbigay, and ecological perspectives. The underlying assumption of most "left" readings of the world is that capitalism itself has changed from a society of "production" to a culture of "consumption," that "labor" has been displaced by "knowledge," and that we have entered a moment in history which is post-class, post-production, post-theory, post-ideology and post-dialectical—in short a "post-al" phase. The post-al, has, in effect, put an end to politics based on "need," "class struggle," "use-value," "collectivity" and the fight against "exploitation," and, in its place, has instituted a politics based on "desire," "difference," "conversation," "consensus," and "coalition." In post-al left journals, social analysis is shifted from the political economy of material practices to cultural politics and poetics, and from the laws of motion of capital to the problematics of representation and (deconstructed) "identity politics." Materiality in the post-al left is not the materiality of class struggle, the mode of production, and "need"—the structure of contradictions and antagonisms in history. Rather, it is the "matterism" of the "body," "language" and "desire."

In opposition to this post-al cultural matterism and its ludic politics" of difference, *Transformation* deploys classical Marxist theory to provide boundary explanations of contemporary capitalism-without-borders and the world order it has legitimated. By boundary work, we mean producing historical materialist analyses that directly engage the most advanced modes of bourgeois knowledges and supersede them. It places classical Marxist theory in new terrains and brings it to bear on the understanding of the emerging contradictions in post-al societies from labor relations to sexuality; from markets to the cyberspaces of virtual reality, from healthcare to "crime" and "family values," from post-al forms of racism to hypercolonialism, and "welfare. . . ."

Transformation is a dynamic biquarterly committed to constantly bringing classical Marxist theories into zones in which they have not often been situated before. At the moment, some classical Marxist writers, in their encounter with new post-al discourses, seem to think that they have offered a helpful critique when, for instance, they denounce bourgeois theory and science for their opaque, elitist language and mystifying "jargon," or when they substitute moral outrage for an explanatory critique of the ethics of "difference," simply dismissing it as narcissistic and decadent. *Transformation* will go beyond such commonsense criticism and, in the tradition of Marx, Engels, Lenin, Luxemburg, Trotsky and other classical Marxist theorists, will not turn away from the "new" and the "post-al." It will confront and historicize them in order to develop class consciousness for transformative praxis.

Transformation is a vanguard journal opposing both nostalgia and utopia and insisting on developing rigorous materialist boundary understandings of post-al social totality—the boundary analyses, in short, that are necessary for a sustained intervention by revolutionary praxis in ending private ownership of the means of production and establishing international socialism. The agent of this historical change is not the singular individual—who spontaneously rebels against the regime of wage labor and capital through the sheer experience of the intensity of exploitation—but is instead the individual as part of a collectivity of workers: what Lenin calls workers as "socialist theorists" whose revolutionary praxis is founded upon a coherent historical materialist theory of the social relations of production and the international division of labor.

We are, of course, aware that the specific political conditions of the post-al moment put our goal to make *Transformation* the site of active classical Marxist knowledges beyond our immediate reach. Classical Marxism has been so violently and systematically excluded from the scene of social struggle and analysis that it will take some time for *Transformation* to become a place for living revolutionary Marxism. But *Transformation* will energetically work towards this goal by activating classical Marxist knowledges among already practicing Marxists and, perhaps more importantly, among younger Marxists, both of whom are forced into silence because their work is marked in the bourgeois knowledge industry as, among other things, "dogmatic" and thus dismissed.

To change these unequal conditions, *Transformation* will provide a place for the articulation of lost and suppressed revolutionary knowledges and praxis. Thus we will publish only those texts that advance classical Marxist theory (or significantly move in this direction). We believe that under unequal conditions (that allow anti-Marxist texts a free reign but impose all sorts of constraints and restrictions on Marxist writings) to provide "equal" space for the texts of right-wing writers or practitioners of the generic left, in the name of an open debate and discussion, is not an open debate but rather a travesty of free inquiry. The dominant bourgeois knowledge industry has, throughout the 20th century, successfully forced radical thinkers and workers into compromise, either by seducing them with the false prospect of an "open debate" or by accusing them of being undemocratic and authoritarian if they do not give equal space to their opponents (who use that space to suppress them). In a society that has been anything but open to revolutionary knowledges and practices, such arguments are aimed simply at further restricting and appropriating the limited space available for radical praxis. The entire knowledge industry, under the regime of wage-labor and capital, is freely available to the opponents of Marxism. Witness the way Derrida's *Specters of Marx*—to take a recent case—is not only a "best seller" but excerpted in the bourgeois new left reviews. To give space to Derrida and other post-al left writers, in the name of open debate, is to fall for the liberal myths of equal and free debate when that formal openness is severely restricted by the actual unequal economic and material resources available to the two sides of the debate. To give room, then, in the pages of *Transformation*, to the opponents of classical Marxism is to further expand the space already abundantly available to them in all sites of culture—from the ludic academy and post-al left journals to right-wing publishing houses and communications, radio and television cartels. One of the projects of *Transformation* is to demystify the deceptive liberal theology of ecumenicism and coalition and to open up a space for emancipatory praxis and knowledges. Since *Transformation* is in contestation with the entire bourgeois knowledge industry, the space of this debate should be understood globally and not locally: those who wish to criticize our praxis can easily do so in the pages of practically all publications of the left and right.

Dorothy Healey on theory—

My concept of what it meant to be a revolutionary was based on a montage of the organizers from the Sinclair novels, along with my childhood memories from Denver. I also began to read an enormous amount of history around this time. I was very taken with Charles Beard—at that point his writing seemed to me to represent great Marxist truths because he talked about the things that high school history never talked about, the underlying economic motives of history makers. I read everything he and his wife Mary Beard wrote. I had started reading Marx and Lenin, but at that point I think Walt Whitman and Henry David Thoreau had more effect on me. What I responded to in my readings were emotional rather than theoretical questions. I was developing a hatred of the brutality of the existing economic system, a hatred of the impersonal degradation of human beings. That's what moved me as a teenager, and stayed with me. . . .

It was action, not theory, that entranced me. I think I was very typical of young and even not-so-young Communists in my attitude. Offhand I would guess that the great majority of Communists, maybe 60 to 70 percent of the Party, never got around to reading much of Marx and Lenin. The Trotskyists were so good at theoretical debates because they had more time to read; they weren't doing the level of activity that we were. When I did get around to reading Lenin later in the 1930s, I read him strictly from my interest in history as history. I wasn't at all interested in nor did I understand the theoretical questions that were involved. It wasn't until the birth of my son in the 1940s, when I was at home for a time, that I reread Marx and Lenin, and the power of their ideas finally hit me. Then theory became exciting. . . .

There was, as I've noted, a lack of genuine theoretical understanding in the Party, for all our talk about theory. We were so busy with day-to-day organizing that we could rarely consider the larger questions facing our movement; in the midst of the Party crisis in 1956 the charge that was made over and over again was that we had been deliberately kept so busy that nobody had time to think. Whether it was deliberate policy or not, it was certainly true that the Party lacked the kind of internal political structures that might have encouraged us to ask substantive questions about the meaning of our own experience. That led to the enshrining of the Party leadership, contributing to their aura of infallibility, and making the likelihood of anyone's challenging what came from them negligible. The fact that by the mid-1930s the international leaders of the Communist movement were advocating changes that made sense in practical terms for American domestic politics only enhanced their authority among us and increased the likelihood that in the future we would continue to accept their leadership even when they were wrong, as was all too often the case. . . .

—*Dorothy Healy Remembers* (New York: Routledge, 1993)

Mas'ud Zavarzadeh

Post-Ality
The (Dis)Simulations of Cybercapitalism

To Terri—City, Critique

Book One[1]

"The Stupidity that Consumption is Just as Productive as Production."
—Marx, *Theories of Surplus-Value*

"I used to think there were only two choices: telling the truth and lying. And now I have found this huge, fantastic gray area. . . ."
—"Coach" (ABC Television)

One

Post-ality is the ensemble of all practices that, as a totality, obscure the production practices of capitalism—which is based on the extraction of surplus labor (the source of accumulation of capital)—by announcing the arrival of a new society which is post-production, post-labor, post-ideology, post-white and post-capitalist. Post-ality, in other words, is a regime of class struggle against the workers that posits a structural change, a rupture, in capitalism: one that severs the past of capitalism from what is regards to be its radically different and "new" present (which unlike its past is now free from exploitation). In doing so, post-ality attempts to solve—in the theoretical imaginary—the historical and material contradictions of capitalism caused by the social division of labor. There is therefore a great urgency among the ideologists of the ruling class to discredit any effort to theorize post-ality (as I am doing here) because such theorization produces knowledge of contemporary capitalism and the strategies that are used to justify it. This discrediting of theories about post-ality takes many forms—as might be expected in the capitalist knowledge industry in which theorists compete for a living with each other in meeting the needs of the agents of capital for ever newer concepts. The most popular form now of deconstructing "totality" (in order to obscure the working of capitalism) is one that questions the very possibility of any "totality" by pointing to the epistemological aporias of the theory of concepts (concept = totality). The strategy, in other words, is to dismantle the frames of intelligibility that make the articulation of such "totalities" as post-ality (and what it justifies, namely "capitalism") possible.

"Totality" is ostensibly put in question, by such theorists of the ruling class as Derrida and deMan, on epistemological grounds. According to them, all concepts are effects of tropes (Paul deMan, *Allegories of Reading* 144-47), and as such, they are language constructs. Moreover, since language is a "field . . . of *play*" (*Writing and Difference* 289, emphasis in the original), all concepts are said to be simply unstable, differential networks of "infinite substitutions" of signs and not an articulation of the real. Thus, there is always "something missing" from concepts— the something that "excludes totalization" (*Writing and Difference* 289). However, these ludic arguments about the playfulness that deprives the concept of its truth ("totality"), exclude themselves from the laws of play and place their own truth (totalizing against totalizing) beyond the differential volatility of substitutions. These ludic theories also forget that play is always a movement of parts within a structure of conflicts and contradictions and these contradictions are effects of class difference and class antagonisms. (This is the line of argument that I will follow throughout my text since I am not interested in simply performing reflexive and deconstructive readings that bring down an argument by putting its founding threads in question.) Thus the very playfulness of play (making sense of playfulness) is a historical effect whose meaning is determined by the social relations of production. What is received as the playfulness of the trope—a lively metaphor— in, for example, Rousseau's *Discourse on the Origins and the Foundations of Inequality among Men* (1754) is a "dead metaphor" in the discourses of Euroamerican Depression (1930's). This historicity of the "playfulness" (its non-self-evidence) necessitates that DeMan and other readers constantly annotate Rousseau's "dead metaphors" to give them "life" and make the "playfulness" of their "play" receivable by readers situated in an entirely different historical situation and material conditions. If metaphors in and of themselves were playful (that is if language was autonomous), there would be no need for annotation. The fact that there is such a need and furthermore that there are fierce contestations over what kind of annotations are appropriate is itself part of the logic of interpretation which is determined by the historical level of class struggle. If "language is about language" as deMan argues (153), the playfulness of the trope should be immanent; an always already of the language confronting itself as a result of the transocial laws of signification. But as deMan's annotation of Rousseau shows, playfulness in a text has to be marked and the marking varies from one period to period another according to the level of class struggle—the struggle, in short, over what is seen to be the "legitimate" ratio of surplus labor. The marking of a text, then, is always class struggle carried on in the tropics of language. DeMan's notion that "all language is about language" (153) is not only a "totalization" but also a part of a class theory of language that posits language as a closed arrangement of signs and reduces all social differences that mobilize signs as interior semiotic differences ("difference within") in which language "confronts itself" and escapes history. However, the totalizations of the ruling class, as I will discuss throughout this essay, are never seen as "totalizations" but as the transhistorical truth of life itself.

The epistemological questioning of "totality," which serves as the basis for rejecting post-ality as a concept, is an ideological alibi to dismantle the theoretical foundation of a coherent knowledge of capitalism as a "totality"—that is, as a systematic and complex set of interconnected economic, cultural, political and theoretical practices. Derrida's idea of *différance* (the founding concept of detotalizing) informs the entire project of postmarxism in which the very notion of society as a totality is decentered and in place of a collective subject of revolution is placed the decentralized, detotalized and differential "hegemony" of a loose coalition. This "war on totality" (Lyotard, *The Postmodern Condition* 82), thus, is not limited to poststructuralist writers but increasingly becomes the project of a generalized "left." For instance, following the announcement that the first issue of *Transformation* would focus on the question of the "Post-al," one "left" writer responded, in a letter to me, with a troping discrediting of the concept, saying that the "Post" meant "mail" and concluded that "hence 'hyper-post-ality'=(?) too many stamps on the envelope, 'post-al (flexi)workplace'=all-night sorting office?" One is hard-pressed to find a difference between the leftist discrediting of concepts and the poststructuralist deconstruction—both marginalize the concepts necessary to grasp capitalism as a totality (the laws of motion of capital). The institutionalized "left" is equally invested in the erasure of concepts and the dispersion of the social totality into an ensemble of the heterogeneous and incommensurate experiences of "agents" in "social movements." When the "rigorous" arguments of the philosopher on behalf of capital fails, the State jokester takes over and defends the rule of wage-labor through "phrases" and "puns"—although in the "witty" writings of such pun(k)sters as Lacan, Derrida, Butler, Ulmer . . . the epistemological and the joke are sutured into the post-al paralogy.

Similiarly Daniel Bell, who draws upon the traditional sociological protocols and research programs, opposes "totality" as vociferously, in his positivist idiom, as Derrida, Lyotard and postmarxists. Moreover, the pop theorists of cybercapitalism, Alvin Toffler and Heidi Toffler, have reproduced and widely disseminated the theories of *différance* in such books as *The Future Shock, The Third Wave, Powershift, Creating a New Civilization*, and through their popular pedagogy of congeniality and anecdotes—especially influencing the corporate elite, their petit bourgeois allies and the Republican Party apparatchiks (whose main function has historically been to build an alliance between the ruling class and petit bourgeoisie by suturing their conflicting economic interests through stabilizing cultural values). In other words, *différance* not only underlies the postmarxist notion of "radical democracy" put forth by Laclau and Mouffe in their adaptation of Derridean deconstruction (and popularized in the knowledge industry by Stanley Aronowitz), but it is also the founding concept of the new aggressive cult of the individual and entrepreneurship that marks both the new "wave" (to use Toffler's metaphor for historical change) conservativism of the 1990's and the rejection of representative democracy by the Tofflers, who would like to replace it with a more or less direct self-representational electronic democracy. The Tofflers' notion that representational democracy is the residue of the Enlightenment and cannot serve the "Third Wave" civil society (*Powershift* 235-360) is rooted in the same philosophical/ideological theories of the sign that has led such ludic theories as Gilles Deleuze and Michel Foucault (in their own rhizomatic versions of *différance*) to denounce the possibility of any representation and instead advocate self-representation. No one, according to this end-of-representation theory, can speak for the other (Foucault, *Language, Counter-Memory, Practice* 206)—each must speak for him or herself. This post-al representation is the informing principle of both the Foucault-Laclau-Mouffe notion of radical democracy and the Tofflers' idea of direct democracy based on the electronic plebiscite. Deleuze and Guattari's rhizomatic democracy of *différance* is the same as the Tofflers' electronic activism (*Powershift* 356-358): both are "rooted" in a post-majoritarian hegemonic democracy of pulsations and lines of flights and "traces" of individual energies.

Electronic activism provides the ideological effects needed by cybercapitalism because it substitutes direct, experiential, affective democracy for a rational critique-al democracy: it is politics without concepts. The rejection of critique (shared by the left postmodernists such as Fredric Jameson and right-wing Third Wavists like Newt Gingrich) serves the purpose of this post-al plebiscitary democracy of direct "reactions." Far from being a "radical" and avant-garde view that definitely marks the "outdatedness" of collectivity, the "war on totality," is the dominant ideology of cybercapitalism in its war against the working class—the collective subject of labor and revolution; the builder of democratic centralism. The anti-totality *différance*, in short, which grounds the political theories of Derrida, Lyotard, Laclau, Mouffe . . . Tofflers, is the theory of decentralization, privatization and devolution of any collectivity that attempts to provide for the common "needs"—putting in its place the self-articulating "desires" of those whose needs have already been met through class exploitation. There is, thus, a direct connection between the notion of hegemonic coalition and electronic plebiscitary democracy; between Ernesto Laclau and Newt Gingrich in their attempts to render the economic interests of an old ruling class as the radically new interests of an emerging cyber civil society.

Situated between the conservative theorists (Bell, the Tofflers) and the ludic left (Derrida, Lyotard, Laclau) in this unified war of the ruling class against totality, are such neo-humanist writers as Edward Said. Writing approvingly of Said's rejection of totalization, for example, one advocate of the post-al common sense, Bruce Robbins writes, "Unlike most Marxists, [Said] has never found much use for "capitalism" as an explanatory term (*Secular Vocations* 166). The reason for Said's resistance, according to Robbins, is that such a use of "capitalism" (or other concepts) "threatens to leave insufficient room for assertion of human will" (166). Behind the facade of difference of all these seemingly diverse theoretical positions, there is a rigid singularity of purpose: to occlude the understanding of the regime of wage-labor and capital in its totality and thus enable transformative practices to change it. As Marx and Engels argue: "the ideas of the ruling class are in every epoch the ruling ideas" (*The German Ideology* 59). Different philosophical idioms (Bell's positivism; Derrida's poststructuralism; Said's pragmatic New humanism), in this, as in all contestations, are simply discursive forms that the ruling ideas take in their local articulations as addressed to different class fractions. Bell's rejection of a totality such as "capitalism" on the ground that capitalism is not "monolithic" (XX) and Derrida's objection to "totality" are both informed by the ruling concept of "difference"—the excessive, rich and plural local diversities. Behind the resistance to totality in the name of *différance*—by the traditional, the postmodern and the positions between— however, is an attempt to make it impossible to draw a line of demarcation between the exploited and the exploited and thereby turn the social into a series of (semi-)autonomous differences that cannot be conceptualized but must be described in their own local terms. According to these arguments, with some variations in their idioms, all concepts are violations of *différance* (whether *différance* is seen in terms of "textuality" or the sheer excessive *différance* of "experience" and the surprising and unexplainable human "agency"). In other words, concepts themselves are self-divided and unable to provide a coherent knowledge ("truth") of a totality such as "capitalism." "Capitalism" as a totality, according to these theories, is far from being a systematic set of practices; it is an ensemble of unceasing *différances*: so much so that the "exploited" and the "exploiter" are both self-divided and there are more differences "within" each than "between" the two. What is called "capitalism" then emerges from these theories of *différance*, as a set of autonomous practices without any necessary relations to one another. Bell thinks that local differences are so intense that the use of "capitalism" as a coherent concept simply distorts the dynamics of the social because no such concept can "explain the complex structure" of a society (Bell, xx).

The ruling ideas, are always "nothing more," as Marx and Engels argue, "than the ideal expression of the dominant material relations, the dominant material relations grasped as ideas" (*The German Ideology* 59), and, as such, they too, like those material relations, are fraught with contradictions. To be precise, post-al theorists—whether assuming an avant-garde posture (Derrida, Lyotard) or defending the complexity of traditional philosophical thought (Bell) or a pragmatic middle-ground (Said)—announce the emergence of a new society such as "postmodern," "postindustrial" or "post-Fordist" which is discontinuous with the past and, as such, not the outcome of exploitation in the accumulation of capital. But at the very time that they propose a present not explainable in reference to the past and also a future which is equally "excessive" and aleatory and thus beyond the laws of motion of capital, they formally oppose the very concept of discontinuity ("post-ality") on the ground that it is the totalization of an "outside" and as such, like all "totalities," constituted by the laws of *différance* that exceed the "inside" and "outside."

Post-ality is thus "formally" the social theory that posits *différance* and play as the dynamics of history and argues for the impossibility of the social as an objective and noncontingent totality (Laclau, "Building a New Left" 15-16). Or, as writers such as Paul Hirst put it, the social is a fractured totality of (semi-)autonomous practices. Hirst's argument moves by specifically decoupling the social and the economic by means of "flexible specialization." "Flexible specialization," unlike "mass production" (which is the synecdoche of classical capitalism here) is a technological mode in which a "range of specialized goods for particular and changing markets" are produced by "using flexible general-purpose machinery and predominantly skilled labor" ("After Henry" 323). What is theoretically and politically important in Hirst's proposal is that, as he puts it, "Flexible specialization can be developed in many social contexts" (324) and that, therefore, there is a discontinuity between the "economic" and the "cultural." Hirst, in other words, makes sure that "no attempt is made to directly derive or deduce wider social and political consequences from a particular type of production technique" (323). The double-structure at work here needs to be (once more) pointed out: "The complex structure" of society which Bell refers to, or the "uncertainty" that Hirst regards to be the mark of "flexibility" do not prevent these and other post-al theorists from using the concept, for example, of "post-industrial" as a coherent (self-identical) and thus "monolithical" concept to describe a new mutation in advanced industrial democracies or from being "certain" that "flexible specialization" is a coherent concept that is effective in the "development of new policies" (328). Complexity, difference, and uncertainty, in other words, have not in any way deterred post-al theory from totalizing contemporary societies as postindustrial, post-Fordist and postcapitalist. The reason given for the injunction against the use of "capitalism" as a coherent concept—as is often the case in post-al theories—is not really epistemological but ideological. The move to deny the possibility of a coherent "concept" that enables knowledge of "totality" is not so much against "totalizing"—post-al theories routinely totalize—but against *historical materialist totalizing*.

The resistance against "capitalism" as a totality is a resistance against the materialist theory of capitalism that foregrounds the laws of motion of capital and places "production" as the central organizing practice in human societies, their institutions and subjectivities. "People won freedom," Marx and Engels write in *The German Ideology* "for themselves each time to the extent that was dictated and permitted not by their ideal of man, but by the existing productive forces" (431). Post-al theory is a utopian theory of entrepreneurial individuality and agency—the "ideal of man"—a voluntarism unburdened by history. "We are," Baudrillard writes in rejecting Marxism, "at the end of production" (*Selected Writings* 128) and moving away from a "capitalist-productivist society to a neo capitalist cybernetic order" (*Simulations* 111) which is nothing short of a historical "mutation." In contrast, positing "production" as a series of determining practices, lays bare the relations of exploitation that underwrite capitalism. Post-ality, however, affirms capitalism by undercutting any causal understanding that might lead to establishing determinate relations between the well-fare of the few and the misery of the many. Again, epistemology is deployed to achieve an ideological goal. Thus Bell, following Karl Popper (*The Poverty of Historicism*), insists that there are "no 'laws of social development'" (Bell xii). Societies move, according to post-al theories, not by inexorable laws but by movements of "desire" which are always aleatory and un-law-full: desire exceeds any law that attempts to explain its surprising movements. Desire shapes two main practices that post-al theories regard to be formative of the mutation of industrialism into post-industrialism: "science" (and its various applications as technology) and "consumption."

Popper argues that human societies do not change by any determinate laws (of production, for example) but by the growth of knowledge. Science, for him, for Lyotard, and other idealist theorists, however, is a form of writing (what Lyotard calls "discourse," *The Postmodern Condition: A Report on Knowledge* 3), and, as such, it is essentially an aesthetic practice motivated by the scientists non-instrumental desire for playfulness and beauty (knowledge for its own sake). In post-al theories transformative science is not "normal" science; it is not an objective inquiry but the but the bold expressions of a heretic scientist whose statements are akin to the non-referential statements of religion, art and literature. There is, for example, no means of traditional "verification" (the test of objective referentiality) for the bold statements of "superstring theory." In the post-al theories of science, the difference between science and writing is regarded to be a modernist one, and, consequently, the lines of demarcation between Heidegger and Heisenberg disappear (Plotnitsky, *Complementarity: Anti-Epistemology after Bohr and Derrida*; David Lindley, *The End of Physics: The Myth of a Unified Theory*).

The anti-productionist and desire-al argument—whether it is advanced by the cultural "right" (Daniel Bell, Francis Fukuyama) or left (Jean-François Lyotard, Jean Baudrillard)—regards post-al societies to be essentially "knowledge societies" (Bell 212, Lyotard, *Postmodern Condition* 3, Baudrillard, *Simulations* 103-152). This, among other things, means that knowledge as "discourse" (Lyotard, *Postmodern Condition* 3) or what Bell calls "theoretical knowledge" is not only the manifestation of prodigal "playfulness" (knowledge confronting itself) but in its formalized articulation—what Bell in his more traditional wording defines as "a set of organized statements of facts or ideas, presenting a reasoned judgment" (175)— it provides the basis of "technology" and is therefore the source of wealth of postindustrial societies. "The games of scientific language become the games of the rich . . . no technology without wealth, but no wealth without technology" (*Postmodern Condition* 45). According to the post-al theorists "labor," in advanced industrial "democracies," is superseded by "knowledge," which is now, more than ever before, the source of "surplus value" (Lyotard, *Postmodern Condition* 45). In the post-al moment, according to these theories, it is "knowledge" and not "labor" that generates capital. "The weight" of post-industrial society, which is "measured by a larger proportion of Gross National Product and a larger share of employment," Bell insists "is increasingly in the field of knowledge" (212). A New Age version of this theory of post-ality ("Soft and weak overcome hard and strong"—*Tao Te Ching*, 36) is put forth by Geoff Mulgan, who, in "The Power of the Weak," argues that the "weak power" of computers and other information devices (mental work) has replaced the "strong power" of the industrial regime. Post-ality is, for him, the triumph of "weak" structures over "strong" ones. One of the implications of the displacement of "labor" by "knowledge" is that in post-al societies, the bipolar structure of class is forever deconstructed by the emergence of the "knowledge class" (Bell 213)—knowledge workers (managers) as well as such other new "classes" as "contingent workers."

I will discuss this deconstruction of "class" later, but here I would like to observe that the very theorists, who denounce historical materialism as deterministic, deploy, in their own articulations of postindustrial society, the most narrow and parochial forms of technological determinism to announce the arrival of a post-al society. And this is the case whether one reads the writings of Bell or Baudrillard (to take the two extremes). The only difference between the two is the local site of their inquiry: Bell focuses on the socio-economic while Baudrillard on the socio-cultural. Bell concludes that technology has transformed capitalism as a social and economic system while Baudrillard regards the entire cultural zone to have been reconstituted by technology and argues that the post-al "real" is itself the direct effect of information technology and cyber practices, as well as their concrete articulation in the media: in postindustrial society the real itself is a simulation; a hyper (post-al) real. "[A]ll of Los Angeles and the America surrounding it are no longer real, but of the order of the hyperreal and simulation. It is no longer a question of a false representation of reality (ideology), but of concealing the fact that the real is no longer real, and thus of the saving of the reality principle" (*Selected Writings* 172). The post-al real, to be more precise, is an "operational" reality: the product of "combinatory models" (167) "information theory and cybernetics" (*Mirror* 122) and not political economy. The assumption that simulation is itself arbitrary and unstable and outside the realm of real/false in no way changes the technological determinism by which Baudrillard arrives at his conclusion. Bell is quite aware that his argument against what he assumes to be determinism (of labor) in historical materialism (49-119) is itself underwritten by what is another form of determinism (by machines). Thus he writes quite defensively that his theory of a postindustrial society is not only not totalizing but "implies no specific determinism between a 'base' and a 'superstructure'; on the contrary, the initiative in organizing a society these days comes largely from the political system" (119). Not only does he not offer any evidence that his theory is not a form of technological determinism but in this part of the book he actually accepts yet another form of determinism: this time the determination of the economic (base) by politics (superstructure).

To posit the source of wealth in post-al societies as "knowledge" rather than "labor" and the source of reality as "images" produced through new configurations of knowledges (cyber-information) means that scattered hegemonies and post-class negotiations—not class struggle—are seen as the source of social change in these societies. Revolution is dead: capitalism is emancipated from labor. However, Bell, Lyotard and other theorists are able to put forth "knowledge"/"information" as the source of wealth only by means of a violent idealism that represses the material conditions of the production of knowledge/information. They see the "images" on TV's and VCR's; listen to the music on the latest CD's, and conclude that the real is being transformed by mediated information. But they bracket the historical fact that these images are constructed and then transmitted by material means (TV sets, VCR players, CD players, cables, satellite dishes . . .) "produced" by the "labor" of workers—the source of whose labor power has in turn been produced by labor. They take the "theoretical" knowledge constructed in laboratories but bracket the material conditions of production of these knowledges: not only are the very instruments of experimentation (which lead to theoretical formulations) "produced" by "labor" but the conditions of possibility of the "experiment" itself (as a science event) are provided by the labor of generations of workers. The buildings in which scientists undertake their work are constructed by "labor"; their food, clothes, cars, telephones, computers . . . are all "produced" by labor.

This bourgeois anti-labor argument is merely a post-alization of the old capitalist argument that it is the ingenuity of the entrepreneur (the creative play of the mind) and not the labor of the proletariat that is the source of wealth. Like the post-al argument for postindustrial society, in this traditional idealist pro-capitalist argument, technology (the machine) plays a prominent role. To this old argument, one has to offer Ernest Mandel's classic counter-argument, what he calls, the "analytical proof" of the labor theory of value (*An Introduction to Marxist Economic Theory* 25-28). He begins by breaking down the price of a commodity into its constituent elements and demonstrates that by carrying this analysis far enough it will become clear that in commodities "only labor will be found" (25):

> If we start by breaking down the average manufacturing cost of commodities into 40% for wages, 20% surplus-value, 30% for raw materials and 10% in fixed capital; and if we assume that 60% of the cost of raw materials can be reduced to labor, then we already have 78% of the total cost reduced to labor. The rest of the cost of raw materials breaks down into the cost of other raw materials reducible in turn to 60% labor—plus the cost of amortizing machinery.
>
> The price of machinery consists to a large degree of labor (for example, 40%) and raw materials (for example 40% also). The share of labor in the average cost of all commodities thus passes successively to 83%, 87%, 89% etc. It is obvious that the further this breakdown is carried, the more the entire cost tends to be reduced to labor, and to labor alone (25-26).

Other arguments based on historical evidence and refuting the claim of post-al theories, in part, on the basis of relying on contemporary statistics, are offered by Alex Callinicos (*Against Postmodernism: A Marxist Critique*) and by David Harvey (*The Condition of Postmodernity*).

Two

Theories of postindustrial society are not only popular in the post-al academy, but also in the popular culture and populist right-wing politics. The writings of such "futurists" as Alvin Toffler have played a significant role in making post-ality part of the popular common sense. In his *Powershift: Knowledge, Wealth and Violence at the Edge of the 21st Century*, for instance, Toffler ridicules theories of production as "material-ismo" (67-80) and marginalizes the role of forces of "production" by writing that "It is knowledge that drives the economy, not the economy that drives knowledge" (413). Both the academic theorists and the pop futurists, of course, theorize knowledge in the tradition of idealist philosophers of the ruling class, for whom "ideas" simply "invent" themselves and emerge from the genius of the scientist. Such idealist theories violently conceal the fact that what is called "knowledge" is itself what Marx calls "dead labor": knowledge, beyond elementary practical everyday problem solving, becomes possible only through the concealed labor of the other—that is, when the social division of labor frees some workers to engage in theoretical analysis. Populist right-wing politicians such as Newt Gingrich have deployed post-ality as a new frame for conceptualizing capitalism, in the 21st century, in the apocalyptic tones so familiar in conservative politics—which is always caught in the contradictions of "cultural conservatism" (holding on to the authority of values that normalize the privileges of the ruling class) and "economic futurism" (breaking new ground in finding innovative ways of increasing the rate of profit). Gingrich uses a semiotics of numbers (a new mode of numerology) to announce the arrival of a post-al moment. In his *Window of Opportunity: A Blueprint for the Future* (written with Marianne Gingrich and David Drake), he states "A year which ends in three zeroes is a rare thing indeed" and continues to say that "As the year 2000 approaches, more and more people will notice that they are about to celebrate something which no ancestor for nearly thirty generations saw" (125).

The most effective arguments against "production" have been made not by scientists or social scientists but by cultural theorists who draw, broadly speaking, upon poststructuralist and psychoanalytical theories to argue for the priority of "consumption" over "production" in terms of personal identity by deploying the notion of "desire." There is of course, as might be expected, a point of convergence between conservative, right-wing politicians and avant-garde philosophers of desire. For Gingrich and other populist theorists, the post-al era—what Toffler calls the "third wave"—acts on the course of history through such devices as computers, fax machines, the space program. . . . Thus, according to Toffler, "the appearance of the computer and new communications media in the mid 20th century smashed Moscow's control" (Toffler, *Powershift* 405) and expanded free-market democracy. The high-tech economy, in Gingrich's view, increases the freedom of the individual and his business opportunity:

> Every American will have a cellular phone, which will probably be a fax, which will probably be a modem, which will probably in some way tie them into the world—whether they want it or not, frankly, every American will be competing in the world market with Germany and China and Japan." (*The New York Times*, December 11, 1994, 4-1)

Post-ality is, for the right-wing, a cybermarket whose flexibility and ever-expanding frontiers defy all regulations—it is a space of unbounded entrepreneurial zones. The post-al theorists of desire also place the individual in a de-regulated space: a site in which no laws can adequately explain or regulate its aleatory shifts and movements. However, they do so by deploying the agency of desire; individuals are seen as free because their practices are motivated not by "reason" and the laws of rationality but by the surprising and unrepresentable substitutions and jolts of desire which defy all laws of reason and modes of explanation. The unmappable trajectories of desire especially articulate themselves in the individual's "consumption"—consumption which is not simply for meeting basic needs but for "pleasure," for stating one's freedom.

To recapitulate, the ostensible basis for the shift from production to consumption in post-al theory is that "Because it reduces the need for raw materials, labor and time, space and capital, knowledge becomes the central resource of the advanced economy" (Toffler, *Powershift* 88). The advanced, symbolic economy, in turn, creates such socio-cultural complexities that no relation of necessity ("determination") holds any longer among the highly layered political, cultural and theoretical practices. Each practice in the social formation is (semi-)autonomous and thus not subject to the laws of an "outside," such as the "labor theory of value." In this post-al situation, the individual is the site of the free play of desire: the alea, contingency, and *différance* annul the laws of motion of labor, and "consumption" becomes the unique expression of subjectivity as an ever moving, indeterminate and shifting frontier. In short, the dogma is that "The Fordist era of mass-production workers and mass consumers confirmed the sense that individual interests could be read off with some confidence from the social blocs formed by production" (Leadbeater 139). In contrast to the Fordist regime in which a "social bloc" (a code for "class" constructed in the social relations of "production") could determine subjectivity, the post-al scene of the social defies such laws of determination of class and production. Consequently, in the post-al society, "the theatre of consumption has become more important. Choice in consumption, lifestyle, sexuality is more important as an assertion of identity. The dynamics of most people's lives is where they can assert their difference from others" (140).

The anti-productionist theories (putting aside the pop post-ality of Toffler and Gingrich) have a wide theoretical and political range—from the postmarxist ("New Times") views of Leadbeater, Aronowitz and ludic feminists, and queer theorists to the speculative philosophical writings of Georges Bataille on "general economy." In this essay, however, I will focus on the writings of Baudrillard since I have discussed in great length these other theories especially the work of Georges Bataille and the role of his notion of "general economy" in the consumptionist theories of post-ality (*Theory and Its Other*). I begin with Baudrillard's violent erasure of what he calls (in *The Mirror of Production*) the "spectre of production." "Today," Baudrillard elaborates in his other texts, "we are surrounded by the remarkable conspicuousness of consumption and affluence," and he regards the emergence of "consumption" to be "a fundamental mutation in the ecology of human species" (*Selected Writings* 29). Since my focus in this text is on the theoretical issues rather than historical analysis, I will simply note that Baudrillard's notion that a "consumer society" emerged "today" is a capitalist story and an ahistorical fantasy. The pioneering writings of Neil Kendrick, John Brewer, and J. H. Plumb (*The Birth of Consumer Society: The Commercialization of Eighteenth-Century England*) as well as the histories of consumption and consumerism that have been brought out since the publication of their work in 1982, have clearly demonstrated—in spite of their historical and theoretical limits—that consumer society is closely tied to the rise of capitalism and the regime of profit: the hegemony of exchange value. Baudrillard's "consumption" is a totalizing concept and not identical with the traditional functional consumption of, for example, food for survival. Rather it is a post-al consumption which is an end in itself, an articulation of an "identity" and an "individuality" that he believes is an expression of those deeper human needs such as giving and receiving: not in a causal and exchange circuit but giving without expecting to receive—that is, for its own sake (pleasure), prodigality and destruction. His notion of "destruction" as an original human need is a conceptual condensation of the conservative views of Bataille and Joseph A. Schumpteter's economic writings (*Capitalism, Socialism and Democracy*) who believed that "creative destruction" and the "social" rather than "economic" forces are central to historical change. For Baudrillard "destruction" means a return to noncommodified and elemental social relations by removing "use" and "value" from an object and thus situating it outside the sphere of causal "exchange." It is a process that in *Forget Foucault* (41) he calls "disaccumulation." For Baudrillard, these anti-productionist, anti-utilitarian acts that affirm the freedom of humans are repressed in capitalism, which is obsessed with "use," "utility" and "trade" (giving for receiving). The Marxist critique of capitalism, Baudrillard believes, is inadequate because it "mirrors" the capitalist preoccupation with production, which is the embodiment of the control ethos of utility, usefulness and functionalism—those very beliefs that are, according to him, responsible for the domination and repression of human beings.

Capitalist domination can be terminated, according to Baudrillard, only by those practices that place human beings beyond the regime of exchange and end the rule of utility. He calls the ensemble of these post-exchange relations, "symbolic exchange": exchanges which are anti-productionist and in the very process of exchange negate the circuit of exchange. In formulating his notion of an extra-economic relations, Baudrillard falls back on Mauss's *The Gift*. In his book, Mauss writes that an awareness of the practice of gift giving in "archaic societies" will resurrect the "elemental" and bring about a radical shift in social life in a way that "once again we shall discover . . . the joy of giving in public, the delight in generous artistic expenditure, the pleasure of hospitality in the public or private feast" (57). Mauss's interpretation of "gift" is part of his larger discontent with "economism": a theme developed in all theories of "consumption" and turned into an axis of interpretation of post-al society by Bataille whose own anti-economistic lessons are the frame of intelligibility of such post-al theorists as Baudrillard, Derrida, Lyotard and various post-al marxists. For Baudrillard, it is through "symbolic exchange"—the gift that places the subject outside economic relations—and not class struggle that a genuine revolution is set in motion and humanity is set free. The symbolic social relation" he writes in *The Mirror of Production*

> is the uninterrupted cycle of giving and receiving, which, in primitive exchange, includes the consumption of the 'surplus' and deliberate antiproduction whenever accumulation (the thing not exchanged, taken and not returned, earned and not wasted, produced and not destroyed) risks breaking reciprocity and begins to generate power. It is this symbolic relation that the political economy model (of capital), whose only process is that of laws of value, hence appropriation and indefinite accumulation, *can no longer produce*. It is its radical negation. What is produced is no longer symbolically exchanged and what is not symbolically exchanged (the commodity) feeds a social relation of power and exploitation" (143).

This noninstrumental "consumption" is a semiotic act; "a system of communication" (*Selected Writings* 46), a mode of forming and disseminating "meanings" above and beyond the functionality of consumption. "A washing machine *serves* as equipment and *plays* as an element of comfort, or of prestige, etc. It is the field of play that is specifically the field of consumption" (*Selected Writings* 44; emphasis added). When one buys a pair of "designer" jeans, one does not simply respond to a "need" (to keep warm, for instance) but acts on the pulsation of "desire": to express oneself and in doing so become involved in a purposeless practice that is essentially an aesthetic act ("play"). For Baudrillard, post-ality is the articulation of this mode of consumption: early capitalism is marked by functional consumption which perpetuates production while post-al capitalism ("consumer society") is a break from this functionalism. Consumption, in post-al capitalism becomes an end in itself, an "excess"ive play: a sheer "waste"—a carnival, a regime of festivities and prodigalities. Consumption in Baudrillard's theory, then, is not determined by such classical Marxist concepts as "use-value" and "exchange" value but by "sign value." The signs and meanings produced through prodigal expenditure are signs that cannot be easily absorbed back into the established system of codes that now controls all significations. Consumption is both anti-production and anti-regulatory: it is a process of excessive signification that cannot be contained by the dominant mode of signification.

"Conspicuous consumption" for Baudrillard is then essentially a resistant semiotic act—an act of intervention in the order of established meanings and representations legitimated by capitalism. Prodigal "consumption" is, according to him, a radical negation of capitalism. The act of consumption therefore is not exhausted by its instrumentality and usefulness (it is, in terms of his later writings, a mode of "seduction" a form of opposition to production and procreation); it is the signifier of an irradicable negative (that cannot be assimilated in a Marxist dialectical synthesis) and constitutes the principle of post-al mutation. The form of capitalism that could be analyzed in Marxist terms of political economy, Baudrillard maintains, has ended and, an entirely new analytics that he calls, the "political economy of the sign" (*Mirror* 121) is needed to make sense of post-al capitalism.

However, Baudrillard's understanding of the Marxist concept of "production" as a "mirror" is not simply a misrecognition but is also ideological in the sense that the logic of its misrecognition is a class logic: it legitimates the (economic) interests of the ruling class. The Marxist theory of "production," contrary to Baudrillard, Habermas, Butler, Cornel West and other critics of the "production paradigm," does not reduce all human activities to "labor"; rather it is a theory of the emancipation of humans from necessity and the freedom from the capitalist form of labor. Baudrillard's notion of "symbolic exchange" is simply a post-al colonial nostalgia for "primitive" society; a transhistorical utopia for the North Atlantic elite who has freed itself from necessity—at the cost of the labor of the other—and now regards the main question of humanity to be not "production" but destructive "consumption." For this class, life is lived ludically: the playfulness that erases the use-value of the objects of necessity in order to turn them into moments of the aesthetic sublime.

Post-al theories, in general, proclaim to "deconstruct" the metaphysics of labor. Consumptionist theories after Baudrillard, however, have used the deconstruction of "production" as their foundation for proving the autonomy of capital from labor and consumption from class/production. One of the main signs of post-al society, according to Stuart Hall, is that "there is a leading role for consumption, reflected in such things as greater emphasis on choice and product differentiation, on marketing, packaging and design, on 'targeting' of consumers by life-style, taste and culture rather than by the Registrar General's categories of social class" ("The Meaning of New Times" 118). One of the un-saids of the displacement of production by consumption is the notion that capitalism is a response not to profit but to the "free choice" (desire) of individuals: it is the consumption and desire for difference that drives capital, and, as such, capitalism is not only not antagonistic to human needs but is in fact a direct response to them. "The private control of the sovereign consumer" is portrayed in these reactionary theories as "real, visible and tangible" (Mulgan, "The Power of the Weak" 358). Consumption in post-al theory has become the trope of the indeterminacy of production.

In its privileging of "consumption," post-al theory privileges individual "choice" over human "needs": it is, in short, a class theory. Thus, even though the displacement of production is a move made in the name of epistemological necessity—to provide a more accurate knowledge of capitalism now—it is, in practice, an ideological alibi for what Hall's statement clearly marks: the removal of "class struggle" from the scene of the social in the interest of increasing the freedom of choice for the upper middle classes within the existing socio-economic structures. These critics announce the end of socialism and with it the outdatedness of the praxis of abolishing private property (that is, congealed alienated labor) in the post-al moment. Instead of abolishing private property, they envision an enlightened radical democracy to supplant socialism (as Laclau, Fukuyama, Mouffe, Cornell West, Aronowitz, Butler and others have advised) and make property holders of each citizen. This, needless to say, is the Thatcherist notion of property-owning democracy represented as a radical differential socialism. For theorists of radical democracy, it is only by means of conspicuous and prodigal "owning" (which enables consumption to become transfunctional and symbolic) that one can be resituated outside the system of exchange and be set free from the repressive utilitarianism of capitalism. The "sign" (constructed through conspicuous consumption) and not "labor" is the formative force in post-al capitalism, and, therefore, it is the "control of the code" (*Mirror* 122) and not seizing of the means of production that is the urgent question for political struggle in the post-al moment. The post-al question, to be clear, is no longer the end of exploitation in the form of putting an end to the extraction of surplus labor (communism) but a more equitable distribution ("consumption") among people, regardless of their race, gender, sexualities, nationalities, of the surplus value produced by the exploitation of the proletariat.

The proliferation of post-al "social movements" (feminism, anti-racism, environmentalism, queer theory, postnationalism) are part of this abandoning the project of the emancipation of humanity from labor under capitalism (exploitation) and instead instituting in its place the libertarian goal of freedom of consumption. The project of emancipation is seen in post-al theories as a universalizing and totalitarian undertaking (Butler, "Poststructuralism") that disregards the difference/*différance*—what Drucilla Cornell calls, "each of us in her singularity" (113). Cornell is, of course, annotating here what Derrida (quoting Levinas) calls "the equitable honoring of faces" ("Forces of Law" 959) of each consumer. In restoring difference/*différance*, post-al theories, in Bell's word, "uncouple" production from consumption. The emergence of theories of consumption, these theorists argue, is the proof that the "political" (the freedom of the subject) is what, in the post-al moment, determines the economic. However, the popularity of consumptionist theories has very little to do with the political or the freedom of the subject: it is a not so subtle device for reducing overproduction. Far from asserting the autonomy of the subject, it, in fact, demonstrates how the freedom of the subject under capitalism is always the freedom that enhances the economic interests of the owners of the means of production.

Baudrillard's notion of "consumption" as a transcendence beyond "production" through symbolic exchange is, of course, only one of the many post-al arguments for the privileging of consumption. A more "activist" version of this argument now has become the hegemonic mode of consumptionism in the knowledge industry. It is regarded to be "materialist" by the ludic academy but is, in fact, a mode of ahistorical, Feurbachian "matterism." It is associated, in its various forms and accents, with the "cultural materialism" of Raymond Williams, the "discourse materialism" of such theorists as Foucault and deCerteau and the "desire materialism" of Deleuze and Guattari. Unlike Baudrillard who tends to focus on the metaphysics of consumption (the system of objects), and the "New Times" theories that foreground the subject of choice, thereby eclipsing "class" and emphasizing the autonomy of capitalism from labor—the ludic activist theory of consumption regards consumption to be more of a practical "everyday" performance of resistance against capitalism.

In these theories, consumption is, for the most part, focused on the activities, or what deCerteau calls "tactics" (of resistance) as opposed to "strategies" (of domination) of the subject-agent of consumption. In a move familiar in post-al theories, ludic activists and matterist performances leave the system alone. Confronted with capitalism, they retreat (in the name of self-empowerment and activism) to local, practical and limited personal defiances. They (like Baudrillard), substitute for global objective conditions of production local and unique subjective circumstances of consumption and see consumption as the assertion of desire (the personal) as the last defense against a society of surveillance and coercion.

The matterist analysis of the performances of the consuming subject-agent are still under the influence of poststructuralist language theories and evolve around the "sign" and not "labor." Like Baudrillard, they too argue that "we are at the end of production," and they too believe that "The super-ideology of the sign and the general operationalization of the signifier . . . has replaced good old political economy as the theoretical basis of the system" (Baudrillard, *Mirror* 122). They too adhere to the notion that the control of the code "that plays on the faculty of producing meaning and difference, is more radical than that which plays on labor power" (*Mirror* 122). However, unlike Baudrillard's increasingly a-political and metaphysical writing, culminating in his break with Foucault (*Forget Foucault*, 1977), the matterist approach to consumption is politico-ethical.

The matterist theories of consumptionism are all founded upon the ludic assumptions of the Foucauldian social theory in which "the discursive" is not simply a separate level or an isolated dimension of the social but, as Laclau puts it, "co-extensive with the social as such" ("Populist Rupture and Discourse" 87). This is another way of saying that "every social practice is production of meaning" (Laclau 87). Consequently, in the post-al dogma, the social is constituted not by forces of production and the social relations that they make possible, but by meaning. In other words, as Fiske puts it, "All the commodities of late capitalism are 'goods to speak with'" (*Understanding Popular Culture* 34). What matters for ending capitalist domination, in other words, is not control of the means of production but the control of the means of signification. The substitution of "consumption" for "production" then is really not an epistemological move: it is done not because such a displacement (as it is claimed) will provide a more accurate understanding of radical structural changes in capitalism but because such a reversal erases "revolution" from the map of social struggle and puts in its place a discursive difference that can be negotiated.

Politics, in the "consumption paradigm," is a matter of changing representations and meanings—discourses—which are post-al nodes of power. This view of politics dematerializes power by decoupling "domination" from "exploitation" and retheorizing power as a diffuse and discursive practice. The post-al theory of power goes beyond Foucault and is based on the notion that the structures of post-al capitalism have become so layered, complex and abstract that one cannot locate a single fixed center from which power issues—moreover power is not even "real." Power in the post-al moment has become so abstract, it is believed, that not even such classic postmodern theories of power (as diffused discourse) put forth by

Foucault can account for it. In *Forget Foucault*, one of Baudrillard's main critiques of Foucault is that although Foucault responded to newer forms of power in his critique of the Marxist notion of power, Foucault's own idea of power has become irrelevant in the post-al moment since power, for Foucault, is still an actuality: lines of force in his institutional analysis are treated as realities. However, in the "consumer society," there are, according to Baudrillard, no "real" lines of force but simply simulations of power: signs that parody power (61). This ludic power is available to all users of signs. The political conclusion is that not only is capitalism not growing more powerful, but it has, in fact, become a source of power-as-simulation for the people. Power in the post-al moment is simulational, and every instance of power is said to give rise to "resistance" which leads to a new form of empowerment within the existing relations of exploitation. Women, people of color, and the queer, in post-al theory, can be empowered without the need to overthrow the system of exploitation that deploys socially produced differences (gender, sexuality, race . . .) to legitimate higher and higher ratios of extraction of surplus labor. The displacing of "exploitation" by "domination" is justified because, as Fiske puts it "The productivity of consumption is detached from wealth or class" (35).

In fact, the post-al knowledge industry has "invented" a whole new interdiscipline called "cultural studies" that provides a new alibi for the regime of profit by shifting social analytics from "production" to "consumption" on the grounds that as de Certeau puts it consumption is simply a "different kind of production" (*The Practice of Everyday Life* 31). Consumption of goods as the deployment of textwares whose "speech potential is not affected by economics" (Fiske 34) is a "festive energizing of the body" (Baudrillard, *Mirror* 44). Post-al "Cultural Studies" has increasingly become the mapping of these festivals of the body (Elizabeth Grosz, *Volatile Bodies*; Angela McRobbie, *Postmodernism and Popular Culture*; bell hooks, *Outlaw Culture: Resisting Representations* especially her text "Power to the Pussy"). To prove its "progressiveness," post-al theory devotes most of its energies to demonstrating how "Every act of consumption is an act of cultural production, for consumption is always the production of meaning" (Fiske 35; see the writings of Constance Penley, Michael Bérubé, Henry Louis Gates, Jr., John Fiske, Andrew Ross, Stuart Hall, Fredric Jameson, Kobena Mercer and Rachel Bowlby among many others). In post-al cultural studies, the *politics* of production is suppressed through various "reading" moves in favor of a poetics of consumption or what de Certeau calls *poiesis*, which is the trope of the post-al for "invention."

Matterist theories, as I have critiqued in detail in *Theory and its Other*, take consumption as *poiesis* to be an act of resistance to capitalism. Briefly, the consumer is placed in a scenario of resistance in which he turns consumption into a practice of "poaching" (de Certeau 31). The consumer, like "indigenous Indians" who diverted the "spectacular victory of Spanish colonization," by the "uses" they made of it "even when they were subjected" (32), can subvert the system of production and power "from within" and "divert" it "without leaving it" (32). Shoplifting and "moving the price tag from a lower-to a higher-priced item before taking to the cashier" (Fiske 39) are among the tactics of resistance as is the practice of "two secretaries spending their lunch hour browsing through stores with no intention to buy. They try on clothes, consume their stolen images in the store mirror and in each other's eyes, turn the place of boutique into their lunch time space, and make tactical raids upon its strategically placed racks of clothes, shoes, accessories" (Fiske 39). But the repertoire of resistance is not exhausted by such acts of transgression. Another "inventive" form of consuming as producing is to intervene into the very existence of the commodities. Since "whole" jeans are connoted with powers that one opposes, "disfiguring them" becomes a way of resisting those powers (Fiske 4).

The shift from "production" to "consumption" is a shift then from "labor" as the constitutive practice of human societies to "pleasure" (of using what is produced) as the post-al shaping force of history. It is done in the name of foregrounding the agency of the subject (who freely chooses and thus resists a monolithic system), but it is in actuality an alibi to divert the subject away from "making" and taking control of the means of making toward what de Certeau posits (29-42) as the ultimate form of post-al resistance, "making do": working within the system and with what the system provides rather than attempting to transform it. It is an ethics of adjustment rather than revolution; it focuses on ways of making do with the world as it exists. All post-al theories of "consumption" as the axis of "social analysis" and "political rallying" and as a marker of what is "most free" and "most truly" ourselves (Robbins, *Secular Vocations* 39), are apparatuses of solving the contradictions of the free-market. In their ruthless competition against their rivals for profit, capitalists produce in an unplanned way. The cycles of crisis (recessions, for example) are the effects of this unplanned "overproduction." Theories of consumption legitimate a subject who is always consuming—regardless of need—and in doing so provides a safety net for the capitalist. Consumptionist theories, in short, are devices to reduce overproduction and in doing so help to realize the capitalist's profit. Theories of post-industrialism, post-capitalism, post-Fordism, are theories that use the alibi of radical structural change within capitalism in order to put forth an argument for the outdatedness of the class struggle and revolution and instead advocate a consensus for a permanent bourgeois democracy.

Three

The "post" in deconstructive semiotics is itself the subject of ludic textuality and marks an indeterminate non-history that occults the material contradictions of capitalism. Post-ality invokes a playfulness that blurs the lines of the "before" and "after" and thus making "post" a waving-wavering "puncept" of undecidability—what Ulmer calls "moira," which is the textual equivalent of the "visual illusion known as the moire effect" ("The Puncept of Grammatology" 179-189)—that obscures its retrograde political valence. This "blurring" is, as I will argue, simply an inaugural move for cutting off—in the pedagogy of "double session"—the relation of the past and present by constructing a history that "has no middle" (Derrida, *Dissemination* 227). "Post" in post-al theory is not the concept of a decided linear temporality in history but the puncept of a crisis-effect "within" history itself (post-ality as what Derrida calls "spacing" across the ages). As such, it is both a "before" and an "after," a supratemporality that contains "The Seeds of Time," to use the title of Fredric Jameson's neoconservative book of, what Hal Foster has called, "untimely meditations" on a theory of history. This atemporal "post" is motivated by the movement not of class struggle but of *différance*, the optics—moire-effect—of the sign. In this reactionary avant-gardism, the waving-wavering effect (moire) gives "post" the "paradoxical ability both to precede and to come after itself" (Elam 12) and turns "post" into a conceptual slippage, a puncept. The notion of history without a middle now informs both right-wing circles and the post-al left, which has fully surrendered to this bourgeois notion of history. As I will argue at the end of this section, left writers such as Fredric Jameson are now in the forefront of a double sessional theory of history.

The notion of *différance* ("post" as "moire" effect) generates a radical fissure that renders knowledge the source of wealth and consequently posits culture and politics as autonomous from the production practices in advanced industrial societies. This enables bourgeois theory to propose a radical break from a "before" to an "after." In its formal discourses, of course, post-al theory vehemently denounces, as historically naive and epistemologically simplistic, any notion of a linear history that could establish a self-identical "before" and "after." It does not regard the "before" as a place of origin and reads the "after" simply as an "after-effect": a complex rewriting of the "before" (Lyotard, "'Re-writing' Modernism"). This disconnecting of the "before" and "after" is itself part of a larger move to exclude causality from the domain of history and with it "historical necessity." The dismantling of "historical necessity" is the project of a post-al science of historiography specified as "genealogy." In place of "historical necessity" and "causality," post-al genealogy installs the "haphazard" (the "event") which is excessive and not subordinate to any "laws" but acts by the *alea*—the chance and randomness of desire (Foucault, *Language, Counter-Memory, Practice* 154).

The need for a "break" (post-ality) is a symptom of a recurrent crisis in the labor practices in capitalism. Bourgeois philosophy "solves" this material crisis in the theoretical imaginary (on the superstructural level) by inventing the "new" (over and over again), that is to say, by producing a post-al state which provides a "beyond" to the crisis—a novel post-al state free from the burden (contradictions) of the past. The turmoil of the contemporary labor force, for instance, is mystified by the post-al discourses on the outdatedness (the "before") of labor and the radically new knowledge worker who is an "after" without any connection to the before. This paradigm of explanation is highly attractive to post-al knowledge industry because it does not have to "explain" the contradictions that transforms the "before" into an "after." Post-al theory simply starts all over again until what is now the "after" itself becomes untenable owing to the increasing contradictions and at which time the "after" is abandoned in favor of a newer "after." Post-al historiography is, in fact, a series of these accelerated "afters" without "befores": a history which "has no middle" and as such does not have to account for its own historicity (what, as I will discuss later) Leo Strauss calls history without historicity and is now the basis of not only academic historiography but also right-wing conservative theory.

In my discussion of the construction of a "post" in post-al theory, I leave aside the writings of such theorists as Foucault and Bell who postulate a "discontinuity" (*Archaeology of Knowledge, Language, Counter-Memory, Practice*) and a "difference" (Bell xiii) between various events and stages of history without at the same time giving up the notion of history as "palimpsests" (Bell xvi) and "discourse" (Foucault). I will focus instead on the more complicated fate of the "post" in Lyotard and Derrida who formally denounce the "break" and the "post"-as-break and instead talk of post-ality as immanent to history: as a continuing rewriting, which is another way of saying the "post" is a crisis of representation across the ages—no age is immune to it.

The declared reason for questioning the "post" as a concept (at the very time that they quietly rely on the unsaid of the "post" in their critique of modernity) is that any "post" assumes a "center" and any "center" is founded upon an idea of "presence"—a self-identical reality which denies *différance* and returns us back to the Enlightenment tradition of "representation." In place of the "post" as discontinuity, Lyotard and Derrida deploy, therefore, the notions of *différance/ differend*—a "prepostal" crisis of the inadequation of the signifier and signified that is transhistorical. Examining the strategies of this "double session, the suppression and deployment of the "post" in the writings of Lyotard and Derrida is important because it serves, on the one hand, as a device for conserving the ideological effects of discontinuity necessary for crisis managing the practices in capitalism and, on the other hand, as a means of denouncing those elements of the dominant ideology that have lost their historical effectivity in the continual renewal of the regime of wage-labor and capital. This conserving and jettisoning has always been the "job" of the petit bourgeois theorist in the division of labor, and he has fulfilled it through various pedagogies of "ambiguity," "undecidability," "subtlety," "depth," and "nuanced readings" which are privileged practices in the *pedagogy of the gray* ["I used to think there were only two choices: telling the truth and lying. And now I have found this huge, fantastic gray area . . . " ("Coach," ABC Television, situation comedy)]. I will focus later, on the exemplary instance of the pedagogy of the gray in Derrida's lesson of the double session and show how well it is learned by Coach Fox (who now disseminates that double science to his "team")—a lesson in which mimesis is both preserved and jettisoned and, in that double science of writing and canceling, a vital theory of knowledge for legitimating the exploitation of wage-labor and capital is rescued. The task of this essay, in part, is to display the elements of the pedagogy of the gray as an ideological ally of the ruling class and to combat it with Red Theory.

I will begin with Lyotard who formally rejects the project of the "post" as discontinuity (*The Postmodern Explained* 76) and speaks instead of history as a textual continuity ("'Re-writing' Modernism" 3-9) or as the "procedure in *ana*-": "a procedure of analysis, anamnesis, analogy, and anamorphosis that elaborates an `initial forgetting'" (*The Postmodern Explained* 80). But in his practices he grounds "the postmodern condition" on the ruins of modernity brought about by the "incredulity toward metanarratives" (*The Postmodern Condition* xxiv): a crisis that cuts off an "after"—an incredulous postmodern which is post-metanarrational, democratic and a nontotalizable ensemble of incommensurate language games— from a "before"—a credulous modernity which is the violent coherence of metanarrational totalitarian and progressive knowledges—(*The Postmodern Explained* 77-79). "After" the incredulity towards the metanarratives of modernity, history takes a fresh, new direction, free from the contradictions of the past which now exists only as a dismembered subjectivity ("anamnesis") and has no coherent objectivity.

Lyotard's rejection of "modernity," under the sign of "totalitarian" progressivism, is an alibi for establishing a post-al state free from the accumulated contradictions of capitalism and colonialism marking bourgeois modernity. It is only by such clearing of ground—separating "now" from "then"; "before" from "after"; "(post)colonialism" from "colonialism"; "pre" from "post"—that Lyotard is able to distance the (post)modern West from the modern West and say that "Capitalism is one of the names of modernity" (*Political Writings* 25). In other words, the (post)modern is the name of (post)capitalism. Modernity is the "before" composed of metanarrational knowledges that gave us "capitalism," but we are now, according to Lyotard, in an "after" (free-market democracy as post capitalism) in which modernity is re-written as an anti-metanarrative free from metanarrational "capitalism"—(post)modernism. "Metanarrative" is the limit sign that disconnects (in spite of Lyotard's formal protestations) the "after" from "before" and constructs a post-al situation in which today's "capitalism" (=propertied radical democracy) is posited as a fresh, new regime unencumbered by the social contradictions of its past.

Derrida's play with "post" takes a more elaborate form. He questions "post," as I have already suggested, as an instance of identity thinking ("totalizing"): a logocentric striving for a center (*Writing and Difference* 278-293). His own retrieving of the "post," like that of Lyotard, takes place by "writing" and "sending" a "post card"—a fractured, aleatory, discontinuous site of migrant textuality. But his own critique of Western metaphysics ("modernity") is founded upon the possibility of a post-al space from which that metaphysics loses its naturalness and thus is seen as metaphysics and subjected to a deconstructive textualization—even if this space is (as he insists) *within* the "general economy" of metaphysics itself (Post)structuralist deconstruction (as distinguished from the non-poststructuralist deconstruction of, for instance, Nietzsche) is a meticulous analysis of "writing" and, like any form of analysis, it requires a post-al "space" whether "immanent" or "exoteric." Derrida, of course, situates his deconstructive analysis as an immanent critique and consequently produces a post-al moment "within" the system itself: the "break" of *différance* in the identity—the difference within.

His most rigorous treatment of the "post" is inscribed in his supplementary reading of history and deconstruction of historical determinism in his *The Post Card: From Socrates to Freud and Beyond*. Here, Derrida textualizes the logic of the "proper" (determinacy) and argues that it is always interrupted by the "heterologic" of the improper; in doing so, he takes the postal system as his example. The postal system—a network of "posts" that is "sites of passage or of relay" (27)—works by forgetting the differences of its "posts" and operates with the identitarian assumption that within it one (identity) can send messages to another (identity) properly. Derrida shows the supplementary (hetero)logics of the postal system by demonstrating its inherent indeterminacy: letters may or may not arrive because the system is never "proper"—"Before posting this card I will have called you" (10).

The "postal principle" (27) is, of course, the synecdoche for the "order" of a reliable communication (history) in which the sender and receiver are connected by their intact message. Derrida deconstructs the "order" of the canonical history (of philosophy) according to which Socrates comes *before* Plato—in the same way that speech (the non-writing Socrates) comes before writing (Plato). He opens up the post-ality within the order and provides a model of historiography for rewriting the history of capitalism as one marked by abrupt shifts, radical reversals and excessive law-less-ness. In *The Post Card*, the post-ality of Plato (of "writing" as a belated sign) is deconstructed but "to deconstruct the metaphysics and rhetorical schema at work" is not "to reject and discard" but "to reinscribe them otherwise" (*Margins of Philosophy* 215). The "post," in other words, is an operational concept in Derrida's analysis. He subjects the "post" to a rigorous reading; he also subjects it to a formalist textualization and questions the possibility of ever moving "beyond" (since "beyond" always creates the illusion of approximating "truth" which is, for him, forever delayed, deferred and spaced)—but he never discards the "post" either. This, in fact, is the lesson of the double session. The double science of deconstructive historiography posits capitalism as a post-ality, whose "direction cannot be situated in the end. There is no destination . . . " (29).

The site of Derrida's pedagogy of the double science of (post)structuralist history is the Bodleian (Oxford) library. In the library, the narrator of *The Post Card* "stumble[s] across" (by the alea of events not any teleological plan) a post card from the frontispiece of Matthew Paris's *Prognostica Socrastis basilei*, a thirteenth century fortune-telling book—the paralogy of chance that Lyotard regards to be the logic of the post-al (*The Postmodern Condition* 60-67). Post-cards for Derrida are "anonymous morsels without fixed domicile, without legitimate addressee, letters open, but like crypts" (53) and as such they are allegories of larger textuaries: "Our entire library, our entire encyclopedia, our words, our pictures, our figures, our secrets, all an immense house of post cards" (53). Post card is then the

Post-ality: The (Dis)Simulations of Cybercapitalism « 27

post-al spacing within the post: the undecidability within the decided.

Derrida's deconstructive history of capitalism is inscribed on the post card the narrator discovers in the Bodleian. On the post card, Socrates is written as a picture in which he is sitting in front of Plato writing. "Socrates, the one who writes—seated, bent over, a scribe or docile copyist, Plato's secretary, no? He is in front of Plato, no, Plato is *behind* him, smaller (why smaller?), but standing up" (9). The stable order of philosophy in which speech comes before writing is reversed; it is Socrates who "writes." The post card opens up a post-al spacing that not only reverses the "order" of the transmission of knowledge but also shows how the history of philosophy—like all histories—is motivated by desire. "*Plato*, teacher, in erection behind *Socrates*" (22); the desire of consummation (consumption?) emerges as the underlying order of history. History, in Derrida, then, contrary to his formal objection to the "post," is, like all idealist historiography "catastrophic" (22). The post-al is a series of unrelated and unrelatable aleatory events, each autonomous from the larger logic of the mode of production. The post-ality of the postal system—fissures within sameness—is not unique but the common feature of history itself, which is also marked by "overturning and inversion" (22). The inversion is the overturning of reason (production) by seduction (consumption).

The "discovery" of the post-al space of desire, erection, seduction and consumption in the order of history places the historiographer in a post-al state in which "reason" is radically fractured by "pleasure": "never have I been so delirious" (17). This is the delirium of post-al "consumption"—"I bought a whole supply of them [post cards]" (10). The post card overturns everything and "allegorizes the catastrophic unknown of the order. Finally one begins no longer to understand what to come . . . to come before, to come after, to foresee, to come back . . . " (21). Whatever the order of "before" and "after," Derrida assumes the catastrophic "post-ality": a fissure, a gap, a disconnection of apocalyptic dimension. History is double session—a double session that "has no middle" (*Dissemination* 227). The post-al "reversibility unleashes itself, goes mad" (13), and any red theorist who attempts to explain this "madness" by the laws of motion of capital is a "bad reader . . . the reader . . . decided upon deciding" (4), like "Comrade Socrates" (38). Marxist revolutionary praxis aimed at ending the "madness" (of the free market) is, according to Derrida, part of the doctrine of the "Platonic party"(38)—a metaphysics. This lesson on the Marxist revolution as metaphysics is "supplemented" by the second session of his lesson in *Spectres of Marx*. In the double session of *The Post Card* and *Spectres of Marx*, Derrida's petit bourgeois pedagogy of the gray comes to its political lucidity: politics is conversation and discursive vigilance.

My point here is, of course, that their formal play with "post" notwithstanding, Derrida, Lyotard and other ludic theorists deny and at the same time institutionalize the "post." This denial and institutionalization is the double science of post-ality which has become the historically necessary pedagogy for post-al capitalism. The "break" (post-ality) that unburdens the present from the past by "catastrophe," allows capitalism to place a "gap," a "slippage," a "differance" between its present moment and its accumulated contradictions from the past. And the "post" (under various names) is repeated over and over again in the guise of innovative knowledges, new modes of understanding, new forms of reading at those historical moments in capitalism when the congealed contradictions delegitimate the efficient economic working of the system to produce an acceptable rate of profit. The role of post-al theory—(post)structuralism, deconstruction, new historicism, ludic feminism, difference (post)colonialism—in the (post)modern knowledge industry is to provide the conditions of conceptual possibility of this necessary post. The knowledge industry, in other words, deals with the recurring crises in capitalism by constantly inventing the "new" (post-al), which is entirely "different" from the "old." In producing a post-al state that promises a way to move (discursively) beyond the crisis and to inaugurate a novel beginning free from the burden of the past, bourgeois "theory" constructs a site unconnected with the practices of the past and offers a pan-historical moment of plenitude free from material contradictions. It is through the regime of post-ality that bourgeois philosophy provides the ideological discourses that make the contradictions of capitalism tolerable by simply explaining them away as belonging to a crude past with which the present has nothing to do. The post-al is the name of that cultural (ideological) space in which various apparatuses of crisis-management are produced in order to iron out the fundamental contradictions that cannot be resolved in present practices.

The conceptual hybridity of the post—its optics of "preceding" itself and coming "after" itself is, like all hybridities in ludic theory, a petit bourgeois mystification of history through the Derridean double-science (Derrida, *Dissemination* 4) that stalls in order to evade and neutralize class antagonisms in the name of epistemological vigilance. The "double science/double session" (*Dissemination* 4; 173-286) is now in the "box of tools" (Deleuze in Foucault's *Language, Counter-Memory, Practice* 199) of the theoretical common sense of the ludic academy, and in the hands of such academics as Ulmer and Elam, it turns the "post" into a reversible trace of repetition without identity, of simultaneous "preceding" and "succeeding"—a waving-wavering puncept of prepostality and postpreality. It is necessary to explore some aspects of this use of the "post" as a discursive stalling apparatus in the post-al knowledge industry because through the ludic semiotics of the "post," petit bourgeois academics have in fact "found this huge, fantastic gray area . . . " within which they can (re)legitimate the way things are (and ought to be) in the bourgeois democracy.

In the gray pedagogy now dominant in counterrevolutionary circles, the crisis of the post is severed from class struggle and represented as an effect of rhetoric through a textual playfulness that marks it as a "pre-post-erous" sign of "crossing, traversing and transcending" historical necessity, which determines, for instance, the political economy of "race." In fact, "race" itself emerges in the post-historical politics of indeterminacy (a history that "has no middle," *Dissemination* 227)— as a "crude" concept and is thus translated into a post-ethnicity (R. Radhakrishnan, "Ethnic Identity and Poststructuralist Difference" 50-71) and a subtle, generalized, "post-whiteness" (*Minnesota Review* No. 46, special issue on "post-whiteness" edited by M. Hill, announced in *College Literature* 21.3, 41). "Post," as taught by Derrida, becomes in the day-to-day negotiations of knowledge in the academy a pre-post-erous sign that acts as the site for a rehearsive deconstruction of historical binaries (that is the fundamental class polarity of workers and owners) and the unleashing of *différance*. A post-ethnicity, then, is put in play to displace social determinacy and to legitimate a new post-al populist petit bourgeois reformism under the sign of the "Rainbow" (Radhakrishnan 65-67). The "pre-post-erous" reduces history to an operation of the epistemology of identity and thus reads materiality itself as the effect of "the mode of production known as binarity" (Radhakrishnan 64). In the post-al scheme of history, the historical materialist understanding of "mode of production" as the material base that "determines the condition of society" and thus necessitates that the "history of humanity" always be "studied and treated in relation to history of industry and exchange" (*The German Ideology* 43) is put aside as belonging to the "Platonic party." Instead history is seen as the pre-post-erous theatre of epistemology. The "pre-post-erous," in other words, views the superstructure as the primary mover of history. It is binarity (the logic of the totalizing sign) that acts as the dynamics of oppression and not the laws of motion of capital. This pre-post-erous idealism, as Marx and Engels explain (*The German Ideology* 61), is part of the dominant ideologies that represent the "rule of a certain class" which is determined by its ownership of means of production, as the "rule of certain ideas" (such as binarism).

In the double-science of the "dangerous supplement" (Derrida, *Of Grammatology* 141-164), the knowledge of the before of the after and the after of the before suspends time in the "always already" of the trope and thus reduces "revolution" to merely a *"topos"* of discourse (Radhakrishnan 67). The lesson of the double session, in other words, is the post-al merging of the "past" and the "future" in the "mimique" ("performance") of the body of Pierrot (*Dissemination* 175). "Like *Mimique,* the double session has no middle" (*Dissemination* 227) and the gestures of Pierrot displace class struggle by locating history in the non-space of the "betweenness" of "hymen (out of which flows Dream)" (Derrida quoting Mallarmé in *Dissemination* 209).

Post-ality in the pedagogy of the gray is the violent erasure of the material "middle"—the now of class struggle—in counter-memory, anamnesis and utopia. The erasure of the "middle" provides the conditions for post-ing history as post-al discontinuities across the ages; history thus becomes, in this representation, a permanent rupture, gap, and the effect of the slippage of desire that inscribes the alea into "events," thereby, annulling all laws of history—"regulatory mechanism(s)" as Foucault (*Language, Counter-Memory, Practice* 154) characterizes them in his post-al effort to occult the laws of motion of capital. The popularity of the notion of history as a double session without a middle is part of the popularity ("domination") of the ruling class pedagogy which teaches fatalism, whether in the guise of textual activism, religion, advertisement or ludic theory: there are, in this version of history, no "laws" that explain the welfare of the few as "caused" by the toil of the many.

History, of course, is not a double session without a middle. This notion of (anti)history, which is now ruling the academy, has its own history—it is part of the on-going crisis of capitalism. The most recent articulations of this crisis, however, arise out of the previous crisis of capitalism (and its colonial intraclass struggle) in Germany and the fascist criticism of modernity and Enlightenment in the works of such precursors of Derrida and Foucault as the right-wing authors Leo Strauss and Heidegger (both avid readers of Nietzsche and "students" of Husserl at Freibourg.) The writings of Leo Strauss and Heidegger are, on the surface, as heterogeneous as the deep structure of their thought and politics is similar. Their heterogeneity, which is used in the ludic academy as a device to resist any analysis that shows the identity of their work, is—as is always the case of *différance* in the capitalist knowledge industry—a local rhetorical maneuver to orient their theories towards a particular class fraction.

The "First Session" of this lesson of post-al history offered by Strauss and Heidegger is the "session" on "reason." Reason, in its dehistoricized and naturalized form, is an ally of capitalism for establishing transhistorical "standards" of "excellence" and is deployed in the retrograde post-al theory to naturalize as "given" the social inequalities that are produced in the material practices of capitalism. Leo Strauss delivers the lesson of reason through his meditations on Socratic panhistorical rationality in which he turns abstract and natural reason into the mover of history. Strauss's focus on reason, it must be reemphasized, is an ideological alibi to assert the priority of "nature" over "history" (*Natural Right and History*). This centralization of reason enables him to normalize the social differences that are the consequences of the laws of motion of capital: some people are "naturally" suited to rule and others to be ruled. His contestation with history (or what he, like all post-al theorists, call "historicism") is that it explains the natural, given "differences" (= inequalities) materially and in terms of social practices (especially economic exchanges). History, in short, according to Leo Strauss is an unreliable source of knowledge because it historicizes privilege and thus points to its lack of natural legitimacy. The "First Session" on "reason" taught by Leo Strauss, then, is a lesson in premodern reason. Unlike Heidegger, he disagrees with Nietzsche that there is only one tradition of reason in the West. Strauss taught that there is a break in rationality in the 16th century that separates the ancient understanding of reason from its modern mode. He regards modern reason, articulated through the Enlightenment, to be a deviation from reason and thus a misguided pursuit since, in its modern moment, especially in the writings of Rousseau and Kant, a notion of reason developed that considers social problems solvable and inequalities as being able to be brought to an end. Leo Strauss, especially in his later writings, regarded Enlightenment's opposition to "tradition," "natural" authority and "inequality" to be opposed to "excellence"—the rule of the "elite." It is this notion of "excellence"—the political alibi for taking the status quo as the effect of laws of nature—that is the lesson of the "First Session" for the owners and high mangers of capitalism and their allies in the academy who argue for "standards." (See, for example, Newt Gingrich's lecture on "Quality and Deming's Profound Knowledge" in his video series "Renewing American Civilization" as well as the writings of such critics as Irving Kristol and Gertrude Himmelfarb.) Leo Strauss's criticism of reason, then, is first a criticism of modernist (namely historicized) reason, and second it is radically different from the critique of rationality by Engels and other Marxists. Engels's critique of Enlightenment rationality is that it is not materialist and thus not historical enough and consequently it becomes a reification of reason. According to Engels, rationality for Enlightenment philosophers eventually becomes an ideological alibi; it amounts to nothing more than "the idealized realm of the bourgeoisie" in which "bourgeois property" is "proclaimed as one of the most essential rights of man" and the "bourgeois democratic republic" becomes the only legitimate form of government (*So-

cialism: Utopian and Scientific 46). The "Second Session" of this history without a "middle" is the session on "desire"—the other of reason, which is the lesson of Heidegger's pedagogy articulated through his notion of "care" (*sorge*) as the "being" of *Dasein* (*Being and Time* 225-273). Heidegger, whom Strauss admired more than any other modern philosopher, deconstructes "reason" in a move that, on the surface, is radically different from Leo Strauss, but this deconstruction is aimed at producing the pedagogy of the gray in which the status of undecidability is naturalized for what Heidegger regards to be the knotted ontological questions of Being. However, in actuality the "undecidable" becomes, in his texts and in the gray writings of his followers, the space of all actual social problems. The ontologically undecidable problems of being, in other words, serve as a paradigm of intelligibility for rendering (as Strauss does) the material contradictions of capitalism as complexities that are beyond the reach of "reason." All acts of "reason" are thus seen as simplistic and ineffective: the complexities are to be appreciated but not analyzed and superseded. Complexities always exceed their explanation since they are beyond the historical systems of representation—they belong to the ineffable. This anti-rationalist view permeates Derrida's early texts in the form of a counter-logocentric anti-conceptuality, and in his later texts, the transconceptuality of the ineffable is articulated through themes of the apocalypse and the sublime. Derrida's post-al anti-conceptuality is now not only a ludic dogma in the writings of such reactionary eclectricians as Gayatri Spivak, Homi Bhabha and . . . but is also the founding practice of ludic queer theory (Morton, "Birth of the Cyberqueer"), of post-al feminism (Ebert, *Ludic Feminism and After*) and of (post)colonial Discourse (*Transformation 3: Imperialism and Ludic (Post)colonial Theory*). Heidegger, through the "care" of Being, and Leo Strauss, through "natural reason," both arrive at the conclusion that difference is natural and thus inequalities are part of the givenness of Being. Racism, homophobia, sexism, colonialism are all questions of Being and Nature not social practices: what seem to be solvable social issues are, in fact, part of the ontological/natural order of existence. Heidegger's "Second Session" is the other of Leo Strauss's deconstruction of history; it is the session of desire that deconstructs Leo Strauss's natural "reason" and provides, by rereading Nietzsche, the logic of the disruptive joys of consumption and care of the consuming self.

Heidegger's and Leo Strauss's right-wing theories are now popularized in the works of a number of contemporary (neo)conservatives who all argue that equality is un-natural and any attempt by the State to bring about a society of equality is discriminating against the chosen. Robert Bork and Allan Bloom are perhaps the best known students of Leo Strauss, but Strauss's lesson is now part of popular culture because of the works of such agents as Rush Limbaugh, Alvin Toffler and Newt Gingrich, who have brought his message to the masses. Heidegger's supplementary pedagogy of difference and panhistorical inequality is not only the gray pedagogy of such high-theorists as Derrida, de Man, Foucault, Judith Butler and Jean-Luc Nancy but it also has become part of the common sense of the popular culture theory through the lessons of Stuart Hall, Eve Sedgwick, Michael Berube, John Fiske, and Andrew Ross. The post-al history of Leo Strauss and Martin Heidegger, of course, converge in the writings of such contemporary post-al theorists as Francis Fukuyama whose book *The End of History and the Last Man* is a Heideggerian-Hegelian reappropriation of Nietzsche for a Straussian pedagogy.

The "double session" is staged, of course, to effect a double deconstruction and, in doing so, put an end to "opposition" (of history to desire, for example) and demonstrate the impossibility of drawing borders. After the double session, desire and history can never again be seen as self-same identities; they are always already inscribed in each other. Derrida's own local lesson in his "The Double Session" (*Dissemination* 173-286) evolves around the double deconstruction of Plato's as well as Mallarmé's notions of mimesis. Plato's theory of "mimesis," Derrida argues, is shown by Mallarmé to be unfounded; it is based on first principles which are metaphysical. However, Mallarmé's own "mimique" (which performs the deconstruction of Plato's mimesis and thus seems to point to an "outside" of mimesis) is, according to Derrida, equally unfounded because it is grounded on a notion of language as gestures without reference. Derrida points out that the nonreferential is, in fact, part of a generalized (non)referentiality as in Plato's notion of referentiality. Mallarmé's "mimique," in other words, far from putting an end to Platonic "mimesis," is part of that regime, and Plato's "mimesis" already deploys a version of Mallarmé's anti-mimetic mimique. The two are inextricably implicated in each other: mimesis is an undecidable project—one can never mark an utterance as referential or nonreferential. The double session is, of course, used, as are all deconstructive moments, as a lesson of critical vigilance: to defer the appeal to clarity and decidability, and herein lies deconstruction's claim to radicality. The State always needs "clear" meanings (patriotism, poverty . . .). But by obscuring the decidable, the deconstructive intellectual reduces the ideological clarity of the State and thus reduces its legitimacy, and in doing so enhances freedom (of individual). However, even though deconstruction represents its lesson as nonpositivistic and a version of what is at times called negative hermeneutic, its political outcome is a mode of "affirmative deconstruction": by rendering the contesting terms (patriotism/internationalism) both obscure, it "affirms" the status quo: the non-state of transnational corporations.

It is this "affirmative deconstruction" that underlies not only Derrida's own so-called political writings but also the post-al social policies of right-wing theorists such as Newt Gingrich. In *The Window of Opportunity* and in the video series, "Renewing American Civilization," Gingrich provides the outlines of social policy for cybercapitalism. More recently Gingrich, in a testimony to the "Ways and Means Committee" of the United States Congress, proposed a "tax credit for the poorest Americans to buy a laptop" computer (*New York Times* January 10, C-6) so that they can receive all the "signs" pointing to the moving of capitalism to the 21st century. In his texts, Gingrich treats "reason" in terms of the panhistorical theories of Leo Strauss and thus regards the State to be the embodiment of that unnatural reason that Strauss thought to be the disease of Enlightenment and the urtheory of equality. The state, Gingrich believes, is the unnatural force that "regulates" (namely deprives from "naturalness") the "desire" (for profit) of the entrepreneur. Through the science of desire Gingrich produces the citizen of post-al capitalism as the seemingly aleatory and free consumer whose consumption does not follow the logic of need but is a trajectory of the eruptive joys of a prodigal use without need. This deployment of desire in post-al theory is, as I have already indicated, the device for reducing overproduction which is the endemic problem of capitalism and a result of the anarchy of the free market. Through desire the crisis of overproduction (recession, for example) is to some extent managed by such psychological stimuli as "consumer confidence"—which is, in fact, an intervention from an "outside" into the free market and its unruly overproduction, but one that is mystified as the workings of the invisible hand of the market itself.

In the same double move, Gingrich subjects "desire" itself to the questions of a panhistorical reason and finds any desire not related to profits and consumption to be a threat to "standards" of "excellence." Like other right-wing thinkers, he has especially targeted such "other" instances of "desire" as having children outside wedlock. In the deconstructed non-space of the double session—the gap of a history without a "middle"—Gingrich "affirms" the non-State of transnational corporations and the natural "desire" of consumers. The emergence of the new cyberorder is the emerging of what, the double session has taught, is the "always already" of "an ageless world" (Derrida, *Specters of Marx*), that is, a history without historicity, which is another way of reinstituting the natural order. As far as Gingrich is concerned this natural order—the consequence of the worldwide rise of capitalism—is blocked by the enormous cost of the unnatural regulatory institution of the welfare system—the depletion of capital by "taxes." The cyberorder simply enhances and extends the "natural" working of the market. In their "affirmative deconstruction," Newt Gingrich's *Window of Opportunity* and Derrida's *The Other Heading: Reflections on Today's Europe* attempt to hold on to the double science of the post: the science of *différance* (de-regulation and erasure of the nontotalitarian state) and the science of desire. Desire and reason, in the "affirmative" deconstruction are not abandoned; they are, to use Derrida's own words in his reading of Mallarmé-Plato, "separated" from each other "by a barely perceptible veil about which one can just say as well that it already runs unnoticed" (*Dissemination* 207). They are each the condition of possibility for the other and, in combination, provide the conditions for the articulation of traditional cultural values such as "family values" (Gingrich) and "plurality of interpretations" (Derrida). Conservative (cultural) values are grafted onto the avant-garde (Derrida) and onto futuristic outlooks which are economic. For instance, Gingrich's futuristic possibilities are, in the words of Andrew Leaky, founded upon the "Opportunity for companies that successfully capitalize on change and turn it into profit, leaving slower competition in their dust" (*The 20 Hottest Investments for 21st Century* 23). This futuristic order, in short, is the order of the "natural," namely the working of the "free market." Gingrich, like Toffler, believes that it is the agency of cyberforces that remove obstacles to the emergence of the "natural." Toffler argues that "the appearance of the computer and new communications media in the mid-20th century smashed Moscow's control of the mind [i.e., unaided, natural reason which set panhistorical "standards"] in the countries it ruled or held captive" (*Powershift* 405). In Derrida the fall of the totalitarian, whether totalitarianism of meaning or of the State, is also tied to a plurality of meaning and the rights of individual. Derrida grafts his conservative cultural values onto the form of avant-gardism that is a Europe without borders. But, like Gingrich's transnational investments, Derrida's Europe without borders is a post-al ideological space within which the transfer of the surplus labor of the South to the North takes place.

The suturing of conservative cultural values onto futuristic/avant-garde economic practices is the mark of the post-al, but it has always marked the fissures within conservative politics. This is another way of saying that the cybersociety which is celebrated in post-al theory is, in actuality, a devolution of the modern city into a medieval village—represented as the postmodern polis: a village that is organized on a post-al ("soft") hierarchy legitimated by the extent of the ownership of the means of production, now wrapped in fiberoptics. Cybersociety is, in short, an allegory justifying the escape of the affluent to the suburb and their abandonment the (inner) city. The craftsman of this new "craft society" is the (computer) hacker who works individually by his/her own ingenuity and skills and has a place of his own (in the Guild of "Information"). The post-al opposition to modernity is an ideological alibi for reaffirming the pre-industrial social order—an order that naturalizes the privileged—and thus reifying class differences. The double session of the conservative and bourgeois progressivism (the futurist/avant-gardist views that legitimate profiteering) marks post-ality from its earliest stages. Arthur J. Penty—a follower of William Morris and such other late Romantics as John Ruskin—writes in the "Preface" to his book *Post-Industrialism* (1922), "From one point of view, Post Industrial connotes Medievalism, from another it could be defined as `inverted Marxism'" (16). Post-ality as a theory of history is a bourgeois fantasy, a retreat into a "back-to-the-future" history.

The double sessional theory of a history with "no middle" is no longer practiced only in the right-wing knowledge industry. It is now the dominant theory of history in the post-al "left." In fact it has become increasingly more difficult to distinguish the politics and practices of what Marx and Engels called a "hybrid sect" of the left, which attempts to "reconcile communism with the ideas prevailing at the time" (*The German Ideology* 457), and right-wing writers. In the dominant post-al "reconciliation" of revolutionary Marxism with free market Republicanism, it has become almost impossible to separate the writings of such hybrid leftists as Fredric Jameson, Stanley Aronowitz, Cornel West, Michel Barrett and Donna Haraway from the retrograde theories of Baudrillard, Derrida, Lyotard, Foucault, Richard Rorty and Judith Butler. The exemplary text of the hybrid left has become Derrida's *Specters of Marx*, while *Capital* is routinely dismissed as a text of unacceptable "scientific Marxism."

In recent years, there has indeed been a race for post-ality among "left" writers and journals, and now, as a matter of course, they try to prove their "progressiveness" to each other by out post-ing one another. An exemplary progressivist "contest" for the post-al is staged in *Marxism in the Postmodern Age* (ed. Antonio Collari and other members of *Rethinking Marxism*). With each writer attempting to be more post-al than the others, an array of hybrid texts are on display here. There are hybrid writings on class analyses, for example, that give up class; economic theory that deconstructs labor (as a modernist metanarrative); theories of sexuality that find Marx's notion that "Our wants and pleasures have their origin in society" (*Wage-Labor and Capital* 33) to be too quaint to be useful in post-production capitalism and thus assert the autonomy of desire from production practices, and finally there are texts that complete the project of ludic anti-conceptuality in the post-al knowledge industry by completely erasing "concepts" and substituting "photographs. In these textwares, exploitation is no longer a class issue—the effect of social relations of production—that can be rationally understood, analyzed and acted on but sheer luminous "experience." These phototexts continue the bourgeois project of diverting attention from exploitation by turning it to an artistic occasion: the "body" of the exploited becomes the site of aesthetic meditation for the post-al leftist-as-photographer.

Marxism in the Postmodern Age, more than any recent text, demonstrates with unequal clarity the collapse of the hybrid left under the pressure of post-al theory and is symptomatic of how the bourgeois left now produces some of the most "effective" texts for the legitimation of capitalism. The collection opens with a post-al reversal of "base" and "superstructure," announcing the "before-ness" of "scientific Marxism" and the arrival of the apocalypse and "The End of Orthodox Marxism" (33-41). In place of "scientific Marxism" aimed at putting in praxis the lessons learned from the laws of motion of capital in order to bring about a communist society, Kellner produces a hybrid form of marxism that he calls "critical marxism"—a marxism devoted to discursive vigilance and adept at negotiation and reconciliation. This is the kind of communism that Marx and Engels described as the product of the imagination of the "literati," a communism that "has lost all its revolutionary enthusiasm and proclaims instead the universal love of mankind" (457). It is a New Age marxism which is further extended in such texts as "Marxism and Spirituality." The communism represented in *Marxism in the Postmodern Age*, it quickly becomes clear, does not turn to "the proletarians but to the two most numerous classes of men" namely "to the petty bourgeoisie with its philanthropic illusions and to the ideologists of this very same petty bourgeoisie" (*The German Ideology* 457). The "essence" of these heavily prefixed (anti)marxisms is that to be an "effective" project Marxism should become "marxism" and give up "its emphasis upon the economic sphere, upon production and the exclusive agency of the working class" (73). This project, which is presented by the editors (with no hint of irony) as a daring new project, is a rather tired rehearsal in the mid-1990's in the United States of some of the anti-communist clichés of the early 1980's (the height of Thatcher-Kohl-Reagan rule) circulated in *Marxism Today* in England. The underlying "argument" of the entire book, which is repeated over and over again in locally different idioms in all the texts (with the exception of Ernest Mandel's text), is that the time of the "proletariat" and "revolution" is already a "before-ness" and the time of the "after" is the post-al time of "reform" and building class alliances. This "theoretical" and "historical" insight is an ideological alibi for resecuring the interests of the ruling class by marginalizing the working class and substituting class coalition for class struggle, hegemonic consensus for class antagonism. This is the very form of "reconciliation" of communism with the most oppressive interests of the ruling class that was advocated by people like Hobsbawm in *Marxism Today* (for example, in the October 1982 issue). I leave aside here that these views are themselves echoes of the Eurocommunism of the 1970's and in turn copies of the platitudes of petit bourgeois writers like André Gorz. The history of anti-communist writing is the history of this discourse chain of crisis management of capitalism by petit bourgeois academics and journalists. The aim of the writers of *Marxism in the Postmodern Age* is to displace the objective interests (the production and exploitation of surplus labor) of the proletariat with the subjective circumstance of identity formation of the bourgeois. This is the politics of the class that has already (by exploiting the labor of the proletariat) fulfilled its "needs" and is now declaring the struggle for "need" a thing of the past and understanding the satisfaction of its own post-al "desire" as the "desire" of all humankind.

The writers/photographers of *Marxism in the Postmodern Age* share the general strategy of the hybrid left in that their only criterion for evaluating political praxis under capitalism is its local, experiential "effectiveness" in terms of the ruling structures, practices and institutions. If the most reactionary persons and institutions ignore/reject/resist/ridicule/marginalize an idea or a particular praxis, this "excluding" is the sure mark for the hybrid left argument that the silenced/ridiculed/resisted ideas/praxis have not been "effective." "Effectiveness" is really an alibi for acceptance by the established institutions for this left which insists that to be effective the ideas/ praxis must be approved by all the (retrograde) elements of the dominant structures. "To forge effective left politics," writes Jeffrey Williams, "it seems to me imperative that we not forget who we are speaking to" ("Where Do We go From Here? A Question of the Left" 87). He then proceeds to indicate whom "we" should "speak" to and under what terms: "Like it or not, the discourses of poststructuralism set the terms of current conversation" (90). In short, the only "effective" discourse is one conducted in the terms set by the dominant theory: if an argument is regarded to be too insignificant/ridiculous/off-the-wall by these terms, then that argument is seen as failing to engage the discourses that "like it or not" are dominant and should be dismissed as a failed discourse. The appeal to this form of bourgeois "effectiveness," as I have argued elsewhere ("The Stupidity that Consumption is Just as Productive as Production"), is a symptom of the cynical pragmatism that is the framing discourse of the post-al left. Having (following the protocols of the ludic) abandoned the objective truth (as a pre-post-terous project of epistemology), the "hybrid sect" is left with defining truth as that which "works"—that is pragmatically and without reference to its truthfulness. And "what works" under the ruling terms is , of course, what supports the existing social arrangements. The only way to be effective in post-al left practices, consequently is to go along ("reconcile") with the ruling institutions and performances of capitalism because, to be effective, as the ludic dogma goes, one must "include" and then reform from "within." Effectiveness, in short, has become an alibi to cooperate ("reconcile") with the system in the hope that the system will open up a space for the cooperators: the inclusion of the cooperators is seen as a mark of their "effectiveness." No intervention from an "outside" (revolution) is thus, from this cynical perspective, "effective," because it is "excluding" and "divisive"—revolution is also a "before-ness" and that too is decided and thus ineffectively divisive. Effectiveness is the political logic of the post-al left at its most ludic hybridity and complicity with the exploiters of the working class; it is an ideological alibi for legitimating "success" in the mainstream life under capitalism and for justifying the system of capital and wage-labor.

In the race for post-ality on the hybrid left, the *Socialist Review* has become one of the most active organs of "marxism in the postmodern age." It is in its pages, for example, that Stanley Aronowitz, recently wrote a "new" version of the narratives of *Marxism Today* for U.S. consumption and announced in excited tones the apocalypse of history without a middle: the sudden death (descent of "before"-ness) of socialism and the arrival of the "after" of "radical democracy" as a fully propertied democracy. Aronowitz's (and *Socialist Review*'s) story of post-al democracy is, however, the predictable repetition of a very familiar story in the history of the crisis of capitalism and an instance of the hybrid left's rush to offer its discursive services to rescue the dominant ideology. What *Socialist Review* enthusiastically unveils as the "news" of the post-al day is, however, an old narrative of accommodation and evasion that Marx and Engels call "true socialism" (*The German Ideology* 455-581) and which is periodically constructed by petit bourgeois theorists to legitimate the economic interests of the ruling class by ever more seemingly "new" and "innovative" discursive apparatuses. The post-al left ideologists of history "innocently take on trust the illusion, cherished by some . . . literary party representatives" and come to believe that history is not a matter of a "particular class" but simply a process of "pure thought" (*The German Ideology* 454). For Aronowitz this "literary" and anti-materialist version of history becomes a matter of semiotics of identity and the politics of representation ("The Situation of the Left" 48-55).

Richard Wolff's "rethinking of marxism" is equally clear in articulating the goals of *Rethinking Marxism*. The "desire" of the journal is, he announces, to "appropriate, for the Marxist tendencies we champion, the critical breakthroughs in bourgeois theories that can be usefully lumped under the heading 'post-modernism' . . . it is some sort of postmodernist Marxism we are after" (Paul Smith, "An Interview with Richard D. Wolff" 13). Wolff seems to think that *Rethinking Marxism* is undertaking a radically novel project. This is, as I have argued, the very project that Marx and Engels critiqued in their historiography of the bourgeois left as the hybrid practice that attempts to "reconcile communism with the ideas prevailing at the time" (*The German Ideology* 457). The goal of the hybridity is, of course, to exclude the proletariat and to suture classes with radically different economic interests into a liberal hegemonic coalition. Hybridity is the name of a reactionary transclass alliance: the very vogue of "hybridity" as a concept in post-al theory (Homi Bhabha's postcolonial psychoanalysis, Jameson's notion of the hybridity of "mode of production" . . .) is owing to the ability of this concept to represent the social as the effect of conversations of diverse constituencies and intertextualities that are "besides" class.

The post-history represented in these "left" texts is, to use Marx's and Engels's words, a "form of propaganda" that displaces class struggle by bourgeois sentimentality about the "universal love of mankind" (457)—that is, the "pluralism" of the post-al coalitionism which liquidates antagonistic economic interests by means of "hegemony." This is the left that, as both *Socialist Review* and *Rethinking Marxism* proudly display, "turn . . . not to the proletarians but to the two . . . classes" of "petty bourgeoisie with its philanthropic illusions and to the ideologists of this very same petty bourgeoisie: the philosophers and their disciples" (457). The petit bourgeois "form of propaganda," which is most effectively carried out in the texts of the hybrid left, is the cutting off of modernism from postmodernism, thereby producing, as I have already discussed, a version of de-materialized history which has no middle. In the writings of Fredric Jameson—who is called by his publisher "the foremost Marxist literary critic in the world today" (Routledge catalog on "Literary and Cultural Studies 1995," 43)—the apocalypse takes the form of the end of "critique." By deploying as his limit text the practice of "critique," Jameson not only arrives at a new version of history-without-class-struggle but at the same time discredits any critique of the interests legitimated by his version of history. He does so by announcing that the "after" of the post, means the "before-ness" (outdatedness) of critique. The termination of the project of critique and the substitution of the sentimentality of "utopian hope" is perhaps Jameson's most valued service to the post-al knowledge industry. Jameson, the terminator, undertakes the ending of critique in the familiar manner of a "true socialist" through his "literary" detours (*The German Ideology* 457). In *Postmodernism or, The Cultural Logic of Late Capitalism*, Jameson posits the end of labor and the emergence of "consumption" as one of the marks of the end of modernism. Postmodernism, for Jameson, has so radically articulated the space and/of identities that the distance between the critic and cultural/political practices no longer exists (as it did in modernism). Postmodernism is thus the regime of the gap (no middle) of desire and not a connecting (middle-ed and thus global) critique: "the cultural critic," he writes, "along with the rest of us, is now so deeply immersed in postmodernist space, so deeply suffused and infected by its new cultural categories, that the luxury of the old-fashioned ideological critique . . . becomes unavailable" (46).

Postmodernism for Jameson, is not simply an aesthetic term; it is equivalent to a theory of history. His goal, in other words, is not a local observation of a particular aesthetic practice but rather to figure out how that practice is symptomatic of the global apocalypse of the end of history and the eruption of a post-history in which one cannot situate oneself in any critique-al way but becomes part of a mediated-constructed landscape (400) in which all categories of historical materialism break down. In the post-al moment, critique, to go back to my discussion of effectivity, is not, according to Jameson, an effective practice: it does not include. In this post-al context, then, Jameson, in his utopia of hope, finds Lenin wanting, because Lenin, according to Jameson, does not have much to say about the "media" and what he has to say about "imperialism" needs to be up-dated to be useful (400). What Jameson says Lenin cannot say about the media is, of course, what Jameson does not want to hear about the media: for Lenin does not regard the media idealistically—in terms of utopian hope—but historically and materialistically. This, according to Jameson, is an ineffective way to deal with the media because it critiques the media which seems to imply that Lenin has an "outside" of culture (not suffused by the media) from which he can offer a critique. The "outside" on which Lenin stands is, as I have discussed elsewhere, the "outside" of the "Working Day"—that is the "outside" of surplus labor ("The Stupidity that Consumption is Just as Productive as Production"). Jameson's quarrel with critique, it now becomes clear, is merely an epistemological skirmish which acts as a distraction from his main goal, which is to obscure the laws of motion of capital by concealing the "outside" of capitalism: the existence of an unassimilable antagonism with capitalism—the practice of extraction of surplus labor from the proletariat by the capitalist. Lenin is radically and materially effective in showing how the media participates in the representation of the "working day" as a natural day. Hope is the valued commodity of the hybrid left because it makes the material contradictions of the "everyday" tolerable. The genealogy of "hope" for the bourgeois left is, of course, a complicated one. But the popularity of the sufi texts of Ernest Bloch (*The Principle of Hope*) and the "after-ist" history of Jameson and now Ronald Aronson (*After Marxism*)—which make Bloch more commonsensical for U.S. readers—all indicate how hope is an ally of capital in its ruthless exploitation of the workers of the world. Utopianism is the ideology of cybercapitalism.

Four

Class is the repressed concept in all theories of post-ality. They declare it dead—as a historical aberration, a pathology of early capitalism—and on the verge of becoming an "anachronism" in the post-al moment (Esping-Andersen, "Post-Industrial Class Structures" 7). But the repressed returns over and over again and haunts all discourses on post-ality. For instance, Esping-Andersen deploys the usual "scholarly" gestures of "on the one hand/on the other hand" ("Mobility Regimes" 225-241) not only to celebrate the end of Fordism and the demise of the working class—along with what he calls the industrial class structure—but also, without any hint of irony, to reproduce class and even the same class structure under the new name of "post-industrial hierarchy" ("Post-Industrial Class Strucutres" 25). His "post-industrial hierarchy" has the same number of class slots, the same hierarchies and the same order of prestige. The radical difference that he finds between "dead" and "living" classes is that the "command structure is obviously less clear-cut within post-industrial hierarchy" (25). The only things that seems to have changed in his Post-Fordist scheme are the names of the class slots (24-25) and his insistence on "hierarchy" as a criterion. Other post-al theorists share a similar logic: Bell, for example, thinks "class" is dead and we should be talking about "status groups," and Bourdieu displaces class with "habitus." All of them deploy what in the bourgeois knowledge industry is perceived as "subtle" and "sophisticated" scholarly "argument" to represent a change in the mechanisms of class exploitation (the mediations of such Fordist or Post-Fordist practices as mobility/flexibility/power) as the abolition of exploitation itself and the end of the extraction of surplus labor, which is the only determinant of class. "Mobility experiences" or class mobility (Esping-Andersen 226), for example, is one of the mechanisms of exploitation in the Post-Fordist order (assuming, for the moment, that class mobility is indeed greater in the Post-Fordist regime than in the Fordist). Class mobility in no way indicates the disappearance of class or a radical change in class structure (Esping-Andersen, "Mobility Regimes" 228-229): it simply means that the subject of exploitation in the Post-Fordist order is a traveling subject. Exploitation itself—the determinant of class—is not mobile; it is permanent. The "old" view "of classes," Esping-Andersen writes, "assumes . . . a 'fordist' type of mobility regime. This however, is *everywhere* coming apart . . . " (emphasis added, 227). Esping-Andersen's announcement of the collapse of Fordism, however, comes at the very time when even he cannot deny (31) that the most brutal form of Fordist Taylorism dominates such frontiers of the post-Fordist "leisure" and "service" sectors as McDonald's fast food restaurants and that "flexibility" itself has become merely a euphemism for the emerging lumpenproletariat of contingent workers—what F. Michon calls "disponible" ("Dualism and the French Labor Market").

Exploitation, the determinant of class relations, is far from being an "old" Fordist practice that has all but disappeared from cybercapitalism, instead it is the condition of possibility for the "prosperity" of post-al societies. *The New York Times*, the voice of U.S. capitalism, has published , a "special report" on "hard labor" on the front page of its February 6, 1995 issue ("Despite Tough Laws, Sweatshops Flourish" A-1; B-4). The article provides more evidence that the exploitation of labor is not only not an "obsolete" practice but is as much an integral part of Post-Fordism as it was of Fordism: the Fordist/Post-Fordist are simply two modalities for increasing the rate of profit. Post-Fordism is not a negation but an updating of the Fordist regime of exploitation. Two months before the appearance of *The New York Times* article, the other organ of transnational capitalism, the *Wall Street Journal*, wrote

> While American industry reaps the benefits of a new, high-technology era, it has consigned a larger class of workers to a Dickensian time warp, laboring not just for meager wages but also under dehumanizing and often dangerous conditions. Automation which has liberated thousands from backbreaking drudgery, has created for others a new and insidious toil in many high growth industries: work that is faster than ever before, subject to Orwellian control and electronic surveillance, and reduced to limited tasks that are numbingly repetitive, potentially crippling and stripped of any meaningful skills or the chance to develop them. (Quoted in "Millions Destined for Poverty as 'High-Tech' Economy Grows," *The People* December 24, 1994, 1).

Opposing Post-Fordism to Fordism is itself one of the strategies for the mystification of bourgeois political economy, the purpose of which is to represent Fordism as the pathology of capitalism and Post-Fordism as the threshold of a new beginning—a post-al cure. However, the constant of both labor regimes (assuming that there are two structurally different labor regimes) is profit and its increase through the expansion of surplus labor.

Post-al theories of class are narratives aimed at obscuring this constant of capitalism by marginalizing production. I need, therefore, to briefly return to my discussion of production/consumption. In my previous critique, I focused on the modes in which consumption was itself represented as a form of production. Here, I emphasize another aspect of consumptionism and will indicate how consumption practices are deployed to found the ludic argument about the outdatedness of class: the notion, in short, that class, as the central locus of collective subjectivity and agency, is dead. In his *Social Theory and the Urban Question*, Peter Saunders writes that a major "fault line" is opening up in post-al societies between those "who can service their key consumption requirements through the market" and those who "remain reliant on an increasingly inadequate and alienating form of direct state provision." This division, which, according to Saunders, rises from the "social division of consumption," is taking the place of "class divisions" (290). Post-al social theory posits that "social relations of consumption" (not "class") articulate such practices as, for example, working class voters supporting the Republican Party in the U.S. ("class dealignment") or voting for post-fascists in Italy. What Saunders obscures is that the difference between the two segments of society he mentions is not one of who has access to the market for private consumption and who has not. Rather the question is what economic and social practices make such a difference possible: what is that gives some people easy access to the market and denies others the same access. The difference between the two is caused not by their mode of consumption. The mode of their consumption is itself an effect of their place in the social relations of production. To divide people according to whether they get bread by giving food-stamps to the cashier or by paying for it with money from their wages is to follow the path of reactionary theorists who have theorized the "proletariat" as the impoverished masses and then placed in the rank of the "middle class" anyone who purchases a TV or a car or who has a mortgage on a house. What separates people is not ownership of consumption items, but ownership of the means of production. The person who pays by food stamp and the worker who pays by his paycheck are in the same class of people: those who do not have access (not to the means of consumption) but to the means of production. The person missing from Saunders's theory is the one whose money is from profit: the owner of means of production. All theories of consumption-as-class erase the antagonism between "wages" and "profit" and treat "money" as the power to purchase consumption items without tracing the source of the money. Post-al theories, such as (post)structuralism, have, by deconstructing "origin," discredited all inquiries about "origin" because such inquiries are all, ultimately, about the "origin" of wealth. In the absence of such knowledge, all monies are simply ahistorical means for purchasing items of consumption, and all private consumers, in Saunders's theory, are equal! Such a theorizing of consumption in isolation from production, predictably, leads to the conclusion that "class" is an "anachronism" in post-al societies.

According to these views, the effective site of social change in post-al theory is not "class" but the incommensurate consuming "identities" obtained in what Angela McRobbie calls the "social relations of shopping" (34). Consumption in post-al theory is "the source of power and pleasure" (Frank Mort 161), and "pleasure" is, of course, the ludic site of "resistance: "Commodities and their images are multi-accented, they can be pushed and pulled into the service of resistant demands and dreams. High-tech in the hands of young blacks or girls making-up are not simply forms of buying into the system. They can be very effectively hijacked for cultures of resistance, reappearing as street-style creed or assertive femininity" (166). Class struggle as the force for social change is, in cybercapitalism, displaced by the "high-jacking" of commodities. In these scenarios of "resistance," the possession of the commodity is always taken for granted: the fact that they need to be purchased and purchasing requires material resources which are determined by the property relations in which the purchasers are situated is always quietly marginalized. In post-al theory pleasure/consumption are seen as identical and as inherently enabling. In her essay "New Times in Cultural Studies," Angela McRobbie argues that the views of the "Orthodox left" on the priority of class have become outdated given the fact that commodities are invested, "particularly by the working class youth" with "new, bizarre, or oppositional meanings" (31). The young working class man who "goes to Armani to buy expensive cashmere jumpers" (pullover sweaters) is not just giving into a "mindless passive activity" of consuming and "social conformity," but instead he is demonstrating an active acquiring of a new identity that is a resistance to the notion of "masculinity" dominant in the working class and a process of "renegotiating" the masculine and overwriting it as "perhaps even a feminization" (McRobbie 34). Since it is assumed that the norm of "masculinity" is ideological and, as such, a class constraint, to break it by wearing an Armani sweater is a form of resistance to class structure under capitalism. In doing so, the buyer of the "expensive" Armani "cashmere jumper" goes against the imposed class norms and defines himself along other axes of identities than "class" and transgresses his social "role." In *Contemporary Capitalism and the Middle Classes*, the well-known communist theorist, S. N. Nadel, engages this very issue: "According to the logic of bourgeois theorists, the ongoing changes in bourgeois society are not the consequences of contradictions, antagonisms and the struggle of different socio-class forces, but only the result of the violation of 'role expectations'" (24). The thrust of reactionary post-al theory is to blur the line between consumption and production and fuse the antagonistic subjects of labor and capital into a hybrid subject. The name of this emerging hybrid subject is "prosumer": a subject in which consumption is indistinguishable from production (Toffler, *The Third Wave* 37-45; 265-288).

In this post-al scenario the proletariat is no longer the revolutionary vanguard but a "shopper," who daringly consumes objects such as cashmere sweaters forbidden for his consumption by the binary representation of bourgeois/proletariat. In doing so, he deconstructs the binary; shows the implication of one in the other; goes beyond "class" lines, and "experiences" guilty pleasures. Guilty pleasures—the transgressions of class codes—are marks of resistance to capital. "Social relations of shopping" thus displace "social relations of production" and transgressive pleasures (role violations), not class struggle become the dynamics of social change in the post-al moment.

The deconstruction of class in post-ality has taken two distinct modes: the (post)structuralist dismantling of class as a binary structure (for instance in Woodiwiss, *Social Theory after Postmodernism*; Dimock and Gilmore, *Rethinking Class*) and the sociological reconstruction of class founded upon "empiricism"—the belief that a new "service class" of managers and professionals have emerged in the post-al societies whose members do not fit the classical Marxist bipolar model (for example in E. O. Wright, *Classes* and his *Interrogating Inequality: Essays on Class Analysis, Socialism and Marxism*). In my discussion, however, I will critique both as part of the general economy of post-al theory since the sociological theory of class—which is not overtly informed by the anti-foundationalism of (post)structuralism—and the (post)structuralist critique—which is anti-empirical—are both effects of changes in the bourgeois knowledge industry caused by the "long boom" in postwar capitalism. In other words, although these two frames of intelligibilities—(post)structuralist textualism and social science empiricism—are commonly regarded as radically different and do use different strategies (empiricism in one and rhetoric in the other) to deal with the question of class, they both perform the dominant ideological task of bourgeois knowledges, which is to construct concepts that remove (or at least reduce) class antagonisms from the social relations of property.

Class is such a significant concept in understanding post-ality because all historical societies are societies of change, and one arrives at radically different views of existing societies depending on whether (and how) the concept of "class" is deployed in the analysis of these societies and their social order. Contestations over class in the post-al moment, in short, are part of the social struggle over the very legitimacy of the ruling order and its underlying existing social formations. Conservative theories marginalize "class" antagonisms and see social change in terms of the great transgressions of "ideas," great "men" (and, occasionally, great "women"), the invisible hand of the market, or a variety of similar factors but not class—that is they do not see social change as the effect of the transformation of material forces and thus do not consider the existing social order (capitalism) to be what it is because of the accumulation of capital as the result of the appropriation of the labor of the many by the few. Even when these theories deploy the concept of class, as in Weberian theories, they theorize class in such a way that it is more an index of political, cultural and psychological practices than economic and material ones.

Marxism explains social change in terms of class: "The history of all hitherto existing society is the history of class struggle" (*Manifesto of the Communist Party*, 40). To be more precise: it explains social change as the effect of conflicts between the forces of production and the social relations of production and not transgressive ideas, roles and ingenuity. As Marx argues:

> The mode of production of material life conditions the general process of social, political, and intellectual life. It is not the consciousness of men that determines their experience, but their social existence that determines their consciousness. At a certain stage of the development, material productive forces of society come into conflict with the existing relations of production of—this is merely expressing the same thing in legal terms—with the property relations within the framework of which they have operated hitherto. From forms of development of productive forces these relations turn into their fetters. Then begins an era of social revolution. The changes in the economic foundation lead sooner or later to the transformation of the whole immense superstructure. (*A Contribution to the Critique of Political Economy* 20-21)

In short, the social relations of production determine whether social products belongs to all members of society (a classless society) or whether they are appropriated by the few who privately own the means of production. Class is the effect of the historical development of a society: its mode of production and the way it places the subject of labor in the social relations of production. Is the subject one who benefits from the labor of others—is he/she an "exploiter" (a "bourgeois," *Manifesto* 41; 43-50) or is her/his labor "exploited" by the owners of the means of production (in which case he/she is a "proletariat," *Manifesto* 41; 51-60). Class, then, is an articulation of the relations of exploitation in class societies. In classical Marxism, therefore, knowledge of class is fundamental to understanding and consequently changing societies.

The general argument of post-al theorists against the Marxist theory of class is that the emerging "realities" of capitalism AFTER capitalism, that is, the freeing of capital from labor (which is said to be the hallmark of post-al capitalism) has brought about structural changes which have displaced "class" as a central category of the social organization of life. The new post-al practices of capitalism, it is said, exceed the analytical range of a class theory which is based on the location of the subject in the social relations of production.

The main evidence used to "prove" the new realities of post-al capitalism is the emergence of managers and non-manual workers, such as clerks, along with the displacement of a stable workforce by contingent workers. These groups are located between the bourgeois and the proletariat, and their in-betweenness, the argument goes, is constitutive of post-al capitalism. Thus they cannot be explained by a bipolar Marxist theory of class, because, according to this view, they are instances of difference *within* class structure itself (not simply difference *between* classes). Such differences within undermine the coherence not only of the classical Marxist theory of class but of the very concept of class itself. This seeming incoherence of class, its self-dividedness, furthermore indicates that no totalizing concept such as class can account for the formation of the subject (differential identities) in the post-al moment when differences are constructed along plural axes of cultural and social practices such as gender, race, sexuality, nationality, religion, region, ethnicity and consumption.

What post-al theories offer as new realities that have rendered class an obsolete category are really changes not in class structures but in the structure of employment (to which I will return later). The convenient mystification of employment (occupation) as class—as I shall argue—is one of the many ideological maneuvers aimed at substituting local mediations and modifications for fundamental structures of exploitation. The change in patterns of employment, in other words, does not contradict Marx and Engels's theory of "class"—"Society as a whole is more and more splitting up into two great hostile camps, into two great classes directly facing each other: Bourgeois and Proletariat" (*Manifesto of the Communist Party* 41). This structure of conflict underlies the shifting patterns of employment and occupations that bourgeois sociology deploys to obscure class structure under capitalism. Patterns of employment constantly vary; they are the effects of the anarchy of "market chances" (the axis of analysis in Weberian class theory). But the structure of class remains stable under capitalism because it is produced by the constant of exploitation.

As a result of the modifications in the structure of employment, the manager has risen to increasing prominence in cybercapitalism and is said to be neither a worker nor a capitalist but rather the difference within the class structure itself. Moreover, the knowledge of the manager—not the labor of the proletariat—is assumed to be the source of post-al power and wealth. The proletariat, it is believed, is equally divided by its own difference within and is for the most part now composed of a core of highly paid workers and an increasing number of service providers. Productionist explanations, according to the post-al argument, are irrelevant to the emerging realities of post-al societies. Contrary to the theorists of post-ality, neither of these "changes" amount to structural changes in capitalism and its class structure. Even at their most radical, such changes are merely knots of mediations in the structure of capitalism, and Marx's labor theory of value and class accounts for these changes within the existing structures of capital and wage-labor. The myth of post-al society (the invention of cybercapitalism as a radically new departure from the exploitive relations that are the source of capital), as I suggested at the beginning of this essay, is an ideological maneuver designed to obscure the fundamental laws of motion of capital and the exploitative character of capitalist society.

Post-al theories do not deploy class as an explanatory concept since they argue that class no longer explains societies that have put production behind them. However, when the concept of class is used, in a limited and (in the Derridean sense of the word) "supplementary" manner to gender, race, textualities, nationality . . . sexuality, it is de-materialized. The major contestations over theorizing "class" are, therefore, between those who theorize it as a "material" inequality brought about people's position in the social relations of production (and thus locate it in the "base") and those who reject the theoretical model of "base" and "superstructure" and read class as a matter of *différance*—that is, as a matter of culture and politics and institutions rather than the economic. But such a reading locates class in the superstructure, in spite of their rejection of the concept. This culturalism is true even of such "Regulation" theorists as M. Aglietta (*A Theory of Capitalist Regulation*) and Robert Boyer ("Technical Change and Theory of Regulation") who regard themselves to be "materialist" and even "marxist."

To recapitulate, the materialist understanding of class regards class to be the effect of the position of the subject in the social relations of production—class, in short, is a question of the relations of property. Accordingly, historical materialism recognizes only two classes in society: the "bourgeoisie" (owners of the means of production) and the "proletariat" (those who do not own the means of production and thus are forced to sell their labor power). The other classes such as the petit bourgeoisie are regarded to be class fractions and transitional: as capitalism becomes more complex it absorbs all the class fractions/transitional classes into one of its two major poles. "In large-scale industry and competition the whole mass of conditions of existence, limitations, biases of individuals, are fused together into two the simplest forms: private property and labor" (*The German Ideology* 85).

Class therefore is not just another "difference" in Marxism but the central force in the social organization and dynamics of history itself. Even in such early materialist texts as *The German Ideology*, Marx and Engels emphasize that class is not simply a cultural or political difference but the articulation of the material interests of people. As such, it is an index of social antagonism—the very social relation, by the way, that post-al theories of class attempt to erase through reading class as a question of "difference" and thus society as a hegemonic organization not of antagonism but of an ongoing conversation to produce consensus. "The separate individuals," Marx and Engels write:

> form a class only in so far as they have to carry on a common battle against another class; in other respects they are on hostile terms with each other as competitors. *On the other hand, the class in its turn assumes an independent existence as against individuals, so that the latter find their conditions of life predetermined, and have their position in life and hence their personal development assigned to them by their class, thus becoming subsumed under it. This is the same phenomenon as the subjection of the separate individuals to the division of labor and can only be removed by the abolition of private property and of labor itself"* (emphasis added, 77).

This "subsuming of individuals under class," they make clear, "brings with it their subjection to all kinds of ideas" (77). Class, in other words, determines all aspects of the life of the individual as part of a collectivity whose formation is economic and not volunteeristic ("coalition").

In classical Marxist theory, class is, therefore, not the outcome of "income" or "status" or "occupation" (as it is in Weberian bourgeois sociology that underlies post-al theories of class). Changes that post-al theory regards to be radical structural change are, from a historical materialist perspective, superstructural changes and not changes in the material base that, in fact, determines class formation. These superstructural changes represent complications in "how" the social relations of production do what they have always done under capitalism: enforce the social division of labor. At stake here is not "how" the exploited surplus value is distributed (as consumptionist theories lead us to believe), but rather the continued practice of exploitation itself. Complications and new mediations in distribution should not obscure the fundamental laws of motion of capital which are the laws of the social division of labor and class structure.

In the "Working Day," Marx argues (*Capital*, 1, 340-416), people either produce surplus value, in which case they are part of the "proletariat," or they exploit surplus value—that is they own the means of production (the "bourgeois") and are in a position to make other people work for them. Class, in other words, is the effect of the subject's relation to the source of "profit" (surplus labor). The fact that the extracted surplus value gets distributed by capitalists through such "new" relays as knowledge-workers and managers (or army officers, teachers, police persons) in no way obliterates the fundamental social and economic division between capitalists and wage-laborers. All post-al theories of class are aimed at substituting the question of "how" surplus value is distributed for the problem of "why" it is extracted: the extraction of surplus labor, in other words, is taken for granted as a natural act because the existence of capitalism itself (which depends on surplus labor) is taken as a fact of nature.

Post-al class theories focus on "how" class structure is "experienced" in daily life and, in doing so, they quietly substitute the observable experiential everyday manifestations of class for its historical and material structures. This maneuver is then deployed to marginalize "exploitation" (the economic) and foreground "domination" (the cultural/political): the material is thus displaced by the cultural, and access to economic resources (capital) is made secondary to access to discourse (power). Post-al theories, in general, are a redeployment of Weberian class theories in which "'classes' and 'status groups' are phenomena of distribution of power within a community" (*From Max Weber: Essays in Sociology* 181). The fact that the "manager" is more "powerful" or has a higher cultural and social status than the worker but is less powerful or has a less prestigious status than the capitalist is seen as the "difference" in the class system. But this is an illusion formed by quietly defining class as the result of "domination" and marginalizing the fundamental material fact of class structure: the position of the subject in the social relations of production and not her place in the social relations of signification (power/status/taste/accent/clothes/ . . .). This illusory view of class is disseminated through (mostly) visual effects in the popular culture: from various TV shows to such monthly and weekly publications as *Time, Newsweek, Vanity Fair, Vogue, GQ*, and by catalogues of goods and services, like *Patagonia, Lands' End*. Also traditional moralist-humanists, such as Christopher Lasch, deploy a similar notion of class (as power) when they define class as an "elite"—that is as a politico-cultural group. Such a view of class not only does not explain the logic of capitalist social relations, but, in fact, like all bourgeois knowledges, it obscures the lines of class antagonism. Lasch, for example, thinks that the "problem" with U.S. society—the most class-divided advanced "democracy"—is that the "elite" has abandoned its moral and social obligation to the ordinary people. The problem, in other words, is "spiritual" and not "economic" (*The Revolt of the Elites and the Betrayal of Democracy*).

These representations disseminate the view that the post-al moment is the moment of individual (not collective) identities articulated by such intersecting factors as sexuality, race, nationality, gender, religion and such other practices as patterns of consumption and taste. These identities acquire their full display, it is said, when the individual has access to the appropriate discourses: it is this access to discourses that allows the lesbian, the African-American, the subcultural "grunge" to become what they are. They are, in other words, not determined by their class but overdetermined (and thus always reversible and open) by multiple factors of difference. Access to discourses is, following Foucault and later Baudrillard, regarded to be access to "power." Therefore, to the extent that class has any place in post-al theories, it is understood not as a matter of "exploitation" but of "domination": emancipation is, thus, a "private" act—freeing oneself from power and thus empowering oneself.

What makes the power/domination theory of class so attractive to post-al theorists is that since power in these theories is seen as a diffuse and non-localized practice open to all, everyone has access to discourse/power. Thus one can, accordingly, empower oneself within the existing social relations of production. (A similar strategy, as I will discuss later, is used in theorizing post-al capital itself as an instance of the diffusion of ownership.) There is, according to these theories, no need for revolution to bring about a different social relations of production; one can be free within the existing society by simply acquiring access to discourses that will allow one to speak for oneself (Deleuze in *Language, Counter-Memory, Practice* 206). Domination, unlike exploitation, is seen, in other words, as a matter of "negotiation," a "conversation," finding one's own "voice," which is another way of saying it is the ability to use discourse to "persuade." (This is, by the way, the main reason for the boom in "rhetoric" in the bourgeois knowledge industry.) The assumption is, of course, that to persuade one does not need "capital" one needs "discourse." If power is available to all, then acquiring it does not depend on acquiring material access: one can be poor but acquire one's identity and voice, for example, as a lesbian or a person of color within the existing social relations of production. This notion of domination/power occults the fact that power, itself, is always produced by material forces (not discourses), that is, in the relations of production. To the extent that power is powerful, it is because it is supported by the ownership of the means of production. Persuasion itself depends on economic access. The persuaded is always persuaded not because of the power of the trope and discourse (although that is how persuasion is represented in ludic rhetoric), but because "the silent compulsion of economic relations sets the seal on the domination of the capitalist over the worker" (Marx, *Capital*, 1, 899). Theories that see class in terms of domination, however, represent power as autonomous—as separated from the material forces that historically produce power—the ownership of the means of production.

The idea of class as domination finds its everyday manifestations in the practical and commonsensical views of class that see class as a social ordering frame (Lasch's elite/non-elite hierarchy for example): who has more (of prestige or money) or better (job). All versions of class as domination, ultimately are versions of a theory of class as a form of hierarchy of power (even though post-al theory, formally, rejects the notion of power as hierarchy). Traditionally, these non-materialist theories of class have posited class in terms of *occupation; status, income,* and *function* and the like. The post-al theories of class are not "explanations" of the objective logic of capital—the historical materialist knowledge of the organization of a society, its division of labor, distribution of wealth and administration of social justice—but rather are "descriptions" of the specific circumstances of individuals; what Weber calls chances in the market, that is, the power to consume. In the name of inclusiveness, post-al theories introduce into their analysis a range of contingencies that occult any sense of social totality. Consequently, the representation of class as occupation, for example, makes it "natural" in post-al theories to raise the issue of women's work (occupational inequality) as an autonomous question: as a matter of gender and not a world-historical problem of the social relation of production. The same is true about the occupational inequalities of persons of color, physically-challenged persons, children's work and the like. Specific, localist descriptions suppress the objective conditions of production that divide people, with rigid clarity, into exploiters and exploited, emphasizing instead the "huge, fantastic gray" zone of differences. The seductive appeal, for the post-al theorist, of the Weberian pedagogy of the gray, in contrast to Marx's red theory of class, is its concern with such contingent factors as "status" and the way it marginalizes social antagonism, installing instead the social semiotics of preferences and prestige. However, for "class" to be a useful concept, it must meet the two criteria put forth by Marx and Engels (as I discussed earlier): it must provide knowledge of the social relations of production and its underlying logic, and, furthermore, such knowledge must provide guidelines for developing a classless society—abolishing the social division of labor.

When class is equated with status, as Alex Callinicos shows (*The Changing Working Class* 1-11), the focus of analysis is shifted from economic exploitation and relations of production to matters of consumption, educational capital and cultural prestige. Like Vance Packard's classic *The Status Seekers*, Paul Fussell's book on the contemporary class situation in the U.S., called *Class*, is an instance of understanding class as status. He spends the entire book discussing accents, eating manners, weight, and clothes. Throughout the book, his main goal is to establish an order of social desirability based on the "mode of shopping" so that he can single out the traits that mark a person's status and show his/her cultural prestige. Class, for Fussell, is a marker of "climbing and sinking and drifting" and not the logic of labor relations. When class is defined as status, status is often implicitly measured in terms of the quality (and quantity) of consumption. What makes people members of the same class, then, is not their position in the relations of production but their quota of consumption. Angela McRobbie's example of the working class youth, who buys the expensive Armani cashmere sweater and thus transgresses, in this calculus of status, the boundaries of the "working class," is founded upon this idealist notion of class. His cashmere sweater, not the surplus labor that he produces, is what (over)determines his social identity. This consumptionist view, furthermore, implies that the lines separating the "working class" from other classes is disappearing since the same item of consumption (a cashmere sweater) is now available to all. Nadel's analysis of the change of ratio of consumption is helpful here: the irresistible development of productive forces, he writes, "ensures that the law of rising requirements acts more intensively than before, enveloping all social layers of the population. It is quite natural that the demands put forward now by the working class substantially exceed the demands of the previous generations of workers" (83). In his *Classes*, E.O. Wright argues that post-al theories that regard class to be a question of status are a continuation of Weberian theories in which "the logic of social order" is explained not by relations of exploitation but by "meaning systems" (108). In this notion of class-as-status-as-meaning-as-textuality, the sociological and the rhetorical approaches to class meet. Post-al theories, of course, regard "meaning" (discourse/signs/textuality) to be "material," but post-al "materialism" is, as Teresa L. Ebert argues in her *Ludic Feminism and After*, a species of "matterism" that Marx critiqued in Feuerbach and other left Hegelians. "Matterism"—the cashmere sweater theory of class—is what covers over the materialist gap between classes. In post-al theory the class gap is always bridged by the "matter" of class-as-meaning-effect: puns and tropes. In his article, "Red London," for example, Gary Gensoko uses a pun to cover over the antagonism that separates Karl Marx from his contemporary, the philosopher of the ruling class, Herbert Spencer, by deploying a language-effect that places both of them in the same punceptual shopping relations. In describing Marx's grave, he writes, "Few miss the irony that Herbert Spencer is buried close to Marx, reminding one of another famous British couple, Marks and Spencer" (37). The (non)argument of this textual ecstasy is that the shopping place (the British chain of stores "Marks and Spencer") is the site of the disappearance of class gaps, since people of various classes (the blue and the white collars) do shop at "Marks and Spencer." Consumption puts an end to class antagonism.

The theory of class as consumption identity informs not only popular works like Fussell's *Class* but theoretical writings such as Bourdieu's *Distinction* and his "What Makes a Social Class?" This is an idealist theory that substitutes semiotic order for materialist logic. Bourdieu, who has become a prominent figure in ludic social theory, for example, substitutes for the social relations of production, the social relations of distinction (that is, "difference") which is for him ultimately a matter of "power" and not "exploitation." For him "capital" is not material but also "social," "cultural" and, most importantly, "symbolic." The major issue for him is, ultimately, the patterns of consumption. Consequently class is no longer a historical objectivity but a differential signification, like "a flame whose edges are in constant movement, oscillating around a line or surface" ("What Makes a Social Class?" 13). The politics of the theory of class as status can perhaps be most clearly seen in the way that such a view of class separates the cultural from the economic and thus allows the ruling class to manage class antagonism by circulating the notion that to be a person of high class (socially desirable) one does not actually need to have access to economic resources. William Safire, the U.S. right-wing *New York Times* columnist, therefore is able to say in his punceptual piece "Middle-Class War" that "We don't need" to embrace "class as a way to categorize American society" because class is not a matter of being rich: "richies can be low-class slobs and *the genteel down-at-the-heels can be high-class povertarians"* (A-19). The goal of the theory of class as status is to obscure the material difference between the "rich" and the "poor" by providing a cultural high place for the noble "povertarians"; what they do not have in material terms is given to them discursively.

Even though the theory of class as "income" seems to be more materialist than the idea of class as status, it is, in fact, equally "culturalist," to use Wright's term (108), because it occults the relations of exploitation which is the logic of capital and wage-labor. In theorizing class in terms of "income," the fundamental historical feature of capitalism is obscured by assuming that all "income," regardless of how it is made, is the same. In other words, to regard class as an expression of "income" erases the social antagonisms that underlie different kinds of "income." There are fundamentally two modes of income, and their different modalities are the differences of the historical formation of classes. The "income" that is constituted of "wages" is not the same as the "income" derived from "profit." In *Grundrisse* Marx defines "wages" as "The price of necessary labor" (570) and in *Capital* (2, 447), he calls it the "value of labor-power." In other words, the income that is made of wages is an expression of the fact that the capitalist has bought "the temporary disposal of labor-power" (Marx, *Theories of Surplus Value* 1, 86). This means that "wages" are always an articulation of exploitation since wages are only a compensation for the worker's labor power, which means that they are always compensation for part of the work done. The unpaid part is the capitalist's "profit," which is "The sum of surplus value" (*Grundrisse* 767). In *Capital* 3, Marx is more explicit about the character of "profit" when he theorizes it as "The converted form of surplus-value, a form in which its origin and the secret of its existence are obscured and extinguished" (139). To say that class is simply a matter of "income" (market chances, in Weberian post-al theory) is to occult the fact that "wages" and "profit" are indicators of a social relation of class antagonism and not of similarity.

In *Wage-Labor and Capital*, Marx makes the antagonism between "wages" and "profit" clear, and indicates how the idea of class as "income" mystifies the most fundamental contradiction of capitalism. "The interests of capital," Marx writes, "and the interests of wage-labor are diametrically opposed to each other" (39). He goes on to say that even in the most favorable situations no matter how the standard of life of the worker might have improved (his ability, for example, as the result of wage increases, to buy a cashmere sweater), such an improvement "does not abolish the antagonism between his interests and the interests of capitalist" (39). Post-al theories like McRobbie's, which equate class with "income," rely on the "embourgeoisment" theory that the increased affluence of the working class has, in fact, eliminated the differences between this class and other classes. The "embourgeoisment" theory is still a very influential one; it is an idealist view in bourgeois sociology that (mis)represents the hold of capital on social institutions, claiming it is a result of the lack of ideological awareness and thus passivity of the working class and not a result of its material-financial resources. Nadel's critique of the "embourgeoisment" theory in his *Contemporary Capitalism and the Middle Classes* is quite to the point here. "A certain growth in worker's wages . . . does not change the principle of capitalist distribution, according to which wages correspond to the value of labor-power only ideally, and profits, always and inevitably, to the value of unpaid labor" (82). The workers rely on wages because of lack of access to the means of production. "It is precisely this lack of means of production, the need to sell his labor-power, and the resulting exploitation by the capital owner that constitutes the essence of the proletarian's condition. *Possession of a refrigerator or a TV set does not change the essence of his condition*" (81-82). Vanneman and Cannon (in spite of their own idealist tendencies that privileges "power" without materializing it) argue in their *The American Perception of Class*, embourgeoisment theories "assume that affluence makes a difference—that workers who live comfortably enough will begin to see themselves as middle class" (275). Vanneman and Cannon clarify that "affluence is a dimension of social status," and they agree that while it may be important for many things, it does not substitute for material power. "What makes" people members of the "working class," they agree, is their exploited position in social relations of production and not "their modest life style" (275). The reason is, as Marx argues, that *"Profit and wages* remain . . . *in inverse proportion"* (39). "Wages" and "profit" stand in inverse proportion because *"The share of (profit) increases in the same proportion in which the share of labor (wages) falls"* (37). Post-al theories of class take the blue collar workers' wage increases, which have made some of their purchasing patterns similar to those of white collar workers, as a sign of irrelevance of class in the post-al moment. They merge "profit" and "wages" into "income" and use it as a marker of class to erase the materialist gap between classes and their historical antagonism.

  Class is mystified in bourgeois sociology and the everyday discourses of the media by yet another conceptual de tour, namely by equating it with the "occupation" and "employment" of the subject. This view not only shapes the pop theories of class (Packard, Fussell, DeMott) but it also underlies the official theories that inform the calculations of the U.S. Department of Labor and dominates the writings of both conservative sociologists (Bell) and the "left Weberians" (Lockwood,

Goldthorpe, Dahrendorf), as well as those such of neo-Marxists as E.O. Wright, whose theory of class in all its various revisions is almost entirely based on the structure of employment. In the official texts/statistics, jobs are usually divided into two major categories, "white collar" and "blue collar." In post-al theories, consequently, all non-manual workpersons are regarded as "white collar" but such a categorization obscures rather than clarifies the logic of social order, because it separates people who have the same material conditions and an identical place in the social relations of productions into different classes. The main reason for this distinction without difference is to expand category of "white collar" in post-al theory since "white collar" is more an ideological than a scientific category and consequently is, in everyday discourses and bourgeois theory alike, synonymous with "middle class." The ideological expansion of "white collar" legitimates the post-al view that the working class has in fact diminished and is in the process of disappearing—class struggle has come to an end in the post-al moment. This is the place to say again: the goal of all post-al theories of class is to assert that

> under contemporary conditions of the scientific and technological revolution, the essence of work is changing, the alienation of the worker in the process of work is overcome, and a new worker is created who, by his education and material standard of living, becomes a member of the 'middle class.' Nadel, *Contemporary Capitalism and the Middle Classes* 80)

The concept of "middle class" in all post-al discourses is not analytical but part of bourgeois propaganda: it is used, as Nadel goes on to argue, "to sustain the myth that the majority of population in capitalist society belong to the 'class' which possesses prosperity and prestige" (91).

The bourgeois propaganda about the "middle class," thus, occults class as the place of the subject of labor in the social relation of production. This move becomes even more clear in the way that this post-al notion of class represents "small business people," who are, in actuality, to use C. Gerry's term, "disguised proletariat" as members of the "middle class"—that is, a class distinct from the proletariat (188). Gerry shows how these seemingly independent "middle class" entrepreneurs with their own distinct "occupation" have identical material conditions with the proletariat: they work in insecurity under the silent compulsion of economic relations and under intolerable conditions—long hours with very low material return, often without vacation and leisure. In other words, the fact that they have an "occupation" that puts them, formally, in a class (invented by post-al theorists) separate from the proletariat does not in any sense mean that they are not "exploited"—the only material-historical basis for class analysis.

"Occupation" is deployed to argue for the *autonomous* existence of a class which does not "fit" into the Marxist theory of class and, therefore, discredits that theory. The occupation of the self-employed, small entrepreneur as the basis of an autonomous "class" is, as Gerry and Nadel demonstrate, more an ideologically necessary device for legitimating right-wing regimes that use individualism and entrepreneurship as a way of reducing endemic unemployment created out of the contradictions of capitalism than a material reality indicating freedom from exploitation. The criterion of "blue collar" and "white collar" is, like "income" and "status," an idealist representation that mystifies the logic of the social division of labor by substituting the order of cultural desirability for objective, material-historical relations of production. If a "car mechanic" is thought to be in a "lower" or "higher" class than a concert pianist, this categorization say more about the working of ideology and the politics of cultural imaginary—desire —than anything about their position in labor relations or their material interests.

One of the effects of deploying "occupation" as the basis of class is that it allows the bourgeois theorists to pluralize classes and in doing so obscure the rigid binary of exploitation. Steven Brint, for example, in his *In an Age of Experts: The Changing Role of Professionals in Politics and Public Life*, posits at least five different "classes" within the "middle class" alone, all based on "occupation": business services, applied science, culture and communications, civic regulation, and human services. In spite of the prevailing theories of bourgeois sociology, there is not a fundamental structural gap between "white collar" and "blue collar" workers. As Marx argues, the "white collar" worker

> belongs to the better-paid class of wage-laborer; he is one of those whose labor is skilled labor, above-average labor. His wage, however, has a tendency to fall as capitalist mode of production advances, even in relation to average labor. Firstly because the division of labor within the commercial office means that only a one sided development of his ability need be produced and that much of the cost of producing his ability to work is free for the capitalist, since the worker's skill is rather developed by the function itself, and indeed is developed all the more quickly, the more one-sided the function becomes with the division of labor. Secondly, because basic skills, knowledge of commerce and languages, etc., are reproduced ever more quickly, easily, generally and cheaply, the more the capitalist mode of production adapts teaching methods, etc. to practical purposes. The general extension of popular education permits this variety of labor to be recruited from classes which were formerly excluded from it and were accustomed to a lower standard of living. This also in-

creases supply, and with it competition. With a few exceptions, therefore, the labor of these people is devalued with the advance of capitalist production; their wages fall, whereas their working ability increases. The capitalist increases the number of these workers, if he has more value and profit to realize. The increase in this labor is always an effect of the increase in surplus-value, and never a cause of it." (*Capital*, 3, 414-415)

The difference between the "white collar" clerical worker and "blue collar" worker is more one of "cultural" and not one of the material and historical relations of "exploitation." The same cultural relation of "domination" (power) marks the relation between the "white collar" clerical worker and "white collar" professionals and managers (the upper segment of the "white collar"). Professionals and managers, as I will argue shortly, do not have an autonomous base: they are part of the antagonism of capital-labor and not independent from it. One should keep in mind that the entire theory of the "new middle class" or "service class" is not whether the middle strata exist but whether these strata are autonomous, that is, whether they are free-floating strata beyond the reach of the class antagonism of labor and capital. My argument is that bourgeois theories use various strategies (some of which I have outlined here) to represent the middle strata as autonomous and, in doing so, argue that the structure of capitalism itself has undergone a radical shift. This is, however, not objectively the case: the middle strata is a class fraction and a transitional one (even ethnographically it is an unstable strata) without any autonomous material base.

Some neo-Marxists such as Barbara and John Ehrenreich have acknowledged that the new middle class is not autonomous from the antagonism of labor and capital but have treated this class (what they call the professional-managerial class or PMC) as a class that, even though it does not own the means of production and is a salaried class, is still different from the workers because the PMC comes into being in the post-al moment to fulfill a new "function." The function of this new class, according to the Ehrenreichs, is as a class fraction—part of the ruling class—separate from the working class. In doing so they have in fact undermined the theory of class as a material location of the subject in the social relations of production and instead proposed a neo-idealist view of class. This neo-idealist theory posits class as a "function": it situates class outside the historical-material relations of production and places it in the superstructure. Barbara and John Ehrenreich invent their notion of class-as-function by stating that post-al capitalism has given rise to the PMC ("Professional-Managerial Class") who do not own the means of production but receive salaries and whose "major function in the social division of labor may be described broadly as the reproduction of capitalist culture and capitalist class relations" (Walker, *Between Labor and Capital* 12). But as Al Szymanski argues, the deployment of the criterion of "function" as a basis for class membership ends up dematerializing class. If PMC is part of the capitalist class because of its function (reproducing capitalist class relations) so are "bank or insurance workers" and "workers in munition industries" because their "labor allows capitalists to maintain a world empire, i.e. because their *economic* function is to *reproduce capitalist class relations*, just as surely as is that of the professionals who propagate ideology" (Walker, *Between Labor and Capital* 51).

The material base of the ruling class is material assets (the means of production) and not merely cultural and technical assets. This has been the case in all phases of capitalism. Cultural and technical assets are always contextual in their usefulness and effectivity (unlike capital which is effective globally). In other words, cultural and technical assets are "assets" only under specific conditions while material assets are assets as such (in the contemporary world dominated by capitalism). The very positing of the professional and managerial class fraction as part of the ruling class is, therefore, an idealist move which attempts to obscure the material base of class since such a move implies that class position is not related to the social relations of production but is a function of the social relations of signification or what Toffler calls, "symbolic and service activities" (76).

Class as "status," "income," "function," and "occupation," in short, are designations of consumption power and markers of the cultural esteem and influence that are associated with that power—again, these are seen as autonomous and isolated from the social relations of production. It is in the context of such idealist theories of class that *maître d*'s, for example, are separated from waitrons because they are on a higher level of "post-industrial command structure" (Esping-Andersen 25). Knowledge of consumption power does not provide any understanding of the social logic of exploitation but is an index of patterns of distribution of social surplus value. But such knowledge is not useful for social change. Rather it is deployed to affirm the existing structures through the manipulation of desire by the ruling class and its agents: the merchants of desire—advertisers and other marketers of "class" images/representations. The diversionist function of such class analyses becomes clear in a recent ordering of the U.S. population reported in the *Washington Post*. According to this report, post-al marketing experts have divided the U.S. population into no fewer than sixty-two separate classes on the bases of wealth, education, mobility, location, ethnic and racial background as well as many other criteria. This classification places people into categories of "Urban Gold Coasters," "Young Literati," "Money and Brains," and "Scrub Pine Flats" (December 24,

1994). "Mobility," "location" . . . (like "income," "status" . . .) are contingencies that are introduced into class theory, as Barbara Foley argues ("class"), in order to obscure the logic of the social division of labor that a historical materialist theory of class foregrounds. "Class," in the words of Esping-Andersen who sums up the post-al position, may have "multiple roots" (226).

Against theories that treat consumption autonomously and as a source of weakening "class," John H. Goldthorpe and Gordon Marshall, although adopting a revisionary notion of class, demonstrate how questions of consumption cannot in any rigorous sense be separated from class. The claim that "education," to take an instance of consumption often treated as an autonomous social power, is "a force of 'class abatement'"—that it is an independent element free from class and produces such social effects as meritocracy which put an end to class—is contradicted, as they show, by "a high degree of resistance . . . to any tendency favoring a reduction of class inequalities. . . . If class differentials in educational attainment are to some extent diminished, then within more advantaged classes family resources can be applied through *other* channels, in order to help children preserve their class prospects against the threat of meritocratic selection" ("The Promising Future of Class Analysis: A Response to Recent Critiques" 390). Even Esping-Andersen cannot deny the conclusions reached by Goldthorpe and Marshall. One of the arguments that he puts forth is that new kinds of jobs render the Fordist-type of mobility regime (that is "class") irrelevant. These jobs, in the post-al societies that are marked by "service" industries, involve labor characteristics of "immeasurable qualities" (that is instances of "excess" from the labor theory of value) "social graces, inter-personal skills." The kind of "human capital" needed in these jobs, however, he admits, "are acquired mainly in family or in expensive elite schools, not in the classrooms of mass education systems. *Inherited privilege may therefore reappear as a decisive class-filter within post-industrial economies* " (emphasis added, 227).

Post-al theories of class substitute the ordering of domination/power for a materialist analysis and, in doing so, cut off power from exploitation and circulate the ideology that one can empower oneself without economic access. Since almost everyone has "power" in a micropractice (parents over their children who in turn have power over other children; bosses over their employees who in turn have power over other employees or over their wives and children; patrons over waitrons in a restaurant who in turn have power over the busboys who in turn have power . . .), the illusion is created that all people are in "different" ways powerful, and the focus is thus distracted from the binaries between the "powerful" (owners of the means of production) and the "powerless" (those who have nothing but their labor power to sell). The post-al conclusion is that power has nothing to do with economic access (ownership of the means of production). This strategy is what allows the culture industry to serve the ruling class by insisting that class is not an economic category but that the "middle class is a state of mind and a set of values deeply embedded in the heart of America" (Anderson B-1; B-6).

The attempt of post-al theory to deconstruct the view that I have outlined is carried out on several levels. I will focus on only one major issue: the emergence of "managers" as a "new class" (I have addressed other issues in *Theory and its Other*). The emergence of managers is used by post-al theorists to argue that only classic capitalism is marked by the binary of "ownership" and "labor" and that post-al capitalism is, above all, distinguished by a radical new class structure in which the "ownership" of capital is separated from its "control." The underlying assumptions here are Weberian as rehearsed by theorists such as Bourdieu, Foucault, Baudrillard and many others: classes are organized not only around "capital" and "labor" but also, as Anthony Giddens argues (*The Class Structure of Advanced Societies*), around "capital" (property), "labor" (physical power) and "knowledge" (qualifications). The post-al theories that posit "managers" as a new class are part of a theoretical frame of social intelligibility in which the "middle class" is seen, as Gingrich and other cybercapitalists propose, as the prototype of a new civilization composed of "new" ("third wave") clusterings, which cannot be explained in terms appropriate to classic capitalism. In other words, for cybercapitalists, "managers" are a synecdoche of an emerging social order evolving not around "capital" and "labor" but around "qualifications" (knowledge). "It is knowledge," writes the popcybercapitalist Alvin Toffler, "that drives the economy, not economy that drives knowledge" (*Powershift* 413). All theories of the "new class" (which are circulated under various names such as service class, new middle class, PMC and the like) are derived from Karl Renner's neo-marxist notion of "service class" (*Dienstklasse*), which is combined, in various mixes, with Weberian and Foucauldian ideas about power and status. They all regard class to be an effect of "institutions" (power/knowledge/status . . .) and not the social relations of production.

Post-al theorists "read" the emergence of "managers" as an indication of the lessening, if not the end, of "exploitation" in this shift which represents the emancipation of capital from materialist labor and its reliance on the consciousness (innovations) of knowledge people. In fact, the appearance of "managers" is used to argue that post-al capitalism is no longer solely focused on "profit." Instead, because of the agency of the managers—who are (assumed to be) more educated and thus have a much more developed social consciousness—post-al capitalism is seen as more concerned with balancing the need for "profit" with the "claims by various groups in the community and assigning to each a portion of the income stream on the basis of public policy rather than private cupidity" (Berle and Means 313). The moves made here (that is, separation of "control" from "ownership"; attribution of policies to the "consciousness" of managers rather than the laws of motion of capital) are familiar ideological moves of bourgeois theory to pluralize and bring about a class detente in order to reduce the tensions of the daily life—a necessity for raising the efficiency of labor. These ideological maneuvers are aimed at arguing that post-al capitalism is marked above all by what might be called the diffusion of capital—capital is no longer, to use Derrida's term, a "proper" regime but has, in the post-al moment, become im-proper. It is, in other words, no longer a centered property but a diffuse regime in which "different" forms of capital, such as cultural capital, skills capital, educational capital, semiotic capital, "supplement" one another. This is a post logocentric and supplementary capitalism, which Derrida defends in his post-al vision of a post-ideological, liberal Europe (*The Other Heading*).

In their "manifesto" for Post-Fordist capitalism, *The End of Organized Capitalism*, Lash and Urry represent the "managers" (and the "service class," in general) in a more postmodern language as a destabilizing, differential and thus autonomous class with their own unique interests that are contradictory with the interests of the owners. This contradiction, they argue, is the force for the emergence of post-al capitalism because the "managers," in protecting their own interests, resist capitalism through (among other things) forming (non-class) New Social Movements. The conflicts between the proliferating and different interests of "managers" and "capitalists," in other words, transforms capitalism into a site of slippage and non-identity by putting an end to "organized" capitalism (that is the self-identical capitalism called "Fordist"), thus making capitalism more democratic, transclass and Postfordist—what Clauss Offe calls "disorganized capitalism," namely a capitalism of fissures and "excess" that defies all explanation and can only be described instance by instance. For Lash and Urry, therefore, the managers—who are, in fact, the most conservative force in contemporary capitalism— are, as knowledge workers, considered the source of social change. They are seen as deploying the strategies of fissures, deconstruction and disorganization in order to liberate the social from the closure of classical capitalism freeing democratic and incommensurate entrepreneurial differences.

This theory of social change by knowledge workers, that is repeated by

Lash and Urry, is founded upon the postmodern recuperation of the old anarchist anti-statist theories. In fact, Lash and Urry regard the main effect of the mangers' revolt to be the collapse (and thus unleashing of freedom) of the state, since the state cannot possibly deal with the increasing, contradictory and fragmented demands of the New Social Movements. Even though they use a more postmodern language, their view is identical with the popcybercapitalism of such right-wing theorists as Gingrich, who find government to be the main obstacle to freedom and difference. The notion of "organized" capitalism and the idea that liberation comes from a "disorganized" post-al capitalism is the "translation" into liberal politics of Gingrich's idea of de-regulation—dis-organizing capitalism to fit the "Third Wave" forces.

As I mentioned before, each post-al theorist has a different explanation of the autonomy of the "new class," and each, accordingly, proposes a different "basis" for it. There are so many different explanations of the new middle class that they cancel each other out. But this is not so much a symptom of "bad" theorizing (an epistemological inadequacy) as the manifestation of the material and historical truth that what is called the "new middle class" is neither a class in itself nor a class for itself—it is a transitional configuration of class fractions. Those theorists, who have attempted to endow the "new class" with a "base," bring its various fragments together, and speak of it, at least, as a class in itself, have all displaced the materialist base of class with an idealist "cultural capital." Nowhere is this more visible than in the class theories of John Goldthorpe, who adopts a version of Karl Renner's views. Goldthorpe believes that the "service class" is autonomous because it has a unique "base" of interest that is radically different from those of capitalist and workers. The new class has a unique base because "These employees, in being typically engaged in exercise of delegated authority or in the application of specialist knowledge and expertise, operate in their work tasks and roles with a distinctive degree of autonomy and discretion; and in direct consequence of the element of *trust* that is necessarily involved in their relationship with their employing organization . . . " (emphasis added, 169). The autonomy of the new class, in other words, is based on a "moral quality" (168) and not on the position of the subject of labor in the social relations of production. The "new middle class" of knowledge workers, in these theories, are neither "bourgeois" nor "proletariat": they are a hybrid whose main work is the invention of signs—cultural innovation and not economic production.

My critique of these theories of the "new middle class" is, of course, founded upon the notion that class is an objective historical-economic category (that is the necessary condition for "class consciousness") and that the concept of the new middle class/service class does not meet the requirement of any sustained notion of class since it is based not on the place of the subject in the social relations of production but on such idealist and ahistorical notions as "trust," "moral quality," "status," "occupation," "income," and "function." In their *Knowledge and Class*, ludic marxists Stephen A. Resnick and Richard D. Wolff, reject the position I have defended. They are aware that the notions of class as "occupation," "income," "function," "status," and the like, eventually lead to a static understanding of class, so, in rejecting the classical Marxist position, they also try to avoid the critique of their views as being static ("deterministic"). However, they erase class as the objective force of social change by some of the same ideologico-epistemological maneuvers I have already described. Resnick and Wolff perform an operation on class similar to what Foucault and Bourdieu and other ludic writers have done to Power and capital: they diffuse class by positing it as a "class process" (109-163). In this diffusionist theory of class, class does not have an objective existence: what might be represented as "class" in their theory, is an overdetermined, non-binary process which is (in the manner of Deleuze and Guattari) seen as rhizomatic and deterritorialized. They perform this operation, in other words, as a poststructuralist critique of foundationalism and in the specific name of de-essentializing class. With Resnick and Wolff, as with all idealist theorists, it is the epistemology that determines the social and not the social that produces the objective conditions for epistemological inquiry (Marx, *A Contribution to the Critique of Political Economy* 21). The main socioecomonic consequence of the notion of class as process is that it completely erases the proletariat-bourgeois binary since, according to them, "individuals . . . participate in more than one kind of class process" (110). In short, there is no marked line between the "exploiters" and the "exploited"; class matters are matters of coalition, alliances and other processes in social life and not a question determined by "production." This is, of course, a return of the pedagogy of the gray in class matters in which the "black" and "white" are seen as reductive and deterministic, and all social processes are thrown into the zone of overdetermined conversations. Class, they believe, is a post-al negotiation ("interaction" 111) which in Esping-Andersen's words, has "multiple roots" (226). In proposing their notion of class as process, Resnick and Wolff, like all post-al theorists, take as their basis the microphysics of class—HOW surplus labor is extracted (115) and erase the question of WHY it is done. Consequently the "exploitation" of one class by the other—which is the source of "profit," the foundation of capitalism and the logic of class struggle—is in the "process" obliterated. "The class process," they write, "has no existence other than as the site of converging influences exerted by all the non-class processes" (116). The "new middle class" is, then, in terms of Resnick-Wolff's theory of class, an instance of diffuse social process.

These moves obscure the fundamental fact that, as J. Scott shows, (*Corporations, Classes and Capitalism*) even within the logic of the separation of "control" from "ownership," the "control" given to the "managers" is merely an operational control of how the long-term goals set and planned by the capitalists, themselves, are articulated and acted on at the local and microphysical level. The significant "control" of long-term projects still remain in the hands of the owners. The emergence of the "managers" is seen in post-al theory as part of those processes in which the "personal" becomes an "impersonal" (corporate) capitalism; this is said to make the regime of "capital" a much more heterogeneous and overdetermined one and, in doing so, diffuse the confrontation between "labor" and "capital." But the class antagonism between "labor" and "capital" is not a matter of "how" the exploitation takes place—directly or indirectly, personally or impersonally. Exploitation is a systemic feature of capitalism: it is the necessary consequence of the laws of motion of capital. It is, to be precise, the outcome of the objective practices of competition.

Each capitalist in order to survive has to make a "profit." It is the priority of the objective fact of "profit," surplus labor, and not "how" it is made (by the mediation of managers or not; through the separation or identity of ownership/control) that dictates the working of capital. Managers, contrary to post-al theorists, do not in any way modify the law of "profit." In fact, as R. Pahl and J. Winkler argue, "managers" are trained to make "profit." Managers, their research found, were not only "more oriented to profit, they were more capable of obtaining it" (118). Their careers, in fact, depend on their skills in making profit. Their use of a portion of profit for "community" (as Berle and Means put it) is itself part of post-al modes of profit making—managerial strategies aimed at increasing the rate of profit and ideologically legitimating it; they are a reinforcement and not a weakening of the principle of profit. "Profit" is the very goal of capital, and how (what cultural and political and social mechanisms are used to obtain it) is a secondary fact: "managers" are part of the secondary mediating mechanisms. Post-al theories are founded upon the micropolitics of mediations: they take mediations as autonomous practices with their own immanent logic and self-determining forces and, thus, treat superstructural experiences as structural features. However, mediations, as I am using the term, are always the mediation of objective forces outside them; they are not autonomous textualities. There are no autonomous textualities.

In fact, the necessity for securing a high rate of profit by what might be called the mangerialization of the workplace has become so necessary under the influence of new cybercultures that even the "managering" is formally diffused as a process throughout the workplace. This diffusion of management is not limited to such post-al industries as electronic and advanced computer concerns in the Silicon Valley but has now become more or less routine even in such fundamentally "Fordist" industries as the auto industry. This style of diffuse management is often modeled after the Japanese practices in which the workers are involved in the managerial processes of decision making.

The mangerialization of the workplace (as the emergence of managers themselves), however, does not eliminate exploitation and the antagonism of the two classes which follows. These managerial techniques simply make class antagonism more tolerable by covering over the contradictions and thus temporarily lowering somewhat the intensity of crisis in daily life so that these do not completely distract workers and reduce their efficiency to an unprofitable level. A worker who is "involved" in decision making processes is still exploited, and the surplus of her labor continues to be appropriated, but she is exploited through the mediation of democratic consensus, which modifies her class consciousness. To take this mediation as a new form of class position is to blur the lines between "exploited" and "exploiters" and thus to legitimate the dominant relations of property. All that the emergence of "managers" show is that the form of ownership has been historically mediated: it is no longer directly personal. It does not mean (as post-al theorists insist) that ownership has been abolished. One has to keep in mind that the "managers"—who in the "experiences" of the everyday seem to be in a radically different intermediary and autonomous class—have no objective material base. The day they lose their job because of the downsizing of IBM, AT&T, GE . . . , for example, it suddenly becomes clear to them that they, too, are wage-earners; that under capitalism there are only two classes: the "owners" and the "workers." Managerial assets (skills, knowledge, credentials), as I have already suggested, are always contextual: outside the specific workplace, they are a very unreliable basis for "power" (let alone "exploitation"). Workplaces are "owned" by capitalists, and their practices are determined by the laws of profit.

The historical "actuality" of the "manager" comes about not because of the disappearance or marginalization of the antagonism of "labor" and "capital," but rather, as Marx explains, it "necessarily arises in all modes of production that are based on opposition between the worker as direct producer and the proprietor of the means of production. The greater this opposition, the greater the role that this work of supervision plays" (*Capital* 3, 507).

Post-al theories of class—in which the manager is seen as a *new*, "excessive" post-class that undermines class structure and whose existence puts an end to class analysis and class struggle—are quite useful for a theory of the subject in the post-al knowledge industry devoted to the construction of a transclass subject of consumption. But the appearance of "managers" and other knowledge/service workers in no way changes the binary class structure under capitalism or points to "contradictory class locations" that require a "revision" of the class theory and the determining role of production in human societies. Managers and other service class people in no sense pose a special case. They are simply class fractions—folds within the existing binary class—and not "excesses" that fracture the binary class structure. Such class fractions ("in the middle") have been discussed and theorized in classical Marxism, contrary to the dominant ludic theory that represents Marxism as unable of recognizing the "middle." In his "'Left-Wing' Communism—an Infantile Disorder," for example, Lenin writes, "Capitalism would not be capitalism if the proletariat *pur sang* were not surrounded by a large number of exceedingly motley types intermediate between the proletarian and the semi-proletarian . . . " (*Collected Works*, 31, 75). Lenin's argument, in sharp contrast with those of post-al theorists, is that "in the middle" is not an "excess" nor does it mark a break, rather it is an integral part of capitalism itself. His interest "in the middle" is to argue for ways to raise class consciousness and to unveil that "in the middle" is never an autonomous class in/for itself. The "semi-proletarian," in other words, is not the site of class slippage and sliding—the effect of the play of the errant tropes of reversible class processes involving the proletariat and the bourgeois. Instead, the "semi-proletarian," according to Marx, is the historical necessity of the opposition between workers and owners of the means of production. The optical illusion that the "semi-proletarian" and others "in the middle" are "new" and "excessive" is caused by the focus of post-al theory on the microphysics of class—the same focus that eventually denies the existence of any collective called "class" because it emphasizes the practices of a singular subject and takes the specificities of the individual to be an "excess" that degrounds the "laws" of class structure. But the laws of motion of capital and its class assert themselves at the level of the everyday all the time. On Monday March 6, 1995, nearly 500 demonstrators marched into a dining room in one Washington, D.C. hotel where county officials were dining and waiting for Newt Gingrich to deliver a speech on the Republican "Welfare Reform." Waving empty lunch trays and protesting against the Republican Party's curtailing of school lunches for children from low income families, the protesters disrupted the gathering. In the middle of the struggle between the demonstrates, police and the guests, one of the guests stood up and shouted at the protesters: "Newt Gingrich is on the right track, he is going to protect us from people like you" (CBS, "Evening News," Monday March 6, 1995). "People like you" is not an errant trope, it is the articulation of the antagonism of "labor" and "capital" in the post-al moment. The difference separating "us" from "people like you" is determined by the social relations of production.

Notes

1. This text is "Book One" of a two-part text on post-ality. "Book Two" will be published in *Transformation 2*.

Works Cited

Aglietta, M. *A Theory of Capitalist Regulation: The US Experience*. London: Verso, 1987.
Anderson, Lisa. "Middle Class's Worries Center Around Security."*Times Union*: Albany, NY, 25 December 1994: B-1; B-6.
Anderson, Perry. *In the Tracks of Historical Materialism*. Chicago: University of Chicago Press, 1983.
Aronowitz, Stanley. "The Situation of the Left in the United States." *Socialist Review* 23.3 (1994): 5-79.
Aronson, Ronald. *After Marxism*. New York: Guilford, 1995.
Atlas, James. "The Battle of Books." *NY Times Magazine* 22 October 1989: 83-100.
Bataille, George. *The Accused Share: An Essay on General Economy*. New York: Zone Books, 1988.
_____. *Visions of Excess*. Minneapolis: University of Minnesota Press, 1985.
Baudrillard. Jean. *The Mirror of Production*. St. Louis: Telos Press, 1975.
_____. *Simulations* New York: Semiotext(e),1983.
_____. "When Bataille Attacked the Metaphysical Principle of Economy."*Canadian Journal of Political and Social Theory* 11.3 (1987): 57-62.
_____. *Selected Writings*. Ed. Mark Poster. Stanford: University of Stanford Press. 1988.
_____. *Forget Foucault*. New York: Semiotext(e), 1987.
Bell, Daniel. *The Coming of Post-Industrial Society*. New York: Basic Books, 1973.
Berle, A. and G. C. Means. *The Modern Corporation and Private Property*. New York: Harcourt Brace & World, 1968.
Berman, Art. *From the New Criticism to Deconstruction: The Reception of Structuralism and Poststructuralism*. Urbana: University of Illinois Press, 1988.
Boyer, Robert. "Technical Change and the Theory of Regulation."*Technical Change and Economic Theory*. Ed. G. Dosi and others. London: Verso, 1988.
Bourdieu, Pierre. *Distinction: A Social Critique of the Judgement of Taste*. Cambridge, MA: Harvard University Press, 1984.

_____."What Makes a Social Class?" *Berkeley Journal of Sociology* 22 (1987): 1-18.
Bowlby, Rachel. *Shopping with Freud.* London: Routledge, 1993.
Brint, Steven G. *In An Age of Experts: The Changing Role of Professionals in Politics and Public Life.* Princeton: Princeton University Press, 1994.
Butler, Judith. *Gender Trouble: Feminism and the Subversion of Identity.* New York: Routledge, 1990.
_____. "Critically Queer." *GLQ: A Journal of Lesbian and Gay Studies* 1 (1993): 17-32.
_____. "Poststructuralism and Postmarxism." *Diacritics* 23.4 (1993): 3-11.
Callari, Antonio et al., eds. *Marxism in the Postmodern Age.* New York: Guilford, 1995.
Callinicos. Alex. *Against Postmodernism: A Marxist Critique.* New York. St. Martin's Press, 1989.
_____ and Cris Harman, *The Changing Working Class.* London: Bookmarks, 1989.
Chambers, Ross. *Room for Maneuver: Reading (the) Oppositional (in) Narrative.* Chicago: University of Chicago Press, 1991.
Chomsky, Noam. *World Orders Old and New.* New York: Columbia University Press, 1994.
Clifford, James. "Traveling Cultures." *Cultural Studies.* Ed. L. Grossberg, C. Nelson, and P. Treichler. New York: Routledge, 1992.
Corlett, William. *Community without Unity: A Politics of Derridean Extravagance* Durham, NC: Duke University Press, 1989.
Cornell, Drucilla. *Beyond Accommodation: Ethical Feminism, Deconstruction, and the Law.* New York: Routledge, 1991.
Derrida, Jacques. *Writing and Difference.* Chicago: University of Chicago Press, 1978.
_____. *Margins of Philosophy.* Chicago: University of Chicago Press, 1982.
_____. *The Post Card: From Socrates to Freud and Beyond.* Chicago: University of Chicago Press, 1987.
_____. "Forces of Law: The 'Mystical Foundation of Autority.'" *Cardozo Law Review* 11. 5-6 (1990): 943-78.
_____. *The Other Heading: Reflections on Today's Europe.* Bloomington: Indiana University Press, 1992.
de Certeau, M. *The Practice of Everyday Life.* Berkeley: University of California Press, 1984.
DeMan, Paul. *Allegories of Reading.* New Haven: Yale University Press, 1979.
_____. *Resistance to Theory.* Minneapolis: University of Minnesota Press, 1986.
DeMott, Benjamin. *The Imperial Middle: Why Americans Can't Think Straight About Class.* New York: William Morrow, 1990.
Dickens, David and Andrea Fontana, eds. *Postmodernism and Social Inquiry.* New York: Guilford, 1994
Dimock, Wai Chee and Michael T. Gilmore, eds. *Rethinking Class.* New York: Columbia University Press. 1994.
Ebert, Teresa L. *Ludic Feminism and After.* Ann Arbor: University of Michigan Press. 1995.
Ehrenreich, Barbara. *Fear of Falling: The Inner Life of the Middle Class.* New York: Harper Perennial, 1990.
Engels, Frederick. *Socialism: Utopian and Scientific.* Peking: Foreign Languages Press, 1975.

Elam, Diane. *Romancing the Postmodern*. New York: Routledge, 1992.
Esping-Andersen, Gosta. "Post-Industrial Class Structures: An Analytical Framework." Ed. Gosta Esping-Anderson. *Changing Classes: Stratification and Mobility in Post-Industrial Societies*. London: Sage, 1993. 7-31.
———. "Mobility Regimes and Class Formation." Ed. Gosta Esping-Andersen. *Changing Classes: Stratification and Mobility in Post-Industrial Societies*. London: Sage, 1993. 225-241.
Fish, Stanley. *There's No Such Thing as Free Speech . . . and It's a Good Thing Too*. New York: Oxford University Press, 1993.
Fiske, John. *Understanding Popular Culture*. London and Boston: Unwin Hyman, 1989.
———. *Media Matters*. Minneapolis: University of Minnesota Press, 1995.
Foley, Barbara. "Class," *Rethinking Marxism* 5.2 (1992): 117-28.
Foucault, Michel. *Language, Counter-Memory, Practice*. Ithaca, NY: Cornell University Press, 1977.
Fukuyama, Francis. *The End of History and the Last Man*. New York: The Free Press, 1992.
Fussell, Paul. *Class*. New York: Summit Books, 1983.
Game, Ann. *Undoing the Social: Towards a Deconstructive Sociology*. Toronto: University of Toronto Press, 1991.
Gates, Henry Louis, Jr., ed. *"Race," Writing, and Difference*. Chicago and London: University of Chicago Press, 1985.
Genosko, Gary. "Red London." *Border/Lines*. No. 34-35 (1994): 36-37.
Gerry, C. "Small Enterprises, The Recession and the 'Disappearing Working Class.'"*Political Action and Social Identity*. Ed. G. Rees and others. London: Macmillan, 1985.
Giddens, Anthony. *The Class Structure of Advanced Societies* London: Hutchinson, 1979.
Gingrich, Newt and others. *Window of Opportunity: A Blueprint for the Future*. New York: Tor Books, 1986.
Goldthrope, John H. and Gordon Marshall. "The Promising Future of Class Analysis: A Response to Recent Critiques." *Sociology* 26.3 (1992): 381-400.
Granovetter, Mark. "Toward a Sociogical Theory of Income Differences."*Sociological Perspectives on Labor Markets*. Ed. Ivar Berg. New York: Academic Press, 1981. 11-27; 40-47.
Gorz, André. *Farewell to the Working Class: An Essay on Post-Industrial Sociaism*. Boston: South End Press, 1982.
Guevara, Ernesto Ché. *Ché Guevara and the Cuban Revolution: Writings and Speeches of Ernesto Ché Guevara*. Sydney: Pathfinder Press, 1987.
Hall, Stuart and Martin Jacques, eds. *New Times*. London: Verso, 1990.
———. "The Meaning of New Times" Eds. Hall and Jacques. *New Times*. London, Verso, 1990. 116-134.
Harvey, David. *The Condition of Postmodernity*. Cambridge, MA: Blackwell, 1989.
Hegel, G. W. F. *Phenomenology of Spirit*. New York: Oxford University Press, 1977.
Hirst, Paul. "After Henry." Eds. S. Hall and M. Jacques. London: Verso, 1990. 321-329.
hooks, bell. *Outlaw Culture: Resisting Representations*. New York: Routledge, 1994.
Jameson, Fredric. *Postmodernism or, The Cultural Logic of Late Capitalism*. Durham, NC: Duke UniversityPress, 1991.
———. *The Geopolitical Aesthetics*. Bloomington: Indiana University Press, 1994.

_____. *The Seeds of Time*. New York: Columbia UniversityPress, 1995.
Kopylov, Yuri, ed. *Leninism and the World Revolutionary Working-Class Movement*. Moscow: Progress Press, 1971.
Laclau, Ernesto. "Populist Rupture and Discourse."*Screen Education* 34 (Spring 1980): 87-93.
_____. "Building a New Left." *Strategies*, 1 (1988): 10-28.
_____. "Beyond Emancipation." *Development and Change*. 23.3 (1992): 121-37.
Lasch, Christopher. *The Revolt of the Elites and Betrayal of Democracy*. New York: W. W. Norton, 1995.
Lash, Scott and John Urry. *The End of Organized Capitalism*. Cambridge: Polity Press, 1987.
Leadbeater, Charlie. "Power to the Person." *New Times*. Ed. Hall and Jacques. London, Verso, 1990. 137-149.
Lenin, V. I. *What is to be Done?* New York: Penguin, 1989.
_____. *The State and Revolution*. New York: Penguin, 1992.
Lèvi-Strauss, Claude. *Structural Anthropology*. New York: Basic Books, 1963.
_____. *The Elementary Structures of Kinship*. Boston: Beacon Press, 1969.
Lindley, David. *The End of Physics: The Myth of a Unified Theory*. New York: Basic Books, 1993.
Lyotard, Jean-François. "On the Strength of the Weak."*Semiotex(e)* 3.2 (1978): 204-212.
_____. *The Postmodern Condition: A Report on Knowledge*. Minneapolis: University of Minnesota Press, 1984.
_____. "'Re-writing' Modernism." *Substance* 54 (1987): 3-9.
_____. *The Postmodern Explained*. Minneapolis: University of Minnesota Press, 1992.
_____. *Political Writings*. Minneapolis: University of Minnesota Press, 1993.
Mandel, Ernest. *Late Capitalism*. London, New Left Books, 1975.
_____. *An Introduction to Marxist Economic Theory*. New York: Pathfinder Press, 1983.
Marx, Karl. *Wage-labour and Capital* & *Value, Price and Profit*. New York: International Publishers, 1975.
_____. "Draft of an Article on Friedrich List's Book *Das Nationale System Der Politichen Oekonomie*." *Collected Works,* Vol. 4. 265-293. New York: International Publishers, 1975.
_____. *The Economic and Philosophic Manuscripts of 1844. Collected Works*. Vol. 3. 229-346. New York: International Publishers, 1975.
_____. *Critique of the Gotha Programme*. New York: International Publishers, 1989.
_____. *A Contribution to the Critique of Political Economy*. New York: International Publishers, 1986.
_____. *The 18th Brumaire of Louis Bonaparte*. New York: International Publishers, 1990.
_____. *Grundrisse*. New York: Penguin Books, 1993.
_____ and Fredrick Engels. *Manifesto of the Communist Party*. Moscow: Progress Publishers, 1952.
_____. *The German Ideology.Collected Works,* Vol. 5. New York: International Publishers, 1976.
Maus, Marcel. *The Gift*. New York: W. W. Norton, 1967.

McLuhan, Marshall. *Understanding Media: The Extensions of Man.* New York: Harper, 1967.
McRobbie, Angela. *Postmodernism and Popular Culture.* New York: Routledge 1994.
McKendrick, Neil, John Brewer, and J. H. Plumb, eds.*The Birth of Consumer Society: The Commercialization of Eighteenth-Century England.* Bloomington: Indiana University Press, 1982.
Mercer, Kobena. *Welcome to the Jungle: New Positions in Black Cultural Studies.* New York: Routledge, 1994.
Michon, F. "Dualism and the French Labor Market." Ed. F. Wilkinson. *The Dynamics of Labor Market Segmentation.* London: Academic Press, 1981. 81-97.
Miller, J. Hillis. *Theory Now and Then.* Durham, NC: Duke University Press, 1991.
Morton, Donald. "Birth of Cyberqueer." *PMLA* 110.3 (1995): 369-81.
Mulgan, Geoff. "The Power of the Weak."*New Times.* Ed. Hall and Jacques. London: Verso. 347-363.
Nadel, S. N. *Contemporary Capitalism and the Middle Classes.* Moscow: Progress Press, 1982.
Nicholson, Linda. *Gender and History.* New York: Columbia University Press, 1986.
_____. "Feminism and Marx: Integrating Kinship with the Economic." Ed. S. Benhabib and D. Cornell, *Feminism as Critique.* Minneapolis: University of Minnesota Press, 1986. 16-30.
Offe, Clause. *Disorganized Capitalism.* Cambridge, MA: MIT Press, 1985.
Packard, Vance. *The Status Seekers.* New York: David McKay, 1959.
Pahl, R. and J. Winkler. "The Economic Elite: Theory and Practice." *Elites and Power in British Society.* Cambridge: Cambridge University Press 1974.
Plotnitsky, Arkady. *Complemenarity: Anti-Epistemology after Bohr and Derrida.* Durham NC: Duke University Press, 1994.
Popper, Karl. *The Logic of Scientific Discovery.* New York: Harper and Row, 1980.
_____. *The Poverty of Historicism.* New York: Harper, 1964.
Poulantzas, Nicos. *Classes in Contemporary Capitalism.* London: Verso, 1978.
Przeworski, Adam. "From Proletarian into Class." *Politics and Society* 7.4 (1977): 343-401.
Radhakrishnan, R. "Ethnic Identity and Post-Structuralist Difference." In *The Nature and Context of Minority Discourse.* Eds. A. JanMohamed and D. Lloyd. New York: Oxford University Press, 1990. 50-71.
Renner, Karl. *Wandlungen der modernen Gesellschaft: Zwei Abhandlungen uber die probleme der Nachkriegszeit.* Vienna: Wienner Volksbuchhandlung, 1953. For English translation of various sections, Tom Bottomore & P. Goode, ed.*Austro-Marxism.* New York: Oxford University Press, 1978.
Resnick, Stephen A. and Richard D. Wolff.*Knowledge and Class.* Chicago: University of Chicago Press, 1987.
Robbins, Bruce. *Secular Vocations: Intellectuals, Professionalism, Culture.* London: Verso, 1993.
Roemer, John. *A General Theory of Exploitation and Class.* Cambridge, MA: Harvard University Press, 1982.
Ross, Andrew. *No Respect: Intellectuals and the Popular Culture.* New York: Routledge, 1989.

_____. *The Chicago Gangster Theory of Life: Nature's Debt to Society*. New York: Verso, 1994.
Ryan, Michael. *Politics and Culture*. Baltimore: Johns Hopkins University Press, 1989.
Said, Edward. *Culture and Imperialism*. New York: Knopf, 1993.
Saunders, Peter. *Social Theory and Urban Question*. London: Unwin Hyman, 1987.
Schumpeter, Joseph A. *Capitalism, Socialism and Democracy*. New York: Harper, 1975.
Scott. J. *Corporations, Classes and Capitalism*. London: Hutchinson, 1985.
Seidman, Steven and David Wagner, eds.*Postmodernism and Social Theory*. New York: Blackwell, 1992.
Shevtsov, M. ed. *Marxism-Leninism on Proletarian Internationalism*. Moscow: Progress Press, 1972.
Smith, Paul. "An Interview with Richard D. Wolff." *Mediations*. 18.1 (1994): 5-17.
Sorensen, Aage. "The Basic Concepts of Stratification Research: Class, Status, and Power. *"Social Stratification: Class, Race and Gender in Sociological Perspective*. Ed. David B. Grusky. Boulder: Westview Press, 1994. 229-241.
Strauss, Leo. *Natural Right and History*. Chicago: University of Chicago Press, 1965.
Timofeyev, T. *The Working Class and The Revolutionary Liberation Movement*. Moscow: Novosti Press Agency Publishing House, 1974.
Trotsky, Leon. *The Struggle Against Fascism in Germany*. New York: Pathfinder Press. 1971.
Touraine, Alain. *The Post-Industrial Society, Tomorrow's Social History: Classes, Conflicts and Culture in the Programmed Society*. London: Faber and Faber, 1974.
Vanneman, Reeve and Lynn W. Cannon.*The American Perception of Class*. Philadelphia: Temple University Press, 1987.
Ulmer, Gregory. "Puncept." Ed. Jonathan Culler. *On Puns: The Foundation of Letters*. Oxford: B. Blackwell, 1988. 164-189.
Weber, Max. *From Max Weber: Essays in Sociology*. London: Routledge, 1961.
Walker, Pat, ed. *Between Labor and Capital*. Boston: South End Press, 1979.
Williams, Jeffrey. "Where Do We Go From Here? A Question of the Left.*College Literature* 21.3 (1994): 84-91.
Wright, Erik Olin. *Classes*. New York: Verso, 1985.
_____. *The Debate on Classes*. New York: Verso, 1989.
_____. *Interrogating Inequality: Essays on Class Analysis, Socialism and Marxism*. New York: Verso, 1994.
Woodiwiss, Anthony. *Social Theory After Post-Modernism*. London: Pluto Press, 1990
Yermakova, Antonia and Valentina Ratnikov.*What are Classes and the Class Struggle?* Moscow: Progress Publishers, 1986.
Zavarzadeh, Mas'ud. "On 'Class' and Related Concepts in Classical Marxism, and Why Is the Post-al Left Saying Such Terrible Things about Them?"*Alternative Orange* 3.3 (1994): 5-12.
_____. "The Stupidity that Consumption is Just as Productive as Production."*College Literature* 21.3 (1994): 92-114.
_____. *Theory and Its Other: Pun(k)deconstruction, Post-theory, and Ludic Politics*. Washington, DC: Maisonneuve Press, 1995.

Robert Albritton

The De(con)struction of Marx's *Capital*

It is the central claim of this paper that the numerous and sometimes fashionable deconstructions of Marx's *Capital* that have been produced in recent years largely abandon any effort to understand the specificity of the economy under capitalism. They usually do so in the name of "anti-economism" or "anti-essentialism," but if capital turns out to have a kind of essence, then their deconstructions would seem to miss the boat. In opposition to what I call "horizontal deconstruction" that dissolves any theory of capital's inner logic, I shall argue for a "vertical reconstruction" that preserves such a theory, but avoids economism by developing relatively autonomous levels of analysis.[1] Thus while capital is seen to have a logic that can be theorized, the causal efficacy of that logic at the level of concrete history cannot be determined without studying the specificity of particular historical contexts in order to clarify the role of capital relative to other social forces.

Marx considered *Capital* to be by far his most important theoretical contribution, hence it has always been a central text for Marxism and for Marxian Political Economy. Different schools of Marxism can be most clearly differentiated according to how they read and utilize the theory put forth in *Capital*. In this paper my aim is to show that the deconstruction of Capital is based on posing choices between false alternatives, confusions over the nature of Marx's theory in *Capital*, and lack of awareness of alternative approaches to the problems of essentialism and economism. My main argument is that Marx's theory of capital's logic can be read in such a way that not only can the excesses of essentialism be avoided without going down the path of horizontal de(con)struction, but also that this theory can provide the basis for a Marxian political economy that has great explanatory power, an explanatory power that can potentially inform transformational strategies. Surely if we live in a world where capitalism is still a force, then a better understanding of this force can contribute to strategies aimed at altering it. At precisely the time in history when we should challenge mainstream economic theory and practice, the deconstructionists abandon the terrain of economic theory.

Resnick and Wolff, for example, collapse Marx's economic theory into a sociology of class. Resnick and Wolff are not alone amongst thinkers on the left in choosing the path that should be marked with the sign "Danger Deconstruction Ahead!" The particular texts that I shall address in this article all (with the possible exception of Mouffe and Ryan) are written by Althusser's progeny. It is not my belief that Althusser's problematic necessarily leads to poststructuralism and deconstrucion even though the thinkers under consideration have chosen this path, while abandoning his modernism and structuralism.

In my view Althusser's Marxism is a unstable ensemble that contained strong modernist and structuralist elements combined with the seeds of postmodernism and poststructuralism. On the modernist and structuralist side Althusser claimed that Marx's *Capital* was the founding work of a new science and that the scientificity of this text was achieved through a series of "epistemological breaks" with previous ideologies. Other central claims included a structuralist ontology that proposed a decentered totality of relatively autonomous practices unified by a "structure-in-dominance," and the view that knowledge has to do with an object of knowledge being both radically distinct from and in some sense adequate to its real object (the forms and types of adequacy would be determined internal to theoretical practice). Poststructuralists modified Althusser by removing some of his conceptions from his basically modernist and structuralist framework. For example, Althusser was anti-essentialist in the sense that he developed a powerful critique of "centered" "expressive" totalities in which the parts were no more than differentiations of a core essence. In the hands of Resnick and Wolff, this anti-essentialist thrust has been removed from Althusser's modernist and structuralist framework and has been absolutized. One might say therefore, that the "essence" of their approach is its anti-essentialism as is evidenced by the identification of their approach as "anti-essentialist Marxism." Or we see, again in the work of Resnick and Wolff, the concept of "overdetermination" cut away from Althusser's notion of structural causality and placed within a totality in which everything participates in the constitution of everything else to the point where the very notion of causality in the sense of some possibility of weighing the possible strength of various influences on an outcome becomes an impossibility.[2]

Some Althusserians who took the path of deconstruction have now become ex-marxists. Cutler, Hindness, Hirst, and Hussain (1977) launch a full scale attack on Marx's *Capital*, under the banner of anti-essentialism. Essentialism in all its forms is seen to be the scourge of Marxist theory, and *Capital* is seen to be the main source of essentialism. According to their interpretation of *Capital*, Marx theorizes capitalism as an economic system in which "All possible capitalist societies are merely the specific localization's or realizations of this economic system and its necessary effects" (vol. 1, 114). In the name of anti-essentialism they abandon the concept "mode of production," they deny that capital has any logic, they reject the theory of value, they denounce the theory of exploitation, and they abjure epistemology in general, arguing that any epistemology must privilege a particular discourse over other discourses.[3] While it is beyond the scope of this paper to critically analyze all these positions, I cannot pass their rejection of the law of value without comment.

The law of value has been rejected by a variety of thinkers for many reasons. Some reject it because they claim that Marx's *Capital* lacks an adequate theory of price determination (especially the neo-sraffians), but Cutler *et al.* reject it for basically two reasons: they argue that an abstract economic law like the law of value is bound to distort the complexity of the concrete, and that when we analyze concrete contexts we see that value is the result of many factors. Marx, however, is not theorizing immediately about concrete contexts but about a purely capitalist society where all production is the capitalist production of commodities with commodified labor power. In such a theoretical context not only can the law of value be defended, but also in my view it is the only basis of value that makes any sense.[4] Furthermore, no matter what the inadequacies of Marx's theory of price determination as it stands in *Capital* Volume Three, there is no reason why an adequate theory of price determination cannot be constructed that is consistent with Marx's law of value and capital's logic. According to Cutler *et al.* , general theory blinds us to the actuality of the concrete, and it follows that our focus should instead be on "the specific conditions in definite national economies" (vol. 1, 153). They do not make it very clear, however, how it is we are to come to <u>know</u> anything about "the specific conditions in definite national economies." They presumably take these positions in the name of improved socialist strategy, but subsequently, and not at all to my surprise, they have become ex-marxists and ex-socialists.

Laclau and Mouffe (1985) push anti-essentialism even further with their claim that the social is radically contingent and precarious. Their epistemology, according to which all that is solid and fixed melts into the flux of process, is little more than the old Heraclitean flux dressed up in poststructuralist terminology. A strong case can be made that reality is a process, but we have to be careful to sort out what we mean by "process." Do we mean simply that change is continual and that change is the result of complex interactions of many factors through time? This may seem unobjectionable. But Laclau and Mouffe go further and claim that process includes the idea that every identity is radically contingent and unstable. As a result there must be a lack of differentiation in their ontology between more persistent and enduring identities and less. And it is precisely in order to make such differentiations that we need the concept "structure." Their concept of process tends to be structureless except for unstable nodal points, and hence the tendency of their ontology is to make reality so fleeting that any effort to understand it in ways that would enable us to transform it rationally would seem to border on the impossible.

As a result of the radical contingency and precariousness of every identity, Laclau and Mouffe see society as radically political. Everything revolves around the struggle for hegemony, which, given its radical contingency, must always be unstable and therefore the focus of intense political struggle. This struggle involves the attempt by rival articulatory practices to capture "floating signifiers" and construct discourses that either reinforce or challenge existing hegemonies. In some ways the emphasis on politicizing all discursive practice might seem quite progressive, but pushed to the extreme, as in their case, it dissolves the economic into the political, making any clear theorization of the specificity of the economic under capitalism an impossibility.

According to Laclau and Mouffe the economic is conceived to be "the last redoubt of essentialism" (75), and their strategy to breach this redoubt is to argue for the thoroughly political nature of the economic just as with all other social realms. It is my claim that the economic is "essentialist" for good reasons; capital does indeed have an inner logic. It is that which enabled Marx to write *Capital*, and it is that which invites us to enlarge and refine the immense breakthrough made by Marx. When Laclau and Mouffe get beyond their conceptual framework of floating signifiers articulated in hegemonic and counter-hegemonic discourses and try to say something substantive about modern capitalism, they borrow from Regulation theory, which according to their own epistemology would have to be considered very essentialist and economistic (160).[5] This peculiar falling back into essentialism is necessitated by the fact that their framework offers them no purchase at all on theorizing the economic under capitalism. In my view their conceptual framework is itself a floating signifier that may have some useful applications to social movements and strategic thinking but beyond that can only be pinned to something substantive in the world by ad hoc borrowings from outside itself.

Having presumably liberated themselves from Marxism's essentialism, they call themselves "post-marxists," while at the same time they borrow their substantive understanding of capitalism from a form of Marxism that from their point of view would have to be considered quite economistic. Resnick and Wolff prefer to call themselves "marxists" rather than "post-marxists." But these differences in label mean very little since the underlying deconstructionist tendencies are very similar. Resnick and Wolff criticize Cutler *et. al* for abandoning value categories, but their radical revision of Marx on this issue means that they maintain value categories in name only.[6] They reject Marx's law of value and Marx's view that capital has an inner logic. Instead value categories are simply used to define class and to develop a typology of class. Indeed with their emphasis on class as the entry point of marxist theory, their version of marxism is bound to be onesidely classist. In order to avoid being so labeled they attempt to connect their abstract typology of class to the concrete by introducing complexity into it. The more historical particularity and contingency is inserted, the more any theoretical explanatory power is dissolved. In Resnick and Wolff there is a real tension between trying to preserve some analytic power to their concepts of class on the one hand, and trying not to privilege "class" or trying to make their concepts of class complex enough to handle the particularity of the concrete. I shall resist analyzing the work of Resnick and Wolff any further at this point, but shall return to it later in the paper.

There are certain refrains we hear over and over again in these deconstructions of Marx's *Capital* that are coupled with a posing of alternatives in such a way that any right thinking rational person must feel compelled to opt for the path of deconstruction. I argue that there are other alternatives than those they pose for us, and that the path of deconstruction is not the option for Marxists to take.

First there is a tendency in these texts to transform Marxism into a straw man or straw monster by exaggerating the tendencies towards essentialism and economism. For example, I do not know any Marxist today who would claim that "a pure logic of capital . . . determines the evolution of the labor process" (Laclau and Mouffe 79) or who would reduce all social relations to the "necessary moments of a immanent law" (Laclau and Mouffe 98), or who would claim that a theory of concentration of capital in the abstract would fully explain concentration in particular times and places (Cutler *et al.* vol. 1, 152). How can one refuse the path of deconstruction if it is posed as the only alternative to such crudely essentialist and reductionist Marxism? Quite easily once one realizes the Marxism seldom has and need not exhibit such crudeness.

Second is the fixation on essentialism as the cardinal sin of theoretical practice, a fixation that leads to an ever more radical and absolute anti-essentialism. "Essentialism" becomes a cover symbol that is used to condemn a variety of sins of omission and commission. The most frequent refrain in this context is the claim that a theory of capital's logic or of capital's basic operating principles necessarily commits one to the position that concrete historical outcomes are determined by or are a function of the immanent laws of motion of capital. Or, in other words, that capital is the essence and history is simply the localization of this essence. In other words essentialism in this context means economic determinism. Of course the theory of capital or any abstract theory can be used deterministically, but there is no necessity that it be so used. It may even turn out that capital does have a logic and that logic can be theorized, but that does not commit one to any position whatsoever on the causal efficacy of that logic at the level of history. Thus to think that we must choose between essential causes and no weighting of causes whatsoever as Resnick and Wolff do is a serious truncation of the range of choice.

Third is the claim that the economic is so thoroughly political that no theory of an abstract economic logic is possible or desirable. While it is no doubt true that the economic is always political at the level of concrete history, it does not follow from this that it is not both possible and desirable to construct a theory of capital's inner logic, a theory that analyzes the workings of capital's commodity-economic logic when not interfered with by extra-economic force. To construct an abstract theory of the economic modus operandi of pure capitalism is to construct an abstract economic theory. Such a theory in no sense precludes consideration of the mutual conditioning between economic and non-economic social elements at more concrete levels of analysis. The question is how to best understand such mutual conditioning, and it is by no means a foregone conclusion that the best way to do this is to collapse the economic into a conceptual soup where, for example, the economic is thoroughly and immediately political and thoroughly and immediately cultural so that we lose all grasp of the specificity of the economic under capitalism.

Fourth is the continual use of concrete diversity to make abstract theory appear to be a procrustean bed imposing overly fixed, one-sided, and simple categories on a concrete reality in a way that does violence to the diversity and complexity of the concrete. It is my contention that we always and necessarily use theories in order to make sense out of the concrete. Some theories may distort more than they reveal or they may be exclusionary in ways that are ultimately oppressive, but good theories help us to better understand and negotiate the concrete. And while we need to be careful with theories that are more abstract and more general because of the dangers of oversimplification and essentialism, if we do take care with such theories, they may end up to be in some ways the most useful precisely because they help us to organize what would otherwise be isolated fragments of knowledge.

Horizontal Deconstruction

Derrida is totally preoccupied with deconstructing, dismantling, and overthrowing reified knowledge structures. Such critical ground clearing operations may sometimes be useful, and it is not the first time that western metaphysics has been radically criticized for its dichotomous structures. While the thrust of Derrida's philosophy may serve as a check on knowledge pretensions, it can tell us very little about what we need to know, can know, and do know.

But isn't a theory of capital's inner logic a logocentric theory of identity or of presence in Derrida's sense, and therefore something to be deconstructed? In the already mentioned "deconstructions" of marxian economic theory, the theory of capital's inner logic is rejected in favor of either a typology of class or a deconstruction of the law of value through the direct introduction of political and cultural concepts. In both cases, the reductionism that follows from imposing the law of value on history is overcome by inserting historical contingency into the law of value and thereby dissolving it. I call these approaches "horizontal deconstructions" because the logical and historical tend to be collapsed together into a single plane of socio-historical discourses, where presumably nothing is to be privileged. In opposition to horizontal deconstruction, I want to advocate "vertical reconstruction." Vertical reconstruction preserves the law of value and carefully mediates the relationship between the logical and historical through relatively autonomous levels of analysis in order to avoid reductionism. In my view this latter approach is potentially far more complex, rich, subtle, and powerful than horizontal deconstruction; and yet Western Marxism has seldom even considered it as a possible option.[7]

The basic work that marxists have relied on to understand capitalism has been Marx's *Capital*, which purports to set forth the laws of motion of capital or the inner logic of capital. Right away this seems to be a very modernist theory opposing a pure inner logic to an exterior that is derivative. It seems to lead to applying abstract economic law to history, making the concrete a function of the abstract. Furthermore, it is a theory that seems to privilege production while ignoring reproduction and consumption. Finally, it seems to reduce the ideological and political to being mere appendages of the economic. The result of applying such a theory to historical analysis would seem to produce a one-sided, exclusionary, and reductionist understanding of history. It is my claim that a theory of capital's inner logic need not commit any of the above "essentialist" sins.[8]

According to Ryan's interpretation of Derrida, western metaphysics has revolved around a series of binary oppositions such as those between pure and impure, or between interiority and exteriority. In his book *Marxism and Deconstruction*, Ryan argues that

> all of the conceptual oppositions of metaphysics which deconstruction undoes can be said to hang on the frame of the interiority/exteriority binary. What is inside, according to metaphysics, is 'own,' proper, good, primary, original, unadulterated; what is outside is other, improper, bad, secondary, derivative, degraded (13).

But the binary oppositions of metaphysics do not simply suddenly and magically appear in discursive formations. The arch metaphysicians of the modern world are not Descartes, Rousseau, Kant, Hegel, Marx, or Husserl. The arch "metaphysician" is capital itself. The binary oppositions of metaphysics arise in a social context conditioned by capitalist production relations. It is not Marx who gives capital an inner logic, it is capital with its logic of self expansion that makes it possible for us to conceive of an inner logic through its commodifying and reifying tendencies.[9]

In a sense Marx's greatest achievement as an economic theorist was to grasp the character of capital's reifying and self-reifying tendencies. I am using reification to mean the tendency to place a profit-maximizing commodity-economic logic in command of human beings. In the extreme, when reification is total, persons are reduced to being simply bearers of the self-expanding motions of capital. To claim that capital is self-reifying is to claim that it has a built-in tendency to expand and deepen its commodity-economic logic. It follows that in the first instance, it is capital itself that continually reproduces invidious distinctions between those who are privileged and those who are exploited, oppressed, marginalized, and silenced. Of course, it is not only capital that does this, but it certainly plays a predominant role. To speak this way of capital may seem to some to be committing an error of reification since capital in a sense is, as a set of reified social relations, also a set of humans. On the contrary, one of Marx's greatest contributions was his understanding of how capitalism, once firmly rooted in society takes on a life of its own such that persons tend to be reduced to mere instruments used by capital for its own self-expansion. Thus it is not the case that I the theorist reify capital, rather capital is self-reifying. If capital is as Marx claims "self-expanding value," then this implies that where capitalism is present there will be a least some tendency for social life to be governed by profit-oriented markets that are at least to some extent self-regulating. There is a self-expanding automaticity built in to capital, and in this sense capital is a set of self-reifying social institutions.

For example, it is undeniably the case that in the leading capitalist countries labor-power does become increasingly commodified between, say, 1600 and 1850, and that in these countries economic life is increasingly governed by the market. The "self-expansion of value" in history involves at least to some extent the increasing commodification of economic life and with it, its increasing reification. Commodification implies reification because the more all inputs and outputs of production become commodified, the more a commodity-economic logic reduces individuals to being mere bearers or personifications of economic categories. If these actual tendencies are extended to completion in theory, then we can theorize an "inner logic" to capital. There can be little doubt that the greatest homogenizing force in the modern world that continually imposes a one-sided identitarian logic upon us is capital itself. And "deconstructing" those socio-economic institutions that we call "capitalism" is a great deal more difficult I'm afraid than deconstructing any metaphysics.[10]

The problem as I see it is how to understand capital's logic of identity in a non-essentialist way. I want to have a clear and accurate theory of that logic, while at the same time I want to understand the exclusionary character of its identities. It is important to understand capital's inner logic, for it helps us to understand the nature of marginalizing tendencies (i.e., inner v. outer) under capitalism. Capital itself does value the inner and devalue the outer, and hence, domestic labor, for example does not produce value from the point of view of capital. It does not produce value and is not valued. Domestic labor, then, is not part of capital's logic. It is devalued by capital.

In our theorizing, which is basically critical of capitalism, we need to fully expose the one-sided, inhuman character of the "inner" or "pure" logic of capital, including the one-sided and inhuman valuing of things that is continually reproduced by capital. In my view an effective theory of capitalism can and must theorize its inner identitarian logic without making exteriority secondary, derivative, degraded, devalued etc. Indeed, we need to turn the tables on capital and reveal that to a certain extent the inner and pure is ultimately destructive to us. We need to become fully cognizant of how capital operates in the abstract and in general precisely in order to understand how it peripheralizes and devalues, without in anyway getting caught up in perpetuating capital's "metaphysics."

If capital's logic of identity is deconstructed by immediately introducing difference into it, then we can never understand that logic and the invidious distinctions between inner and outer that are continuously reproduced throughout capitalist history.[11] The problem then is how to move from capital's logic to more concrete levels of analysis without getting trapped by it ourselves?

The way that I propose to do this is by conceiving of levels of analysis which have different logics without any of the logics being considered in any way inferior in relation to each other. Indeed, in a sense, the most "exterior" logic, the logic of historical analysis, is the most important, because what we most need to understand in the end is change at the level of the concrete. Moreover, the most "inner" logic, the law of value, is morally the most objectionable because in this logic humans are reduced to mere puppets of profit maximization. Thus if a category is not considered in the inner logic of capital, it is not because it is in anyway inferior or unimportant, it is because it is not sufficiently reified to be effectively thought about through capital's commodity-economic logic. For example, the fact that gender considerations do not enter the inner logic of capital does not imply that they are not of fundamental importance to the understanding of modern history. They are excluded only at this level of abstraction in theorizing capital because we are assuming total reification. The reason for their exclusion is that capital's inner logic is purely structural in the sense that it is a theory of structural economic positions without consideration of who fills those positions. At this level of abstraction there are capitalists and workers, but we do not know whether they are male or female, white or black, young or old, straight or gay, or what have you. Thus not only are gender differences not considered, but also all personal differences are not considered, whether they be of gender, race, age, or sexual-orientation. For example, from the point of view of capital's inner logic, whether workers are black or white, young or old, male or female, heterosexual or homosexual is of no concern and of no interest. It is not inconsistent with capital's inner logic that all capitalists be female.

In the context of a purely capitalist society, capital is only concerned with labor in the abstract, labor as profit creating activity and not with its personal characteristics. This exclusion from the most abstract level does not imply that at more concrete levels when we consider categories such as race and gender, that they must be considered in some sense secondary or inferior add-ons. Paradoxically, we can actually understand the relation between capital and gender better by excluding the consideration of gender from capital's inner logic. This is because being clear about the inner logic is crucial to understanding how and in what ways it articulates with gender, including its tendency to devalue domestic labor precisely by excluding it from the self-expanding motion of value.

I am suggesting that with horizontal deconstruction we lose all critical distance from capital and hence our ability to understand it. By letting capital have its way in theory as we do when we theorize pure capitalism, capital exposes itself for what it is. The theory of pure capitalism brings out capital's logic to the fullest, precisely so that we can gain critical distance from it and not be fooled by it. And the price for not gaining critical distance from capital's metaphysics is to be caught up in that metaphysics in ways that simply perpetuate it.

Resnick and Wolff's De(con)struction of Marxian Economics

In the considerable body of work by Resnick and Wolff, we do not find Derrida's method of deconstruction in the strict sense, but in a looser sense their approach can be considered a deconstructive one because of the centrality of radical anti-essentialism. Their work displays in a very clear way what I have called "horizontal deconstruction" or what could also be seen as a kind of ontological homogenization or leveling.

The central concept of their social ontology is "overdetermination" according to which all of the processes that make up social life influence the constitution of each other. Or in their own words overdetermination implies that "all qualities of any one process, as well as its very existence, depend completely on (are constituted by) all the other processes in society" (Resnick and Wolff, 1987a 137). Further, they reject causal analysis, for the weighing of one cause more heavily than another "privileges" that cause and any such privileging commits the sin of essentialism.[12] Thus they assert that "Among the different relations between any one entity and all those others that over-determine it, none can be ranked as 'more important' or 'more determinant' than another" (Resnick and Wolff, 1987b 4). Such tolerance, such egalitarianism, and such radical pluralism could be seen to represent intellectual virtue of angelic proportions. In my view, on the contrary, it presents a flattening out of the intellectual landscape and an unwillingness to take a position on substantive knowledge about the world.

Their ontology is also homogenizing because it assumes that society is made up of processes all of which mutually constitute each other. But this may not be the case. Society may be made up of things other than processes, or at least not all social entities may be fully or well comprehended through the concept of "process." Too much emphasis on process may make social entities incomprehensible by reducing them to flux, and some entities may change very slowly and be quite fixed while others may be radically unstable and contingent. In short, in social theory we need both the concepts of process and structure, and we need at least the possibility of considering that some social objects may be ontologically quite different than others and that therefore different types of causal analysis may be appropriate to different objects or to different levels of analysis.[13]

Resnick and Wolff flatten out the social into a sea of processes that can only be voluntaristically, locally, and tenuously grouped together into categories of analysis. Indeed the grouping principles are called "entry points" and these turn out to be quite arbitrary. In *Economics: Marxian versus Neoclassical*, we find no discussion of the commodity-form with its accompanying value and use-value, no discussion of value form theory, and no discussion of Marx's labor theory of value. With regard to crises, they simply assert that "Cycles do not result from some essential cause or group of causes" (1987a 187). And while it is true that the causes of particular concrete crises may be highly complex and controversial, in the context of a theory of a purely capitalist society, we can reduce this complexity in order to explore the possible causes of crises that can exist within a pure commodity-economic logic. They completely ignore this possibility because they wrongly believe that such an approach must necessarily do violence to the diversity of the concrete. Abstract economic theory is evacuated of content by Resnick and Wolff because of the complexity of the concrete, but it is precisely because of the complexity of the concrete that we need abstract theory. It is ultimately theories that help us make sense of our experience and find our way around and through the complexities of everyday life. It is even plausible to argue that the very meaning of our concepts derive from theories.

Elsewhere they (1990 110) claim that "In Marxian economics, the emphasis is on the historical conditions that complexly determine production and expanded reproduction, distribution, and consumption, and especially on the conditions that give rise to a multiplicity of class processes and positions." But this is not at all what Marx does in *Capital*; his project is not one of primarily writing a history of capitalism. The history of capitalism is enormously complex. To explore "the historical conditions that complexly determine" economics in the United States in 1994 would be impossibly complicated if we assume that there can be no ranking of causes and that everything constitutes everything else. Such an approach has nothing to do with the project that Marx undertook in *Capital*. It completely mires our thinking at the level of the concrete and undermines the efficacy of theory.

In *Economics: Marxian versus Neoclassical,* Resnick and Wolff focus little on the substance of Marxian economic theory and instead devote their attention to the different "entry points" that distinguish Marxian from neoclassical theory. They make it clear that they "mean by 'entry point' the concept or concepts a theorist uses to enter into, to begin, discourse about some object of analysis" (1990 121). Given this definition, the entry point of Marx's *Capital* would be either "commodity" or "value." They simply assert that the entry point of marxian economics is "class," but this seems rather dogmatic. "Class" is not the concept that Marx begins with, and though it is a concept of fundamental importance, there are other concepts that may be as important—for example, "capital." In short, it is not clear why there must be one entry point and why it must be class. Indeed, by making class the entry point, they collapse Marx's theory of capital's inner logic into a sociology of class. Marxian economic theory as formulated in Marx's original research project disappears altogether. Instead particular concepts are extracted from the theory and mined for what they can yield for class analysis. But the concept of surplus value upon which their typology of class rests is meaningless without the law of value, and they explicitly deny that there is any such thing as a law of value.

Furthermore, why should we prefer one entry point over another, if as they claim (1987a 9) all entry points are equally biased? Resnick and Wolff have a totally subjectivist and pragmatist approach to theory. We simply voluntaristically project any theory we want on to the world. And we create the world by the theories we project on to it. No theory is any truer than any other theory, but theories do have different practical consequences when put into effect. This totally politicizes theoretical practice—the theory with the most adherents wins. A theory that claims that certain races are biologically inferior is not false and cannot be proven false; and indeed, if it can recruit enough followers, it may become hegemonic.

There are numerous problems here, and I will not try to go into all of them. One very major problem with such an extreme form of pragmatism is the impossibility of knowing what the consequences of holding a theory will be. At least some if not most theories are not easily or univocally connected to determinate social outcomes. Or some theories may have very good intentions and very bad outcomes. At one point Resnick and Wolff (1987a 22) claim that we should choose the entry point of class because it will produce social justice. But if it is not possible to weigh the various causes of anything, then it is not possible to know what consequences will follow from adopting their theory. If we cannot know the consequences, then the selection of entry point is totally arbitrary and there would be absolutely no reason to be a Marxist. They explicitly state that "class exploitation is no more a cause of historical development than any of the other nonclass and noneconomic components of a society" (1987a 21). It would seem to follow that we cannot claim that class is any more important to historical development than hopscotch.[14]

Capital's Distinct and Complex Ontology

In modern social science the debate over whether or not there is a unified scientific method spanning the natural and social sciences usually touches on ontology because the debate comes down to the cognitive possibilities of the objects in the social as opposed to the natural sciences. It is widely assumed that the social is ontologically homogeneous and that therefore the same methodology with minor modifications can be used throughout the social sciences. Contrary to this assumption, a careful analysis of Marx's *Capital*, has lead me to conclude that the social is ontologically heterogeneous. And if this is true, it has very radical implications.

Capital seems to be a uniquely self-reifying social reality in the sense that it continually expands and strengthens itself by feeding off human and natural resources. In history the damage wrecked upon the human and natural environment by capital's pure profit orientation is of course continually resisted, and in the process capital is continually altered. But this need not stop us from understanding the thrust towards total reification embedded in capital's fundamental dynamics. Thus we can theorize a purely capitalist society where total reification reigns and all production is the capitalist production of commodities and where all inputs and outputs are totally commodified including labor power. Total commodification implies total reification because it implies that socio-economic life is organized entirely by the motion of commodities, money, and capital; and, as a result, socio-economic relations between persons are always mediated by things as in Marx's expression "cash nexus."

I am not aware of any other social object of knowledge that has an inner logic in the same sense as capital. This means that in theorizing capital, political economy has been aided in its abstractions by the fact the capital is self-reifying to some extent in history. By identifying capital's self-reifying tendencies, political economists have been aided in theorizing capital's logic. But in order to avoid the essentialist errors of economic determinism and reductionism, it is necessary to be cognizant of the fact that at the level of concrete history capital's logic is to some extent disrupted and it is only one social force amongst others (certainly one of the most powerful). Moreover at the level of concrete history only a portion of economic life is strictly speaking capitalist (e.g., peasant labor, self-employed labor, domestic labor, voluntary labor, forced labor etc. are not capitalist). Hence the central problem of Marxian political economy is moving from the inner logic of capital which theorizes the economic to concrete history where the economic is only partially capitalist, and is conditioned by the non-economic in complex ways.

In my view and I believe in Marx's view, *Capital* is primarily a theory of capital's basic operating principles or inner logic.[15] It is a theory of capital in the abstract and in general or a theory of pure capitalism in which all means of production are owned by capitalists and landlords, and all commodities are produced by workers for a wage. Indeed pure capitalism is an "inner" logic only in so far as it can be conceived of as self-expanding value. But in order for value to be self-expanding all inputs and outputs of production must be totally commodified so that value can expand itself through a commodity-economic logic without reliance upon any outside supports and particularly not extra-economic force or organized human intervention. As previously mentioned, this condition of total commodification can also be referred to as total reification because social relations are mediated by commodities and money such that individuals are reduced to being mere bearers or personifications of economic categories. The extreme subjectification of individuals through private property, competition, and the prevailing cash nexus is the counterpart of the extreme objectification of individuals as they become mere objects for the use by capital in its own self-expansion. This seemingly paradoxical juxtaposition of subjectification and objectification is at the very heart of capitalist reification. And it is only through the study of a purely capitalist society that we can come to fully grasp the implications of this all too real contradiction.[16]

The theoretical object of marxian political economy, as I understand it, is capitalism. But capitalism is a unique object of knowledge in its self-reifying character. At one level of theory we can conceive of pure capitalism, and this is not a one-sided exaggeration that we create in our imaginations, but rather it is an extending to completion in theory of the reifying tendencies that capitalism presents in history. It is neither a simple reflection or copy of "reality," nor is it simply an artifice produced by us. Rather it is an abstraction made possible by the evolution of the discourse of political economy as it interacts in complex ways with the history of capitalism of which it is a part. Thus as capitalism evolves and with it greater reification of social life, political economy as a theoretical practice becomes more possible and up to a point helps clear the path for capitalism by recommending policies that free up markets (especially Ricardo). At the same time, in order for Marx to be able to make his "epistemological break" with classical economics, class divisions had to have become increasingly apparent. In short the evolution of economic reality assists theory construction and theory construction influences the evolution of economic reality. Theory is not in any sense a direct copy, reflection, or representation of reality, but it is in complex ways reality-assisted.[17]

Although capital never becomes totally reified in history, it continually shows itself to be a powerful reifying force, subduing and subsuming all manner of pre-capitalist and non-capitalist social forms. Indeed it is the only social phenomenon that is self-reifying in the sense that it continually expands and deepens its commodity-economic logic until it runs up against obstacles that require dependence on outside supports. Because of its strong self-reifying tendencies, capital has a tendency to shape other social forms more than they shape it. For example, history is replete with instances where capitalism seems to bring about similarities or convergence between radically distinct cultural formations.[18] But this is not to say that the logic of capital always prevails at the level of the concrete. The purchase of capitalism on history is only partial. It is one social force amongst others, and on the one hand, all things being equal, one would expect the reifying force of capital to prevail in the long run (at least as long as capitalism exists or is not highly compromised as it might become in a phase of transition away from capitalism), but on the other hand, things are seldom equal, and the logic of capital may in various ways and to varying extents be refracted, deflected, dispersed, counteracted, defused, or blocked. Furthermore, capital does not engulf all of social life or even all of economic life even if its role is often preponderant. In my view, capitalism cannot be equated with the economic because the economic is only partially capitalist at the level of the concrete. Furthermore, the economic is not the base, nor is it always determinate in the last instance, rather it is a particularly powerful and persistent set of social forces that to the extent that it has capitalist components tends in the long run to shape other social forces more than it is shaped by them, but which may be thwarted or compromised either partially or totally in particular circumstances.

The theory of capital's inner logic can be considered a theory of capital's essence, but it does not follow that such a theory is "essentialist" in the usual meaning of the concept.[19] First, because capital's essence is the entire theory of its inner logic, it is a complex essence. Second, because capital is a social construct, it is a socially constructed essence. Now this may seem like a contradiction in terms, but it is not because of reification. Although human beings construct capitalism, once constructed, it achieves a certain automaticity or life of its own, and it is precisely this reified character that is the necessary condition for theorizing an inner logic. Third, it is an historically specific essence in the sense that capitalism is an historically specific mode of production. Fourth, it is an essence that is active in history, but history is not a function of this essence since historical outcomes are complex combinations of capital's logic with other social forces. It follows that the relation between capital's inner logic and history is nothing like a simple essence/appearance relation.

If we look at Marx's historical writings, such as *The Eighteenth Brumaire*, it is apparent that in history persons are not simply personifications of economic categories and historical outcomes are not simply the localizations of capital's logic. But Marx saw the dawning of monopoly capital as the death knell of capitalism, and hence was not too concerned to focus on just how the inner logic of capital was to be used to understand history.[20] It is here that I differ the most from Marx, for I see a much more problematic relation between the inner logic of capital and concrete history than he did. I agree with Marx that capital has an inner logic that can be theorized, but the effectivity of that logic at the level of history cannot be assumed, but instead must be explored in each concrete context in relation to the other significant social forces at work.

We have already seen that implied by Marx's writings are at least two distinct levels of social ontology. At the level of capital's logic, persons are bearers of economic categories and at the level of history persons may exhibit various forms of agency. It follows that the types of logics used at these two levels must be different. At the abstract level capital reproduces itself and expands via a commodity-economic logic without any outside intervention by human agency. Humans become simply objects of capital's self-expansion, and hence the logic used is distinctively necessitarian. In sharp contrast, at the historical level, humans combine into various types of collective agencies that may resist and disrupt capital's logic in all sorts of ways at the same time that capital's logic conditions those same agencies. Furthermore, collective agencies tend to be complex so that the sort of logic used must be appropriate to the complex processes of action, reaction, resistance, and transformation by non-homogeneous collectivities.

What underlies the different logics at these two levels is fundamentally differences in degree of reification. At the level of pure capitalism reification is total and persons are simply bearers of structures. At the level of history where reification is not total, persons actively engage in political struggle to better their lives. It seems that capital is both ontologically distinct from other social objects and ontologically complex and layered internally.

In my view the logical and historical study of capital are sufficiently ontologically distinct that they require separate logics and separate theories. Indeed, the ontological gap is sufficiently great that I believe a mediating level of theory (mid-range theory) is necessary.[21] Such a theory would attempt to periodize capitalist history in accord with the qualitatively different types of capital accumulation that were characteristic of different stages of capitalist development.[22] It would translate capital's inner logic into patterns of structures, policies, practices, and institutions characteristic and typical of capital accumulation in a stage-specific temporal and spatial frame. And it would explore the interconnections between the economic, the ideological, the legal, and the political.

The three levels of analysis theorize structure/agency relations differently. At the level of pure capitalism, human agency is subsumed to the agency of capital and the self-organization of humans is subsumed to the self-expansion of capital. At the level of mid-range theory, abstract types of agency characteristic of stage-specific forms of capital accumulation are considered. Here the focus is not on the actual complexities of change but on characteristic types of domination and resistance. At the level of historical analysis structures are more or less agencied and agencies are more or less structured in an on-going process of struggle and change. At this level change may be successfully studied in all its complexity precisely because the analysis of it is informed by more abstract levels of theory. Also at this level, theory may be used to inform thinking about transformational strategies.

Conclusions

While I agree with Althusser's claim that *Capital* is the founding work of a new science, I do not accept what I consider his excessive modernism nor am I at all tempted by the path of deconstruction. Where I fundamentally differ from Althusser is on the nature of this "new science." For Althusser *Capital* is the founding work of the science of history, and he extracts from this text a structuralist epistemology for the social sciences. In contrast I consider *Capital* to be the founding work of the science of capitalism, and I consider capitalism as an object of knowledge to be ontologically distinct and ontologically complex or layered. But if capitalism is ontologically distinct, it implies not only that there can be no general epistemology for the social sciences, but also that the epistemology employed must be specific to this object with its unique ontology. Finally, if capitalism is ontologically layered, it implies distinct epistemologies or at least distinct logics for each layer to the extent that it is ontologically distinct. Elsewhere (1992) I have argued that the theory of capital's logic employs a dialectical logic, mid-range theory employs a predominately structural logic, and historical analysis predominantly a logic of process (though not in the sense of Laclau and Mouffe).

A crucial point that remained unsettled in Althusser's epistemology and that I find unsettling is his claim that knowledge occurs to the extent that the object of knowledge "cognitively appropriates" or "is adequate to" the real object. I can agree with Althusser's firm rejection of crude empiricism and of the problem of guarantees as it would occur in crude copy or reflection theories of knowledge. But having driven such a wedge between the object of knowledge and the real object, terms like "cognitive appropriation" hardly seem adequate. And indeed with Resnick and Wolff the problem is solved by the disappearance of the real object altogether. Resnick and Wolff's deconstructive epistemology is marked by rhetorics vying for power, by the endless play of signification unable to make contact with reality, by an arid ontological homogeneity, by an anti-theory leveling or horizontality, and finally by a cynical intellectual universe where the best propagandist wins. Resnick and Wolff abandon the terrain of economic theory in favor of a sociology of class at an historical conjuncture when capitalism appears to be in permanent crisis. Their aim is no doubt a radically pluralistic marxism, but when pluralism becomes too radical it tends towards its opposite—a kind of monism, which is not only a monism but a kind of mush precisely because anything goes. The deconstruction of Marx's *Capital* has, no doubt, been good intentioned, but the consequences I'm afraid are producing a desertification of the terrain of Marxian political economy. Indeed, Resnick and Wolff have already abandoned Marxism despite their continued use of the label. The tendency of their theory is insidious and should be strongly resisted.

Notes

I would like to thank Banu Helvacioglu, Stephanos KourKoulakos, Michelle Mawhinney, and Jennifer Welsh for their helpful comments on earlier drafts of this essay.

I read Lehmann (1993) after I had written the first draft of this article, and discovered that quite independently she also arrived at the concept "de(con)struction."

1. Resnick and Wolff and others have followed a path that has lead from Althusser's "relative autonomy" to positions of extreme pluralism that effectively undermine all causal analysis. I do not believe that the concept need lead to this position, and hence, in this essay I use it and also clearly defend causal analysis. I use the concept primarily to refer to the complex ways that different levels of analysis remain distinct while informing one another.

2. Both of these tendencies are exemplified in the works of Resnick and Wolff and their followers.

3. The only way they can escape epistemology is by not being explicit about their own epistemological assumptions.

4. See Sekine (1984, 1986) for a rigorous reconstruction of Marx's law of value including a demonstration of the necessity of the labor theory of value and a theory of price determination connected to the theoretical context of value categories.

5. See my article "A Critique of Regulation Theory" in Albritton and Sekine (forthcoming) for an in depth analysis of the economistic tendencies of regulation theory.

6. They have no interest in any law of value, which was of course central to Marx. Instead they are only interested in value categories in so far as they help to define their typology of class.

7. Many individual Marxist theorists and schools of Marxian political economy have paid lip service to the idea of levels of abstraction or levels of analysis, but few have seriously considered in any extended way how relatively autonomous levels of theory might be constructed or how the complex problems associated with separate logics that inform one another across levels might be formulated. In my view this is perhaps the central problem of contemporary Marxism.

8. It is beyond the scope of this paper to show in detail how all these sins can be avoided. I have written on them elsewhere however (see especially 1991 and forthcoming).

9. For more on this point see Albritton (1991). It is beyond the scope of this paper to demonstrate at length that capital does have an inner logic. This is perhaps best done in Sekine's two volume *Dialectic of Capital*.

10. "Deconstruction" is totally inappropriate in this context. It is possible to transform capitalism, but it is not possible to deconstruct it.

11. By introducing politics directly into the law of value, Ryan unwittingly dissolves the law of value and with it our ability to understand capital's inner logic.

12. Causality is, of course, a complex issue. Althusser, for example, writes of linear causality, expressive causality, and structural causality. No doubt one could come up with other types and forms. However, it seems to me that if one is unable to rank at all the various influences that bear upon an outcome, then no meaningful conception of causality is possible. We clearly need to understand causality in some sense in our daily lives in order to survive. Why, then, should we deprive ourselves of at least some conception of causality in our theoretical practices.

13. The analysis of types of causal analysis is beyond the scope of this paper, but clearly our choice is not simply between essential causes and no weighting of causes as Resnick and Wolff (1987a 19) make it out to be.

14. See Suchting (1991 note #78) for an Althusserian critique of Resnick and Wolff's solipsism and relativism.

15. My interpretation of *Capital* is heavily influenced by Sekine (1984; 1986), who in his *Dialectic of Capital* not only reconstructs Marx's theory as a rigorous dialectical logic with explicit parallels to Hegel's *Logic*, but also convincingly deals with numerous problems of economic theory such as the "transformation problem."

16. In Albritton (1991) there are extended analyses of how this peculiar subjectification/objectification affects capitalist law, politics, and ideology.

17. I realize that what I am arguing here goes against the grain of most poststructuralism, which is ontologically anti-realist. From the character of my argument, it is obvious that I hold a version of a realist ontology. For an extended and interesting defense of a realist ontology read the works of Bhaskar. It is also the case that Althusser holds to a realist ontology.

18. Three examples come to mind. Germany and the United States in the late nineteenth century had very different cultural and political arrangements, but the pressures of capitalism produced similar ways of managing labor power, produced similar tendencies towards monopoly, and similar expansionist nationalism. After World War II the United States and Japan had radically distinct cultures, but they both went through a McCarthyite type period when the left was purged from the trade union movement. Also there seems to be some cultural convergence between Japan and the United States today as capitalism increasingly weakens traditional authority structures in Japan. Finally in the 30s fascist movements sprang up in the most diverse cultures, suggesting that forces at work at the level of global capitalism may have played an important role.

19. The usual meaning of essentialism in this context is economic determinism and class reductionism. See Albritton (1993) for a more extended discussion of this point, and see Albritton (1991) for an initial effort at actually theorizing stages of capitalist development in non-reductionist ways.

20. " . . . the stock company is a transition toward the conversion of all functions in the reproduction process which still remain linked with capitalist property, into mere functions of associated producers, into social functions. . . . This is the abolition of the capitalist mode of production within the capitalist mode of production itself, and hence a self dissolving contradiction, which prima facie represents a mere phase of transition to a new form of production" (Marx 1971 Vol. 3 436-8).

21. For an effort to construct a mid-range theory that periodizes qualitatively different modes of capital accumulation that predominant in different periods of capitalist history, see Albritton (1991).

22. When I use the word "stage" I do not mean to imply any sort of teleology. It is simply a term for periodizing capitalist history by developing a mid-range theory.

Works Cited

Albritton, Robert. *A Japanese Reconstruction of Marxist Theory*. London: Macmillan, 1986.

_____. *A Japanese Approach to Stages of Capitalist Development*. London: Macmillan, 1991.

———. "Levels of Analysis in Marxian Political Economy: An Unoist Approach." *Radical Philosophy* 60 (1992).
———. "Marxian Political Economy for an Age of Postmodern Excess."*Rethinking Marxism*, 6.1 (1993).
——— and Thomas Sekine. *A Japanese Approach to Political Economy: Unoist Variations*. London: Macmillan, Forthcoming.
Althusser, Louis. *For Marx*. New York: Vintage, 1969.
——— and Etienne Balibar. *Reading Capital*. London: New Left Books, 1970.
Amariglio, Jack, Stephen Resnick, and Richard Wolff. "Division and Difference in the 'Discipline' of Economics." *Critical Inquiry*, Fall (1990).
Cutler, Anthony, Barry Hindness, Paul Hirst, and Athar Hussain. *Marx's Capital and Capitalism Today*. London: Routledge and Kegan Paul, 1977.
Laclau, Ernesto and Chantal Mouffe. *Hegemony and Socialist Strategy: Towards a Radical Democratic Politics*. London: Verso, 1985.
Lehmann, Janet. "The Undecidability of Derrida/The Premature Demise of Althusser." *Current Perspectives in Social Theory* 13 (1993).
Marx, Karl. *Capital* 3 Vols. Moscow: Progress, 1971.
Resnick, Stephen and Richard Wolff.*Economics: Marxian versus Neoclassical*. Baltimore: The Johns Hopkins Press, 1987a.
———. *Knowledge and Class*. Chicago: University of Chicago Press, 1987b.
———. "Marxian Theory and the Rhetorics of Economics."*The Consequences of Economic Rhetoric*. Ed. A. Klamer, D. McCloskey, R. Solow. Cambridge: Cambridge University Press, 1988.
Ryan, Michael. *Marxism and Deconstruction*. Baltimore: Johns Hopkins Press, 1982.
Sekine, Thomas. *The Dialectic of Capital,* vol. 1. Tokyo: Yushindo Press, 1984.
———. *The Dialectic of Capital,* vol. 2. Tokyo: Toshindo Press, 1986.
Suchting, W. A. "On Some Unsettled Questions Touching the Character of Marxism, Especially as Philosophy." *Graduate Faculty Philosophy Journal* 14. 1 (1991).
Uno, Kozo. *Principles of Political Economy: Theory of a Purely Capitalist Society*. Trans. Thomas Sekine. Sussex: Harvester Press, 1980.

Alex Callinicos

Wonders Taken for Signs: Homi Bhabha's Postcolonialism

P ostcolonial thought is the last refuge of the postmodernist. The philosophical foundations of what has come to be known as postmodernism were laid by thinkers such as Derrida, Foucault, and Deleuze, whose work in turn—despite the considerable differences among them—was packaged under the common label of poststructuralism in the English-speaking world. Now the various ways in which these theorists sought to continue Nietzsche's metaphysics of power have been subjected to searching, arguably devastating critical examination, above all in Habermas' *Philosophical Discourse of Modernity*, but also in the work of other writers, notably Peter Dews (1987). Nothing resembling an adequate response to the questions raised by Habermas, Dews, and others has yet to appear. Derrida's blustering comments on the *Philosophical Discourse* simply provide yet more evidence—were it still needed—of his apparent inability to cope with criticism (Derrida 1988: 156-58, n. 9).

At the same time, equally severe political objections to postmodernism were raised by several Marxist writers (Anderson 1983, Eagleton 1985, Callinicos 1989). In particular, they argued that its ostensible philosophical radicalism concealed a powerful tendency to depoliticize critical theory. The theme, for example, in Foucault's last writings of an "aesthetics of existence" seemed to imply that political action be redirected away from any intervention in the public sphere towards a restyling of the self—a line of thought which fitted in comfortably with the narcissistic obsessions with lifestyle and the body so typical of the 1980s. Postmodernism, in other words, seemed like a way in which the sometime radical intellectual could learn to stop worrying and love late-capitalist consumption. Certainly Rorty's pragmatist refashioning of poststructuralism involved the elimination of any critical distance from the liberal-democratic status quo. Thus the adoption of an ironic stance towards his beliefs—based on the claim that no "final vocabulary" can be shown to be rationally preferable to any other—allows Rorty to continue being sentimentally patriotic about America, willing to grant that it could slide into fascism at any time, but proud of its past and guardedly hopeful about its future" (Rorty 1993: 47; see also Rorty 1989, and for a hilarious critique, see Eagleton 1990).

The significance of what has come to be known as postcolonial theory is that it gives postmodernism a political inflection it previously lacked. Homi Bhabha, postcolonialism's subtlest thinker, makes explicit in *The Location of Culture* the kind of reorientation involved: "Driven by the subaltern history of the margins of modernity—rather than by the failures of logocentrism—I have tried, in some small measure, to revise the known, to rename the postmodern from the position of the postcolonial" (1994: 175). This "renaming" of postmodernism involves doing a certain amount of theoretical violence to it. Bhabha acknowledges that Rorty, for example, is "steeped in a Western ethnocentrism" (192). Yet he attacks "the damaging and self-defeating assumption that theory is necessarily the elite language of the socially and culturally privileged" (19). "Are the interests of 'Western' theory necessarily collusive with the hegemonic role of the West as a power bloc?" he asks (20). No, Bhabha replies, because one may distinguish between "the institutional history of critical theory and its conceptual potential for change and innovation" (31).

Robert Young makes an analogous case for postmodernism in a book, *White Mythologies*, which constructs, in effect, the philosophical genealogy of postcolonialism. Young responds to Frank Lentricchia's charge that poststructuralism involves a "denial of history" (1983: xiii) by seeking to demonstrate that the very different attempts by Sartre and Althusser to construct a Marxist theory of history foundered on the same rock: conceptualizing society as a totality required the exclusion of difference, of the heterogeneous and the discontinuous, but could not prevent the return, whether covert or open, of the repressed. Moreover, the Marxist drive to totalize was not simply a philosophical impossibility, but a concealed form of domination: what it excluded was the world outside of, but subject to, the West. Thus in Fredric Jameson's Hegelian Marxism, "[n]o one apparently is allowed a history outside the "us"—that is, Western civilization and the Western point of view" (Young 1990: 113). Poststructuralism, however, with its hostility to totalization and privileging of difference, represents a break with this kind of Eurocentrism: "Postmodernism can best be defined as European culture's awareness that it is no longer the unquestioned and dominant center of the world" (Young 19). Young thus seems to differ from Bhabha in holding that poststructuralism carried with it an explosive political charge from the start; nevertheless, he explores the ways in which postcolonial theorists such as Bhabha himself and Gayatri Spivak have made explicit and further developed the subversion of Eurocentrism allegedly effected by Derrida and Foucault.

Young's argument raises large claims about the relationship between, not simply Marxism, but the Enlightenment whose heir and critic it is, on the one hand, and the multiplicity of forms in which the Western powers have over the past five centuries succeeded in constituting and maintaining themselves as globally dominant, on the other. I cannot directly address these questions here, though I discuss them elsewhere, in *Theories and Narratives*. My concern here is rather with Bhabha's particular version of postcolonial theory. The publication of a collection of his essays, *The Location of Culture*, provides an occasion critically to assess his work. I shall try to show that, *pace* Young, Bhabha's refashioning of postmodernism involves precisely the fault with which its critics constantly charge this current—namely that it evacuates critical theory of its historical and political content. I should perhaps emphasize that my argument is not intended to deny the urgency of decentering theory—that is, of developing forms of analysis which do not treat the history and civilization of Europe and its North American extension as the measure of human experience. This task, in turn, cannot be separated from a political identification with the plight of those subject to a Western imperialism which the Gulf War of 1991 showed to be very much alive and kicking, and in particular with the struggles which continue to challenge its domination (see Callinicos *et al.* 1994). But precisely because developing anti-imperialist theory matters so much, it is essential rigorously to inspect the credentials of intellectual work purporting to challenge Western domination.

This is especially important because the label "postcolonialism" covers a theoretically and politically heterogeneous collection of tendencies. It embraces, for example, what involves, in the guise of a decentering—of a critique of Eurocentrism—a tacit *re*centering of theory and practice. Typically this consists in deploying a conception of the Third World as a dehistoricized, homogenized rhetorical construct whose chief function seems to be as a source of intellectual authority allowing the user to dismiss the claims and arguments of others not entitled to use it (the repeated, almost ritualized invocation of "US Third World feminism" in Dhaliwal 1994 is an example of what I have in mind). As Aijaz Ahmad has so forcefully argued, this kind of usage of the expression "Third World" ignores the historical specificity and divergent development of the societies falling under it. But the question of what relation this imaginary "Third World" bears to its supposed referents is in any case beside the point, since, he argues, its role is chiefly to speak to the situation of intellectuals from the former colonies but now located in the Western academy (Ahmad 1992).

There are, however, other strains of postcolonial thought. Edward Said's *Orientalism* is in many ways the founding text of this entire intellectual current. In a brilliant discussion of Said, Ahmad highlights what he calls the former's "inability to make up his mind whether 'Oriental Discourse' is a system of representations, in the Foucauldian sense"—that is, a body of statements functioning within an apparatus of power-knowledge whose operation requires the construction of a particular "truth"—"or of misrepresentations, in the sense of a realistic problematic," in which case Orientalism must be understood as a set of false assertions capable, in principle at least, of being confronted with more accurate representations of the social formations it subsumes under the ideological category of the East (Ahmad 185-86). Young explores the same equivocation in Said's writing from a poststructuralist perspective (see 1990: ch. 7). Ahmad notes, but does not, in my view, place sufficient stress on, what he acknowledges is Said's "partial distancing from Foucault" since *Orientalism* was first published in 1978 (199). Yet Said's more recent writings contain increasingly strong hints that the promise of universal emancipation offered by the Enlightenment is not irredeemably Eurocentric, but can be fulfilled through what Habermas has memorably called "the radicalized Enlightenment"—through the development of a theory and practice of emancipation that is genuinely universal (Habermas 1986: 158).

Consider, for example, this comment on the work of Ranajit Guha and the other Indian historians associated with the journal *Subaltern Studies*:

> if subaltern history is construed to be only a separatist enterprise—much as early feminist writing was based on the notion that women had a voice or room of their own, entirely separate from the masculine domain—then it runs the risk of just being a mirror opposite [of] the writing whose tyranny it disputes. It is also likely to be as exclusivist, as limited, provincial and discriminatory in its suppressions and repressions as the master discourses of colonialism and elitism. In fact, as Guha shows, the subaltern alternative is an integrative knowledge, for all the gaps, the lapses and ignorances of which it is so conscious. Its claim is that by being subaltern it can see the whole experience of Indian resistance to colonialism more fairly than the partial histories provided by a handful of dominant native leaders or colonial historians. This is a claim not dissimilar in its moral force to Lukács' theory of 'proletarian' consciousness, where in a

world of impoverished and yet fantastically widespread 'reification,' in which everything from the human soul to the product of human labor turned into a commodity or an inert thing, only the viewpoint of the human *thing* itself can comprehend and resist the enormity of what has happened. (Said 1988: viii)

Said thus rejects any attempt to base critical theory on a Manichean opposition between dominant and subaltern groups, between oppressor and oppressed; at the same time, he seems to follow Lukács in advocating the adoption of a totalizing perspective in order to grasp the nature of, and the means of challenging the relations of oppression. Bhabha, by contrast, takes the first step but not the second. Thus:

The language of critique is effective not because it keeps forever separate the terms of the master and the slave, the mercantilist and the Marxist, but to the extent to which it overcomes the given grounds of opposition and opens up a space of translation: a space of hybridity, figuratively speaking, where the construction of a political space that is new, neither the one nor the other, properly alienates our political expectations, and changes, as it must, the very forms of our recognition of the moment of politics. (Bhabha 1994: 25)

Bhabha makes very strong claims for the strategic (if not ontological) priority of the questions addressed by postcolonial theory: "Questions of race and cultural difference overlay issues of sexuality and gender and overdetermine the social allegiances of class and democratic socialism" (175). But cultural difference—"race," nationality, and other forms of "ethnic" identity—is not to be conceptualized as the self-assertion of primordially given collective subjects. On the contrary, "the articulation of cultural differences" occurs in "'in-between' spaces" where identities are formed through a process of hybridization: "It is in the emergence of the interstices—the overlap and displacement of domains of difference—that the intersubjective and collective experiences of *nationness*, community interest, or cultural value are negotiated" (1-2). This stress on the hybrid character of identity is closely related to Bhabha's preoccupation with the experiences of the displaced and the migratory, that is, of those whose conditions of life compel them to cross borders and occupy "'in-between' spaces"—with "the history of postcolonial migration, the narratives of cultural and political diaspora, the major social displacements of peasants and aboriginal communities, the poetics of exile, the grim prose of political and economic refugees" (5).

In themselves, these themes are in no way peculiar to Bhabha's writings. Hybridity—the constant formation and reformation of identity as a synthesis of diverse influences and experiences—is, for example, explored by Said in his recent book *Culture and Imperialism*. And the experience of exile and migration is one of the major reference points for postcolonial thought more generally—though, as Ahmad suggests, often without sufficient attention being paid to the different forms of displacement from Third to First World, and the variety of social destinations to which those undergoing them have traveled (Ahmad 1992, esp. chs. 2 and 4). What is distinctive to Bhabha's work is the particular manner in which he explores these and other themes. The spin he gives postcolonialism consists in his conceptualizing domination and resistance by means of a poststructuralist philosophy of language influenced especially by Lacan's appropriation of Saussure. Bhabha is describing his own method when he writes: "To provide a social imaginary that is based on the articulation of differential, even disjunctive, moments of history and culture, contemporary critics resort to the peculiar temporality of the language metaphor" (176).

The master-concept deployed in Bhabha's resort to "the language metaphor" is that of ambivalence. He insists on "the historical connectedness between the subject and object of critique so that there can be no simplistic, essentialist opposition between ideological misrecognition and revolutionary truth" (26). It is through the psychoanalytical theme of ambivalence that he explores this "historical connectedness." "The concept of cultural difference focuses on the problem of the ambivalence of cultural authority: the attempt to dominate in the *name* of a cultural supremacy which is itself produced in the moment of differentiation" (34). Several of Bhabha's essays examine in depth—and indeed sometimes in the obscurity often unfortunately characteristic of Lacanian theorizing—the ambivalences constitutive of colonial discourse. Their force derives from the fact that "the body is always simultaneously (if conflictually) inscribed in both the economy of pleasure and desire and the economy of discourse, domination and power": the colonized is at once desired and despised (67). More specifically, "colonial discourse as an apparatus of power . . . turns on the recognition and disavowal of racial/cultural/historical differences" (70). Bhabha explores the resulting ambiguities and contradictions notably in his discussion of colonial mimicry—the efforts by both colonizers and colonized to make the latter more like the former. He calls mimicry "an ironic compromise," "the desire for a reformed, recognizable other, as a subject of a difference that is almost the same but not quite" (86). The British colonial state in India, for example, aspired to transform the beliefs and behavior of its subjects. Had, however, these efforts been successful, had Indians been remade into Englishmen, then the rationale for British domination of India—the difference between rulers and ruled, the racial inferiority of Asians to Europeans—would have been removed. A "flawed colonial mimesis" was both presupposition and result of this form of domination (87):

> Mimicry is thus the sign of a double articulation; a complex strategy of reform, regulation, and discipline, which 'appropriates' the Other as it visualizes power. Mimicry is also the sign of the inappropriate, however, a difference or recalcitrance which coheres the dominant strategic function of colonial power, intensifies surveillance, and poses an immanent threat to both 'normalized' knowledges and disciplinary powers. (86)

"[T]he ambivalence of mimicry—almost but not quite" implies a process of displacement that makes it "the affect [sic] of hybridity—at once a mode of appropriation and of resistance, from the disciplined to the desiring . . . as discrimination turns into the assertion of the hybrid, the insignia of authority becomes a mask, a mockery" (91, 120). The process of imitation of the colonizer's culture is at the same time one of subversion. For example, the evangelizing efforts of Christian missionaries in nineteenth-century India were frustrated, not only by outright rejection, but also by the combining of Christian beliefs with the apparently contradictory doctrines of Hinduism, or by the fetishistic incantation of Biblical formulas. Bhabha quotes one Anglican clergyman's complaint in 1818: "If you urge them with their gross and unworthy conceptions of the nature and will of God or the monstrous follies of their fabulous theology, they will turn it off with a sly civility perhaps, or with a popular and careless proverb" (121).

Bhabha's explorations of colonial ambivalence—pursued as they are with great (sometimes excessive) subtlety—are undoubtedly of real interest and importance. But they do raise the question of the nature of the differences he analyses. Here, his answer is perfectly explicit. They are '[t]he work of the word' (124). The following passage is the closest that Bhabha comes to developing and justifying this claim:

> The reason a cultural text or system of meaning cannot be sufficient unto itself is that the act of cultural enunciation—the *place of utterance*—is crossed by the *différance* of writing. This has less to do with what anthropologists might describe as varying attitudes to symbolic systems within different cultures than with the structure of symbolic representation—not the content of the symbol or its social function, but the structure of symbolization. . . . The linguistic difference that informs any cultural performance is dramatized in the common semiotic account of the disjuncture between the subject of the proposition (*enoncé*) and the subject of enunciation, which is not represented in the statement but which is the

acknowledgment of its discursive embeddedness and address, its cultural positionality, its reference to a present time and an open space. (36)

This "enunciative split" produces "an ambivalence in the act of interpretation," since it involves an ineffaceable gap between the content of a proposition and its discursive context (36). More generally, it seems that the intrinsic heterogeneity of discourses is a consequence of "the structure of symbolic representation." Cultural difference turns out to be Derridean *différance*, the endless process of displacement from one signifier to another, in which a transcendental signified that would halt this flight of meaning is at once constantly posited and indefinitely deferred. Bhabha is well aware of the obvious objection that these claims are a particularly flagrant example of what Deleuze and Guattari denounced as "the imperialism of the signifier" (Deleuze and Guattari 1980: 84). "I may be accused," he acknowledges, "of a form of linguistic or theoretical formalism" (Bhabha 57). His reply amounts to the assertion, already encountered, that transforming poststructuralism into postcolonialism provides the former with the political content it had previously lacked, explicitly at any rate. Thus, "if the interest in postmodernism is limited to a celebration of the fragmentation of the 'grand narratives' of post-enlightenment rationalism then, for all its intellectual excitement, it remains a profoundly parochial enterprise." (Bhabha 4) The problem of cultural difference rescues postmodernism from the fate of merely proliferating "a self-perpetuating series of negative theologies" by giving it a definite historico-political location (171). Indeed, Bhabha advances the even stronger claim that the ambivalences of the colonial experience somehow anticipated the deconstructions of Derrida and the genealogies of Foucault:

> My growing conviction has been that the encounters and negotiations of differential meanings and values within 'colonial' textuality, its governmental discourses and cultural practices, have anticipated, *avant la lettre*, many of the problematics of signification and judgment that have been current in contemporary theory—aporia, ambivalence, indeterminacy, the question of discursive closure, the threat to agency, the status of intentionality, the challenge to 'totalizing' concepts, to name but a few. (173)

The trouble with this line of argument is that Bhabha's analyses of colonial power are themselves so thoroughly imbricated with poststructuralist concepts—those of Saussurian philosophy of language read through Lacan and Derrida—that they cannot provide any independent support for the claim there is a privileged relationship between these concepts and "colonial textuality." One rather has the feeling that some sort of card trick is going on: colonial discourse is invoked to give poststructuralism much needed political and historical content, but this discourse turns out itself to be a poststructuralist construct (as the terminology involved—"discourse," "textuality," etc.—indicates. This impression is reinforced when one notes the way in which Bhabha tends to rewrite the other texts—and particularly those concerned with the struggle against imperialism—he discusses. So, for example, he concentrates on those aspects of Fanon's work which highlight "the psychoanalytic ambivalence of the Unconscious," rather than those that posit "a Hegelian-Marxist dialectic" pointing towards "the total transformation of Man and Society" (40-41). There is, of course, nothing wrong with selectively interpreting, and reinterpreting texts—how else, after all, are traditions are creatively continued? It is, however, the particular drift of Bhabha's rewritings that is revealing. Again and again, the interest of various struggles against colonial domination turns out to be the way in which they instantiate "aporia, ambivalence, indeterminacy," and all the other items of the poststructuralist repertoire. Far from the experience of subjection and resistance to Western imperialism politicizing postmodernism, that experience is reduced to yet another variation on the well-worn theme of the endless flow of signification.

This process is perhaps best illustrated by the way in which Bhabha appropriates Ranajit Guha's studies of peasant rebellions in colonial India. Thus he seizes on Guha's discussion of the circulation of chapatis (unleavened bread) from village to village during the development of the Indian Mutiny of 1857, a phenomenon regarded by colonial historians as part of the build-up of rumors which helped to precipitate the revolt. For Bhabha, "[t]he indeterminate circulation of meaning as rumor or conspiracy, with its perverse, psychic affects of panic, constitutes the intersubjective realm of revolt and resistance" (200). Rumor is constitutive of revolt, and rumor is itself an effect of the process of signification:

> The *semiotic* condition of uncertainty and panic is generated when an old and familiar symbol (chapati) develops an unfamiliar social significance as sign through a transformation of the temporality of its representation. The performative time of the chapati's signification, its circulation as 'conspiracy' and/or 'insurgency' turns from the customary and commonplace to the archaic, awesome, terrifying. This reinscription of a traditional system of organization through the disturbance, or interruption, of the circulation of its cultural codes . . . bears a marked similarity to the conjunctural history of the Mutiny. (202; emphasis added)

The greatest single rebellion against British imperialism in India is thus conceptualized primarily in terms of an "interruption" of the signifying chain. Bhabha doesn't go so far as explicitly to *reduce* the Mutiny to this: he is careful to note other, non-discursive conditions of the revolt (202-20). But this takes up merely a paragraph in an essay devoted to "those *signs* by which marginalized or insurgent agents create a collective agency" (199; emphasis added). It is not difficult to demonstrate the difference between this problematic and the chief preoccupations of Guha's writing. It is true that the interpretation of Guha's work is not free of controversy. Both Ahmad and Said call him a poststructuralist (Ahmad 1992: 68; Said 1993: 296). But this judgment—from which each draws directly opposed conclusions about the merits of Guha's historiography—seems to me mistaken. His initial programmatic statement for the collective project of *Subaltern Studies* takes as its reference point the concept, central to orthodox Communism in India as elsewhere, of "a bourgeois-democratic revolution" of "a more modern type" than 1789, which would achieve victory "under the hegemony of the workers and peasants": understanding why the independence struggle did not culminate in this revolution, or even a more conventional bourgeois revolution, "constitutes the central problematic of the historiography of colonial India" (Guha 1988a: 43). Guha thereby situates his writing within the process of collective reflection by the Indian left— and indeed by what used to be the international Communist movement and its revolutionary critics—on the achievements and limitations of the great anti-imperialist struggles which dominated the mid-twentieth century.

He does, however, break new ground, in two important respects. (I am indebted for a better understanding of Guha's historiography to T. V. Sathyamurthy's "Indian Peasant Historiography.") First, he rejects the assumption that modern Indian history is the work of an elite—whether it be, as it was for colonial historians, the British imperial state, or, as nationalist and Stalinist historiography insists, the Indian National Congress. This assumption implies, in the study of peasant rebellions,

> a refusal to acknowledge the insurgent as the subject of his own history. For once a peasant rebellion has been assimilated to the career of the Raj, the Nation or the People, it becomes easy for the historian to abdicate the responsibility he has of exploring and describing the consciousness specific to that rebellion and be content to ascribe to it a transcendental consciousness. (Guha 1988b: 82)

Secondly, in seeking to recover the actuality of "insurgent consciousness" (as opposed to the "Ideal Consciousness" posited by historians whose aim is to fit colonial risings into a teleological narrative of Indian nationalism) and in particular to grasp the specific role played by religious beliefs and practices, Guha resorts to concepts and techniques derived from structuralist and poststructuralist linguistics (1988b: 83; see also the references to Barthes, Beneviste and Jakobson at 53-63). Yet the primary theoretical influence here seems to be, not any variant of poststructuralism, but Gramsci's conception of contradictory consciousness. Thus:

> Insurgency was indeed the site where the two mutually contradictory tendencies within this still imperfect, almost embryonic, theoretical consciousness—that is, a conservative tendency made up of the inherited and uncritically absorbed material of the ruling culture and a radical one oriented towards a practical transformation of the rebel's conditions of existence—met for a decisive trial of strength. (Guha 1983: 11; see also Gramsci 1971: 333.)

The distance between Guha's Marxist historiography and Bhabha's poststructuralism is made clear in some remarks of Gayatri Spivak's on *Subaltern Studies*. She argues that

> their work presupposes that the entire socius, at least insofar as it is the object of their study, is what Nietzsche would call a *fortgesetzte Zeichenkette*—a 'continuous sign-chain.' The possibility of action lies in the dynamics of the disruption of this object, the breaking and relinking of the chain. This line of argument does not set consciousness over against the socius, but see it as itself constituted as and on a semiotic chain. (1988: 5)

Spivak thus discovers in *Subaltern Studies* a perspective very similar to Bhabha's, in which historical agency is a consequence of the "disruption" of the "semiotic chain," a chain that embraces, not merely consciousness, but the social in its entirety. She proposes that Guha and his collaborators adopt a self-consciously "deconstructive approach," which would make explicit the tacit assumptions of their historiographic practice (Spivak 9). But, she also notes with regret, "[t]hey fall back on notions of consciousness-as-agent, totality, and upon a culturalism, that are discontinuous with the critique of humanism" (10). The casual way in the *Subaltern Studies* historians use various metropolitan theorists, ignoring their "historico-political provenance," seems to Spivak "a repetition as well as a rupture from the colonial predicament: the transactional quality of inter-conflicting metropolitan sources often eludes the (post)colonial intellectual" (10). This rather patronizing explanation, which gently taxes the "(post) colonial intellectual" with failing to appreciate the nuances of the Western ideas he or she eagerly but uncritically imports—rather like a Third World state that runs up vast debts importing the latest technology from the North, ignores the possibility that, for Guha at any rate (for the contributions to *Subaltern Studies* imply a variety of theoretical perspectives), the main issue simply isn't how to conceptualize rebellions as disruptions of the signifying chain. For one not wholly preoccupied by the latest trends in literary theory, to read Guha's attacks on colonialist and nationalists historians for "denying a will to the mass of the rebels themselves and representing them merely as instruments of some other will" (1988b: 82) is to be reminded irresistibly of Edward Thompson, and in particular of the famous "Preface" to *The Making of the English Working Class*, which begins by declaring that "[t]he working class . . . was present at its own making," and goes on to promise to rescue the "losers" of history "from the enormous condescension of posterity" (1980: 8, 12). To note Guha's and Thompson's common preoccupations with understanding the oppressed and exploited as historical subjects, and with recovering the actual consciousness, in its complexity and ambiguity, of specific, and often forgotten struggles is not to elide the differences between them. Thompson was famously hostile to any attempt to import Parisian theories into Marxist historiography; Guha has been sharply critical of Thompson's blindness to the gulf separating colonial and metropolitan conditions (1989: 277). For all that, they seem more natural companions than do Guha, on the one hand and Bhabha and Spivak on the other.

Another way of putting this is to say that there is, after all, a Marxist tradition to which, in their idiosyncratic ways, Guha and Thompson both belong. To say this is in a certain respect to highlight the difficulties with Guha's historiography, since two of the most important concern the relationship between the critical but ambiguous concept of the subaltern and a more straightforward class analysis, and the need for an explicit confrontation with the origins of his writing in the debates within the Communist movement. Moreover, registering the distance separating Bhabha and Guha does not settle the question of which offers the better way of making sense of imperialist domination and the struggles against it. I shall offer two reasons for preferring Guha's, despite the problems mentioned above.

The first concerns the explanatory power of different interpretations. There is a sense in which Bhabha is right. Any rebellion involves a disruption of the signifying chain. And any such disruption is likely to involve a reconfiguration of existing beliefs, the redeployment of traditional concepts and practices for the purposes of resistance, however specific its purposes and local its scope. The role played by spirit-mediums in the Zimbabwean war of liberation of 1972-80 is a particularly striking insistence of this kind of process (Lan 1985). None of this implies, however, that such struggles can be reduced to the displacements in the sign-chain they involve, as Bhabha and Spivak in effect assert when they claim that the possibility of historical action depends on the disruptions of this chain. On the contrary, the work of Bakhtin and his school suggests that proper weight can only be given to discourse, and in particular to the immanence within it of social conflict, if account is simultaneously taken of the extra-discursive historical context of the utterance (see Callinicos 1985 and 1995b). In principle it would seem difficult for a poststructuralist approach, in which historical action arises from displacements in the signifying chain, more than to allude to the material conditions of this chain, and this in a manner which draws them into the chain and transforms them into signifiers, that is, into mere links. In practice, Bhabha's essays suggest that on these assumptions historical interpretation reduces to rounding up, again and again, in whatever situation, the usual suspects—ambivalence, indeterminacy, and the like.

Secondly, and more fundamentally, there is the politics of Bhabha's postcolonialism. Consider, for example, the following passage:

> From the perspective of negotiation and translation, *contra* Fanon and Sartre, there can be no final discursive *closure* of theory. It does not foreclose on the political, even though battles for power-knowledge may be won or lost to great effect. The corollary is that there is no first or final act of revolutionary social (or socialist) transformation. (30)

Bhabha begs various questions here. Who, for example, advocates a "final discursive *closure* of theory"? It is doubtful if either Fanon or Sartre did. Certainly the classical Marxists didn't: for them knowledge was (as Engels put it) an infinite process of successive approximations to the truth. But there still is a serious issue at stake here. Bhabha seems to believe that structures of power can never be overturned by the revolutionary action of the oppressed. He approvingly quotes (in a less qualified form than her original formulation which began by saying "It is possible that . . .") Veena Das' claim that "subaltern rebellions can only provide a night-time of love"—and not, she adds, "a life-time of love" (192; compare Das 1989: 315). At best, it seems, the dominated can "re-negotiate" the terms of their oppression by exploiting the ambivalence inherent in any power-relation and displacing the flow of signifiers through which domination functions, in the way in which the Indian subjects of the Raj subverted Christianity with their "sly civility."

Resistance in all its forms, however subtle and oblique, is to be welcomed: one of the most challenging tasks of the radical historian is to recover and reconstruct these forms. It is, however, absurd and a symptom of the current ideological conjuncture that it should be necessary to say, indeed to insist, that revolution—large-scale social and political transformation—is both feasible and desirable. Disillusionment currently surrounds so many past revolutions that I shall use a contemporary struggle to highlight what Lukács calls the actuality of revolution.

The removal of the apartheid regime in South Africa is surely a most inspiring and moving example of a successful liberation struggle. But the negotiations (of a more conventional kind than those forming the focus of Bhabha's argument) which led to the transfer of political power to the representatives of the black majority were only possible because of a series of insurrectionary mass struggles between 1976 and 1986 which forced the old regime to the negotiating table. And these risings involved the development of a revolutionary popular consciousness intransigent in its refusal to compromise and its demand for a fundamental and comprehensive transformation of South Africa. The negotiated transfer of political power thus depended on revolutionary struggle. The irony of the current situation is that the terms of its pact with the old regime (and, implicitly, with local and foreign capital) the African National Congress must restrain the dynamic popular movement which brought it to office—a contradiction that may lead to the indefinite deferral of the radical socio-economic changes for which that movement fought as much as it did for citizenship rights (Callinicos 1994). The debate between negotiated compromise and rapid transformation—between reform and revolution—goes on, not because of the fading influence of some totalizing grand narrative but because of social realities that are far from unique to South Africa.

Bhabha's postcolonial rewriting of poststructuralism thus involves both an idealist reduction of the social to the semiotic and a narrowing of political horizons. To reverse the title of one of his own essays, "Wonders (are) taken for signs" (ch. 6). Political struggle seems to come down to exploiting the intrinsic ambivalence of the dominant discourse. But is it really too late to hope—and, above all, to fight—for "a life-time of love"?

Works Cited

Ahmad, Aijaz. 1992. *In Theory*. London: Verso.
Anderson, Perry. 1983. *In the Tracks of Historical Materialism*. London: Verso.
Bhabha, Homi. 1994. *The Location of Culture*. London: Routledge.
Callinicos, Alex. 1985. "Postmodernism, Poststructuralism, Postmarxism?" *Theory, Culture & Society*, 2:3: 85-101.
_____. 1989. *Against Postmodernism*. Cambridge: Polity Press.
_____. 1994. "The End of Apartheid," forthcoming in *Economic and Political Weekly*.
_____. 1995a. *Theories and Narratives*. Cambridge: Polity Press.
_____. 1995b. "The Missing-Link?"
_____. and others, eds. 1994 *Marxism and the New Imperialism*. London: Bookmarks.

Das, Veena. 1989. "Subaltern as Perspective" in R. Guha, ed., *Subaltern Studies VI*. Delhi: Oxford University Press, 310-24.
Deleuze, Gilles, and Felix Guattari. 1980. *Mille plateaux*. Paris: Éditions de Minuit.
Derrida, Jacques. 1988. "Afterword: Toward an Ethic of Discussion" in Derrida,*Limited, Inc*. Evanston: Northwestern University Press. 111-60.
Dews, Peter. 1987. *Logics of Disintegration*. London: Verso.
Dhaliwal, Armapal. 1994. "Response to Aronowitz," *Socialist Review*, 23.3: 82-98.
Eagleton, Terry. 1985. "Capitalism, Modernism and Post-Modernism,"*New Left Review*, 152: 60-72.
_____. 1990. "Defending the Free World," in Ralph Miliband and Leo Panitch, eds., *Socialist Register 1990*. London: Merlin. 85-94.
Gramsci, Antonio. 1971. *Selections from the Prison Notebooks*. London: Lawrence and Wishart.
Guha, Ranajit. *Elementary Aspects of Peasant Insurgency in Colonial India*. Delhi: Oxford University Press.
_____. 1988a. "On Some Aspects of the Historiography of Colonial India," in Guha and Spivak 1988: 37-44.
_____. 1988b. "The Prose of Counter-Insurgency," in Guha and Spivak 1988: 45-86.
_____. 1989. "Dominance Without Hegemony and Its Historiography," in Guha, ed., *Subaltern Studies VI*. Delhi: Oxford University Press.
_____. and Gayatri Chakravorty Spivak, eds. 1988. *Selected Subaltern Studies*. New York: Oxford University Press.
Habermas, Jürgen. 1986. *Autonomy and Solidarity*. London: Verso.
_____. 1987. *The Philosophical Discourse of Modernity*. Cambridge: Polity Press.
Lan, David. 1985. *Guns and Rain*. London: James Currey.
Lentricchia, Frank. 1983. *After the New Criticism*. London: Methuen.
Rorty, Richard. 1989. *Contingency, Irony, and Solidarity*. Cambridge: Cambridge University Press.
_____. 1993. "Trotsky and the Wild Orchids" in Mark Edmundson, ed., *Wild Orchids and Trotsky*, New York: Penguin. 29-50.
Said, Edward. 1985. *Orientalism*, Harmondsworth: Penguin.
_____. 1988. "Foreword" in Guha and Spivak 1988: v-x.
_____. 1993. *Culture and Imperialism*. London: Chatto and Windus.
Sathyamurthy, T. V. 1990. "Indian Peasant Historiography,"*Journal of Peasant Studies*, 18.1: 92-144.
Spivak, Gayatri Chakravorty. 1988. "Subaltern Studies: Deconstructing Historiography," in Guha and Spivak 1988: 3-32.
Thompson, E. P. 1980. *The Making of the English Working Class*, Harmondsworth: Penguin.
Young, Robert. 1990. *White Mythologies*. London: Routledge.

Teresa L. Ebert

(Untimely) Critiques for a *Red Feminism*
—For Helen Reguerio Elam

One

Historical materialism haunts feminism.[1] Most postmodern feminists—whom I shall call "ludic feminists"—have suppressed "objective reality" in discourse and regimes of signification. Nonetheless, they are feeling (however indirectly) the historical pressures of the return of the suppressed "objective reality." The increasing polarization of wealth, feminization of labor and impoverishment of women in the world are all historical processes whose objectivity cannot be blunted in discourse. The issue of materialism—of a reality independent from the consciousness of the subject and outside language and other media—is thus gaining a new urgency for feminists after poststructuralism. Many are beginning to ask whether there is "an outside to discourse," as Judith Butler does in her *Bodies that Matter*, and attempt to articulate this material reality. The issue is especially pressing for Anglo-American neo-socialist feminists, who by-and-large have substituted Foucault for Marx, discourse for ideology, and have joined other poststructuralist feminists in embracing a cultural or discursive materialism while rejecting any "positive" knowledge (knowledge free from the consciousness of the subject and independent from language) as positivism. (I am using the term "neo" here because this "socialism" is one with little interest in "labor," "exploitation," and other global issues). Perhaps the best-known neo-socialist feminist to make this shift recently is Michele Barrett, who announces in the preface to her *The Politics of Truth: From Marx to Foucault* that she is moving from Marx's "economics of untruth" "being," as she says, "Marxism's account of ideology, used to show 'the relation between what goes on in people's heads and their place in the conditions of production'"—to Foucault's "*politics of truth*, being his own approach to the relationships between knowledge, discourse, truth and power." In so doing, she announces that, "I am nailing my colours to the mast of a more general post-Marxism" (vii). But as Renate Bridenthal asks: "Where is this ship sailing to? This is not a time for intellectuals to be sailing away on a sea of indeterminacy" (220).

The retheorization of materialism in postmodern feminism follows two related paths. The first is a reunderstanding of materialist feminism coming out of the Marxist tradition. But this is itself a contradictory and divided site—involving a conflict between those feminists reclaiming historical materialism and those who, following postmarxism, marginalize historical materialism as "positivism." These postmarxist feminists largely subscribe to the continued dominance of poststructuralist knowledges and are caught in the contradictions between the political necessity of materialism and its displacement by the ludic priority given to discourse. They end up substituting discursive determinism for what they reject as an economic determinism in classical Marxism, as Barrett does in *The Politics of Truth*. The second mode of materialism is non-Marxist and is developed entirely out of feminist encounters with poststructuralist theories (especially those of Derrida, Foucault, Lacan and, with some recent modifications, Bourdieu) and rearticulates materialism as what is, in fact, a mode of idealism—what I call "matterism": the "matter" of the body, the "matter" of sexuality, the "matter" of race, the "matter" of media, and, above all the "matter" of language.

In its engagement with "materialism" ludic postmodern feminism has reached a political crisis. But it attempts to represent and deal with this crisis as an exclusively epistemological question—as if epistemology itself is not partisan. We, therefore, need to examine some of the reasons why "materialism"—after the serious epistemological and political challenges from poststructuralism, postmarxism, post-Heisenbergian physics and New Historicism—continues to remain a fundamental issue in feminism and how ludic feminism (as the avant-garde of discursivist social theory) has theorized materialism in the post-al moment.

It is important to point out that the "ludic" is not a rigidly defined category but a widely shared social "logic" that is articulated in a number of diverse and even conflicting ways by various ludic theorists and feminists. The crux of all ludic postmodern and feminist theories, however, is the rewriting of the social as largely discursive (thus marked by the traits of linguistic difference), local, contingent, a-systematic and indeterminate. In many cases, this move is accompanied by a rearticulation of power as diffuse, a-causal and aleatory—most notably as articulated by Michel Foucault and elaborated by a number of feminists, especially Judith

Butler. Social systems (totalities) become, for ludic postmodernists, merely discredited metanarratives rather than social "realities" to be contested. According to ludic logic (which is itself a meta-narrative that forgets its own meta-narrativity), not only history but also the social are seen in semiotic terms: as "writing," as traces of textuality (Jacques Derrida), as "given by the universe of the phrase" (Jean-François Lyotard), and as a regime or genealogy of discursive practices and power-knowledge relations (Michel Foucault), as the "risk" of reappropriating through the materiality of literature what is lost in conceptuality (Jean-Luc Nancy, *The Experience of Freedom*). In all these cases the fundamental nature of the social is without center or determination: for Derrida this is expressed as the absence of any grounding ("transcendental") signified, such as "revolution," resulting from the play of *différance*; for Lyotard it is articulated in terms of the "differend," while for Foucault, it is accounted for by the a causal, aleatory nature of power. Nancy, in his *The Inoperative Community*, of course, posits the social as a community without a collectivity (of production).

The political consequences of this idealist move—in which, as Derrida says, "everything became discourse" (*Writing and Difference* 280)—are clearly articulated by the post-Marxist political theorist, Ernesto Laclau, who develops a ludic social theory "identifying the social with an infinite play of differences" ("Transformations" 39). Following Derrida, he argues that "to conceive of social relations as articulations of differences is to conceive them as signifying relations." Thus, not only is the social "de-centered," according to Laclau, but social relations, like all "signifying systems," are "ultimately arbitrary" and as a result "'society' . . . is an impossible object" ("Transformations," 40-41). By reducing the social to "signifying relations," that is, to a discursive or semiotic process, Laclau renders social relations "ultimately arbitrary" (like any sign). This means that social relations cannot be subjected to such determining relations as exploitation since they are "arbitrary," and if social relations are not exploitative (determined), they no longer require emancipation. In other words, Laclau and other ludic theorists, from Derrida to Drucilla Cornell, Foucault to Judith Butler, are not only rewriting the basic "struggle concepts" necessary for social change (e.g., "society," "surplus labor," "history," "class," "exploitation," "use-value," and "emancipation") as a series of tropic metanarratives, but they are also turning the *realities* that these concepts explain into "arbitrary," indeterminate, "signifying relations." Ludic theorists, in short, are troping the social. In so doing, they de-materialize various social "realities," cutting them off from the material relations of production, and turn them into a superstructural matrix of discursive processes and a semiotic, textual play of *différance*.

However, as long as ludic feminism continues to address the question of "women"—and does not simply collapse into a merely textual or epistemological meditation on the fate of the sign—that is, as long as it follows the feminist imperative of praxis, ludic feminism (unlike other varieties of postmodern discourse) is pulled into debates over the actual conditions of the lives of women. But, no serious engagement with these conditions can possibly bracket or evade the matter of materialism. Ludic feminism is thus constantly drawn into arguments and counterarguments over questions raised by "materialism" and its epistemological "other"—idealism. Some ludic feminists, however, have tried to obscure the problem of materialism and prevent a full critique of the issues involved. Ironically this "new" debate replays an old and familiar strategy described by Lenin nearly a century ago in his critique of idealism (*Materialism and Empirio-Criticism: Critical Comments on a Reactionary Philosophy,* 196-255). Describing the writings of the Machians, Lenin says that one thread that runs through their texts is their rejection of binaries, their claim that they have "risen above" materialism and idealism and "have transcended this 'obsolete' antithesis." This gesture, Lenin writes, is no more than an ideological alibi because in their actual practices, they "are continually sliding into idealism and are conducting a steady and incessant struggle against materialism" (354). Like Machians, ludic feminists declare that the debate over "idealism" and "materialism" is an "outdated" binary and, in the ecumenical spirit of postmodernist eclecticism (which underwrites liberal pluralism), provide a reconciliation of the two. Judith Butler, for instance, offers her theory of "performativity" to, in effect, "think through" the binary of what is "characterized as the linguistic idealism of poststructuralism" and a "materiality outside of language" (*Bodies that Matter* 27-31). Similarly, Drucilla Cornell offers her notion of remetaphorization" and the "performative power of language" as a way of avoiding "pit[ting] 'materialist' feminism against feminine writing" (*Beyond Accommodation* 3). However, as Lenin writes, any such "hybrid project" is in fact an alibi for the legitimization of idealism (*Materialism*, 350).

The politico-epistemological crisis that "materialism" has produced in ludic feminism has to do with its class politics. Ludic feminism becomes—in its *effects,* if not in its intentions—a theory that inscribes the class interests of, what bourgeois sociology calls, the upper-middle classes and of Eurocentrism. It does not acknowledge the "materiality" of the regime of wage-labor and capital. Nor does it acknowledge the existence of a historical series independent from the consciousness of the subject and autonomous from textuality. Such a recognition would lead to the further acknowledgment of the materiality of the social contradictions brought about by the social relations of production founded upon the priority of private property. Ludic feminism cannot accept a social theory that finds private property—the congealed surplus labor of others—to be the cause of social inequalities that can be remedied only through revolution. Ludic feminism is, in *effect*, a theory for property holders. Nor can ludic feminism simply revert to an a-historical, essentialist position and posit the "consciousness" of the subject as the source of social reality. Such a move would go against the general poststructuralist constructivism and consequently would lead to, among other things, a reinscription of logocentrism and the phallocentrism that underlies it. Ludic feminism therefore needs to "invent" a form of materialism that gestures to a world not directly present to the consciousness of the subject (as classic poststructuralism has done), but not entirely "constructed" in the medium of knowing (language) either.[2] It has simply become "un-ethical' to think of such social oppressions as "sexism," "racism," and "homophobia" as purely "matters" of language and discourse. Ludic feminism is beginning to learn, in spite of itself, the lesson of Engels' *Anti-Duhring*: the fact that we understand reality through language does not mean that reality is made by language.

The dilemma of ludic feminism in theorizing "materialism" is a familiar one. In his interrogation of Berkeley, Lenin points to this dilemma that runs through all forms of idealism: the epistemological unwillingness to make distinctions between "ideas" and "things" (*Materialism* 130-300), which is, of course, brought about by class politics. Ludic feminism, like all forms of upper-middle class (idealist) philosophy, must hold on to "ideas" since it is by the agency of ideas that this class (as privileged mental workers) acquires it social privileges. Although posed as an epistemological question, the dilemma is finally a class question: how not to deny the world outside the consciousness of the subject but not to make that world the material cause of social practices either. Ludic feminism, like Berkelian idealism, cannot afford to explain things by the relations of production and labor. This then is the dilemma of ludic feminism: the denial of "materialism" leads ludic feminism to a form of idealism that discredits any claims it might have to the struggle for social change; accepting materialism, on the other hand, implicates its own ludic practices in the practices of patriarchal-capitalism—the practices that have produced gender inequalities as differences that can be deployed to increase the rate of profit. This dilemma has lead feminism to an intolerable political crisis: a crisis that is, in fact, so acute it has raised questions about the viability of feminism as a theory and practice itself.

Two

Given its class politics, ludic feminism has attempted to overcome this politico-epistemological crisis by theorizing materialism in a way that reconciles its contradictory interests. On the one hand, it is primarily a theory of "upper-middle class" (to use the term of bourgeois social theory) Euroamerican women and, on the other hand, it claims to be interested in social change for all women. These "solutions" have taken two historically determined forms.

In the early phases of its "romance' with poststructuralism—roughly from the early 1970's (as in the writings of Hélène Cixous and Julia Kristeva) to the mid-1980's (as in such early writings of Teresa deLauretis as *Alice Doesn't*)—ludic feminism understood materialism mostly as a matter of "language" ("sign"). This idea of the material as the "matter" of language is perhaps most comprehensively performed in a book published at the end of this phase of ludic materialism namely, *Textualizing the Feminine* by Shari Benstock (1991). By the time Benstock's book was published, materialism-as-language theory had become institutionalized in feminism. Benstock's conventional reading of what I am calling ludic feminism does not directly engage the question of "materialism," but her book is basically an instance of the emergence (and decline) of the notion of (mostly Derridean-Lacanian) textuality in contemporary feminism. Such feminists as Mary Daly, who are not in any conventional sense poststructuralists, also have a ludic understanding of materialism as a matter of language, as is clear from her tropic books such as *Gyn/Ecology*.

In theorizing "materialism" as a "matter" of language, ludic feminism essentially deployed the concept of "textuality" in Derrida (for example, in *Of Grammatology*, especially 141-164), the idea of the "sign" in Lacan (*Écrits*, particularly, 30-113 and 146-178), and also the notion of language as discourse in Foucault (*Archeology of Knowledge*, especially 40-49 and "The Discourse on Language"). For Foucault "discourse" has an exteriority of its own ("Politics and the Study of Discourse" 60); it is a reality in its own right and not simply a reflection of an independent reality outside it. In his elaboration on this view of "discourse," Ernesto Laclau goes so far as to say that "The discursive is not, therefore, being conceived as a level nor even as a dimension of the social, but rather as being coextensive with the social as such" ("Populist Rupture and Discourse" 87). Understanding materialism as a matter of language has led ludic feminism to rethink politics itself. If the "matter" of social reality is "language," then changes in this reality can best be brought about by changing the constituents of that reality—namely, signs. Therefore, politics as collective action for emancipation is abandoned, and politics as intervention in discursive representation is adopted as a truly progressive politics. Since language always works in specific contexts, the new progressive ludic politics was also deemed to be always "local" and anti-global. From such a perspective, emancipation itself is seen as a metaphysical metanarrative and read as totalizing and totalitarian (e.g., Lyotard, *Postmodern Condition*). Following the post-Marxism of Laclau, ludic feminists like Judith Butler, proclaim the "loss of credibility" of Marxist versions of history" and "the unrealizability of emancipation." Emancipation for Butler has a "contradictory and untenable" foundation and thus becomes part of a sliding chain of significations ("Poststructuralism and Postmarxism"). Social change, thus, becomes almost entirely a matter of superstructural change, that is, change in significations. Political economy, in short, is displaced by an economy of signs.

With minor local modifications in the works of various ludic feminists, this notion of materialism is maintained in ludic theory from the early 1970's to the mid-1980s. However, from the mid-to-late 1980's (around the time of publication of Jane Gallop's *Thinking Through the Body* in 1988) the idea of "materialism" as solely a matter of language loses its grip on ludic theory. After the publication of Paul deMan's *Wartime Journalism*—when questions of "ethics" suddenly become foregrounded in contemporary high theory—and under the increasing pressures from New Historcism, ludic feminism has made new attempts to rearticulate materialism in a less discursive manner. The pressures on reunderstanding "materialism" as a non-discursive force have not been entirely internal to theory. At the end of the 1980's, as a result of conservative social policies in the U.S. and Europe (for example, new tax laws), a massive transfer of wealth from the working class to the owning class has taken place. Moreover, the working of postmodern capitalism has literally affected "everyday" life in U.S. and European cities (homelessness, crime in neighborhoods devastated by unemployment, abandoned children. . .). In the face of such conditions, the idea of progressive politics as simply a question of changing representations and problematizing the "obvious" meanings in culture has become too hollow to be convincing. As part of the emergence of "ethics" in critical theory and the decline of "high theory" itself, ludic feminism has been rethinking its own understanding of "materialism." In the 1990's materialism in ludic feminism is no longer simply the "matter" of language, rather it has become the resisting "matter" of the non-discursive, or as Diana Fuss puts it in her *Essen-*

tially Speaking, "the body as matter" (52). The main theorists of this new version of "materialism" are writers such as Judith Butler and Elizabeth Grosz. (Increasingly the notion of materialism deployed by Eve Sedgewick and other queer theorists is to a very large extent influenced by Butler). The idea of the non-discursive ("the real or primary relations") is, of course, available even in the early work of Foucault himself (*Archeology of Knowledge,* for example 45-46; 68-69). Butler, whose recent writings are increasingly marked by her engagement with something called the non/extra-discursive is, of course, a close reader of Foucualt. (Butler's doctoral dissertation, later published as *Subjects of Desire,* it is helpful to keep in mind, is focused, in part, on Foucault).

What is of great importance in any theory of materialism is the way in which the relation of the material to the non-material is articulated. In his earlier works such as *Madness and Civilization,* Foucault had posited a more causal relationship between the discursive and non-discursive. The "innovation" in *Archeology* (and in the writings that followed) is that causal explanation (in fact any explanation) is dismissed as a modernist search for origin. In the post-*Archeology* writings the discursive and the non-discursive exist side by side without any "necessary" relation between them. The Marxist principle that the extra-discursive explains the discursive ("It is not the consciousness of men that determines their existence, but their social existence that determines their consciousness," Marx, *A Contribution to the Critique of Political Economy* 21) is abandoned in favor of indeterminacy. In fact, the "indeterminateness" of the relation between the discursive and non-discursive is central to the idea of the "material" in ludic feminism. Through indeterminacy, ludic feminism—like all idealist theory—argues for the freedom of agency and proposes a theory of the social in which the bourgeois subject is still the central figure. The subject in ludic feminism does not, of course, always appear in its traditional form. However, it is commonly affirmed through a trope or a practice, such a the practice of performance in Butler: it is, for example, impossible to think of a performance, no matter how performative—without a performer. It is, therefore, important to say here that Foucault and ludic feminism ostensibly reject any causal explanation in order to acquire the freedom of the agent, but in actuality the only determinism that they are opposing is the determinism of the material (labor, class, and the relations of production). In spite of their formal objections to explanation and causality, they, in fact, establish a causal relation in their theories between the discursive and non-discursive in which the Marxist theory of the social is reversed. In ludic theory it is the discursive that silently explains the non-discursive. Dreyfus and Rabinow (hardly opponents of Foucault!) put it this way:

"Although what gets said depends on something other than itself, discourse dictates the terms of this dependence" (*Michel Foucault* 64). In other words, not only is discourse autonomous, it is also determining: it organizes the non-discursive. In short, the non-discursive is more of a formal(ist) gesture towards an "outside" which might be regarded as "material." The decidability/undecidability of the relation between the discursive and non-discursive—and not the mere acknowledgment (as in both Foucault and ludic feminism) that there is an extra-discursive—is the central issue in theorizing materialism.

The result of this ludic positing of a relation of indeterminacy is a materialism that does not act materially; it does not determine anything: it is an inert mass. For the poststructuralist feminist, such as Butler, Cornell, or Fuss, this non-determinate relation is what makes the theory of the non-discursive in postmodern feminism "progressive" and non-reductionist. However, this is a very conservative and constraining understanding of the non-discursive and its relation to the discursive. The indeterminacy that it posits as a mark of resistance and freedom is, in actuality, a legitimization of the class politics of an "upper-middle class" Euroamerican feminism that is obsessed with the freedom of the entrepreneurial subject and as such privileges the "inventiveness" of the sovereign subject—in the form of what Butler calls "citationality," Cornell calls "remetaphorization," and what more generally is understood as creativity, agency—over the collective social relations of production. This individuality is materialized in the uniqueness and irreplaceability of each body.

The non-discursive for ludic feminists in the 1990's, thus, becomes more and more a question of not simply that which exists outside the discursive but as that entity which is resistant to the discursive—and the body is put forth as the prime site for this resistance. What I have said so far about the history and theory of "materialism" in recent feminist theory should not conveniently be read to mean that, for example, no feminist theorist before the mid-to-late 1980's talked about "materialism" as a matter of the body or that no feminist theorist, at the present time, regards "materialism" to be a matter of language. My point is that, at the present time, the notion of materialism as "language" is, to use Raymond Williams' terms, a "residual" concept (writers such as Barbara Johnson, who have shown an interest in feminism in their more recent writings, for example, still, by and large, regard materialism to be a matter of language). The idea of "materialism" as a matter of body—as, in short, a force resisting the discursive—is an "emergent" theory. We see the effort to suture these two theoretical tendencies together in the work, for example, of Judith Butler.

In his move from the project of "archeology" (questions of language and knowledge) to "genealogy" (issues of power and practice), Foucault has concluded that the only possibility of social change is through an entity that can resist the all inclusive and all-encompassing regime of the dominant "episteme" that he himself had so thoroughly analyzed in *The Order of Things*. Since the episteme defines and controls all that was intelligible, to move beyond its regime, one has to appeal to an entity that is non-thinking, non-intelligible and has the power to resist the episteme. This entity, for Foucault, is the body, and the power of the body is acquired through its relentless seeking of purposeless pleasure: pleasure not as the reward for performing the task of reproduction. As Foucault elaborated in his later works, such as *History of Sexuality* and *Discipline and Punish*, the body has its own materiality that enables it to "exceed" and "escape" discourse and its associated regimes of power-knowledge. This, of course, does not mean that the body is not conditioned, inscribed, and molded by discourse. However, it does mean that power-knowledge never succeeds in completely overcoming the body: culturalization is never total and the body always exceeds the power-knowledge that attempts to completely control it. This "exceeding" is possible partly because of the internal conflicts and contradictions among the various discourses that attempt to control the body.

The notion of the body as a resiting site in Foucault, however, is a highly political one and is devised in part to inscribe a bourgeois ludic "materialism" (of pleasure) in place of historical materialism. Foucault himself is quite clear on this point. In his "Body/Power," Foucault states that

> The emergence of the problem of the body and its growing urgency have come about through the unfolding of a political struggle. Whether this is a revolutionary struggle, I don't know. One can say that what has happened since 1968, and arguably what made 1968 possible, is something profoundly anti-Marxist. How can European revolutionary movements free themselves from the 'Marx effect....' This was the direction of the questions posed by '68. In this calling in question of the equation: Marxism = the revolutionary process, an equation that constituted a kind of dogma, the importance given to the body is one of the important, if not essential elements. (*Power/Knowledge* 57)

The politics of Foucault's theorizing of the body as a site of resistance materialism becomes even more clear when he says, "I wonder whether, before one poses the question of ideology, it wouldn't be more materialist to study first the question of the body and the effects of power on it" (*Power/Knowledge* 58). The materialism of the body in Foucault, then, is specifically designed to oppose collective revolutionary praxis by substituting individual regimes of purposeless pleasure—pleasure as a mode of the Kantian "sublime," a pleasure that is an excess of all systems of representation and an escape from discourse and all social meanings. Social meanings—it is assumed—are all ideological, and the true freedom of the subject is attained by transcending ideology: pleasure deconstructs ideology (the preordained obviousness upon which the metanarratives of a society are founded) and arrives at surprising encounters that can only be called novel "experiences" (Foucault's formal opposition to "experience" notwithstanding).

This legacy of Foucauldian inferential materialism has dominated the ludic feminist notion of the non-discursive and the material. Materialism in ludic feminism (as in Berkeley and other idealist philosophers) is, in fact, more a theological category than a materialist one. It is a form of what Lenin in his critique of Berkeley called "objective idealism" (Lenin, *Materialism* 23). The masquerading of this objective idealism—or what, in the context of Lenin's discussion of Berkeley, could be called spiritual materialism—as "materialism" in ludic feminism has not escaped the attention of ludic feminists themselves. Kathryn Bond Stockton, herself a ludic feminist theologian, describes the prevailing mode of "materialism" in ludic feminism in this way:

> I mean materialism in its strongest sense: the material onto which we map our constructions, 'matter on its own terms' that might resist or pressure our constructions, or prove independent of them altogether. This materialism is the nondiscursive something poststructuralist feminists now want to embrace, the extradiscursive something they confess necessarily eludes them. ("Bodies and God" 131)

Unlike historical materialism, which foregrounds the historical praxis of the materiality of labor, materialism, for the ludic feminist in the 1990's, is not an actual historical praxis that determines other practices, rather it is a purely "inferential" entity. It is, in fact, the consciousness of the subject that creates ("invents") this ludic "matter." Any understanding of "matter" as a positive entity (labor) is dismissed in ludic feminism as vulgar determinism/positivism. The "matter" of ludic feminism, in short, is a non-determining matter that depends on the subject and, as such, it is a reinscrpition of traditional Euroamerican idealism—this time represented as postmodern (non-positivist) materialism—to cover up the contradictions and crisis of patriarchal-capitalist. Materialism becomes (through such practices as "performance") that which exceeds the existing systems of representation—an escapes from socially constructed meanings. In ludic feminism, then, materialism (as a resisting matter) is an "invention." The seemingly "antitranscendental" element that materialism is supposed to bring to bear upon social analysis for ludic feminists, as Stockton herself realizes, "only masks their deep dependence" upon "mystic unfathomable Visibilities" (132). Ludic spiritual materialism, in Stockton's words, "stands as a God that might be approached through fictions and faith but never glimpsed naked" (131). Stockton's analysis is a conservative and local one: she simply observes the striking similarities that exist between spiritual materialism in ludic feminism and Victorian theological thought. In so doing, she blocks a more global understanding of ludic materialism: ludic materialism is an outcome of the contradictions of the social divisions of labor in class society. Spiritual materialism is, in short, is a strategy for managing the crisis of class relations.

Materialism, in other words, is "invented" in ludic discourses to bring back transcendentalism in a more postmodern and thus convincing rhetoric. Moreover, as I will discuss more fully below, the trope of "invention" and theories of "invention" are introduced in contemporary theory as a means to overcome the impasse of "constructivism." Constructivism effectively combated humanism along with humanist and essentialist notions of the subject, but it also left the subject and subjectivity too determinate: "upper-middle-class" ludic theorists have not been able to accept any theory that circumscribes the freedom of the subject (of capital). However, what is commonly represented, under the guise of invention, as "materialism" in ludic feminism, is merely a re-invention of the very familiar technocratic imagination so valorized in capitalism: materialism as *technoludism*. The most well-known example of technoludism—that is, the conjuncture of technocratic fancy, inventionism and spiritual materialism—is Donna Haraway's "Cyborg Manifesto" which has become for many the manifesto of new, post-socialist ludic materialism. An apt commentary on the writings of Haraway and other feminist technotheorists is provided by Marx and Engels. In their critique of idealist philosophers, Marx and Engels called them "industrialists of philosophy" who live on "absolute spirit," and this description remains valid for (techno)ludic feminists today (Marx and Engels, *The German Ideology* 27, *Collected Works*, Vol. 5). It is necessary to recall that Haraway's essay ends with what Stockton calls the trope of the "Christian Pentecost" ("Bodies and God" 138): Haraway claims that "Cyborg imagery . . . is a dream not of a common language, but of a powerful infidel heteroglossia . . . a feminist speaking in tongues" (*Simians* 181). This spiritual materialism—this ludic matterism in its various forms from cyborgian technoludism to Butlerian "citationality"—is now the dominant theory of materialism in the postmodern knowledge industry. It is a materialism that does not determine the non-material but is, in fact, determined by the consciousness of the subject that infers it and thus constitutes it. Ludic materialism, then, whether perceived as the matter of sign/textuality or as the matter of the body is an invention to overcome the determinism of social constructionism: it is a device to return the freedom of the subject and the contingency and non-necessity of the social with a newly legitimated force to the entrepreneur and patriarchal-capitalism.

Materialism, however, is neither a matter of "language" (sign/discourse/textuality) nor is it an a-historical, inert, "resisting" mass (of the body) whose existence can be inferred by "faith or fiction," by performativity, resignifications and other ludic rituals. In its most radical rendering, ludic postmodern materialism leads to a form of Feuerbachian materialism about which Marx writes: "As far as Feuerbach is a materialist he does not deal with history, and as far as he considers history he is not a materialist" (Marx and Engels, *The German Ideology* 41). Materialism, is not a matter of inference. It is the objectivity (of "surplus labor"). Moreover it is an active objectivity: a praxis—the praxis of labor through which humans "act "upon external nature" and change it, and in this way simultaneously change themselves (Marx, *Capital* 1, 284). As a praxis, it is historical, and as labor, it is conflictually structured between the owners of the means of production and those who have nothing but their own labor power to sell. Materialism, in short, is a historical praxis and a structure of conflicts that determines other practices. Unlike the Foucauldian and ludic inert non-discursive, it does not simply exist side by side with the discursive: it make the discursive possible; it "explains" the discursive. Explanation is, of course, the very thing that Foucault's theory of the autonomy of discourse is designed to erase. For Foucault all explanations (why) are ideological: only description (how) of discourse is a legitimate form of knowledge. Materialism is not an inert resistance to discourse, that has to be inferred by "fictions and faith." Instead materialism is (as Marx meticulously describes it in *Capital*, 1, 340-416) what confronts the subject of labor in "the working day": the working day is the site in which the material and historical process of extracting surplus labor from the worker by the capitalist takes place.

Three

Theories that approach materialism as a matter of language, as discourse, base their argument on the assumption that discourse/textuality have an opacity and density of their own, a physicality, which makes language "mean" not simply by the "intention" of the author and speaker or by her conscious "control" but by its own autonomous and immanent laws of signification. This understanding of "materialism" is transhistorical: it refers mostly to the material in the sense that I have already described as inert matter, "medium" or "thingness" and is, in short, a form of "matterism" rather than materialism. Or as Marx says in his "Theses on Feuerbach," "The chief defect of all hitherto existing materialism"—and we can add poststructuralist materialism to the list—"is that the thing, reality, sensuousness, is conceived only in the form of the object of *contemplation*, but not as *human sensuous activity, practice*" (*The German Ideology* 121). And "human sensuous activity" is above all, for Marx, labor: the way people "*produce* their means of subsistence" and thus "indirectly produce their actual material life" (*The German Ideology*, 42).

It is, then, especially surprising to see a neo-socialist-feminist like Michele Barrett define materialism in Marxist thought as "the doctrine seeing consciousness as dependent on matter" without realizing that "matter" in Marxism is not inert mass but the praxis of labor and the contradictions and class conflicts in which it is always involved. Barrett goes on to pose the poststructuralist debate over materialism as one between "words and things," "matter" and "meaning" ("Words and Things" 202, 201). However, "words and things," to use her terms, are not finished a-historical entities: they are the product of the social relations of production. To pose the question the way Barrett does is to erase the dialectical project of Marxism and to occlude the structure of conflicts in capitalism. Historical materialism is an explanation of these conflicts. Barrett's misreading is symptomatic of a more serious problem over the issue of materialism within Marxist and socialist feminism. This is fundamentally the problem of the place of the relations of production in feminist theory and political practice. It is the question of whether feminist knowledge should give priority to the way people "produce their means of subsistence" (labor)—to the material reality and historical struggles of the relations of production—or whether, as Seyla Benhabib and Drucilla Cornell argue, "the confrontation between twentieth-century Marxism and feminist thought requires nothing less than a paradigm shift . . . the 'displacement of the paradigm of production'" (*Feminism as Critique* 1). This is not simply a debate among materialist feminists. The "displacement of the paradigm of production" by a majority of postmodern, Anglo-American neo-socialist feminists has significantly contributed to the occlusion of the economic and suppression of the problem of exploitation in most other feminist theories and consequently in contemporary social theory in general. It has produced a ludic or post-al socialist feminism *without* Marxism, turning it into a general left-liberalism, and has participated in the ludic substitution of a discursive politics of individual, libidinal liberation for a revolutionary politics of collective socio-economic transformation.

Why should this displacement matter? The erasure of Marxism from feminism and (ludic) postmodern knowledges has become so pervasive that the importance of these issues has been largely suppressed, and the question itself can no longer even be asked without requiring extensive explanation. It matters because, as Marx and Engels say, "the free development of each is the condition for the free development of all" (*The Communist Manifesto* 75), and there can be no "free development" unless the fundamental needs of each person are met: unless production fulfills needs instead of making profits (Marx, *The Gotha Program* 10). Making profits, in short, is the denial of the needs of the many and the legitimization of the desires of the few. As a revolutionary (not a post-al) socialist feminist, Nellie Wong argues,

> Without overthrowing the economic system of capitalism, as socialists and communists organize to do, we cannot liberate women *and* everybody else who is also oppressed.
>
> Socialist feminism is our bridge to freedom. . . . Feminism, the struggle for women's equal rights, is inseparable from socialism. . . . ("Socialist Feminism," 290).

A revolutionary socialist feminism is based on historical materialism. It insists that the "material" is fundamentally tied to the economic sphere and to the relations of production, which have a historically necessary connection to all other social/cultural relations. The "material," in other words, contrary to ludic theory does not simply exist autonomously as a resisting mass, side by side with autonomous discourse. Materialism, as Engels puts it, means that "the degree of economic development," in a society forms "the foundation upon which the state institutions . . . the art and even the religious ideas . . . have been evolved, and in the light of which these things must therefore be explained instead of *vice versa* " ("The Funeral of Karl Marx" 39). It is—to repeat what is so violently erased in idealist theory—therefore, not "the consciousness of men that determines their existence, but their social existence that determines their consciousness" (Marx, *A Contribution to the Critique of Political Economy* 21). In short, Marx argues that "the nature of individuals thus depends on the material conditions determining their production"—"both with *what* they produce and with *how* they produce" (*The German Ideology* 42).

For a red feminism this means that issues about the "nature of individuals"—gender, sexuality, pleasure, desire, needs—cannot be separated from the

128 » Teresa Ebert

conditions producing individuals: not just the discursive and ideological conditions but most important the *material* conditions, the relations of production, which shape discourses and ideologies. Thus the struggle to end the exploitation and oppression of all women, and in particular of people of color, lesbians and gays, within the metropole as well as the periphery, is not simply a matter of discursive or semiotic liberation or a question of the resisting "matter of the body," but a global social relation: it thus requires the transformation of the material conditions—the relations of production—producing these forms of oppression.

Historical materialism thus means the primacy of women's and men's productive practices—their labor processes—in the articulation and development of human history and in the construction of their own subjectivities. As Marx argues in *Capital*, through labor the subject "acts upon" external nature and changes it, and in this way the laborer simultaneously changes her/his own nature (v. 1, 283). Such a view of materialism also understands "reality" to be a historically objective process: reality exists outside the consciousness of humans—ideas do not have an autonomous existence and thus reality is not merely a matter of desire of the body, or the operation of language (or, on the other hand, of the "thingness" of things). This does not mean that reality, as we have access to it, as we make sense of it, is not mediated by signifying practices. But the empirical fact that reality is mediated by language in no way means, as Engels and others have argued, that it is produced by language. Social relations and practices are, in other words, prior to signification and are objective. The subjugation of women, then, is an objective historical reality: it is not simply a matter of representation by self-legitimating discourses. The extraction of surplus labor is an objective social reality in class societies and all social difference are produced by it, whether directly or through various mediations. Transformative politics depends on such a view of reality since if there is no objective reality there will be little ground on which to act in order to change existing social relations. Transformative politics, in other words, does not simply "redescribe" the existing social world through different discourses as does ludic politics (e.g., see Rorty, *Contingency* 44-69), but rather acts to change the "real" social, economic—the *material*—conditions of the relations of production exploiting women and determining our lives.

Four

It is by now commonplace among ludic postmodernists and feminists, including many socialist feminists, to dismiss the insistence on relations of production as economic reductionism and to discredit the concept of any determination of the "superstructure" (e.g., the cultural, ideological, representational, political, juridical, etc.) by the economic base. This is, for instance, the core argument *against* historical or dialectical materialism and for cultural materialism in Donna Landry and Gerald MacLean's *Materialist Feminisms* (e.g., 61-62). It is necessary to discuss this book at some length since it articulates many of the questions I have raised in this chapter—the problem of feminism, critique and materialism—in direct opposition to my own argument. A critique of their book, therefore, will provide a more open contestation between my argument and that of ludic feminism. Landry and MacLean's book attempts "to present a history of the debates between Marxist and feminist social and cultural theorists in the 1960's, 1970's and early 1980's, primarily in Britain and the United States, and to analyze what has happened to transform those debates in recent years" (ix). But as deconstructionists they are quite ambivalent about the project of writing a history and end up with what they themselves describe as a "schematic and inconsistent" "chronological narrative." *Materialist Feminisms* is especially representative of the discursive, post-Marxist turn in socialist feminism and demonstrates some of the limitations of this ludic mode.

They begin their book by saying that "this is a book about feminism and Marxism written when many people are proclaiming the end of socialism and the end of feminism. . . . We find these claims to be both premature and misleading" (vii). However, the authors are deeply invested in poststructuralism, especially deconstruction, as the ground of their knowledges, and this leads them to turn Marxism into a *textuality* that they try to deconstruct. In fact, the book expends considerable energy trying to displace and erase Marxism altogether from materialism and from feminism. Thus, while the book begins by treating Marxist, socialist, and materialist feminism as nearly synonymous, it concludes by saying: "Need materialism be only an alias for Marxism? We hope that by now the distinction between Marxist feminism and materialist feminism is clear" (229). But in writing a materialist feminism *without Marxism*, the book offers little more than a left-liberal, poststructuralist "identity politics of undone identities."

The core of Landry and McLean's notion of materialism is an adaptation of Raymond Williams' notions of "cultural materialism" and "green socialism" which they graft onto deconstruction. While they continue to call their position "historical materialism" (following Williams' revisions), they, in fact, fundamentally break with the tradition of historical materialism and instead subscribe to the, by now, dominant *discursive* conception of materialism:

> the production of signs, of signifying systems, of ideology, representations, and discourses is itself a material activity with material effects. Instead of arguing that the material or economic base produces certain effects, like culture and ideology, as part of its superstructure, a cultural materialist would argue that ideology and the discourses generated by social institutions are themselves located in material practices which have material effects that affect even the economic structures of the base. (61)

This issue of the "materiality of the many signifying practices" and whether or not cultural, ideological and discursive practices (superstructure) are determined by the "material or economic base" is the basic conflict between a cultural/discursive materialism and historical materialism. As Landry and MacLean explain, "from a cultural materialist position, arguments for the determinism of the "base" suffer from economic reductionism" (61-62).

But it is not really "reductionism" that disturbs Landry and MacLean since they seem to have no trouble at all in accepting the postmarxist view of Laclau and Mouffe that "history and the real *are* discursive" (140), which is itself quite a reductionist and deterministic position. What Landry and MacLean, like other poststructuralists and postmarxists, are doing is simply replacing "economic reductionism" with a "discursive reductionism" and calling it a new non-deterministic materialism.

Thus, Landry and MacLean claim that the "more adequately materialist feminist reading" is one that reads both Marx and the world "as texts," for the world and history are "always discursively constructed" (139-140). Their main argument against Marx (and for deconstruction), thus involves reading "Marx's concept of value," following Gayatri Spivak, "as a catachresis or pun," which "not only shifts the grounds of debate from a tendency towards economic reductionism but opens potentially productive contradictions in Marx's texts" (64). But "surplus value" in Marx is the profit gained from the appropriation and exploitation of the contradictions in the social divisions of labor in production. To turn it into a linguistic pun, not only erases a powerful explanatory concept, but it also "shifts the grounds of debate" from social contradictions over the exploitation of people's lives and labor to the play of textual differences. The ultimate goal of such readings of the "labor theory of value" in Marx is to turn it into a concept analogous to "value" in Saussure (*Course in General Linguistics* 111-122). However, "value" in language is a "local" condition of meaningfulness (Saussure 116). Signs acquire their "value" by "opposition," to use Saussure's own term, but this "opposition" is itself the outcome of prior material oppositions which Voloshinov effectively discusses as the oppositions of classes: language is "an arena of class struggle," that is, a site in the struggle over the extraction of surplus value (*Marxism and the Philosophy of Language* 23). The meaning of the sign "black," in other words, is not determined simply by a local, immanent "opposition" to white but by the way "black" and "white" are constructed and given meaning in the process of production. Immanently it would be difficult to explain why "black market" is a term of derogation and "white lie" is a term of justification and thus acceptance. "Black" in black market is negative because of what is outside discourse: the race and class antagonisms over the social divisions of labor and expropriations of surplus value—antagonisms which are made intelligible and fought out in the arena of discourse. "Surplus value" in the labor theory of value, in short, determines not only the value of the sign but of all systems of intelligibilities in class societies (Alex Callinicos, *Race and Class* 16-39).

However, for discursive materialists, in spite of their formal protests, discourse in their practices determines not only the "real" but also social and political change. Materialist feminism, then—as put forth by Landry and MacLean and the majority of ludic postmodernists and feminists—becomes a discursive "politics of difference" sensitive to the "leaky distinctions" among "questions of race, sexuality, ethnicity, nationality, postcoloniality, religion, and cultural identity, as well as class and gender" (90). Materialist feminism is reduced, in short, to what Landry and MacLean celebrate as a poststructuralist "identity politics of undone identities." But such an identity politics completely displaces the transformative struggle against "interlocking systems of oppression—racial, sexual, heterosexual, and class oppression" called for by earlier materialist feminists, such as those of the Combahee River Collective (145). This substitution of a politics of difference reunderstands power relations, following Foucault (*History of Sexuality*, 1, 85-102), as reversible relations of difference and rearticulates binaries, oppositions and hierarchies as discursive categories and practices that can be "reversed . . . [and] displaced" by a "deconstructive reading." But such a rhetorical displacement of binaries does not eliminate the real existing social and historical binaries between exploiter and exploited. It simply covers them over, concealing their grounding in the social divisions of labor and the relations of production.

Five

At the core of discursive materialism is the poetics of invention. The post-al politics of "invention" is a politics of discursive transformation that seeks to move "beyond" established codes into a "utopian" space of unencumbered (semiotic) freedom through the subversion of existing regimes of discourse and hierarchies of representation, language games, and signifying relations. It is a politics of local, contingent acts generating new phrases, idioms, linkages and rules of judgments for each particular situation without any pre-existing criteria. Such judgments, according to Jean-François Lyotard, have "to be always done over again" because they concern incommensurable linkages among *differends*—linkages that must be "always done over again" in order not to suppress some other *differend*, some other linkage (*Differend* 140). Politics is thus reduced to discursive alterations and subversions: what Lyotard calls the "invention of new idioms" for the *differend*.

As I earlier suggested, part of what is at stake in the emphasis on "invention" by ludic postmodern and feminist theorists (not only Lyotard but also Derrida, Butler, and Cornell, as well as Luce Irigarary, Hélène Cixous, Gregory Ulmer and others) is the crisis of social constructionism. Structuralism and, later on, poststructuralism critiqued traditional humanism for its metaphysics of presence—by which it secured its basic categories (self, consciousness, gender, sex, race . . .) in nature. They offered, as a "supplement" to this theory of the subject, the notion that the subject was not naturally created but was socially constructed. By now, the idea of social construction as opposed to a "natural" essentialism has become the ludic orthodoxy, and the conflict between "essentialism" and "constructionism" has become one of the most contested scenes in feminism. Recently, however, the theory of the subject as socially constructed is turning into an impediment for ludic feminists and postmodern theorists, for whom constructionism seems too deterministic and restrictive of the agency of the subject. Ludic theorists are thus attempting to problematize this determinism through the trope of "invention"—the multiple, indeterminate, reversible play of significations that subverts any stable, definite meanings. For these ludic critics, the subject's inventiveness—that is, her/his participation in the discursive "play" of language games, metaphors, significations—enables her/him to overcome the determinacy of social construction and move into the terrain of a utopian future.

This move first to a semiotic constructionism and then to invention involves a double displacement of historical materialism. By construing social construction largely in terms of a discursive construction, structuralists and poststructuralists have substituted a linguistic determinism for a historical materialist concept of construction as determined by the forces and relations of production. Now the more recent ludic rejection of even linguistic determinism entirely eclipses the historical actuality of determinism without having to address its materialist and economic forms.

This valorization of a liberating inventiveness and complete erasure of any form of necessary relation is clearly evident in Drucialla Cornell's "utopian feminism" with its strategies of "remetaphorization" (*Beyond Accommodation*). But perhaps one of the fullest articulations of this eclipse of historical materialism in the shift from constructionism to invention is developed by Judith Butler in *Bodies that Matter*.

Butler's work combines a deconstructive textualism with a Foucaultian analytics of power. It is thus important to briefly critique here the basic presuppositions of Foucault's notion of power. Power in Foucault is not understood as primarily textual, although it is irrevocably linked to the operation of discourse and knowledge relations. Rather power, according to Foucault, "must be understood in the first instance as the multiplicity of force relations immanent in the sphere in which they operate and which constitute their own organization" (*History of Sexuality* 92). Moreover, these "force relations" of power are, according to Foucault, self-constituting, immanent, local, diffuse and a-systematic. Power, in other words, is "aleatory" (that is, marked by chance and arbitrariness); contingent (rather than historically determined); heterogeneous (divided by difference within), and unstable—by provoking "resistance" it "undoes" itself. Foucault's analysis of the local, specific and contingent, however, is based on a quite abstract, static, a-historical and mystified concept of power: for Foucault "Power is everywhere . . . comes from everywhere . . . is permanent, repetitious, inert"—it is always already with us and always will be. Moreover, Foucault turns resistance into a nearly automatic, immanent response to the exercise of power: "where there is power, there is resistance" (95-96). For "Resistances," Foucault declares, "are inscribed in the [relations of power] as an irreducible opposite"—rather like a natural resistance to a physical force (96). Such a theory of power substitutes a logic of contingency for the logic of social necessity. In so doing, it preempts any need for collective, organized social transformation—any need, in other words, for emancipation, and more important, it dispenses with the necessity for organized social and political revolution to overthrow dominant power relations. All we need to do, according to this ludic logic, is recognize and validate the local "multiplicity of points of resistance" that power itself already generates.

Perhaps the most "appealing" aspect of Foucault's theory for most "left" critics and feminists is that it offers, as Foucault himself says, "a non-economic analysis of power" as opposed to the "economism in the theory of power" in Marx as well as in the juridical-liberal notion of power (*Power/Knowledge* 88-89). Foucault conflates these two quite opposed understandings of power by equating a trope with a theoretical explanation—he follows the ludic assumption that explanation/concepts are, in fact, tropes. He characterizes the juridical-liberal notion of power as a form of economism simply because it relies on the trope of commodity exchange. Whereas, in "the Marxist conception of power," he says, "one finds none of all that" (88). What one does find—and what Foucault's entire theory of power is an attempt to displace—is, as Foucault describes it: "an economic functionality of power . . . power is conceived primarily in terms of the role it plays in the maintenance simultaneously of the relations of production and of a class domination which the development and specific forms of the forces of production have rendered possible" (88-89). In opposition to a Marxist theory of power—which always insists on the *dialectical* relations of power and the economic—Foucault (the former student of the Marxist philosopher Louis Althusser) develops an unrelentingly *anti*-historical-materialist theory of power. He severs power from its material connection to the social relations and contradictions of production, and reduces it to an abstract force confined to the superstructure. His is an anti-dialectical theory that substitutes an analytics of localized, reversible domination for a theory of systematic global exploitation. This ludic displacement of historical materialism has made Foucault one of the main articulators of post-Marxism in late capitalism and given him an extraordinary influence among academics, professionals and other middle and upper class knowledge-workers, especially in the West.

Building on Foucault's theory of a localized, diffuse, a-systematic power, Butler rewrites constructionism, specifically the construction of gender/sexed bodies, as indeterminate. In short, she rewrites it in terms of invention—what she calls "performativity" or "citationality." In *Bodies that Matter*, Butler specifically contests, what she calls, "radical linguistic constructivism" which "is understood to be generative and deterministic" and forms a "linguistic monism, whereby everything "is only and always language" (6). According to Butler, "what ensues," from this position, "is an exasperated debate that many of us are tired of hearing" (6): a debate over determinism and agency, over essentialism and constructivism. She decries the way structuralist and radical linguistic theories reduce "constructivism" "to determinism and impl(y) the evacuation or displacement of human agency" (9). This is an especially important issue in Butler's work. She is committed to the preservation of "agency"; in fact, it is the priority of her post-al politics. But she rejects both the "voluntarist subject of humanism" and the "grammatical" subject of structuralist and classical post-structuralist theories. She thus dismisses those who "construe" construction "along structuralist lines," because they "claim that there are structures that construct the subject, impersonal forces, such as Culture or Discourse or Power, where these terms occupy the grammatical site of the subject" (9). In other words, she objects to what she considers to be a personification of "discourse or language or the social" that posits a grammatical subject as initiating the activity of construction. Butler attempts to displace this grammatical logic of structuralist and "radical linguistic constructivism" (the logic of subject and predicate) with a more open rhetorical or discursive logic of agency as "reiteration": in other words, with a notion of agency as *invention*, which she variously calls "performativity" or "citationality."

She argues that Foucault's "view of power" should be "understood as the disruption and subversion of this grammar and metaphysics of the subject" (9); it is an analytics of power that, for Butler, accounts for the generation of subjectitivities without in turn positing a determining subject. This enables Butler to understand construction as "neither a subject nor its act, but a process of reiteration by which both 'subjects' and "acts' come to appear at all. There is no power that acts, but only a reiterated acting that is power in its persistence and instability" (9). In other words, subjects/agents, are for Butler, effects of the agency of a reiterative power that she calls performativity. Butler is asserting a localized and localizing theory of power and construction (performativity) that is determinate yet indeterminate; involves subjectivities but not a "Subject," and an agency that constructs its own agents.

Invention or performativity enables Butler to posit a mode of inquiry—into the construction of the subject—that she claims "is no longer constructivism, but neither is it essentialism," because there is, Butler asserts, "an 'outside' to what is constructed by discourse" (8). However, this is an "inventive" rather than a conventional notion of "outside": as Butler says,

> this is not an absolute 'outside,' and ontological thereness that exceeds or counters the boundaries of discourse; as a constitutive 'outside,' it is that which can only be thought—when it can—in relation to that discourse, at and as its most tenuous borders. (8)

In other words, the very "outside" to discourse that allows us, according to Butler, to escape the dichotomy of constructivism/essentialism, is itself *invented* through the play of discourse. By this she means that "the extra-discursive is delimited, it is formed by the very discourse from which it seeks to free itself" (11). However, this is not so much a move beyond the "exasperated debate" as it is yet another ludic displacement of fundamental issues through a tropic play that conflates differences through a logic of supplementarity.

The limits of this discursive "invention" of the outside (the "extra-discursive") are made especially clear in Butler's ludic articulation of matter/materiality. She reunderstands "the notion of matter, not as a site or surface, but as a *process of materialization that stabilizes over time to produce the effect of boundary, fixity, and surface we call matter*" (9). In other words, Butler is substituting "materialization" for construction, but in so doing, she puts forward a concept of "materiality," "matter," "materialization" that breaks both with the common sense understanding—where these terms refer to a reality or referent *outside* language—and with a historical materialist understanding, in which these concepts refer to the objective reality of the actual historical conditions produced by the mode of production. Instead, Butler rewrites materialization, itself, as a form of discursive practice: as she says, "*materialization* will be a kind of citationality, the acquisition of being through the citing of power" (15). Citationality—that is, the practice of "citing," repeating, summoning sexual norms and "laws"—is, in turn, also a form of performativity. Performativity, a concept Butler originally developed in *Gender Trouble*, is a form of performance, but its meaning, for Butler, cannot be simply reduced to performance, especially theatrical notions of performance as role playing. Butler argues that "performance as bounded 'act' is distinguished from performativity insofar as the latter consists in a reiteration of norms which precede, constrain, and exceed the performer . . . further, what is 'performed' works to conceal, if not to disavow, what remains opaque, unconscious, unperformable. The reduction of performativity to performance would be a mistake" (*Bodies* 234). The meaning of performativity, in other words, slides into a kind of "speech act" that enacts, repeats or "cites" the norms of sex. In fact, one of the main concerns of *Bodies that Matter* is "the reworking of performativity as citationality," so that Butler now defines performativity as "the reiterative and citational practice by which discourse produces the effects that it names" (14, 2).

Butler's "outside" to discourse, in other words, is what discourse itself constructs through "exclusion, erasure, violent foreclosure, abjection." But this "outside" is itself supplementary: it is a "disruptive return" that constitutes what excludes it. For example, the primacy of masculinity in Western metaphysics is, Butler argues, "founded . . . through a prohibition which outlaws the spectre of a lesbian resemblance" (the lesbian phallus); masculinity, then, is an "effect of that very prohibition . . . dependent on that which it must exclude" (52). The "outside" (the excluded lesbian), in other words, is the necessary ground "constituting" the "inside" of masculinity and heterosexuality. Butler is following here the classic poststructuralist erasure of the boundaries between inside and outside, that is, "supplementarity" (Derrida, *Grammatology* 144-145). But this supplementarity—

what Butler insists is the "indissolubility of materiality and signification" (30)—also locates us as always already in an infinite semiotic loop: a kind of discursive Mobius strip. Butler reduces materiality to the materiality of the signifier and the effects of signifying processes, notably citationality. As she declares, "it is not that one cannot get outside of language in order to grasp materiality in and of itself; rather, every effort to refer to materiality takes place through a signifying process which . . . is always already material" (68).

Thus, sex, for Butler, is not "a bodily given . . . but . . . a cultural norm which governs the materialization of bodies" (2-3). The "construction" of sexual identity is an activity of performativity in which the body "assumes" or "materializes" its sex through a process of "citationality"—that is, a speaking in and through bodies in which the symbolic laws, norms and discourses of heterosexuality are "cited" in the same way, according to Butler, that a judge "cites" a law (14). There is in Butler's theory then an equivalency or rather a tropic sliding and linking together of materialization, performativity, citationality as all forms of discursive reiteration. In other words, "matter" (the body) is given its boundaries, shapes, fixity and surface—it is "materialized" (sexed)—through the "citationality" of discourse, through the "reiteration of norms." The materiality of sexuality, then, is not outside language but is the *effect* of discourse.

However, in a footnote, Butler specifically disclaims that materiality is "the effect of 'discourse' which is its cause" (*Bodies* 251, n. 12). But, she is able to make this disclaimer only through a series of dissimulations that in turn validate "dissimulation," itself, as the crux of her theory of materiality/materializations. She does so by deploying Foucault's theory of power, which, as I have already indicated, posits power as diffuse and dispersed without a cause or originary source. Foucault's aleatory and contingent notion of power enables Butler to, as she says, "displace the causal relation through a reworking of the notion of 'effect.' Power is established in and through its effects, where these effects are the dissimulated workings of power itself" (251, n. 12). Butler is, in short, deconstructing causality (following Nietzsche's re-reading of causality through its effects in his *The Will to Power*) into a circuit of supplementary relations in which the "cause," as Nietzsche claims, is itself the effect of its own dissimulated causality, or the "effect" is itself the causality of its own dissimulated effects. This move enables her to rewrite materiality as the "effect of power": according to Butler, "'Materiality' appears only when its status as *contingently constituted through discourse* is erased, concealed, covered over. Materiality is thus the dissimulated effect of power" (251, n. 12, emphasis added). In Butler's ludic argument, materiality is thus entirely confined to the level of the "superstructure," to discourse. Moreover, this ludic articulation of materiality is an extended ideological re-mystification. In the name of openness, it puts forth an understanding of power as a closed, self-legitimating operation. It completely suppresses the real material conditions of what Marx calls the "working day": the production of profit (surplus value) through the exploitation of our unpaid and subsistence labor.

Butler's suppression and mystification of the materiality of materialism—the materiality of labor—is quite explicit in two brief references she makes to Marx's historical materialism. The first is an offhand reference in which she attempts to appropriate Marx to her position by linking him to her rereading of classical notions of matter as "temporalized" and as positing the "indissolubility of . . . materiality and signification" (*Bodies* 31). She attributes this temporalization to what she claims is Marx's understanding of "'matter' . . . as a principle of transformation" (31). However, Butler is able to appropriate Marx for a genealogy of (idealist) theories of matter, only by profoundly misreading him and completely excluding the issue of labor from his work. In a footnote to her observation on Marx, she specifies that her reading is based on the first of Marx's "Theses on Feuerbach," in which, she says, Marx "calls for a materialism which can affirm the practical activity that structures and inheres in the object as part of that object's objectivity and materiality" (250, n. 5). She goes on to argue that on the basis of "this new kind of materialism that Marx proposes . . . the object is transformative activity itself and, further, its materiality is established through this temporal movement. . . . In other words, the object *materializes* to the extent that it is a site of *temporal transformation* . . . as transformative activity" (250, n. 5). This reading is a remarkable act of mystification and idealist abstraction, for it completely suppresses the fundamental element in Marx's "new kind of materialism": this "practical activity," this "transformative activity," constituting the object *is labor*. Marx's reunderstanding of materiality in the first *Theses on Feuerbach* as "*sensuous human activity, practice*" is the insistence on materiality *as labor*. To reduce labor to mere temporality is to exclude its materiality and do exactly what Marx opposes: to substitute "interpretation" for "transformation" of the world. As Marx writes in *Capital*, "Labour is, first of all, a process . . . by which man, through his own actions, mediates, regulates and controls the metabolism between himself and nature. . . . Through this movement he acts upon external nature and changes it, and in this way he simultaneously changes his own nature" (*Capital*, Vol. 1, 283). Labor, of course, takes place in a temporality, but this is a specific "history" (i.e., a particular articulation of a mode of production), not an abstract, idealist, immanent "temporality" of *différance*. However, Butler does indeed reduce this transformative activity to basically an abstract (and quite idealist) notion of "temporal movement." Of course, the notion of temporality informing Butler's concept of materiality—as well as her concepts of performativity and the differences-within reiteration and citationality—is not a historical, materialist temporality but rather the deconstructive trope that is one of the core principles of the Derridean notion of *différance*.

In "basing" her theory of materiality on Foucault's notion of a diffuse, autonomous, contingent and aleatory power, Butler, like Foucault, makes power, itself, the *constitutive* "base" of society and all social processes, substituting it for the Marxist concept of a *determining* economic base. But how effective is such a move, especially when we also consider that Butler has articulated Foucault's analytics of power in relation to a deconstructive logic of supplementary, thus generating a circular logic that quite outdoes Foucault? As I have already suggested, Butler constructs a supplementary circuit in which all the fundamental concepts of her social analytics are equivalent—or tropically slide one into the other. She declares not only that "'materiality' designates a certain effect of power or, rather, is power in its formative or constituting effects" (34), but also that "performativity is one domain in which power acts as discourse . . . [as] a reiterated acting that is power" (225). Moreover, Butler insists, as we have already seen, on the "indissolubility of materiality and signification" (30) and that "*materialization* will be a kind of citationality" (15), that is peformativity. In other words, power is not only the constitutive base of the social, immanent in all processes, but, through a series of tropic slippages *power is materiality is discourse is citationality is performativity*. Such an understanding of power and materiality becomes so closed and circular as to border on the ludicrous. It does not so much explain processes of power and social construction as avoid explanation altogether by inventing a series of tropic displacements. Butler is, of course, following Foucault, who claims that "power is everywhere . . . comes from everywhere" (*History of Sexuality* 93). But as Nancy Hartsock rightly points out, "Power is everywhere, and so ultimately nowhere" (170). Such a notion of power is so broad and idealist, it is both absurd and quite ineffectual. How much more absurd, then, is Butler's supplementary logic in which *power is materiality is discourse is citationality is performativity*? Not only is power everywhere and nowhere, but power is everything and nothing.

While this may be a quite ineffectual theory of power for any politics of social transformation, it is nonetheless a very appealing and popular one among ludic feminists and theorists, precisely because it provides an analytics of power in which we do not have to confront the global relations and systematicity of power;

in which we do not have to deal with the most serious consequences of power operating in dialectical relation to the mode of production and division of labor— the consequences, in other words, of *exploitation*. By construing power as immanent in all processes, as operating as discourse, as citationality—and thus as a "reiterative acting" divided by differences-within—this ludic logic constitutes power as reversible, as generating its own resistances. The "compulsory power relations," that Butler argues operate through multiple local sites to "form, maintain, sustain, and regulate bodies" (34), are themselves "unstable" and indeterminate: generating and sustaining resistance along with regulation. Moreover, the privileged place ludic theories accord discourse means, as Foucault argues, that "Discourse transmits and produces power; it reinforces it, but also undermines and exposes it, renders it fragile and makes it possible to thwart it." The agency of change, in other words, is discourse itself or power *as* discourse. More, specifically, it is what Butler calls "resignification."

The politics of such a ludic theory is that it blurs the lines between the powerful and powerless, oppressor and oppressed, and produces a social analytic that turns the historical binaries of social class into reversible matters of discourse in which exploiter and exploited become shifting positions in the (Lacanian) Symbolic, open to resignification. This means that, through the play and invention of discourse (resignification), every subject, everyone, always already has access to the power imminent in discourse without any connection to the position of the subject in the social division of labor. In other words, in this analytics of power, the social relations of production—class relations—are covered up and concealed. Everyone is always already located in multiple sites of resistance no matter what their location in property relations may be. This view occludes the source of power: the fact that power is always constructed at the point of production. In contrast, power for historical materialists is always linked to relations of production and labor. In any society divided by the unequal division and appropriation of labor, power is a binary relation between exploiter and exploited; powerful and powerless; owner of the means of production and those who have nothing but their labor power to sell. Power, thus, cannot be translated into a plurality of differences as if all sites of power are equally powerful. The resolution of these binaries does not come about through a linguistic resignification but through revolutionary praxis to transform the system of exploitation and emancipate those it exploits.

We especially see Butler's assertion of the agency of invention (citationality) as a de-materialized site of reversible power in her efforts to account for the way "sex is both produced and destabilized in the course of this reiteration" of norms

(10). Not only does citationality invoke the "chain of binding conventions," but it is also "by virtue of this reiteration that gaps and fissures are opened up," producing instability, and "this instability is the *de*constituting possibility in the very process of repetition, the power that undoes the very effects by which 'sex' is stabilized" (10). In other words, as supplementary processes, citationality, reiteration, and performativity, all simultaneously constitute and "deconstitute"; regulate and deregulate; "produce and destabilize" the materialization—sexing—of the body. The process of reiteration (citationality/performativity) is, *in and of itself*, a process of *invention*: the reversible, de-stabilizing, de/reconstituting play of significations that subverts any stable, definite meanings. What this means is that the "regulatory power" of norms—which is established through reiteration—is itself reversible: it is also a deregulatory power.

However, contrary to ludic claims, this diverse deployment of deregulating invention by Butler, as well as by Cornell, Lyotard, Derrida and others (whether as performativity, citationality, resignification, remetaphorization, refiguring, the differend, *différance* . . .) is not a progressive move beyond (free of) the bounds of existing systems and their material conditions. Rather invention is a way of avoiding the consequences of the structural forces in society—the social relations of production. The logic of invention is a double move that attempts to displace exploitation. Again, it does so by first construing material structural forces either as discourse or as so heavily mediated by discourses as to be "indissociable" from them, as Butler does. Then it reinterprets these structures in terms of the trope of invention and a differential logic (*différance/differend*/difference-within), thereby defining them as, in themselves, heterogeneous, indeterminate, self-deconstructing processes. In other words, within this ludic logic, structures are always already being *undone* by their own destabilizing processes, their own differences-within. This means, in effect, that, for ludic theorists, there are no exploitative or determining *structures* or *systematic* relations, including production, because such structures would always already be in the process of *undoing* themselves and their effects. Of course, ludic critics do not deny oppression (that is, domination as opposed to exploitation), but they largely confine both their recognition and explanations of the occurrences of oppression to particular, local events and gestures of power that are, by definition, reversible, that generate their own resistances. What this means is that there is no need for revolution or class struggle since any oppressive "structure" is itself a deconstituting process that undoes its own effects (oppression). Domination is especially seen as undoing its own attempts to regulate subjectivities. As Butler argues, "'sexed positions' are not localities but, rather, citational practices instituted within a juridical domain," which attempts to "confine, limit, or prohibit some set of acts, practices, subjects, but in the process of articulating that prohibition, the law provides the *discursive occasion* for resistance, a resignification, and potential self-subversion of that law" (*Bodies* 109). Liberatory politics, for Butler, is thus a matter of invention, of resignification: the difference-within every citation or repetition of norm that opens up a space for reinventing the norm and its symbolic regime, as in the regime of heterosexuality.

However, by trying to explain heterosexuality as regulatory regime of discourse, a compulsory symbolic law operating through "citationality," Butler confines "the regime of heterosexuality" entirely to a scene of the superstructure, to a discursive order. She suggests *how* it may operate, but she is not able to explain in any way *why* it does so; *why* it has the social and historical power it does; *why* it deploys (cites) the norms that she thinks it does. In cutting off heterosexuality—as well as materiality—from the material conditions of production, she isolates the "regime" of heterosexuality from any relation to patriarchal capitalism. This move then enables her to substitute the *symbolic regime* of heterosexuality for the *social formation* of patriarchal capitalism (which she entirely occludes) as the determining structure constructing our lives, gender and sexuality. Moreover her post-al politics posits invention as the latest trope for the freedom of deregulated subjectivities and unbounded desire—unconstrained by the "truth" of needs. But in actuality, the deployment of invention justifies, normalizes and, in the name of deregulation, regulates the subjects of the new World Order. None of these ludic modes of invention—Butler's resignification, Cornell's remetaphorization, Haraway's recoding, Lyotard's ode to the pleasures of inventing new phrases—break the logic of the dominant ideology of capitalism which produces subjects according to the needs of the moving forces of production.

Butler's own analysis points up the limits of her ludic privileging of the discursive. Class, labor and the relations of production are the suppressed, "covered over," "exclusionary" and "constitutive outside" of her own theory. Her notion of citationality, for instance, is unable to *explain* the material reality, of lesbian and gay oppression. Thus, she briefly moves toward a class analysis of resisting sexualities in order to ask, "For whom is outness a historically available and affordable option? Is there an unmarked class character to the demand for universal 'outness'" (227)? However, following her notion of citationality, Butler regards class, itself, to be a performance: an individual quoting of the texts of power. In other words, class, for Butler, is based on "power" as access to discourse and is contingent and individual; it does not concern the position of the subject in the social relations of production. But class is not the "effect" of power; rather it is the construct of production and, as such, it is a collectivity of practices.

For historical materialist feminists and lesbian/gay critics, however, "outness," and the possibility of exploring alternative sexualities is not simply a matter of individual "desire" nor is class a series of individualities. This is not to deny that one "experiences" sexuality on the level of individual experience, rather it questions whether sexuality can be *explained* on the level of experience. Butler's question about the "affordability" of "outing" both hints at and withdraws from dealing with the historical forces that, in fact, make "individual" experience socially possible. In his text, "It's Not Natural," Peter Ray demonstrates how the

> industrial revolution of the eighteenth and nineteenth centuries broke down the traditional bonds and constraints of a society which had been tied to the land by economic necessity. Millions began to work in the cities for money wages, and for some at least the possibility arose of living outside the traditional family arrangements. Heterosexuality and homosexuality were concepts developed by the medical, moral and legal authorities at that time, in order to police the new society by demarcating acceptable and unacceptable behaviour. Male homosexuality was not specifically outlawed in Britain until 1885. (32)

Similarly John D'Emilio's work develops a sustained argument for the way alternative sexualities are tied to the labor relations of capitalism (*Making Trouble*). In her intimate critique, "A Question of Class," the contemporary lesbian theorist and writer, Dorothy Allison offers an explanation of alternative sexualities and class that is an effective intervention in the ludic reading of queerity. She argues that "Traditional feminist theory has had a limited understanding of class differences and of how sexuality and self are shaped by both desire and denial" (*Skin* 15). Focusing specifically on lesbian sexualities, she writes:

> I have known I was a lesbian since I was a teenager, and I have spent a good twenty years making peace with the effects of incest and physical abuse. But what may be the central fact of my life is that I was born in 1949 in Greenville, South Carolina, the bastard daughter of a white woman from a desperately poor family, a girl who had left the seventh grade the year before, worked as a waitress, and was just a month past fifteen when she had me. That fact, the inescapable impact of being born in a condition of poverty that this society finds shameful, contemptible, and somehow deserved, has had dominion over me to such an extent that I have spent my life trying to overcome or deny it. I have learned with great difficulty that the vast majority of people believe that poverty is a voluntary condition. (*Skin* 14-15)

No matter how much ludic theorists try to erase questions of class, poverty and the economic from their work, their analysis is haunted by the relations of production and divisions of labor. We find this "return of the repressed" of the relations of production in Butler's ludic analysis in the opening chapter of *Bodies that Matter*, in which she attempts to "discern the history of sexual difference encoded in the history of matter" through a "rude and provocative" rereading of Plato (54, 36). She begins by positing matter within the metaphysical binary of matter and form, and confines her argument to this metaphysical circuit. But at two points in her text, when she attempts to explain why Plato has constituted the category of the "excluded" in the way he has, she is forced to move beyond the domain of discourse to the *relations of production and the division of labor*. As Butler explains, "This xenophobic exclusion operates through the production of racialized Others, and those whose 'natures' are considered less rational by virtue of their appointed task in the process of *laboring* to reproduce the conditions of private life" (48, emphasis added). And again, she says, "There is no singular outside, for the Forms require a number of exclusions; they are and replicate themselves through what they exclude, through not being animal, not being the woman, not being the slave, whose propriety is purchased through property, national and racial boundary, masculinism, and compulsory heterosexuality" (52). All these exclusions are part of the same "singular outside": the material relations of production which construct all of the social divisions and differences around labor and the appropriation of social resources. In other words, for all Butler's discursive displacements, the concealed, sutured over *base* of her own theory—as it is of any theory or knowledge practice—is still the (occluded) *economic base*.

We can see the consequences of these different theories of materialism by briefly examining the construction or "materialization" of female gender—what Butler calls "girling." To describe this process, Butler adapts Althusser's concept of "interpellation" which means the ideological process of "calling" a person to take up (identify with) the position "named" (e.g., girl). According to Butler,

> medical interpellation . . . (the sonogram notwithstanding) . . . shifts an infant from an 'it' to a 'she' or a 'he,' and in that naming, the girl is 'girled,' brought into the domain of language and kinship through the interpellation of gender. . . . The naming is at once the setting of a boundary, and also the repeated inculcation of a norm. (7-8)

Butler understands this naming ("girling") as placing the infant in a "regulatory regime" of discourse (language and kinship). But for historical materialists, ideological interpellation does not simply place the infant in discourse, but more important it also places the child in the relations of production, in the social division of labor (according to gender, hetero-sexuality, race, nationality). Butler's theory of performativity completely eclipses this dialectical relation between ideology and the economic. Butler is concerned with changing how "bodies matter," how they are valued. But without relating ideological "interpellation" to the relations of production, no amount of resignification in the symbolic can change "What counts as a valued body"—for what makes a body valuable in the world is its *economic value*.

This *truth* is painfully clear if we move beyond the privileged boundaries of the upper-middle class in the industrialized West (for whom basic needs are readily fulfilled) and see what is happening to "girling" in the international division of labor—especially among the impoverished classes in India. Here the "medical interpellation" (naming) of infants/fetuses, particularly through the use of the sonogram, immediately places "girled" fetuses not only in discourse but also in the gender division of labor and unequal access to social resources. About 60 per cent of the "girled" fetuses are being immediately aborted or murdered upon birth (female infanticide) because the families cannot afford to keep them. The citational acts, rituals, and "performatives" by which individuals are repeatedly "girled"—such as expensive ear-piercing ceremonies and exorbitant bride dowries—are not simply acts of discourse, but economic practices. In India, under postcolonial capitalism, the appropriation of women's surplus labor is increasing to such an extent that these rituals and "performatives" of "girling" are becoming highly popular and widely exploited sources of capital and direct extraction of surplus labor. So much so, the unmarried woman's *family* is itself being "girled" in order for its combined labor to collectively produce the surplus value taken from the "girled body" (e.g., bride dowries). Revolutionary praxis and not simply "resignification" is necessary to end the exploitation and murdering of hundreds of thousands of economically de-valued "girled" bodies.

Six

How is making discourse or the matter of the body the ground of politics and social analytic any less reductive than the economic base? Yet, while economic reductionism is to be avoided at all costs according to ludic theories, a discursive reductionism or a theological matterism is widely embraced as a complex, sophisticated, and open multiplicity. The issue here is not whether "reductionism" is negative: it is not—ask any rigorous scientist (Weinberg, "Two Cheers for Reductionism"). To articulate the relations connecting seemingly disparate events and phenomena is in fact a necessary and unavoidable part of effective knowledge of the real. Rather the question is why are some reductions—particularly those connecting the exploitation and gender division of labor to the accumulation of capital—suppressed and rendered taboo in ludic (socialist) feminism while other reductions—such as the discursive construction of sex/gender or a matterist resistance as performance—are championed and widely circulated? The answer, of course, does not lie in the "logic" of the argument, although that is the way it is commonly represented. On a purely epistemological or logical level both moves establish a necessary relation between two phenomena. Instead, the answer is in the economic, social and political interests these two forms of "reductionism" support and the power of bourgeois ideology to discredit historical materialist knowledges.

Thus what is at stake in this displacement of the economic by discourse is the elision of issues of exploitation and the substitution of a discursive identity politics for the struggle for full social and economic emancipation. Marx and Engels' critique of the radical "Young Hegelians" applies equally to ludic cultural materialists:

> they are only fighting against '*phrases.*' They forget, however, that to these phrases they themselves are only opposing other phrases, and that they are in no way combating the real existing world when they are merely combating the phrases of this world. (*The German Ideology* 41)

This is not to say that the conflicts over ideology, cultural practices and significations are not an important part of the social struggle for emancipation: the issue is how do we explain the relation of the discursive to the non-discursive, the relation of cultural practices to the "real existing world"—whose objectivity is the fact of the "working day"—in order to transform it? Obviously this relation is a highly mediated one. But for ludic materialists the relation is so radically displaced that it is entirely suppressed: mediations are taken as autonomous sites of signification and consequently the actual practice of ludic cultural analysis is confined entirely to institutional and cultural points of mediation severed from the economic conditions producing them. The analysis of "mediations" becomes a goal in itself, and the operation of "mediations" is deployed to obscure the "origin" (surplus labor) and the "end" (class differences) that in fact frame the "mediations." It is only in the context of historical materialism that one can point up the politics of this erasure of "origin" (arche) and "end" (telos) in poststructuralist theory. In ludic feminism the arche and telos are erased as if they were merely metaphysical concepts. My point is that the erasure of arche and telos serves a more immediate and concrete purpose: it makes it impossible to connect the "mediated" to other social practices, and consequently the inquiry into and analysis of the "mediations," themselves, take the place of knowledge of the social totality in which mediations are relays of underlying connections. For historical materialist feminists, however, cultural and ideological practices are not autonomous but are instead primary sites for reproducing the meanings and subjectivities supporting the unequal gender, sexual and race divisions of labor, and thus a main arena for the struggle against economic exploitation as well as cultural oppression. The untimely time of red feminism has come.

Notes

1. The theoretical and political issues addressed here are developed much more fully in my book, *Ludic Feminism and After*.

2. On the politics of invention, see *Transformation 2:The Invention of the Queer: Marxism, Lesbian and Gay Theory, Capitalism*. (Washington, DC: Maisonneuve Press, 1995).

Works Cited

Allison, Dorothy. *Skin: Talking about Sex, Class and Literature*. Ithaca, NY: Firebrand Books, 1994.
Barrett, Michele. *The Politics of Truth: From Marx to Foucault*. Stanford: Stanford University Press, 1991.
_____. "Words and Things: Materialism and Method in Contemporary Feminist Analysis." *Destabilizing Theory*. Ed. Barrett and Phillips. Stanford: Stanford University Press, 1992. 201-219.
Benhabib, Seyla and Drucilla Cornell, eds.*Feminism as Critique: On the Politics of Gender*. Minneapolis: University of Minnesota Press, 1987.
Benstock, Shari. *Textualizing the Feminine*. Norman: University of Oklahoma Press, 1991.
Bridenthal, Renate. "Rev. of *The Politics of Truth*, by Michele Barrett."*Science and Society* 58.2 (1994): 218-220.
Butler, Judith. *Bodies that Matter: On the Discursive Limits of "Sex."* New York and London: Routledge, 1993.
_____. *Gender Trouble: Feminism and the Subversion of Identity*. New York: Routledge, 1990.
_____. "Poststructuralism and Postmarxism." *Diacritics* 23.4 (Winter 1993): 3-11.

Callinicos, Alex. *Race and Class*. London and Chicago: Bookmarks, 1993.
Cornell, Drucilla. *Beyond Accommodation: Ethical Feminism, Deconstruction, and the Law*. New York: Routledge, 1991.
Daly, Mary. *Gyn/Ecology: The Metaethics of Radical Feminism*. Boston: Beacon, 1978.
de Lauretis, Teresa. *Alice Doesn't: Feminism, Semiotics, Cinema*. Bloomington: Indiana University Press, 1984.
D'Emilio, John. *Making Trouble: Essays on Gay History, Politics and the University*. New York and London: Routledge, 1992.
Derrida, Jacques. *Of Grammatology*. Trans. Gayatri Spivak. Baltimore: The Johns Hopkins University Press, 1974.
_____. *Writing and Difference*. Trans. A. Bass. Chicago: University of Chicago Press, 1978.
Dreyfus, Hubert and Paul Rabinow. *Michel Foucault: Beyond Structuralism and Hermeneutics*. 2nd. ed. Chicago: University of Chicago Press, 1983.
Ebert, Teresa L. *Ludic Feminism and After*. Ann Arbor: University of Michigan Press, 1995.
Engels, Frederick. "The Funeral of Karl Marx." *When Karl Marx Died: Comments in 1883*. Ed. Philip Foner. New York: International Publishers, 1973.
Foucault, Michel. *The Archaeology of Knowledge and the Discourse on Language*. Trans. A. Sheridan Smith. New York: Pantheon, 1972.
_____. *Discipline and Punish*. New York: Vintage-Random House, 1979.
_____. *The History of Sexuality*. Vol. 1. Trans. R. Hurley. 1978. New York: Pantheon, 1984.
_____. "Politics and the Study of Discourse." *Ideology and Consciousness* 3 (1973): 7-26.
_____. *Power/Knowledge*. Ed. C. Gordon. New York: Pantheon, 1980.
Fuss, Diana. *Essentially Speaking: Feminism, Nature and Difference*. New York and London: Routledge, 1989.
Gallop, Jane. *Thinking Through the Body*. New York: Columbia Press, 1988.
Grosz, Elizabeth. *Volatile Bodies: Toward a Corporeal Feminism*. Bloomington: Indiana University Press, 1994.
Haraway, Donna. "A Manifesto for Cyborgs: Science, Technology and Socialist Feminism in the 1980s." *Simians* 149-181.
_____. *Simians, Cyborgs, and Women: The Reinvention of Nature*. New York: Routledge, 1991.
Lacan, Jacques. *Écrits: A Selection*. Trans. A. Sheridan. New York: Norton, 1977.
Laclau, E. "Beyond Emancipation." *Development and Change* 23.3 (1992): 121-137.
_____. "Populist Rupture and Discourse." *Screen Education*, no. 34 (Spring 1980): 87-93.
_____. "Transformations of Advanced Industrial Societies and the Theory of the Subject." *Rethinking Ideology: A Marxist Debate*. Ed. S. Hanninen and L. Paldan. New York and Bagnolet, France: International General/IMMRC, and Berlin: Argument-Verlag, 1983.
Laclau, Ernesto and Chantal Mouffe. *Hegemony and Socialist Strategy: Towards a Radical Democratic Politics*. London and New York: Verso, 1985.
Landry, Donna and Gerald MacLean. *Materialist Feminisms*. Cambridge, MA and Oxford: Blackwell, 1993.
Lenin, V. I. *Materialism and Empirio-Criticism*. 1927. New York: International Pub, 1970.

Lyotard, J-F. *The Differend: Phrases in Dispute*. Trans. G. Van Den Abbeele. Minneapolis: University of Minnesota Press, 1988.
_____. *The Postmodern Condition*. Trans. G. Bennington and B. Massumi. Minneapolis: University of Minnesota Press, 1984.
_____. and J-L. Thébaud. *Just Gaming*. Trans. W. Godzich. Minneapolis: University of Minnesota Press, 1985.
Marx, Karl. *The Communist Manifesto*. Ed. Frederic Bender. New York: Norton, 1988.
_____. *A Contribution to the Critique of Political Economy*. Ed. M. Dobb. New York: International Publishers, 1970.
_____. *Capital*, 1. New York: Vintage, 1977.
_____. *Critique of the Gotha Program*. New York: International Pub, 1966.
_____ and F. Engels. *The German Ideology*. 3rd rev. ed. Moscow: Progress, 1976.
Nancy, Jean-Luc. *The Experience of Freedom*. Stanford: Stanford University Press, 1993.
_____. *The Inoperative Community*. Minneapolis: University of Minnesota Press, 1991.
Ray, Peter. "It's Not Natural." *Living Marxism* (Dec. 1992): 31-32.
Rorty, Richard. *Contingency, Irony, and Solidarity*. New York: Cambridge University Press, 1989.
Saussure, Ferdinand de. *Course in General Linguistics*. 1959. New York: McGraw, 1966.
Stockton, Kathryn Bond. "Bodies and God: Poststructuralist Feminists Return to the Fold of Spiritual Materialism." *Feminism and Postmodernism*. Ed. Margaret Ferguson and Jennifer Wicke. Durham: Duke University Press, 1994. 129-165.
Voloshinov, V. N. (Mikhail Bakhtin). *Marxism and the Philosophy of Language*. Trans. L. Matejka and I. Titunik. Cambridge: Harvard University Press, 1973.
Weinberg, Steven. "Two Cheers for Reductionism."*Dreams of a Final Theory*. New York: Pantheon, 1992.
Williams, Raymond. *Marxism and Literature*. Oxford and New York: Oxford University Press, 1977.
Wong, Nellie. "Socialist Feminism: Our Bridge to Freedom."*Third World Women and the Politics of Feminism*. Ed. C. Mohanty, et al. Bloomington: Indiana University Press, 1991.

Greg Dawes

A Marxist Critique of Post-Structuralist Notions of the Subject

Does Marxism have a theory of the subject? Is it able to answer satisfactorily questions about the inner recesses of consciousness? For a host of intellectuals on the left the response has been and continues to be negative. Louis Althusser, for instance, remarks that "there is nothing in Marx that could provide the foundations of a theory of the psychic" (Althusser 21). Perhaps the most renowned spokesperson for the psychoanalytical theory of the subject is Julia Kristeva. In a post-1968 article she alleged that:

> Marxist theory, still a powerful tool for understanding the economic determinants of social relations, has little to say on the crisis in question: it is not a theory of meaning or of the subject. There is no subject in the economic rationality of Marxism; there is in Marxist revolution, but the 'founding fathers' have left us no thoughts about it, while academic Marxologists of today can hardly wait to get rid both of meaning and of the subject in the name of some objective process. (Moi, *The Kristeva Reader* 31-32)

Since the foundation of the Frankfurt School, we have witnessed a major shift in the stances of potential or actual Marxists with respect to consciousness and the notion of the subject. The most influential and numerous group of Marxist cultural critics has overwhelmingly opted for an incorporation of Freudian metapsychology within the epistemological framework of Marxism. The reasons for this integration of Freudianism and Marxism are many and they are beyond the scope of this essay.

Now psychoanalysis comes into the picture because it levels a complaint against Marxism for its lack of a theory of the subject. This theory, according to Freudians and neo-Freudians consists of an attempt on the part of psychology to come to grips with and explain the vagaries of individual consciousness and behavior—above all their irrational, pathological aspects—in terms of a deeper, psychic process. Psychoanalytic theory attempts to interpret the subjective experience of individuals as essentially shaped by their formation *as subjects*—a process which is understood as taking place in a *pre-conscious* state of being. For Freud, this "unconscious" is largely construed as biological. For Lacan and neo-Lacanians, it is identified with "language"—or rather, unconscious desire, like the linguistic process of signification, can never be fulfilled in some plenitudinous moment of "meaning." Desire always lacks its object, in the same way that the symbolic dimension of language never fully gives us the "object" itself. Thus Freud, in V. N. Voloshinov's words, "psychologizes the organic," whereas Lacan, as we might paraphrase it, "psychologizes the linguistic."

Marxism would argue that subjects—that which we perceive ourselves to be as individuals—are not merely empirical givens. Subjects, in the process of being socially constituted, are not fully nor necessarily conscious of this procedure. In other words, subjects are not always conscious of the complex social factors of which they are a composite. Human beings appear in a state of becoming in the course of socialization, of social intercourse and relations. Thus, while becoming socialized is not necessarily a completely conscious process it is, nonetheless, thoroughly *social*.

In *The German Ideology* and *The 1844 Manuscripts*, Marx and Engels contend that as human beings become more conscious of their social nature they begin to see themselves as alienated in capitalism and note that their society does not reflect their social composition. Briefly put, their social nature, the reflection in society of their "species being" is objectified, it is robbed from them. Once human beings become conscious of the contradiction between their collective nature and the means of production, they seek to alter and appropriate these means. All this would be one level of abstraction.

According to Marx's early writings, however, alienation can manifest itself in four fundamental ways for the worker.[1] The primary form of alienation relates directly to the worker's production. He or she produces something that is then turned into a commodity on the market by the capitalist. The number of hours the worker devotes to producing this commodity are compensated by the capitalist in the form of wages. Hence, the worker is, at this stage, doubly alienated: he has no jurisdiction over his product and he receives a partial compensation (in the form of wages) that does not fully account for the amount of labor he has put into the product nor the sale value of the same. The capitalist's financial interests, then, are in opposition to those of the worker. While the capitalist attempts to maximize his profit by selling these commodities, he can only do so by making the life of the worker more miserable (by lowering his wages and benefits, and by increasing his work hours). Thus, as a class, workers are all subjected to this type of alienation. By uniting collectively and taking over the means of production from the capitalist, Marx believes that the workers will be able to rid themselves of this type of alienation.

But in order to unite with other workers, this worker would have to overcome another form of alienation: from the other workers. One of the ways the capitalist can ensure his profits is by pitting workers against one another. If a certain sector of the working force in a given factory is given financial privileges over the rest of the workers, or if workers are used as strikebreakers when the primary workers are holding out for raises, the capitalist stands to benefit from these and similar circumstances. When one worker is alienated from others, the collective well-being of the working class as a whole is in jeopardy. All of these types of alienation ultimately undermine the interests of the proletariat. Returning to the Marxist notion of subjecthood, this then is the undergirding of the social conception of the subject.

One could file an objection to Marxism at this point by stating that if in fact the conscious experience of subjecthood is not the result of processes that antedate the entrance of the subject into a network of social relations, but is rather a fully social reality, then how do we explain the presence of society in subjective consciousness? What can justify the simultaneous property of consciousness as it appears to the individual subject and yet also exists outside that subject on the objective plane of social relations?

It is a truism, generally speaking, that Marx and Engels did not devote any major efforts to solving this problem—and that, in this sense, Marxism as it appears in the classical texts does not provide a fully elaborated and detailed account of the theory of the subject. But they did indicate where they thought the answer to lie: in *language*. In their analysis of German philosophy and society in *The German Ideology*, Marx and Engels refer to language as "practical consciousness." The experience of conscious subjecthood presupposes language as consciousness in its objective, "practical" form as well as the individual as linguistic communicant. Society constitutes the subject in a plurality of ways: as a differentiated participant in social labor, say, or in human reproduction and kinship relations. But language is that specific instance of a social relation that not only shapes social units as subjects, but also provides a medium in which the individual so formed can become conscious of himself as subject. Language enables the social subject to relate *to others* and *to himself* in a social manner.

In this essay I argue that in the standard indictment of Marxism for its lack of "theory of the subject," Freudianism and neo-Freudianism reveal their own inability to break with idealist notions of consciousness. In other words, whereas Freudianism attempts a critique of consciousness as classically represented in bourgeois ideology—the Cartesian subject, or the Romantic notion of the individual ego (Fichte)—its "rupture" with this ideology can only occur through the postulation of an unconscious in which the individual is grasped not in truly sociological but in biological, pre-social terms. Consciousness itself, as Voloshinov notes, becomes an object of "distrust." But the effect of this stance is merely to leave consciousness in the grip of its bourgeois-ideological representation—a representation that is only abstractly refused, not fully overcome.

By contrast, Voloshinov's studies, *Freudianism: A Critical Sketch* and *Marxism and the Philosophy of Language*, build a structure for understanding consciousness based upon the Marxist observation that language is practical consciousness.[2] Voloshinov, as I maintain below, re-thinks the "subject," as represented in bourgeois philosophy and ideology generally, as an instance of "inner speech," the source of which lies in the larger, objective sphere of "behavior ideology," viz., "that atmosphere of unsystematized and unfixed inner and outer speech which endows our every instance of behavior and action and our every "conscious" state with meaning" (Voloshinov, *Marxism* 91). However, Voloshinov's critique does not always make apparent the connections between this form of consciousness, class consciousness, and the class struggle. In what follows, I suggest a Marxist alternative to poststructuralist notions of the subject and consciousness based, to a large degree, on Voloshinov's writings.

Toward a Marxist Theory of Consciousness

Following the observations that Marx and Engels made about language and consciousness, V. N. Voloshinov's *Freudianism: A Critical Sketch* and *Marxism and the Philosophy of Language* supply us with a pathbreaking, materialist understanding of the notion of the subject and the whole question of the unconscious and consciousness. They allow us to see consciousness as a type of continuum with different stages, ranging from what Voloshinov calls "unofficial" to "official" consciousness. The key to grasping these concepts is to see the mediation reality undergoes through language. For Voloshinov, as I will show below, language is always already attached to every act and every thought, and human beings are, consequently, thoroughly social. He believes that the Freudian isolation of psychic processes and bifurcation of consciousness and the unconscious in the individual are symptomatic of the decay of social relations in capitalism. In point of fact, argues Voloshinov, it is in moments of social disintegration that the privileging of the sexual and the condemnation of consciousness gain increasing popularity.

Given the historical moment in which Voloshinov was writing (the 1920s and 30s), and based on his works, we could surmise that he shared the view that the collapse of capitalism as an economic system was, in a certain sense, inevitable. This would explain why he frequently refers to the "decline" or "decadence" of the system. The missing link here is a Leninist notion of political organizing. Without a highly organized, class conscious vanguard party, there is little chance that a revolution can take place. This in itself, and not the inexorable development of the productive forces, explains why a workers,'' revolution took place in an underdeveloped country like Russia. Yet there is even more to all this. The vanguard party and the working class must have a developed form of class consciousness and a keen sense for the strengths and weaknesses of the party as well as of the bourgeoisie, and they must have a special understanding of the strategies that must be followed in order to take power. In spite of the strengths of Voloshinov's work, he does tend to underestimate the role of political agency in his works.

Another weakness that should be underscored before we proceed is that Voloshinov's argument that in times of crisis sexuality becomes more prominent seems to carry with it certain moral overtones. While it is true that the sexual can be overemphasized as the bourgeoisie as a class feels more and more threatened by the proletariat, it is also true that there are certain egalitarian strides made in that direction precisely because of the stress on sexuality—the liberation of women and men from traditional gender constraints being prominent among them. One could speculate that Voloshinov's stance vis-à-vis sexuality might be tied to the "free love" movement in Russia in the 1920s and 30s. Marxism maintains that unequal gender relations begin to inflame with the advent of class society and private property. As an institution marriage frequently exacerbates the inequalities extant in capitalism among different social classes and genders. Marxists argue that by abolishing private property and social classes these social inequalities will begin to be rectified and the base for a more egalitarian society can then be put in place.[3] On a Marxist view, that continues to be the central issue with regards to subjectivity under capitalism. While this would get to the root of the issue, one still has to analyze such social phenomena—such as sexuality—as they develop under capitalism. From a Marxist vantage point this would involve looking at the growth of egalitarian political movements under capitalism that were able, in spite of the limitations of the system, to institute reforms which did improve the lives of, say, women and African-Americans. Yet these social movements would be gauged according to their own class delineations within the system.

Factoring in these modifications, Voloshinov's critique of Freudianism and its underestimation of consciousness serves as a useful starting point to begin to rethink the whole notion of a Marxist theory of the subject, not only because there are historical parallels to be drawn here, but also because psychoanalysis is generally incompatible philosophically and politically with Marxism. The intent in this section is not to undertake a critical and necessarily thorough reading of Freud's works, but rather to study Voloshinov's indictment of Freudianism and, perhaps more importantly, his development of a Marxist philosophy of language and consciousness.[4] A primary interest in this essay is to show how Voloshinov's works contribute to a Marxist understanding of consciousness, language, and the formation of the subject.

Voloshinov begins by noting the skeptical attitude that psychoanalysis has maintained with respect to consciousness. In Freud's work, consciousness is principally associated with biological and not with historical existence (Voloshinov, *Freudianism* 10). Human beings ostensibly become aware of themselves biologically and psychically on almost neutral grounds without the direct intervention of socio-historical factors. Hence, according to Voloshinov, Freud manages to underscore subjective psychological or biological categories over against objective, socio-economic ones (Voloshinov, *Freudianism* 12). As in the case of other bourgeois philosophies of Freud's time, human beings almost become abstractions extracted from their natural environment (society)[Voloshinov, *Marxism* 15]. Human beings are not seen as developing and consisting of a plethora of social relations, but rather as somehow, for the sake of experimental isolation, responding to metapsychological phenomena. In other words, as the human psyche is reified in Freudian thought, it appears to us as a separate realm with its own history and its own internal relations. Furthermore, according to Voloshinov, the root of this individual behavior is biology: consciousness itself is judged not by historical but rather by biological development. The core feature of this biological given is sexuality (Voloshinov, *Freudianism* 10). In fact, argues Voloshinov, the physiological aspect of our existence takes precedence over consciousness as the latter becomes more suspect in bourgeois thought.

The major irony involved in granting higher status to the biological, as Voloshinov keenly discerns it, is that Freud's argument rests on biological suppositions even though he only indulged in meticulous biological research in the first stage of his career (Voloshinov, *Freudianism* 34, 71). Thereafter, Freud relied almost exclusively on his clinical interpretations (between the patient and himself). It is this contradiction, as well as his general "distrust of consciousness," according to Voloshinov, that weakens the interpretations he makes about consciousness, the unconscious, and the patient. By isolating the individual clinical case to the general neglect of the social, Freud's theory takes on centripetal characteristics which do not account fully for the historical and social forces of his time. Ultimately, this movement creates a type of dualism between consciousness and the unconscious, the objective and the subjective, and the social and the individual (Voloshinov, *Freudianism* 25, 77). The last one of these pairs in most every instance takes precedence over the first of these. It is not, of course, that Freud ignores history *en bloc*, but that he is unable to transcend the limits of the bourgeois notion of the individual.

For Voloshinov, as we shall see shortly, consciousness is based upon the way linguistic utterances interact, the manner in which they socially engage one another. This will allow Voloshinov, the linguist, to dissect the social meaning of the utterance as well as the larger question of social communication and, consequently, the social formation of human subjects. By contrast, Freud does not penetrate any deeper than the level of interpretation when he analyzes his patient's psychical condition and assumes a priori that the solutions to a given psychical disorder are due to the individual's own personal and/or family history:

> Freud's whole psychological construct is based fundamentally on human verbal utterances; it is nothing but a special kind of interpretation of utterances. All these utterances are, of course, constructed in the *conscious sphere of the psyche*. To be sure, Freud distrusts the surface motives of consciousness; he tries instead to penetrate to deeper levels of the psychical realm. Nevertheless, Freud does not take utterances in their objective aspect, does not seek out their physiological or social roots; instead he attempts to find the true motives of behavior in the utterances themselves—the patient is himself supposed to provide him the information about the depths of the "unconscious" (Voloshinov, *Freudianism* 76).

Since language, for Voloshinov, is the very basis of consciousness and since it is social by its very nature, Freud's studies are constrained—in Voloshinov's eyes—by his limited knowledge of what we now know as socio-linguists and, by implication, of consciousness. Freud's introspective method of uncovering psychic processes, then, is circular—it remains in the inner recesses of the individual psyche in order to confirm its hypotheses as particular complexes in the unconscious. In other words, Freud's method does not take into account more completely the toll that economic, political, and sociological factors can have on individuals. The complexes that Freud perceives in the unconscious are, Voloshinov suggests, symptoms of social or political conflict that have not been fully understood by the individual and are not just due to internal tension. But that, in Voloshinov's view, does not make these symptoms "unconscious" nor governed by the "pleasure principle" in opposition to the "reality principle."

In the second phase of Freud's work the unconscious gains greater stature; prior to that Freud had considered it as something "incidental."

> [T]he unconscious becomes an essential and extremely vital component of the psychical apparatus of every single human being. The very psychical apparatus itself becomes *dynamic*, that is, is set into perpetual motion. The conflict between the conscious and the unconscious is declared a constant and regular form of psychical life. The unconscious, moreover, becomes a productive source of psychical forces and energies for all domains of cultural creativity, especially for art. At the same time, the unconscious can become the source of all nervous disorders whenever its conflict with the conscious goes awry (Voloshinov, *Freudianism* 35).

The content of the unconscious is no longer composed of incidental or spontaneous matters, but rather of specific complexes which are of a primarily sexual character. Confronted by the demands of the "reality principle," the individual undergoes repression of his most intimate, pleasurable desires.

Fueled by instinctual drives, these complexes operate in the unconscious, but they can be harnessed, according to Freud, through psychoanalytic sessions. As Voloshinov points out, Freud relies increasingly on unconscious methods in order to facilitate the interpretation of dreams—such is the case of "free association." This procedure allows the psychoanalyst to sort out the dream images—the symbolic representations—that appear to the patient. But these symbols can only partially compensate the patient for the lack of satisfaction that she feels. The patient is permitted in her dreams to return—in some unfulfilled form—to the paradise lost of her infancy (Voloshinov, *Freudianism* 52). Thus, according to Voloshinov, psychoanalysis does not provide us with a more detailed portrayal of material life, but rather furnishes us with what we might call "psychical narratives" that are based on clinical sessions with patients.

> The concept of the unconscious, therefore, does not move the psyche the slightest bit closer to material nature; its implementation does not in

the least help us connect a psychical system of laws with the objective system of laws for nature in general. The rift between the inner-subjective sphere and the material sphere remains exactly the same in psychoanalysis as in the psychology of consciousness (Voloshinov, *Freudianism* 70).

The result of this method is that objective reality per se becomes the "reality principle"; a functioning unit within Freud's own system of thought that never escapes the limitations of philosophical subjectivism. Consequently, in Voloshinov's estimation, psychoanalysis ends up studying interpretations of interpretations. Hence the distance implied in the Oedipus Complex which, as Voloshinov has painstakingly demonstrated, asks material reality to comply with this ideological construct rather than proceeding vice versa.

In sum, Voloshinov's critique of Freudian psychoanalysis hinges on his contention that the latter does not conduct physiological research after the first phase of Freud's career; that he does not engage in linguistic studies even though Freud maintains that consciousness depends on language; that if he had carried out that research he would have realized that language, by its very nature, is thoroughly social; that this, in turn, would have led Freud to the conclusion that consciousness is a social product and not a "thing-in-itself" (individual); finally, that, had he concluded the above, Freud would have never been inclined to give so much credence to the quasi-separate realm of the unconscious.

What does Voloshinov suggest as an alternative to this type of troping of objective reality? How is his theory of consciousness any more objective than Freud's? The key aspect of consciousness that Freudianism ignores and Voloshinov underlines is the social role of language. Returning to Marx and Engels' initial intuition that language is "practical consciousness," Voloshinov embarks on a thorough Marxist study of the role of language in the formation of consciousness. To become "self-conscious" for Marx and Engels entailed becoming socially conscious as human beings engaged in production together as mental or manual laborers and as a *class*. Both philosophers believed that language was the material expression of consciousness. "Language is as old as consciousness, language is practical consciousness that exists also for other men, and for that reason alone it really exists for me personally as well; language, like consciousness, only arises from the need, the necessity, of intercourse with other men" (Marx and Engels 51). As a linguist, Voloshinov believed that Marxism had remained relatively silent on the question of language and he felt that it was the paramount task of his day to lay the foundation down so that a materialist understanding of such disciplines as literature, religion, ethics, as well as science itself could be secured (Voloshinov, *Marxism* 9).

A Marxist Critique of the Post-Structuralist Subject « 159

For Voloshinov, the basic and most essential element of consciousness is the sign:

> The reality of the inner psyche is the same reality of that of the sign. Outside the material of signs there is no psyche; there are phsysiological processes, processes in the nervous system, but no subjective psyche as a special existential quality fundamentally from both the physiological processes occurring with the organism and the reality encompassing the organism from outside, to which the psyche reacts and which in one way or another it reflects. By its very existential nature, the subjective psyche is to be localized somewhere between the organism and the outside world, on the *borderline* separating these two spheres of reality (Voloshinov, Marxism 26).

The relation between the "outside world" and the organism is, however, dialectical—both accrue meaning as they relate to each other. They have no immanent meaning in and of themselves. In Voloshinov's judgment, the question of human consciousness is anchored in language (in the sign) and can be expressed by examining the dialectical interaction between inner and outer signs.

The sign acts as a mediator for reality; it absorbs a wide variety of physiological or linguistic emissions. As a major component of the psyche it consists of any "organic activity or process: breathing, blood circulation, movements of the body, articulation, inner speech, mimetic motions, reaction to external stimuli (e.g., light stimuli) and so forth" (Voloshinov, *Marxism* 29). In short, then, signs are the raw material of our daily and lifetime experiences as they are actively registered in the psyche. According to Voloshinov, it is a mistake of abstract objectivists (like Saussure) to assume that the psyche can be pinned down solely to physiological characteristics because it actually "enjoys an extraterritorial status in the organism": it is a type of social entity that lives inside the body of every individual (Voloshinov, *Marxism* 39). Hence, to reduce it to a mere inter-organic, or metaphysiological existence is to misrepresent its relation with the "outside" world.

In Voloshinov's works, the psyche is composed of inner and outer signs which reflect biological and biographical matters in the first instance, and ideological questions in the second example. By "ideological" Voloshinov means, throughout most of *Freudianism* and *Marxism*, a system of ideas which is the product of social relations. Human thought then consists of the dialectical relation between the psyche and the ideological:

> My thought, in this sense, from the very start belongs to an ideological system and is governed by its set of laws. But, at the same time, it belongs

to another system that is just as much a unity and just as much in possession of its own set of laws—the system of my psyche. The unity of the second system is determined not only by the unity of my biological organism but also by the whole aggregate of conditions of life and society in which that organism has been set (Voloshinov, *Marxism* 35).

Even introspection, for Voloshinov, has an expressive character, that is, it is able to move from an inner to an outer sign within the psyche. There are gradations of understanding—of associating one inner sign with another—even within the realm of introspection, so that inner thought is also a social process. This is so because of the internal dynamics of inner signs relating to one another and because of their negotiation with incoming outer (social) signs. When an individual "receives" an outer sign—a sign from the "outside" world—he must refer it to other known inner signs if he wants to understand it (Voloshinov, *Marxism* 11). This process, of course, is an on-going one of constant inward and outward flows of signs that are being processed or are left unprocessed.

On a more general level, all of our thoughts can proceed, at one time or another, from inner to outer, although it is possible that they will remain in the inner phase for quite some time or forever. As our ideas move from inner to outward expression they inherit a higher measure of complexity and, consequently, they approximate objective reality to a larger degree. In the terms of Voloshinov's objective psychology, this amalgam of inner and outward speech that permeates our conduct is called behavioral ideology (Voloshinov, *Freudianism* 88). Succinctly put, behavioral ideology is the foundation for the production of thought and for all of our physical expressions. All of this, then, constitutes what Voloshinov perceives as consciousness.

Pace Freudians and neo-Freudians, as we will see below, Voloshinov valorizes consciousness and proposes a new formulation of the "unconscious." Since the Freudian notion of the unconscious does not differ significantly from consciousness, Voloshinov's critique confirms that the unconscious loses its power as an explanatory medium (Voloshinov, *Freudianism* 85). A better option, he suggests, is the idea of unofficial and official conscious. If consciousness (or official conscious) is "that commentary which every adult human being brings to bear on every instance of his behavior," the "unconscious" (or unofficial conscious) consists of ideas, images, desire etc. that are being processed, that have not been able to crystallize sufficiently to enter the official conscious (Voloshinov, *Freudianism* 85). Thus, unconscious motor reactions or thoughts represent a lower development in consciousness; they are as yet unprocessed or they may never be fully processed—such is the case of breathing, digesting food, or urinating. From this we can see that in Voloshinov's works the unconscious is quite frequently associated with the biological and that both of these are deemed to be simpler forms of psychic processes. In Freudian and neo-Freudian studies, by contrast, the biological occupies the center of attention as does the unconscious.

Having reconstructed Voloshinov's argument regarding consciousness from the ground up, we still need to weigh the social implications of his theory. If we return for a moment to the utterance as an expressible medium of communication—whether with oneself or with others—we will recall that Voloshinov considers it to be dialogic or intrapersonal. Consequently, all communication, even introspective mental activity is thoroughly social. There is only one situation in which the individual comes to "possess" the word in any way or form, and that is as he or she articulates a word. The physical act of articulation is, organically, individual by the very nature of our material composition as human beings—we are all physically unique (Voloshinov, *Marxism* 86). Beyond this, the whole of linguistic production and of thought itself is socially oriented; language is an intimate part of social relations in any society. However, Voloshinov's great contribution to sociolinguistics and to literary theory is his observation that if there are these close ties between social relations and language then one's place in these relations (one's class) has a determining effect on language and, therefore, on consciousness.

For Voloshinov, then, self-consciousness is always social. Class consciousness, and, I should hasten to add, gender and race identity, are major components of self-awareness. According to Volshinov, these are the "*objective roots* of even the most personal and intimate reactions" (Voloshinov, *Freudianism* 87). The heart and soul of bourgeois ideology is an individualism which requires one to rely very heavily on biological and biographical experience at the expense of social relations. In drawing the lines of demarcation for the subject, capitalism distorts the greater potentiality of human beings, it retards their growth, and thus, produces alienation. As a subject increasingly concentrates on the biological (the sexual, for instance) and the biographical to the detriment of the socio-economic and historical, the more *alienated* is the individual from his or her fellow workers, the more *alienating* is the society. For Voloshinov, as well as for Marx and Engels, in bourgeois society there is a false sense of value that is attributed to the individual in isolation as though he or she were trans-social or not a part of a social class. But following the logic of Voloshinov's linguistic and sociological study, this is an abstraction, for only the articulation of the utterance (physiologically) is an individual expression. In spite of this uniquely individual act (the utterance), consciousness always remains and is social. Consciousness is always an expression of *social class*. (Although it must be underlined in passing that Voloshinov does not always make this connection evident.)

But why then—one might object—is this individualist attitude so prevalent in capitalism? Why do individuals belonging to the bourgeoisie feel so confident that the "survival of the fittest" is the "law of the jungle"? Voloshinov maintains that this individualist tendency among bourgeois thought is also a social product:

> Individualistic confidence in oneself, one's sense of personal value, is drawn not from within, not from the depths of one's personality, but from the outside world. It is the ideological interpretation of one's social recognizance and tenability by rights, and of the objective security and tenability provided by the whole social order, of one's individual livelihood. The structure of the conscious, individual personality is just as social a structure as is the collective type of experience. It is a particular kind of interpretation, projected into the human soul, of a complex and sustained socioeconomic situation (Voloshinov, *Marxism* 89).

In Marxism this analysis is known as "false consciousness": the bourgeoisie, precisely because of its class position in capitalism, is generally unable or unwilling to perceive the total social ramifications of its individualism, hence, it only "abstracts"—to borrow Bertell Ollman's term—a limited number of aspects of an issue (Ollman 23-83). Generally speaking, for instance, the bourgeoisie sees its own economic well being as something that is tied to its own internal prowess, that is the result of its own individual efforts when, if we take into consideration a greater number of factors, we find that that idea has little foundation in the material reality of capitalism. The subject thus conceived becomes a metaphor for the bourgeois class, whose economic interests are in opposition to those of the working class. To concentrate on the role of the subject per se is not, of course, a negative thing, but to devote all one's energy to the analysis of the individual to the detriment of one's own class and the class struggle, constitutes a distortion of real life conditions in capitalism.

It might help, at this point, to return to Voloshinov's notion of "behavioral ideology" to explain Voloshinov's conceptualization of consciousness more precisely. Behavioral ideology is composed of unofficial and official ideology, or inner and outer expression. Moreover, this notion entails a series of gradations or steps within the individual and society at large that vary from the lowest, "most fluid" level to the upper strata of our behavioral ideology (our consciousness). To the first of these levels, as it suggests, belong such things as "vague and undeveloped experiences, thoughts, and idle, accidental words that flash across our minds" and these "lack any sort of logic or unity." Those elements belonging to the second stratum "are a great deal more mobile and sensitive: they convey changes in the socioeconomic basis more quickly and more vividly" (Voloshinov, *Marxism* 92). Creative energy is stored in this second area which gives the upper level the opportunity to challenge or radically restructure (socio-)ideological systems. This maneuverability comes about in the upper level of consciousness where the ideological system has already had the occasion to "solidify" or to develop a higher degree of complexity. Consciousness, then, is not some incidental affair nor is it dependent upon the unconscious, rather while still:

> inside a conscious person's head as inner-word embryo of expression, is as yet too tiny a piece of existence, and the scope of its activity is also as yet too small. But once it passes through all the stages of social objectification and enters into the power system of science, art, ethics, or law, *it becomes a real force, capable even of exerting in turn an influence on the economic bases of social life* (Voloshinov, *Marxism* 90; my emphasis).

Once consciousness has reached this stage it gains the potential to become revolutionary; to challenge the legitimacy of the official ideology in the human subject and in society. In periods of economic and political decline—such as the Great Depression—Voloshinov concludes, a greater gap is created between official and unofficial ideology, so that a mental division of labor clearly emerges and prevents inner speech from manifesting itself in outer speech. "Motives under these conditions begin to fail, to lose their verbal countenance, and little by little really to do turn into a "foreign body" in the psyche. Whole sets of organic manifestations come, in this way, to be excluded from the zone of verbalized behavior and may become *asocial* (Voloshinov, *Freudianism* 89). In fact, however, Voloshinov's observations may only hold true for the bourgeoisie. This divide created between official and unofficial ideology may indeed become the modus operandi among the bourgeois class, which would rather forget or suppress the economic and political forces that allow it to be the ruling class. But the working class would presumably become more class conscious and, in the process, produce a species of synthesis of official and unofficial ideology, however, relying on the former more than on the latter. Revolutionary consciousness, then, would entail a high development of official ideology that would be the fruit of class struggle. Voloshinov recognizes this implicitly when he states, in another context, that the sign becomes the arena of class struggle (Voloshinov, *Marxism* 35). Following this logic, class consciousness too would be a product of the struggle among classes in capitalism.

Of course, there is not a direct correspondence between one's social class and one's class consciousness. The working class has the *potential* to assume power if it gains revolutionary consciousness, but, as we know, this development happens among *certain* sectors of the working class who then unite with other like-minded revolutionaries from different social classes to take over the means of production. Or it may not happen at all during that period in history. As left-wing political activists know, it requires a great deal of political agitation for revolutionary class consciousness to gel.

According to Voloshinov, one of the symptoms of societal decay, or of alienation, is the excessive emphasis on biological (the sexual in particular) and biographical factors. In Voloshinov's view, as the gap between outer and inner speech increases an accumulation of asocial and antisocial forces take hold that overestimate the place of the sexual or create an asocial (read: individual) sexuality. Moreover, this highlighting of the sexual generally comes about when the bourgeois family as an institution—and, by extension, the society as a whole—is disintegrating. It is important to underscore in passing that by "decay" and "disintegration" of capitalism Voloshinov refers to the heightening of the class struggle in the nation space and worldwide. Individualism—not individuality—is a symptom of this class strife.[5]

In essence, as the bourgeoisie's power begins to be threatened by other social classes or other bourgeois forces, as the institutions associated with the bourgeoisie's power come under fire, the ideology of this class begins to retreat back into itself, to look for ways that it might protect itself and reestablish its hegemony. The primacy of such social characteristics as individualism, inordinate attention to sexuality and the unconscious, is, in Voloshinov's estimation, symptomatic of the extreme alienation of the bourgeoisie and the petite bourgeoisie in capitalism. In this case it is true that Voloshinov's analysis does not devote enough attention to the question of the actual political and economic conflicts under capitalism that lead to this type of alienation. His study veers frequently from a close examination of the principal forms of alienation that are highlighted in Marx and Engels' work—in particular the class antagonism between the working class and the capitalist. Yet one must recognize, it seems to me, that Voloshinov decides to focus on linguistics and consciousness precisely because he believes that Marxism must develop a more sophisticated understanding of these areas of study.[6] In spite of these limitations, Voloshinov's work provides us with a provocative argument in favor of the connection between language, class consciousness, and subject formation, and a compelling antidote to poststructuralist notions of the subject.

In what follows, I argue that in the attempts of Lacan, Kristeva, Deleuze and

Guattari to supplant the ostensible lack of a subject in Marxism by importing psychoanalysis into its theoretical framework they follow a separate course that takes them away from Marxism and they do little, in fact, to build upon Marx and Engels' works.

Neo-Freudianism and the Mirror Stage in Lacan

One of the most influential psychoanalytic theorists to have a major impact on cultural studies, at least since the 1960s, is Jacques Lacan. His forays into the pre-conscious stage of human development, the concept of desire, the reconceptualization of the unconscious, and, particularly, the relation between language and subjectivity have left a lasting impression on anyone who engages in literary criticism in particular or cultural studies in general. The general thrust of Lacanian and post-Lacanian arguments finds its support in his theory of the "mirror stage" and in the pre-conscious formation of the subject. The former is said to be the primary stage of identification, the moment in which a human being gains perceptual knowledge of him or herself as a being separate or distinct from others. Succinctly stated by Lacan it is:

> drama whose internal thrust is precipitated from insufficiency to anticipation—and which manufactures for the subject, caught up in the lure of spatial identification, the succession of phantasies that extends from a fragmented body-image to a form of its totality that I shall call orthopaedic—and, lastly, to the assumption of the armour of an alienating identity, which will mark with its rigid structure the subject's entire mental development (Lacan 4).

In sum, in the mirror stage the subject sees himself as fragmented—as a series of images which are not yet one—and has fantasies about these different images of himself. He is, of course, not a self in the proper sense of the word during this stage. At this moment, then, the human subject is immersed in what Lacan terms the "Imaginary"—a pre-social, pre-linguistic state of being. Once human beings move on to the world of language and, thus, participate in society, they can never completely recover these original fantasies. These sensory desires, however, continue to comprise part of the subject's living experience. From this moment on, if you will, there is a kind of division of labor between the production of the imaginary in the unconscious and the production of symbols in consciousness. We are vexed by our (fragmented) desires which cannot entirely be redeemed in our adult life.

According to Lacan, this organic development takes place before what he terms the "social dialectic." Thus, significantly, the imaginary phase in one's life attains an almost autonomous status in the unconscious and can only be accessed by consciousness in the form of the symbolic. One's entry into the symbolic order establishes forever the priority of the social over the individual. In Lacan's analyses, the individual experiences reality heretofore through the mediation of language and becomes part of the symbolic order. It is at this stage that the subject develops as an effect of the symbolic—he becomes a "social being." However, once the subject has been initiated into the "social dialectic" or regular social relations, he or she is affected by the lack of oneness with his or her surroundings and is henceforth consigned to desiring the unattainable "other." For Lacan it is the moment that:

> decisively tips the whole of human knowledge into mediatization through the desire of the other, constitutes its objects in an abstract equivalence by the co-operation of others, and turns the I into that apparatus for which every instinctual thrust constitutes a danger, even though it should correspond to a natural maturation—the very normalization of this maturation being henceforth dependent, in man, on a cultural mediation as exemplified, in the case of the sexual object, by the Oedipus complex (Lacan 5-6).

From this moment on argues Lacan, the individual desires what he or she cannot fully grasp and he or she attempts to fill this gap via the symbolic, the very raw material—as we noted above—of the subject. Lacanian psychoanalysis, then, aims at uncovering the desire that pervades the inter-subjective domain, at dissecting the multiple signifieds unleashed by this desire:

> What is at stake in an analysis is the advent in the subject of that little reality that this desire sustains in him with respect to the symbolic conflicts and imaginary fixations as the means of their agreement, and our path is the inter-subjective experience where this desire makes itself recognized (Lacan 68).

The urgency of the analyst—and subsequently of the cultural critic—is to arrest desire, which is expressed in symbols and which Lacan says "envelop the life of man in a network so total that they join together, before he comes into the world" (Lacan 68). As becomes apparent, the social individual as such continues to suffer on the symbolic level and is never quite able to retreat to the abandoned "mirror stage." Desire, meanwhile, runs rampant and it is the analyst's duty to identify it in language and to allow the patient to divulge, through a type of metaphor of the mirror stage, what is plaguing him or her (81). The subject is always operating at a distance; he is incessantly pursuing his desires or fantasies in the real and these are negated concrete fulfillment. And this happens because the gap never existed in the preconscious stage, and because the symbol murders the thing, as Lacan puts it, and "this death constitutes in the subject the eternalization of his desire" (Lacan 104). Thus, desire is an ephemeral goal which will never be attained and the subject consistently undergoes what Lacan calls *méconnaissance*, that is, the individual faces something other than what he or she wants in the form of desire. It is then a question of forever being alienated from, or chained to, these unconscious desires. However, the genesis for this alienation takes place before the subject's entry into language. Thus, it is not social alienation to which Lacan refers here; but rather a type of phenomenological alienation: one is never able to fully perceive the world nor oneself. As Peter Dews notes it is not that Lacan abandons completely the social implications of this alienation, but rather, for Lacan the:

> fundamental problem consists in the rise of modern individualism, and the consequent 'increasing absence of all those saturations of the super-ego and ego ideal that are realized in all kinds of organic forms in traditional societies, forms that extend from the rituals of everyday intimacy to the periodical festivals in which community manifests itself' (Dews 238).

This alienation can best be summarized by turning to Lacan's theory of language and consciousness. As we noted above, the principal corpus of the symbolic is located in language, whose structure Lacan tells us, is in consciousness and the unconscious (Lacan 298). For Lacan, the unconscious and what is produced in it have linguistic properties. Thus, for example, dreams have the structure of a sentence, a psychological symptom is also structured like language, and the unconscious per se is part of "concrete discourse" (Lacan 49). But how, then, does one distinguish between consciousness and the unconscious? Lacan believes that the latter is "that part of concrete discourse, in so far as it is transindividual, that is not at the disposal of the subject in reestablishing the continuity of his conscious desire" (Lacan 49). At other moments he describes the unconscious as a "blank" or as "occupied by a falsehood" (Lacan 50). In any case, the subject is, of course, composed of the combination of consciousness and the unconscious, and all forms of consciousness rely on language for their substance. But what complicates the matter of subjecthood is that it entails more: it also includes the inheritance of preconscious material collected in the "mirror stage" as well as images—the stuff of the imaginary—which are not recorded in language. Lacan contrasts the symbolic, a representative of the social order and of language, with the imaginary relation that connects the ego to its fragmented images—its fantasies. In defining consciousness Lacan, then, encounters his first major obstacle in the idea of the imaginary because it is not "specific" and is not "determinant" (Lacan 191). Unlike other processes in the unconscious or consciousness, the imaginary is less concrete; it cannot be more or less pinned down in language.

But the main problem that prevents Lacan from undertaking a materialist analysis of consciousness is the Saussurian theory of language. Since language, for Saussure, as well as for Lacan, is a closed order, and since there is an arbitrary relation between the signifier and the signified, language, according to Lacan, becomes an imperfect medium. Consequently, it is an "illusion" to believe that the signifier represents the signified (Lacan 150, 166). To be sure, it would be foolhardy to claim otherwise; the signifier can only be a social approximation of the signified. But the turning point to observe here is that Saussurian theory impedes Lacan's understanding of consciousness because it conceives of the system of language, as Voloshinov argues, as "an objective fact external to and independent of *any* individual consciousness." Voloshinov sees a paradox in the fact that Saussurian linguistic theory contends that language is outside of individual consciousness at the same time that it can only be scrutinized within the realm of individual consciousness (Voloshinov, *Marxism* 65). Thus, Voloshinov contends, reality according to the abstract objectivists, is unmediated; it does not pass through language as a social system any more than it navigates through human subjects (Voloshinov, *Marxism* 67). Following this logic, Lacan's theory of consciousness (and of language) is severely impaired by his adoption of Saussurian linguistics. At the same time he is aware that linguistics, at least as it is formulated by Saussure, cannot fully account for consciousness and the unconscious. Thus, Lacan speaks of the human subject's enslavement to language and of its limitations (Lacan 148-50).

Consequently, Lacan's skeptical attitude toward language parallels his stance vis-à-vis consciousness. In spite of the fact that language is the product of intersubjectivity, we have seen that the signifier never grasps completely the heterogeneity of the signified, and so the subject undergoes a continual process of alienation. However, this is not the type of alienation that derives from one's social or productive relations, rather it is the result of alienation in the process of becoming. The only sense of plenitude the subject achieves is in the pre-conscious, mirror stage, which is anterior to his socialization, his entry into the symbolic order. Since consciousness is based on language, the subject cannot consciously access his lived experience in the pre-conscious phase of his life. The unconscious, we might recall, also relies upon language and, in fact, the psychoanalyst's duty includes some sort of untangling of the language of the unconscious and the interpretation of that language. In short, then, it is not wholly inaccessible to the subject thanks to psychoanalysis. But the real and the imaginary, for Lacan, extend almost beyond the reach of the subject. Once the subject enters the symbolic order, he forfeits his claim to the real—which is the raw material outside or before language. Nor can the individual communicate with the imaginary; instead he relegates himself to substituting objects for the utopian stage of the imaginary. Hence, both of these realms of his life experience are not part of his conscious intention. In the end, the unconscious, in Lacan's view, involves the subject's impossible representation in inter-subjectivity and language, and the inaccessibility of the pre-conscious mirror stage, while it haunts human beings all their lives. More importantly, since there is a fissure in communicative possibilities at the level of language, and since consciousness is based on language, then conscious action can be perceived, in many ways, as hopeless. In contrast, it is worth recalling that for Voloshinov "behavioral ideology" extends not only to language (both oral and written), but also to all human gestures, thus, consciousness, in Voloshinov's estimation, can be objectively defined or described.

Thus, in concluding, while Lacan goes beyond Freud by shifting the emphasis in the study of consciousness from the biological to the linguistic, he adheres to Saussurian linguistics rather than socio-linguistics and thus de-emphasizes the social dimension of the relation between human beings and language (Dews 51-53). By extension, Lacan ends up psychologizing consciousness from an abstract objectivist point of view because, consciousness, like language, is a closed system that cannot intrude upon the pre-conscious state of being. A subject's "becoming" in an ontological sense becomes the primary focus of his work. The result of Lacan's analysis is that social or productive relations or even one's class, race, or gender appear to have little bearing upon one's formation as a subject, upon one's consciousness. Lacanianism, then, breaks with Marxism the moment it posits the formation of the subject as an asocial product. Consciousness per se becomes an a-social a priori which then rules over the subject even after human beings have entered the realm of the "real," and this, besides creating an operating dualism in Lacan's thought, contradicts the founding principles of classical Marxism. From the angle of Lacanianism one can only voluntaristically impute to a subject some class, gender, or racial social descriptions. Yet even if one does so, as a Lacanian, he or she must recognize the privilege accorded to the pre-conscious and pre-social in Lacan's works, which only serves to undermine the intent of the Lacanian.

Supplementing the Gap? Kristeva's Theory of the Subject

At the beginning of this essay I cited a passage from Kristeva's "The System and the Speaking Subject," which was published at a stage in her career when she perceived a need to correct the "inadequacies" of a Marxist theory of the subject. She contends, as we have seen, that while Marxism is able to furnish a very effective explanation of social relations in society it has no theory of meaning or of the subject (Moi, *The Kristeva Reader* 31-32). I have argued that while it is true that Marx and Engels did not devote the bulk of their work, nor even a major treatise to the study of linguistics or the "theory of the subject," they did, nonetheless, indicate the direction in which a materialist analysis of consciousness might lie. Rather than building on these Marx and Engels' initial intuitions on this issue, she borrows from systems of thought that are philosophically incompatible with Marxism, and, thus, seems to undermine her own project. It is only by surrendering key concepts in Marxist thought that Kristeva can introduce a theory of language and the subject into Marxism. For this reason, although her writings have been considered to be congruous with Marxism, they represent a significant departure from it.

If my hypothesis is true, then why would Kristeva not pick up on these original insights? What prevents her from conceiving of subjectivity in the main of Marxist epistemology? First, her studies of Marxism take place during the post-1968 era in French left-wing politics. She engages in Marxism at an historical moment when the PCF had advocated the primacy of the productive forces to the detriment of the social relations of production. Thus, the dialectical relation between the two elements of production is somewhat obscured by the reign of this specific type of Marxism in France. So the question of subjecthood and of meaning do indeed *appear to be* extraneous to Marxist thought. Second, her training as both a linguist and psychoanalyst leads her to the conclusion that these disciplines might provide an answer for the lack of a "theory of the subject" and of "meaning" in Marxism. Kristeva then forges a concept of meaning and of the subject based on the fundamental premises of semiotics. But her version of semiotics is one that has psychoanalytic overtones. Semiotics becomes, as we will see below, a voice for the unconscious. Third, her neo-Saussurian linguistic research guides her to the major aporia of Saussurianism: the signifier cannot possibly due justice to the multiplicity of the signified. Once Kristeva detects the crack in the foundation, she then looks to supplement it with what we might term her "psychoanalytic semiosis." For Kristeva semiotics becomes a method for explaining the development of subjectivity in the unconscious as well as its general processes.

It is against this background that she launches her theory of the subject and meaning. This history helps us understand why it is that a rift opens up between theory and practice in her works. Kristeva's objective is to establish a semiotics within scientific practice and theory, but the latter is consistently developed at the expense of the former. Thus, she envisions semiotics as a "mode of thought where science sees itself as (is conscious of itself as) a theory" (Moi, *The Kristeva Reader* 77). From the start, then, the practice of science is not as much of a concern for Kristeva as is the *theory* of science, or, as she terms it later, a "science-theory of discourse" (Moi, *The Kristeva Reader* 85). Given the history that we sketched out above, the division created between the productive forces and the relations of production, Kristeva attempts to construct a bridge between these two realms. Following the Althusserian tradition of the imaginary as the locus for the interpellation of the individual with the social, Kristeva posits semiotics as the glue that will hold these two spheres together. The result of her investigation is that her work is unable to transcend the Althusserian threshold of production within theory on the one hand, and infinite imaginary (or semiotic) production on the other hand. Social relations, in Kristeva's studies, therefore, are for all practical purposes dissolved. Consequently, in working out what she conceives of as a materialist representation of the subject and of meaning, her theory is unable to fully fill the gap established between the theoretical framework—her own version of semiotics— and the practical or objective world.

Thus, while there are some fundamental differences between Freud and Kristeva, I would argue that the three major charges leveled by Voloshinov at Freud can equally be applied to Kristeva's case: 1) Life in the biological sense stands at the center of her philosophical system; 2) she explores the unconscious because of her "distrust of consciousness"; 3) she puts subjective psychological and biological factors ahead of socio-economic ones (Voloshinov, *Freudianism* 12). For this reason, as I maintain below, Kristeva's theory is an idealist theory of the subject and of meaning that renounces conscious, class representation.

To begin with Kristeva's work let us consider her two most pressing areas of investigation: the attempt to elaborate a Marxist linguistics (or semiotics) and a post-Freudian theory of the subject. In the first instance, she appends a science of language to Marxism in order to engage the whole notion of linguistic representation. And the birth of language coincides with the inauguration of the social nature of the subject. But Kristeva wants to lay down the foundation for an area of study that she considers to be dangerously set aside by Marxism: the moment before

172 » **Greg Dawes**

one's initiation into the socially symbolic world before—and this follows the Althusserian reading of Lacan—one can interpellate oneself with the world. In short, her objective is to investigate the operations of the unconscious or of the pre-social state of being. To legitimize this type of research she first must prove conclusively that this is indeed a vital area for understanding human nature and that Marxism has neglected this domain.

For Kristeva, a new, rehabilitated neo-Saussurian semiotics involves doing a Marxist analysis of communication which somehow relies on the best of Marx's methodology—his studies of the value that underlie distribution, social consumption and production—while also going beyond Marx:

> But Marx clearly outlines another possibility: another space where work can be apprehended without any consideration of value, that is, beyond any question of the circulation of merchandise. There, on a scene where work does not yet *represent* any value or *mean* anything, our concern is with the relation of a *body* [a body of goods according to Marx] to *expenditure* [of human force]. Marx had neither the wish nor the means to tackle this notion of productive labor prior to value or meaning. He gives only a *critical* description of political economy: a critique of the system of exchange of signs (values) that hides a work-value (Moi, *The Kristeva Reader* 82).

Following Marx ostensibly, Kristeva claims that communication involves distribution, social consumption and production, and labor is its basis. In other words, communication is a form of production which exists thanks to labor. However, Kristeva feels that not enough attention has been paid to work before it becomes fully social and begins to rely on exchange value:

> In this way, Marx is led to study work as *value*, to adopt the distinction between use value and exchange value, and while still following the laws of capitalist society, to limit himself to a study of the latter. Marxist analysis rests on *exchange value*, that is, on the circulating *product* of work that enters the capitalist system as value ('a unit of work'), and it is in this way that Marx analyses its combinatory forces (workforce, workers, masters, object of production, instrument of production). (Moi, *The Kristeva Reader* 81)

The reasoning process is the following: if she can prove that Marx limited his research to the role of exchange value and not use value, then she must begin to examine the nature of this neglected use value which exists prior to its socialization. But this move, which purports to remedy the ills of Marxism, is a misreading of the notion of value in Marx's works. According to Marx, on the surface the commodity seems to consist of exchange value and use value. But if we dig deeper into the matter we find that each commodity is the fruit of abstract labor which is congealed in it. So the commodity is actually made up of the form of the appearance of value (exchange value) and value (the materialization of abstract labor). In Marx these two facets of the commodity must viewed dialectically: value creates the grounds for exchange value which is already latently present in value in capitalism. Therefore, exchange value is not external to value, but rather a living, albeit distinct, part of it. Thus while it may be true that much of Marx's work was dedicated to exchange value, in no way can one then say—as Kristeva does—that he limits himself to exchange value alone. Instead Marx looks at the way value is created by productive forces and relations in capitalism.

Since Kristeva believes that there is a terrain outside of exchange value that has been left untouched—the pre-conscious—she works Freud into the analysis because Marx purportedly cannot account for work done before its socialization and because Freud permits one to "think of the work involved in the process of signification as anterior to the meaning produced and/or the representative discourse; in other words, the dream-process" (Moi, *The Kristeva Reader* 83). Freud's method provides a way of digging up the development of "'thinking' before thought" (Moi, *The Kristeva Reader* 84). Thought refers to conscious mental processes, whereas thinking prior to this rational procedure is deemed unconscious (dreamwork). Thus, the unconscious becomes the unexamined raw material—in this instance biological—on which pyschoanalysis will lay its claims. The rupture between exchange value and use value which Kristeva observes in Marx's work therefore serves as the springboard for the break between consciousness and the unconscious. As Kristeva sees it, the challenge for semiotics is to "look at the difference between the types of signifying production prior to the product (value)" (*The Kristeva Reader* 85).

Once she putatively establishes the limits of Marxism, she then maps out her exploration of the unconscious, which will increasingly occupy her research. One of the most salient features of her reading of Freud, on the other hand, is the unsurmountable tension that arises between the institutions in society and the drives or "energy charges" of the subject before he is constituted as such. This pre-subject or subject in the process of being—very Heideggerian in nature—consists then of *chora*, or a "non-expressive totality formed by the drives and their stases" (Moi, *The Kristeva Reader* 93). In concert with Lacanianism, meaning or value prior to our socialization as human beings is inaugurated during this stage of our lives:

> The theory of the subject proposed by the theory of the unconscious will allow us to read in this rhythmic space, which has no thesis and no position, the process by which significance is constituted (Moi, *The Kristeva Reader* 94).

So it is that the subject's conception of meaning and value is constructed in the unconscious and not in a conscious phase of development. The notion of the subject *per se* also remains just beyond the reach of consciousness and can only be opened up by studying the signifying system in the unconscious.

Having purportedly validated her contentions about Marxism's weakness in the area of the unconscious, Kristeva must then defend a theory of meaning which is firmly anchored in linguistics. For Kristeva semiotics is a self-critical science for analyzing signifying systems of all sorts. This method pays particular attention to the mediation between image and object—the symbolic (Moi, *The Kristeva Reader* 101-103). In following the work of C. S. Peirce, Kristeva posits the symbol as the lowest common denominator in semiotics. According to Peirce it consists of a replica (the signifying unit) and an object (the interpretant, the idea, the signified). What semiotics must do is to look at the relationship between the replica and the object as well as "the series in which these replicas can be placed" (Moi, *The Kristeva Reader* 64). Part of Kristeva's own interest in the unconscious might have been enhanced by Pierce's belief that an unconscious existed before perceptual judgments, or, our first stage of cognition. Therefore, in this linguistic theory too, Kristeva discovered that language had a proverbial point of no return—it simply could not faithfully act as a mediator. Kristeva also finds support for the Freudian idea of the symbolic in the work of Saussure, for whom the sign undergoes arbitrariness while the symbol does not (Moi, *The Kristeva Reader* 25, 68, 91). Here, as we will maintain below, we come upon the same type of problem that emerged in Lacan: the arbitrariness of the sign leads to the "unfixity" or impossibility of language itself; language falls shy of communicating our conscious life.

Kristeva's major contribution to both linguistics and psychoanalysis may be her identification of the origin of signification for human beings. Since the unconscious is the locus of subjectivity and meaning, when does one emerge from this state into a social state of being? As we remarked above, according to Kristeva, in the pre-conscious phase of development human beings are centers of *chora* or a "non-expressive totality formed by the drives and their stases in a motility that is as full of movement as it is regulated" (Moi, *The Kristeva Reader* 93). Or, as she puts it later, *chora* is analogous to "vocal or kinetic rhythm" (Moi, *The Kristeva Reader* 94). More importantly perhaps, this is the stage at which human beings have not yet formulated a linguistic sign; in other words, it is pre-linguistic. Thus, the theory of the unconscious proposed by psychoanalysis elaborates a theory of the subject which "allows us [psychoanalysts, Semioticians] to read in this rhythmic space, which has no thesis and no position, the process by which significance is constituted" (Moi, *The Kristeva Reader* 94). The constitution of meaning begins once one reaches the *thetic* stage and is thus initiated into the symbolic, which, as in the case of Lacan, is the equivalent of the social. One consequently passes from what Kristeva calls the *genotext* (the pre-symbolic) to the *phenotext* (language for communication, the symbolic).

It is important to observe that Kristeva replaces Lacan's notion of the imaginary with the semiotic, which, along with the symbolic composes the total signifying process. At the same time that the semiotic participates in the signifying process, according to Kristeva, it is marginal to language, it is outside conscious knowledge. Since the late 1970s her investigations have concentrated primarily on the deviations from the linguistic or symbolic order. In her Maoist years, in the 1960s and 70s, the symbolic order was associated with patriarchy, capitalism, or spaces that language could not map out (e.g., the chora). By the late 1970s and early 80s it was delimited to meaning any disruption of the symbolic in language. The chora's heterogeneous flow cannot be fully repressed under the symbolic order and it is this semi-autonomous status that allows the chora to keep the symbolic order in check, to test the limits of the symbolic.

In her later essays, then, notably in "Psychoanalysis and the Polis" (1981), Kristeva's theory is further intensified and loses much of its rational grounding. Meaning itself comes to be equated with infinite production because of the pulsation of desire (Moi, *The Kristeva Reader* 312). The very purpose of existence for human beings is relegated to a search for the Other via desire (Moi, *The Kristeva Reader* 311). And one particular symbolic figure emerges among the signifying system, the *abject*, which is the locus of needs, attraction and forbidden desire and which is anterior to the difference between subject/object (Moi, *The Kristeva Reader* 317). All of these declensions of desire cannot manage to find their complete or even partial expression in human activity because desire, like meaning, reproduces *ad infinitum*. This emphasis on desire comes at the expense of a stable or reliable conception of reference. As the abject takes on greater proportions in Kristeva's theory, the possibility of describing objective reality becomes something less feasible. Consequently, it appears that the philosophy which she espouses becomes increasingly tied to relativism and subjectivism. For instance, in a passage on delirium "subjective truth" becomes just as legitimate as "objective truth," it:

masks reality or spares itself from a reality while at the same time saying a truth about it. More true? Less true? Does delirium know a truth which is true in a different way than objective reality because it speaks a certain subjective truth, instead of a presumed objective truth? (Moi, *The Kristeva Reader* 308).

This, then, is as good as a place as any to begin with a critical appraisal of Kristeva's work. This last passage illustrates very clearly the idealist tendency in her thought because what it does ultimately is to question the validity of objectivity reality. The gist of her philosophy could essentially be: is there an objective reality? This query explains the whole movement of her works: she cannot accept the existence of an objective reality which would somehow gain the upper hand on subjective reality (read: on the "autonomous" nature of the unconscious). And in the heart and soul of this autonomy, this sanctimonious domain of freedom, lies the privileging of the unconscious or of the pre-conscious stage of human development which, it should be noted, relies on Freud and Lacan's theory of the unconscious.

Let us retrace the logic of Kristeva's argument in order to question its very premises. Her principal aim is to supplement Marx with a "theory of meaning" or "the subject" because, as she alleges, Marxism has neglected these areas. But Kristeva's premise is falsified from the very start by its equation of the category of value with a process of pure semiosis. Because, according to the labor theory of value, labor comes to be represented by a quantity of exchange value, Kristeva concludes that value itself, including use value, must, like meaning, be understood along purely semiotic lines. This constitutes already a complete break with Marxism, for which value, despite its capacity under capitalism to assume abstract, symbolic expression, is not just a sign or a representation but rather an objective reality based on society's productive and reproductive needs. Thus, Kristeva pretends to find, within Marxism, an unexplored area requiring the supplement of Freudian theory for its illumination. This is misguided. Her thinking is idealist from the beginning, and her attempt to provide a Marxist foundation for what she is proposing is based upon the fallacy of equating value with meaning.

How does this idealist tendency come about in Kristeva's writings? She, like Lacan, relies on Saussurian linguistics for the construction of a theory of consciousness and the unconscious. Once she perceives a rupture in the possibility of the signifier to represent the signified, then she gives up conscious representation altogether. Consequently, like Lacan, Kristeva does not transcend the closed order that operates in Saussurian linguistics nor does she seem to want to understand the mediational role that language plays in the formation of history. Instead, in accordance with the Saussurian view, linguistics becomes an "autonomous," self-regulating, objective system that functions independent of human subjects. This idea of language leads Kristeva to perceive it as an almost pure production devoid in any real sense of social relations.

Let us turn to the relation between language and the formation of the subject. As in the case of Lacan, the subject experiences a sense of plenitude prior to his entrance into the symbolic order, into language. As we noted above, Kristeva's intent is to prove that this pre-social state of being and dreamwork have a determining effect on the formation of the subject and of meaning. However, in the process, Kristeva, in a return to Freudian theory, reinforces the primacy of the biological and subjective nature of subjecthood. For what the chora suggests is that the individual is an unmediated form of organic energy in the pre-linguist phase and that this phase in one's life is driven by the unconscious. In positing the unconscious as a semi-autonomous realm which takes charge of such matters as desire and need, Kristeva essentially duplicates the Saussurian isolation of language in her notion of the unconscious as well as in her theory of the subject. Consequently, one ends up with an individual who comprises three generally self-sufficient areas: language, the unconscious, and (conscious) social life. However, it is the "uncontrollable" unconscious that really defines the "essence" of subjecthood—one's desires and needs—independently of social relations. Given her Saussurian linguistic orientation, like Lacan, Kristeva believes that the signifier simply cannot satisfy the plethora of meanings that the signified generates any more than society can satisfy the wants and fantasies of human beings.

Thus, in spite of her intentions to remedy Marxism by supplying it with a theory of meaning and of the subject—which it ostensibly lacked—Kristeva, in both her linguistic and psychoanalytic studies, veers in the direction of subjectivist philosophy. Her position on the subject and Marxism is established by setting reflection theory up as a philosophical strawman: "naive reflection theory," so the argument goes, fails to register the subtleties of the interaction between linguistic and social phenomena. Reflection theory collapses subject and object; linguistic and social. But this is only so if one prescribes to a mechanistic, undialectical reflection theory. In reaction to this reflection theory, Kristeva, herself, abdicates before mediation and opts for pure production.[7]) In so doing, she abandons a materialist understanding of consciousness and subject formation in favor of an idealist narrative. In attempting to fill a gap in Marxist theory—the lack of a theory of the subject—Kristeva imports idealist thinking and tries to integrate it with Marxist philosophy, but this move proves to be detrimental to Marxism, for it negates its foundational principles rather than building upon them.

Deleuze and Guattari's Schizoanalysis

In their controversial pioneering work, *Anti-Oedipus: Capitalism and Schizophrenia*, Felix Guattari and Gilles Deleuze claim to lay the grounds for a materialist analysis of political, linguistic, and philosophical representation. Their work has gained a great deal of legitimacy in cultural studies, appealing mostly to anarchist or "new democratic" political expressions in the United States and in Europe. At their hands, the canonicity of psychoanalysis certainly undergoes a radical and welcome rereading. Indeed, it is this aspect in particular that makes their writings attractive to literary critics, because they are able—at least initially—to unmask the metaphorical guise of Freud's conception of the Oedipus Complex. In *Anti-Oedipus*, however, Deleuze and Guattari counter with what they perceive to be a materialist understanding of the psyche that, on closer inspection, rests on the premise that the unconscious and material, social reality are perfectly congruent. To be sure, there are parallels that can be drawn between the two in Voloshinov's sense: the unconscious as "unofficial ideology," as an alienated form of "inner speech." Nevertheless, for Voloshinov there is never an *immediate* identity between the unofficial ideology and the potential decline of capitalism. Consciousness, according to Voloshinov's argument, always involves the *mediation* of speech and of language. But Deleuze and Guattari see this relation in the opposite way: the real itself is declared to be simply a "product" of the unconscious; it is the unconscious that produces social reality, not vice versa, as in the writings of Voloshinov. By positing the relationship between the unconscious—consciousness itself is set aside—and the real as one of "production" rather than representation, Deleuze and Guattari believe they have taken the road to materialism. This is analogous to Kristeva's fallacious equation of value with meaning. In both cases these thinkers isolate one of Marx's prominent categories of analysis, drain it of its specific meaning in this context, and then proceed to make it the centerpiece of their neo-Freudianism. In so doing, they break with Marxism from the very start.

By selecting production as a substitute for representation, Deleuze and Guattari establish an a priori that does not consider representation in production from its mediation with human subjects. Desire, for Deleuze and Guattari, "produces" but it does not "represent." With this supplementation, they think they have solved the problem of subject; for production, unlike representation, can be conceived as occurring without conscious mediation. But this move compounds the problem. Since they ostensibly erase representation and, hence, yield to "pure production," human agency as a potential mediatory transformer of historical circumstances is also erased. Ultimately, as John McCarthy has lucidly observed, the flow of the pure intensities of desire capitulate to the open flow of capitalism itself and to the further dehumanization of the human subject.[8]

In political terms, by collapsing desire into material forces in capitalism (the economy), and by discarding representation in toto, they have given up the tools to change it. Non-representability, or the open flows of desire, are an impossibility; some type of representation exists and will exist everywhere and it is our duty as revolutionaries to seize those means of mediation or to create our own. In other words, proletarian self-representation (read: egalitarianism) in the aesthetic, political, and economic realms can only be crafted when we have appropriated the means of representation and production in those realms and changed the contour of mediation itself.

Let us commence with Deleuze and Guattari's theory of the subject or of the psyche: their critique of the Oedipus complex in particular and Freudian psychoanalysis in general. According to Deleuze and Guattari, once we accept the Oedipus complex and its structural expectations, then we confine ourselves within an ideological construct or within a symbolic configuration and thus lose sight of desiring production:

> The fact is, from the moment that we are placed within the framework of Oedipus—from the moment that we are measured in terms of Oedipus—the cards are stacked against us, and the only real relationship, that of production, has been done away with. The great discovery of psychoanalysis was that of the production of desire, of the productions of the unconscious. But once Oedipus entered the picture, this discovery was soon buried beneath a new brand of idealism: a classical theater was substituted for the unconscious as a factory; representation was substituted for the units of production of the unconscious; and an unconscious that was capable of nothing but expressing itself—in myth, tragedy, dreams—was substituted for the productive unconscious (Deleuze and Guattari 24).

The Oedipus complex then misguides psychoanalytic theory from the original object of its research: the production of the unconscious and of desire. For Deleuze and Guattari, Freudian psychoanalysis triangulates the unconscious—which becomes equated with desire or open flow—and thus limits its energy to symbolic representation. By rejecting the legitimacy of the Oedipus complex, Deleuze and Guattari do indeed step beyond the borders of symbolic representation—and beyond the interpretations of both Lacan and Kristeva—to embark on an ambitious assessment of psychology from what they allege is a materialist standpoint. Their goal ultimately is to bypass mediation and to encourage self-representation:

> Wouldn't it be better to schizophrenize—to schizophrenize the domain of the unconscious as well as the sociohistorical domain, so as to shatter the iron collar of Oedipus and rediscover everywhere the force of desiring-production; to renew, on the level of the Real, the tie between the analytic machine, desire, and production? For the unconscious itself is no more structural than personal, it does not symbolize any more than it imagines or represents; it engineers, it is machinic. Neither imaginary or symbolic, it is the Real itself, the "impossible real" and its production (Deleuze and Guattari 53).

According to Deleuze and Guattari the unconscious represents itself; it needs no forms of mediation and any form of representation necessarily obstructs its activity. At Freud's hands, in other words, the unconscious—specifically the Oedipus complex—becomes a species of ideology because he reduces its field of influence. To schizophrenize, for Deleuze and Guattari, is to unchain the unconscious; to allow it to flow. Hence, while these authors applaud psychoanalysis for the discovery of the unconscious, they feel that the Oedipus complex succumbs to idealism. For them, desire runs rampant and is trapped or repressed by myriad forms of representation which drain it of its energy. The production of desire, as they note in Chapter One, is real:

> If desire is productive, it can be productive only in the real world and can produce only reality. Desire is the set of *passive syntheses* that engineer partial objects, flow, and bodies, and that function as units of production. The real is the end product, the result of the passive syntheses of desire as autoproduction of the unconscious. Desire does not lack anything; it does not lack its object. It is rather the *subject* that is missing in desire, or desire that lacks a fixed subject; there is no fixed subject unless there is repression. Desire and its object are one and the same thing: the machine, as a machine of a machine. Desire is a machine, and the object of desire is another machine connected to it (Deleuze and Guattari 26).

Note that Deleuze and Guattari speak of "autoproduction"; there is no regulation of production in the unconscious. The subject appears as decentered or in flux unless he or she is being socially repressed. The ideal or fulfilled moment that Deleuze and Guattari depict, is for the subject to be open to the multiplicity of the forces of desire without any intervention in his or her affairs. As we can see, they do coincide with Kristeva and Lacan at least in this: capitalism restricts the flow of desire through repression and thus retards the growth of the subject. For Deleuze and Guattari, however, the issue goes even further: all representative entities (whether they are the Oedipus Complex or the State) cannot fully contain the flows of desire no matter how they might attempt to do so (Deleuze and Guattari 66-68). Hence, we might paraphrase the authors for a moment and claim that democratic forces (or self-governing groups) cannot be held back regardless of the repressive barriers that are placed before them. The self apparently finds a place in this scheme as a major architect of his or her future.

Now this auto-representation crosses what would be commonly conceded domains, from sexuality to the political and economic to the linguistic. Thus, for instance, in language the signifier is perceived to be "despotic" because it constrains the multiplicity of meaning and centralizes or totalizes its expressiveness. Instead of allowing open communication between the self, nature, and society, previous layers of linguistic tradition prevail as the hegemonic interpretations of the world. Linked to the ruling class, this dominant version of meaning is absolutist, it skews the multiple intentionality of linguistic production. For Deleuze and Guattari a revolutionary position consists of acknowledging and allowing the infinite complexity of meaning to play itself out endlessly:

> [O]ne is struck by the complexity of the networks with which it covers the socius: the chain of territorial signs is continually jumping from one element to another; radiating in all directions; emitting detachments wherever there are flows to be selected; including disjunctions; consuming remains; extracting surplus values; connecting words, bodies, and sufferings, and formulas, things, and affects; connoting voices, graphic traces, and eyes, always in a polyvocal usage—a way of jumping that cannot be contained within an order of meaning, still less within a signifier (Deleuze and Guattari 204).

Here, and throughout *Anti-Oedipus*, Deleuze and Guattari seem to be aiming their attack at some sort of rigid, mechanistic rationalism that is unable to perceive the subtleties and nuances involved in the nexus between language and the world. The signifier, as they observe in the same chapter, never gets to the heart of the question, "What does it mean?" but rather dismisses it from the outset (Deleuze and Guattari 208). According to Deleuze and Guattari, the proliferation of meanings generated in language in some way resembles the production of the unconscious: both productive processes are arrested systematically in order to create a fixed form of meaning or symbolic interpretation.

The final stage to focus on in *Anti-Oedipus* is the political dimension. The direct correlative of the representation they have been addressing in sexuality and language is self-representation. What Deleuze and Guattari appear to be arguing is that a heterogeneous revolutionary movement should seize the state apparatus and the means of production and, in doing so, govern itself. The society, then, would move from capitalist to post-capitalist forces and relations of production. However, the most important ingredient in their work is that this revolution would not be carried out by a vanguard (a party), but rather, by "spontaneous groups" (Deleuze and Guattari 255-56). In spite of the historical tradition that shows this revolutionary tactic to be disastrous, Deleuze and Guattari advocate this "strategy" because they believe it is more consistent with "communist" principles and because they see "real socialism" in a process of decay—and ultimately of regression—in the Soviet Union and in the Eastern Bloc. One can understand their reaction to the old communist movement given the way it pushed for an economist agenda. While a critique of this movement and its tactics is surely needed and a rethinking of vanguard politics the paramount issue of our day, Deleuze and Guattari's solution to the question of revolutionary agency (and of agency in general) is insufficiently elaborated. As much as one would want to advocate socially egalitarian political and economic systems, to believe in self-representation, how do these movements avoid centralization? Moreover, an open-ended assertion of "self-representation" risks glossing over class, gender, and race differences. On a Marxist point of view, there would be no "self-representation" available to the capitalist class—their representation as class would begin to wane after the workers' revolution. Only working people would be allowed to "represent themselves." However, in Deleuze and Guattari's works there is no such clarification.

In sum, Deleuze and Guattari's defense of the unconscious or of desire as a "revolutionary" force does not, to my mind, find the needed support in the sociohistorical domains. When consciousness "strait-jackets" the unconscious and becomes yet another mode of repression in *Anti-Oedipus*, then do they not bequeath to capitalism all the capacity to act rationally (Deleuze and Guattari 338)? Does not rationality lose its potential to become revolutionary? Claiming that the unconscious is the motor force of change is tantamount to giving up revolutionary struggle all together—and thus opting for "micro struggles"—or to repeating the errors of the past and inviting capitalist forces to crush the spontaneist, revolutionary movement. Deleuze and Guattari's argument fits into the very framework that the capitalist system would like to envision for all "oppositional groups"; the ruling class would be delighted to know that the organizational and rational features of a potential class enemy have been dropped in favor of points of resistance or "escapes" from systemic oppression. When Deleuze and Guattari contend that escaping is a type of social investment that has a revolutionary potential, one can only think that this proposal involves a definite class bias which assumes that people have the free time and the money to create those alternative life styles and that the ruling class will simply sit back idly while individuals or communities take on this project (Deleuze and Guattari 341). In fact, of course, as long as the changes in a people's lifestyle do not interfere with the accumulation of capital, the ruling class will not be terribly disturbed by these transformations. Indeed, the ruling class might even grant certain concessions in the realm of sexuality say, because it could easily increase—and not decrease—the productivity of workers and enhance the consumption of commodities.

Is this, then, a new materialist philosophy? It is not for two reasons in particular: 1) it critiques dialectics indirectly and thus loses the relation between quantity and quality, a negation of a negation, and the interpenetration of opposites; 2) it ends up positing desire, in almost a pantheistic fashion, as the transcendental origin that is decentered. The most salient aspect of the first point is that the subject/object relation collapses in their analyses and, consequently—in spite of Deleuze and Guattari's analysis and development of the schizo—there is no human subject which can conceivably change the status quo except through "escapes." Human beings are quite simply subjected to the flows of the unconscious, which in the *Anti-Oedipus* becomes a synonym for material reality (Deleuze and Guattari 283). The problem is that if the unconscious represents areas of the physical world which are outside the realm of rational apprehension at the moment, then do we not give up our ability to shape the present or the future? Do not human beings, as John McCarthy has poignantly remarked, dissolve into "quantum epistemology"? The results of this type of nihilism, as McCarthy has conclusively shown is that:

> we might regard Deleuze and Guattari's reduction of the complex texture of individual and social relations to an essential constitution of rampant particles of desire as a Nietzschean desire for power through deconstruction. In postmodernism this will to power draws on the fluid epistemology of the quanta of modern physics and uses it to fragment social spaces and structures. The play of particles so formed is that of a cultural positivism in which the signifier behaves probabilistically in the form of the number. It is at this point of the rendering of culture into its elemental quantum numerics that the social field is most permeable to the passage of capital" (McCarthy 29).

What Deleuze and Guattari's philosophy offers, then, is something akin to abstract objectivism. The "desires" of the individual and the existence of human agency—in the form of conscious action—get lost in the plethora of "particle flows." Following this logic, human beings themselves become part of the particle flows, they become producers of the "intensities of desire" and nothing more. Thus, if one is to speak of Deleuze and Guattari's theory of the subject, one would have to yield immediately to the open field of new physics. This idea is encapsulated in McCarthy's description of the type of alienation that the subject undergoes in *A Thousand Plateaus*, "[T]he subject is deconstructed into its elemental particles and individual desire drawn out to join the cosmic flows of quanta. Dialectic of individual and social is ended and the individual is lost, both as a container and an agent for ethico-political concerns" (McCarthy 3). Gone, then, too is any concept of revolutionary agency.

Conclusion

All three of the neo-Freudian tendencies within poststructuralism that we have critiqued in this essay abandon the Cartesian "cogito" or the Fichtean romantic "ego," but they fail to supersede its constraints. In their attempt to replace these bourgeois theories of consciousness with more radical, materialist alternatives, they return unwittingly to their point of departure. In the cases of Lacan, Kristeva, Deleuze and Guattari, they all, like Freud in Voloshinov's critique, reify and treat as a transhistorical and pre-social category an alienated subject that is in fact a symptom of class relations under capitalism. Rather than focusing on the economic and political system that is at the root of the formation of the human subject, they focus on the inner recesses of the individual psyche, they "liberate" the unconscious and "treat" the subject. For Voloshinov, however, the key to attending to the alienation of individuals is to change the society, liberate the new, healthier form of social relations stirring within it, and the problem of the subject will become solvable. In Voloshinov's work, his analysis of inner and outward speech functions in social relations in general and in the type of relations prevailing in a given society. However, as I have noted in this essay, the relation between subject and class is not always that clearly articulated. This is especially true if we analyze capitalism dialectically. In spite of the various types of alienation that capitalism produces, subjects are able to counteract this alienation through political struggle. When these subjects—in particular of the working-class—are able to overcome this alienation through class solidarity, they can create more humane social and economic conditions within the space of capitalism even as they ultimately organize to dialectically transcend it because the antagonism between labor and capital continues to persist under capitalism.

Notes

I would like to thank Neil Larsen for his reading of and comments on this article.

1. See especially Marx's "Economic and Philosophical Manuscripts" in *Early Writings*, trans. Rodney Livingstone and Gregor Benton (New York: Vintage Books, 1975). See also Bertell Ollman's *Alienation: Marx's Conception of Man in Capitalist Society*, second edition (London: Cambridge University Press, 1976).

2. It is curious to note the way this more "orthodox" view of human nature has been either disregarded off-hand, or been appropriated and confused by post-structuralism. A prime case of this re-writing of history takes place in the so-called Voloshinov/Bakhtin controversy. It is not my intent to demonstrate that *Freudianism: A Critical Sketch* and *Marxism and the Philosophy of Language* were written Voloshinov and that he was not acting as a ghost writer for Bakhtin. Instead, these works are illuminating because the ideas expressed in them represent an organically Marxist whole and not some sort of collage pasted together in order to please the censors. In short, in pointing out some of the redeeming values of a Marxist theory of the subject, that one finds worked out in a specific way in Marx and Engles' writings as well as in Voloshinov's works, the objective is not so much to delve into the intricacies of this "crisis of authorship," as it is to evaluate Voloshinov's contributions to a Marxist critique of the bourgeois subject and to a Marxist conception of consciousness.

While I come down on the side of I. R. Titunik, Gary Saul Morson and Caryl Emerson with respect to this controversy, the fundamental issue is not *who* wrote these works, but rather *why* they were surreptitiously buried in Bakhtin's oeuvre. It seems to me that Voloshinov's credibility has been tarnished and subsumed by Bakhtin in the critics' eyes precisely because the real issue that lays behind all this controversy is Marxism itself, which can only be conceived, in the case of Clark and Holquist for instance, as mechanical Marxism. Marxism can only be imagined in the most rudimentary ways because of the historic events which have led to the fall of the Eastern Bloc and of the Soviet Union and to the momentary triumph of international capital and the persistence of anti-communist and Cold War thought. But it is equally true, that if these political defeats (or disasters) took place it is because of the erroneous conclusions reached by the Third International, and it is not due to the failure of Marxism as a whole. Hence the urgency to re-examine the detours that were taken along the way. Here I am confining myself to cultural theory, and in particular, to the theory of the subject, so hastily appended to Marxist epistemology from the very start.

An appropriate place to start is the flight from Marxism in one of pioneering works on the Voloshinov/Bakhtin case: that is, Katerina Clark and Michael Holquist's major work, *Mikhail Bakhtin*. To begin, it seems logical to assume, that if *Freudianism* and

Marxism were originally published in Voloshinov's name, then it is the critic's burden of proof to contradict and convincingly establish that this was not so. In my estimation, Clark and Holquist are never able to carry this through. At the beginning of their chapter on the "disputed texts," they even declare that "there is nothing on paper to resolve this controversy once and for all" (Clark and Holquist 147). Yet they continue to allege that these works were not so much the result of Bakhtin's *direct* intervention as the product of studies developed in the Bakhtin Circle and, hence, written under his tutelage (Clark and Holquist 149). They further maintain that both of these studies generally reflect Marxist strands of thought not because of the philosophical inclination of this circle, but rather because of the enormous pressure exerted on them by the "party dogmatists" of the 1920s and 30s. Thus, they conclude, "the reality is that all three, Bakhtin, Medvedev, and Voloshinov, became more Marxist in their writings of the late 1920s, as was necessary to ensure plausibility" (Clark and Holquist 155).

This is the recurring theme in their book: that Voloshinov and Medvedev (the author of *The Formal Method*) were mere collaborators or even students of Bakhtin who needed to pass as Marxists in order to be inaugurated into Soviet intellectual circles. The paramount issues of this debate relate in some way to the discrediting of Marxism *in toto* and not just to the critiquing of a particular type of Marxism. To take one example, Clark and Holquist engage in what could almost be seen as a willful misreading of the Marxism in *Freudianism* and *Marxism* by analyzing this epistemology reductively. The Marxism found in these two works, according to Clark and Holquist, is actually a "shrewd, well-worked-out strategy" by Bakhtin to slip these books past the censors (Clark and Holquist 159). And this Marxism, as these authors note, is less dogmatic than its counterpart because it challenges the assumptions of positivism, "vulgar sociologism" and "class hysteria" (Clark and Holquist 168). What this study dealing with authorship leads to most significantly is to a misconception or distortion of Marxism at the hands of Clark and Holquist. Their book says more about their lack of understanding of Marxism than it does about the actual authorship of either Bakhtin or Voloshinov. The Marxism attacked by Bakhtin is made synonymous with positivism, class hysteria, and a certain type of monolithic totalitarianism—which would prevent the publication of these works. To be sure, mechanical Marxism has been guilty of oversimplifying dialectics and materialism. But at no time can Marx and Engels' work itself be accused of exalting the values of positivism, class hysteria, or as veering away from a concept of "objective reality" (Clark and Holquist 159).

What is it that *Freudianism* and *Marxism* propound that ignites such a reaction in the minds of critics? If they are just other books in Mikhail Bakhtin's repertoire with a sufficient amount of window dressing to get them past the censors—then why do they stir up such virulent attacks on Marxism? Furthermore, why all the debate surrounding the question of authorship? What would be lost ultimately if the authorship were conceded to be Voloshinov's?

There is a political position involved which places both the *Marxism* and *Freudianism* books in a different category from Bakhtin's other works. Of course, this is not to deny some of their similarities, particularly as relates to linguistic research. But one of Voloshinov's most important contributions to Marxism, expounded upon in the last of these works, is his questioning of pre-conscious subject formation, the dichotomy created between consciousness and the unconscious as well as his critique of ideological nature of Freud's conception of subject formation, which, is incompatible with dialectics and historical materialism. See V.N. Voloshinov, *Marxism and the Philosophy of Language* , trans. Ladislav Matejka and I. R. Titunik (Cambridge, MA: Harvard University Press, 1986); and *Freudianism: A Critical Sketch* , trans. I. R. Titunik (Bloomington and Indianapolis: Indiana University Press, 1987).

3. For the classic account of this argument see Fredrick Engels' *The Origin of the Family, Private Property, and the State* (New York: Pathfinder Press, 1972). Among the Marxist/Feminist interventions, I find Nancy Hartsock's *Money, Sex, and Power: Toward a Feminist Historical Materialism* (Boston: Northeastern University Press, 1985) to be very insightful.

4. I have double-checked Voloshinov's observations with Sigmund Freud's *A General Introduction to Psychoanalysis* (New York: Garden City Publishing Co., 1938) and with John Rickman, M.D. ed. *A General Selection from the Works of Sigmund Freud* (New York: Doubleday, 1989).

5. For a remarkable study on communist individuality and the notion of moral realism, see Alan Gilbert's *Democratic Individuality* (Cambridge: University of Cambridge Press, 1990). "Democratic" and "communist" become virtually synonymous terms in his conception of a *real* democracy.

6. See Voloshinov's introduction to *Marxism and the Philosophy of Language* (Boston: MIT Press, 1986)

7. See Toril Moi's contradictory discussion of Kristeva's notion of language production in *Sexual/Textual Politics* (London and New York: Routledge, 1985), 157-171.

8. See McCarthy's critique of postmodernism, "Postmodern Pleasure and Perversity: Scientism and Sadism." *Essays in Postmodern Culture.* Eds. Eyal Amiran and John Unsworth. New York: Oxford University Press, 1993. I have cited from the original, unpublished manuscript.

Works Cited

Althusser, Louis. "Marx and Freud." *Rethinking Marxism* 4.1 (1991).
Bakhtin, M. M. and P. N. Medvedev. *Formal Method in Literary Scholarship: A Critical Introduction to Sociological Poetics.* Trans. Albert J. Wehrle. Cambridge, MA: Harvard University Press, 1985.
Clark, Katerina and Michael Holquist *Mikhail Bakhtin* Cambridge, MA: Harvard University Press, 1984.
Deleuze, Gilles and Felix Guattari. *Anti-Oedipus: Capitalism and Schizophrenia.* Trans. Robert Hurley, Mark Seem, and Helen R. Lane. Minneapolis: University of Minnesota Press, 1983.
Dews, Peter. *The Logics of Disintegration: Post-Structuralist Thought and the Claims of Critical Theory.* London: Verso, 1988.
Engels, Fredrick. *The Origin of the Family, Private Property, and the State.* New York: Pathfinder Press, 1972.
Freud, Sigmund. *A General Introduction to Psychoanalysis.* Trans. Joan Riviere. New York: Garden City Publishing Co., 1938.

_____. *A General Selection from the Works of Sigmund Freud.* Ed. John Rickman, M.D. New York: Doubleday, 1989.
Gilbert, Alan. *Democratic Individuality.* Cambridge: Cambridge University Press, 1990.
Hartsock, Nancy. *Money, Sex, and Power: Toward a Feminist Historical Materialism.* Boston: Northeastern University Press, 1985.
Lacan, Jacques. *Ecrits.* Trans. Alan Sheridan. New York: Norton, 1977.
Marx, Karl. "Economic and Philosophical Manuscripts."*Early Writings.* Trans. Rodney Livingstone and Gregor Benton. New York: Vintage Books, 1975.
_____. and Fredrick Engels. *The German Ideology.* Ed. C. J. Arthur. New York: International Publishers, 1977.
McCarthy, John. "Postmodern Pleasure and Perversity: Scientism and Sadism." Manuscript form. Published in *Essays in Postmodern Culture.* Eds. Eyal Amiran and John Unsworth. New York: Oxford University Press, 1993.
Moi, Toril, ed. *The Kristeva Reader.* New York: Columbia University Press, 1986.
_____. *Sexual/Textual Politics.* London and New York: Routledge, 1985.
Ollman, Bertell. *Alienation: Marx's Conception of Man in Capitalist Society.* London: Cambridge University Press, 1976.
_____. *Dialectical Investigations.* New York: Routledge, 1993.
Voloshinov, V. N. *Freudianism: A Critical Sketch.* Trans. I. R. Titunik. Bloomington and Indianapolis: Indiana University Press, 1987.
_____. *Marxism and the Philosophy of Language.* Trans. Ladislav Matejka and I. R. Titunik. Cambridge, MA: Harvard University Press, 1986.

Donald Morton

Queerity and Ludic Sado-Masochism: Compulsory Consumption and the Emerging Post-al Queer

One

Sexual practices—like other social practices—are undergoing radical changes in late multinational capitalism through modifications of the systems of "exchange." These changes are caused by objective forces that can neither be controlled by moral or ethical appeals to the individual—either from the Right ("Abstinence Until Marriage!") or the Ludic Left ("Do Your Own Thing!")—nor ultimately explained on subjective grounds. Changes in material forces require correspondingly different patterns of production, exchange, consumption, social organization—and also correspondingly different forms of ideological reproduction and subjectivity. It is in this light, for example, that the appearance on the cultural plane of such recent films as *Exit from Eden* (on sado-masochism) and *Ed Wood* (on transvestism) has to be understood. While conservatives and liberals—as two branches of the same camp of guardians of bourgeois morality, one more and one less "progressive"—regard these as "break through" movies signaling an increased tolerance for other sexualities that the one group fears and the other favors, these films are instead symptoms of the new ideological training needed to produce the different forms of subjectivity required by contemporary capitalism. These films point to the fact that, in a new form suitable for the 1990's, sex radicalism is itself being "mainstreamed" and erotic practices that were once regarded as "avant-garde" and thus "marginal" are now becoming "popular." Today's sex radicalism makes its claims in a theoretical/cultural/social/economic . . . environment quite different from that of 1960's sex-liberationism. Post-al theory has performed the ideological work late capitalism needs to have done by changing the very concept of radicality itself, so that the "radical" has lost its decided oppositionality. The sex radicals of the past (de Sade, Bataille, Henry Miller, Anais Nin, Jean Genet, Phil Andros/Samuel Steward) accepted—and even enjoyed—the rarefaction of their marginal positions. They asked, more or less, to be left alone in an uncompromisingly oppositional "bohemia" or adversarial "sub-culture" to pursue their interests in conscious antagonism with the bourgeois, which they recognized as by definition "marginal" interests which those in the "center" would not share. Today's post-al sex radicals and theorists want not merely to make the non-norm (margin) the norm (center), but to disrupt normativity itself. Since advanced bourgeois post-al theory substitutes for an identitarian logic (in which distinct entities have distinct identities) a Derridean supplementary logic (in which there is a playful "differential" relation between all entities in culture and no distinct identities), those occupying the place of the social and sexual "center" (if such a thing can be posited) are supposed to have a "share" in the interests of the social and sexual margins.

It has been clear for some time now that, as one of the main marginal sexual practices, homosexuality has become a central ideological focus in dominant academic and intellectual circles; has undergone—like sex radicalism in general—a thorough retheorization by bourgeois philosophers, critics, and commentators; and been reshaped in Queer Theory. As an "advanced" branch of (post)modern thought specializing in the reunderstanding of questions of desire and sexuality, Queer Theory serves a signal role in late capitalist ideological indoctrination—not just for those who identify themselves as queer/lesbian/gay but for everyone. What we are witnessing today is the emergence of the "post-al" queer which Queer Theorists represent as a set of social practices and a form of subjectivity that are said to be "progressive" because in addition to being supposedly non-natural, non-essentialist, and textuo-socially "constructed" they are differential and non-exclusionary and therefore "change-able." The claims to political "progressiveness," however, come into conflict with the underlying post-al theoretical assumptions: the claim to provide a pathway for the subject's "freedom" conflicts with the deconstructive notion of the undecidability of meaning at large and thus with the very problematization of any binary, including "the free"/"the unfree." In broad terms, for Queer Theory the queer subject is constructed by the processes of signification—"Homosexuality is textuality," one queer critic has declared (Bredbeck 255)—which, if one takes (post)structuralism on its own terms, are fundamentally aleatory, non-teleological, and anti-foundational and thus cannot provide the basis for moving the social formation in any particular direction. These contradictions lead to a crisis of "agency" in which the (post)structuralist subject, as a site of textual play driven by the liberation of repressed desire, is robbed of its ability to "act" in the familiar sense but "resolves" this contradiction by celebrating such "liberation" as a new form of "self-invention." In other words, this queer "textual constructionism" (as opposed to social constructionism) is ultimately a form of post-authorial "invention."

In her pre-post-al essay, "Compulsory Heterosexuality and Lesbian Existence," written before ludic (post)modern theory, deconstruction, and Queer Theory had made their broad impact on thinking about sexuality, Adrienne Rich argued that the oppression of lesbians is part of the gendered oppression of all women and is seen in the operations of the *structure* of an institutionalized heterosexuality: "heterosexuality," she said, "needs to be recognized and studied as a *political institution*" (232). Drawing on and extending the work of Kathleen Gough, she outlined the ways in which heterosexist structures enable gender-defined "male power" to be exercised materially over women: "*to deny women* [their own] *sexuality . . . or to force* [male sexuality] *upon them . . . to command or exploit their labor to control their produce . . . to control or rob them of their children . . . to confine them physically or prevent their movement . . . to use them as objects in male transactions . . . to cramp their creativeness . . . to withhold from them large areas of society's knowledges and cultural attainments*" (233). Rich also relied on the rigorous work of Catharine MacKinnon delineating "the intersection of compulsory heterosexuality and economics" that produces woman's "structurally inferior position in the workplace" (234). "We need an economics," she declares, "which comprehends the institution of heterosexuality, with its doubled workload for women and its sexual divisions of labor, as the most idealized of economic relations" (245). In the end, however, Rich is not arguing from a Marxist position, not arguing for the "determinateness" of structures: she proposes instead that women can liberate themselves largely voluntarily by choosing "woman identification [as] . . . a source of energy" and as "a potential springhead of female power" (244).[1] Lesbian sexuality, as Rich saw it, was significant as a practice that breaks through the structures of compulsory heterosexuality. While she opened herself predictably for critique from a broadly (post)structuralist perspective for the "structuralism" and "essentialism" implied by her essay, as for a critique from the historical materialist perspective for her "voluntarism," the essay's basic idea remains in the air today that what ultimately produces lesbian/gay oppression is compulsory heterosexuality. Yet this thesis is very difficult to maintain in the 1990's when bourgeois institutional structures are being liberalized so that, for instance, lesbian and gay couples can and do in fact receive the same employee benefits awarded to heterosexual couples. At the time Rich was writing the ideological "queering" of the social that would situate all subjects under the same regime of commodification had not yet occurred. Today the fact that under the regime of late multinational capitalism the homosexual wage laborer can be rewarded like the heterosexual wage laborer suggests that while Rich was right to call attention (however limitedly) to oppression in relation to structures and economics, ultimately she underestimated, among other things, the degree to which capitalism's changing imperatives would itself put pressure on an exclusively heterosexual structuring of desire. Seen in this light, the ultimate determinate structure is not one which promotes compulsory heterosexuality but one which promotes *compulsory consumption.*

Queer Theory has become a principal ideological arm of late capitalism because—as I have indicated elsewhere[2]—it promotes the elevation of desire and the near exclusion of the question of need. Queer Theorists have themselves helped to make this case: classical Marxist analysis will not be productive when applied to the queer subject, as one queer critic says, because urban gay male culture "is anything but external to advanced capitalism and to precisely those features of advanced capitalism that many of the left are most eager to disavow" (Warner, *Fear* xxxi). "Post-Stonewall gay men reek of the commodity," Warner continues, and "give off the smell of capitalism in rut" (xxxi). Such remarks only echo the post-Marxist cliché that there is no outside of the commodification process and that consumption itself "liberates." In today's supposedly post-production consumer society, Warner's urban gay male becomes exemplary. Since Queer Theory proposes itself as an explanation of the operations of desire relevant to all, it follows that all subjects are irresistibly subject-ed to the ever-expanding regions of commodity-fetishism. On this view, the public sphere is not a structured space of commonality for contesting the principles by which a just society can be ordered, but a cultural site overrun by an endlessly proliferating multitude of consuming libidinalities governed by "playful"—and thoroughly commodified—desire. Warner emphatically equates capitalist commercial institutions and practices such as bars, discos, brand-name recognition with such social practices as "camp" and "promiscuity" which he sees as the salient features of homosexual subjectivities. From this perspective, all subjects have been "queered"—that is, have become "cruising" Deleuzean nomads seeking to make themselves and others as "immediately consumable" (commodifiable) as possible—subjects, in other words, who regard living "from moment to moment"—without the capacity for or interest in rational calculation about the future—as the only life worth living. Thus, the glamorization throughout the culture industry of the "queer life-style" (a concept-subverting, reason-minimizing, pleasure-seeking mode of living) as a model of consumption on the international market. If lesbians seem to have been left out of this analysis as somehow "slower" than urban gay males to be drawn into commodifying processes, Danae Clark's recent essay on "Commodity Lesbianism" clearly shows they are very quickly "catching up." Indeed a recent commentator on "the lesbian postmodern" suggests that, like Warner's urban gay males, she and, by extension, other "(post)modern lesbians" are finally "helpless" before the processes of commodification (Doan 2ff). If lesbians have been "slower" to be drawn into "commodification," this by no means a question of their lack of sophistication and unawareness of contemporary fashions and pleasures (or theories about fashions and pleasures) but a result of the fact that as a group (because of the economic disadvantages of women in general) their buying power is not quite as high as that of gay males. Living from "moment to moment" has to be the mode of life under capitalism because it assigns priority to the extraction of surplus value from the labor of workers (maximization of profit) and not to the citizenry's basic needs for food, clothing, shelter, health care, education. . . . Under these conditions everyone is uncertain about the future (even the very short-term future). Thus a variety of bourgeois theorists—but especially Queer Theorists—have stepped in to justify the desperation of life under capitalism (its uncertainties) by proposing that an "undecidable," "moment-to-moment" life full of Deleuzean "intensity" is the best of all possible lives! Queer Theory's subject of desire (for whom desire is autonomous and unrelated to need) is a subject for whom the question of social responsibility (for fulfilling the citizenry's needs through rational calculations) is oppressive because it hints at collectivity and collectivity for the queer and the entrepreneur alike means "collectivism."

It is urgent to mark how the very understanding of homosexuality in mainstream intellectual and cultural circles has changed under the impact of accelerating capitalist commodification and under the ideological tutelage provided by (ludic) Queer Theory. The lesbian/gay subjects of the earlier gay liberation movement were subjects who, while recognizing the marginality of their sexual practices nevertheless put forward their demands for a place in the community by identifying themselves as oppositional citizens with something to offer the larger society by working for the right to their form of sexuality while locating sexuality itself as only one—if important—region of their subjectivity and their citizenship. They understood themselves as contributors to a generally beneficial process of social production which necessarily relied on rational calculations guiding whatever productive work activity is required to meet the needs of society at large both now and in the future. Even mainstream gay commentators like Frank Browning, who have examined it, have concluded that today's queer "culture of desire" is "on a journey separate from that of equity, democracy, and justice" (104). Without exaggerating the success of the earlier lesbian/gay movement in working in solidarity for the interests of all, I would argue that to a significant degree they accepted the notion that like all citizens they were, first and foremost, *subjects of need* and took on the responsibility of struggling over *which* kinds of rational and conceptual calculations (which theories about *need*) would make for a just society.[3] Under the ideological regime of Queer Theory, the subject is—first, last, and always—the *subject of desire* who takes the form of Warner's "cruising" (commodified/commodifying) subject and Deleuze and Guattari's "desiring machine" and lives for the "intensities" of the moment. The queer subject is utterly distrustful (incapable?) of rational calculations which inevitably "constrain" desire. The queer subject is, in other words, the model "consuming" subject for the regime of late capitalism.

Here I wish to inquire into the ongoing cultural and social shifts in the sexual arena by examining the connection of post-al queerity to the increasingly popular interest in the practices of sado-masochism. The next section of my discussion inquires into the structure of compulsory consumption and the emerging post-al queer under late capitalism by focusing on two bourgeois accounts of sado-masochism that reveal its increasing "popularity" as a result of shifting exchange values and corresponding changes in political economy. The last section inquires into and critiques a well-known historical materialist theorization of changes in sexual practices.

Two

In the mid-1980's Jeffrey Weeks described S/M practitioners as "the most radically transgressive members" of the "'sexual fringe'" who "remain marginal to the mainstream of most people's sexual lives" (85). Yet in her recent book, *Sadomasochism in Everyday Life* (1992), Lynn Chancer observes that "sadomasochistic sex figures more and more prominently in current U. S. practices and cultural imagery" and then offers a broad set of examples from the role of S/M in contemporary pornography and as a staple in the repertoire of practicing male and female prostitutes to the S/M clubs in many large U. S. cities to S/M's appearance as motif in contemporary films and even in television ads for Calvin Klein products and Guess jeans to a "suburban Tupperware-style party at which the display of S/M paraphernalia was greeted not with surprise but with curiosity" (20-22). As with Queer Theory, which has had an enormously affirmative reception in the culture industry and especially in both academic and commercial publishing, the increasing attention being given to sado-masochism immediately raises the question of the politics of its "popularity."

The new "popularity" of marginal sexual practices has to be historicized: the "popular" is not—as idealism proposes—the sign of a spontaneous irruption of a new phase in human consciousness but is instead the result of changes in the social relations of production which are ultimately determined by changes in the mode of production. Under capitalism, the "popular" is those goods (Nike sneakers), practices (eating low-fat foods) and people (winning politicians) that are successfully packaged, advertised, and sold as commodities with high *profit*-ability. Unlike the sales of luxury items (Mercedes-Benzes, diamonds . . .), where profit-ability is more or less "obvious," in the popular arena, the extraction of "profit" taken over large masses of people serves the ideological need to cover up the fundamentally economic interest. While the commodification process is, at one level, a matter of turning goods into sell-able items, at another level, it is a matter of "training" people to be "good" consumers—creating in them a state of mind which finds the goods for sale to be "unquestionably" "desire-able." As Marx explains, "Production thus produces not only the object but also the manner of consumption, not only objectively but also subjectively. Production thus creates the consumer . . . " (*Grundrisse*, 92). In historical materialist terms, the training of the "good" consumer (the interpellation of the subject as a dependably "spontaneous" buyer) has several dimensions. For one thing, the "good" consumer is a subject whose mystified consciousness is *incapable* of recognizing the conceptual distinction between "use-value" (which corresponds to the evaluation of goods-for-sale in relation to the subject's need) and "exchange-value" (which corresponds to the occlusion of the question of need in order to keep the exchange process—the circulation of "unneeded" goods—going for the sake of profit). Furthermore, the "good" consumer—and the new "queer" subject is the perfect instance—is not simply the subject who "forgets" to measure commodities against her actual "needs" but one who is agile enough (whose "desires" are sufficiently "fluid") to keep up with the constant shifts in exchange values under capitalism. Exchange values are historically variable. As Marx also observes, the process of exchange under capitalism can turn what was not a "need" into a "need": exchange, he says, "is subject to changes, because needs are produced just as are products and the different kinds of work skills" (*Grundrisse* 527). Thus, as capitalism opens up new terrain for commodification and produces new "markets" for goods that did not previously exist, new products, new worker skills and new exchange values also appear. It is in these terms that we must read today's mainstreaming of marginal sexual practices: not as a matter of people's "changing autonomous sexual tastes" but as a question of the changes in late multinational capitalism's exchange values. "Queer," it is often argued, refers to a space of utter flexibility and fluidity that includes all kinds of differences (homosexuals, bisexuals, transsexuals, transgendereds . . .) not the space of a particular difference.[4] Thus Lynda Hart writes: "One of the most important things that queer theory has to contribute to discussions of subjectivity formations is that not only are identities fluid across and between categories but they are also always unstable and shifting *within* the categories themselves" (91). The post-al "queer" subject is not then the specifically "homosexual" subject at all but the endlessly fluid, agile, and—I would add—consuming subject living—nomadically—for the moment. Ultimately, the queer subject is also not a specifically sexed, raced, gendered . . . subject but the *subject of sensation.* Post-al theory represents the queer subject's fluidity not simply as something that "happens to" the subject but in which the subject "actively" engages: eager to find a sense of "agency" when some fundamental premises of post-al theory seem to rob the subject of agency, queer theorists encourage the subject to "affirm" and celebrate its own "shiftingness" as a form of "self-deconstruction" which is a form of performative "self-invention." Yet as even Warner's account of the queer subject suggests, this newly celebrated fluidity is actually nothing more than a new level of adaptability to late capitalism's shifting exchange values.

On this view, the current interest in sado-masochism under the regime of late multinational capitalism has to be understood not as a frontier of new "rights" in the expanding regime of the liberal state but rather as a boundary-moment in the formation of new consumer-subjectivities that open previously unavailable terrain to capital. In other words, against the commonsense notion that sado-masochistic practices are to be understood as voluntary acts of submission and domination (on the part of the "bottom" and the "top") that should be evaluated on the basis of whether or not they are engaged in "consensually," it is much more urgent to understand that the ideological function of the new sex radicalism is to interpellate all subjects as basically "subjects of sensations" who live in the moment (an eternal, de-historicized present) by responding to immediate appeals to their senses as opposed to "subjects of concepts" who can make rational calculations about their own and the general social good and about how their own and society's future needs will be met.

The emergence of post-al queerity as a new stage of compulsory consumption marking a shift in exchange values can be grasped through an examination of two recent texts on sado-masochism: Mark Thompson's collection on *Leather-Folk: Radical Sex, People, Politics, and Practice* (1991) and Anne McClintock's special issue of *Social Text* on "Sex Workers and Sex Work" (1993). Although published just a few years apart, the two collections rely on two different conceptual and theoretical substructures and correspond to two different understandings of political economy and reveal the unevenness with which changes in relations of production take place.

Against the background of contemporary bourgeois thought, *Leather-Folk* seems intellectually and theoretically "backward," a "throw-back" to an earlier era (which never heard of "*différance*" or "text/sex") because it is framed within traditional modes of understanding and is dominated by essentialist, experientialist, empiricist, and patently idealist discourses, all of which are deployed to represent leather-folk as a rarefied and suppressed minority interested not in mainstreaming its practices but in protecting its "right" to do what it wants "in private." The book prides itself, for instance, on being "the first co-gender, nonfiction anthology" on "sadomasochistic sexuality" (xi) and thus implicitly promotes an older "egalitarianism" in which "differences" are "clear-cut" and "decisive and thus not ludically "queered." It furthermore relies on an updated idealist (New Age) vocabulary: "When mystery enters our lives, and stays there, we are set off from others . . . [and] certainly there is no group more cloaked with the mystery and wonder of gay life than leather-folk" (xi). It draws on the (linear) quest-romance tropes and topoi of "adventure," "exploration," "wandering," "seeking," "ritual," "initiation," "coming of age," and "enlightenment." When it turns "scientific," its science is empiricist, as in Geoff Mains's discussion of the biological basis of pain-pleasure and the operation of endorphins in "the molecular anatomy of leather" (37ff.) Its primary epistemological premise is that knowledge is derived from experience rather than the—(post)modern—reverse. And its theory of the subject is classic humanist: "Consensual sadomasochism reinforces only concepts of individual freedom" (35). This old-fashioned experientialism (not to be confused with the new-fangled "experientialism" of [post]modern theory), implicit in various writers descriptive accounts of their own and other people's sexual practices (as in the texts by Tucker, Mains, Allison . . .), is also articulated by the editor as one of the book's informing principles: "S/M practices, composed of highly potent sex games, increases our awareness about ourselves and others" (xvii). Ultimately the collection frames its discussion of sexuality in more or less Reichean and Marcusean terms (setting itself the goal of liberating "erotic potential from the dour puritanical ethics that still rule our culture and our libidos, [as] a prerequisite to establishing a more sane and forgiving society" [xvii]). Thus to the bourgeois reader trying to keep up with the latest theory, *Leather-Folk*'s conceptual substructure will seem dated after the Foucauldian critique of the "repressive hypothesis" and in a time when sexual liberation is supposed to be an actuality, not a mere desideratum.

By contrast, the *Social Text* collection on "Sex Workers and Sex Work" is post-ally up-to-date: it constructs sado-masochism as a form of ludic "theatre" and "performance." This framing of the issues is immediately evident in the collection's visual texts. The photographs in *Leather-Folk* are "snapshots" of men and women in leather, on the one hand, and of unclothed young men in outdoor settings, on the other, a combination which links S/M activities with the "primitive naturalness" of initiatory and mythic rituals (the one exception, a "documentary"—that is, "informative"—indoor shot of unoccupied slings and empty Crisco cans at the Catacombs does little to offset this impression). *Social Text*'s many photographs of men and women in leather gear of various kinds and in various poses evoke the techno-cultural (self-consciously "artificial"—"theatrical," "performative") construction of the sado-masochist as "queer" subject. For instance, the essay on transvestism by (man/woman) Robert/"Stella" is accompanied by eleven queerly-angled photos of various stages of Robert's prosthetic "reconstruction" into "'Stella'" which involves the exchange of one set of commodities (suit, white shirt, tie . . .) for another (rubber dress, net stockings, high-heeled thigh length boots . . .). Thus whereas *Leather-Folk* embraces "nature," *Social Text* not only proposes that S/M is "against nature"(89) (the dominatrix defies the laws of nature by enacting the subjection of "man") but that the proper mode of understanding sexualities is representational, differential, textuo- and techno-cultural, and not essentialist, empiricist, or natural. (I shall return shortly to this naturalism/anti-naturalism contrast, which demands further evalutaion.) In other words, the "sophisticated" *Social Text* collection explores the post-al notion that—as Barbara Kruger phrases it another context—"Images . . . dictate the seemingly real through the representative" (210).

Editor McClintock frames the *Social Text* inquiry into sado-masochism in bourgeois terms and traces the genealogy of S/M to the Enlightenment and its new modes of "discipline," in particular to Enlightenment juridical models which devised "a new technology of the power-to-punish" (107) which turned "punishment" into "the rationally calculated, causal effect of the crime, and the administrators of punishment" into nothing "more than the dispassionate ministrants of rational law" (107). On this view, S/M is a "scandal" because it

> radically disarrange[es] the right-to-punish [and] stages the right-to-punish, not for the civic prevention of crime, but for pleasure, parading a scrupulous fidelity to the *scene* and costumery of the penal model, while at the same time interfering directly with the rules of *agency*. Hence the intolerable affront embodied in the dominatrix and her client. How can punishment be established in the minds of the public as a logical calculus of criminal *cause* and penal *effect*—the rational execution of Truth—if members of the general public can take up, on whim, the birch, the rod, the handcuffs, the whipping block, and declare sentence not for the prevention of crime, but for the delirious excess of pleasure? For it is as subversive of the modern penal economy to enjoy a punishment without having first committed a crime, as it is to commit an unpunished crime. (107-108)

True to the Foucauldian principle of the "reversibility of power," McClintock then argues that "heterosexual commercial S/M subverts the gendered economy of the right-to-punish, putting the whip and the money in the woman's hand, and exhibiting the man on his knees" (108). More "scandalous" still in her view is the shift from the "commercial" to the "recreational": "lesbian and gay S/Mers parade punishment not as the dutiful exercise of civic prevention, but as a recreational theater of power, denying the state its penal monopoly and provocatively exposing the right-to-punish not as Reason's immutable decree, but as the irregular product of social hierarchy" (108).

McClintock's seemingly "reasonable" attention to the operations of "reason" here is meant to suggest that the *Social Text* approach to sado-masochism takes reason seriously. However, in true post-al fashion, what it ultimately does—as McClintock's discourses ("stages," "scene," "costumery," "exhibiting," "parade," "recreational theater," "exposing") indicate—is to turn both the supposedly "conservative" juridical uses of "reason" and the "liberatory" fight against "oppressive" reason through parody into "spectacle." This takes attention away from determinative and causal factors and focuses it on *the speculary*, on the actions of proponents and opponents of sexual "freedom" as forms of "representation" *for consumption by the eye*. The effect of this shift in perspective forces one even to reconsider the relationship of the graphic (patterning perceived visually, that is, sensuously) to the textual (signification implicated in the conceptual): it suggests that the subordination of the "snapshots" to text in *Leather-Folk* is "old-fashioned" and that, as instantiations of "spectacle" in the *Social Text* collection, the photographs there take on greater prominence—as if the graphics were readable not simply as "illustrations" of the text but even in a sense "on their own." The trajectory of these gathering implications is that the graphic/sensuous is autonomous from the textual/conceptual. On the political and ideological plane, in the foregrounding of "spectacle," the position of today's "sex radicals" converges with that of their "opponents." A recent episode in the culture wars shows the continuing fascination on both the bourgeois right and the bourgeois left with "scandalous" spectacle masquerading as reason.

Following the Sixth North American Lesbian, Gay, and Bisexual Studies Conference held at the University of Iowa in November, 1994, the right-wing group "Accuracy in Academia" offered its hostile analysis of the event in its publication *Campus Report* (January 1995). Under the front-page headline ("'Queer' Activism Promoted at Gay Studies Conference: Keynote Speaker Bares All in Night Act for Iowa U.-Sponsored Event"), a "scandal" was revealed: that "Tim Miller—a keynote speaker at the conference—stripped off his clothes and talked to his penis" (Hill 1). Both the performance of the keynote speaker and the discourses of the unsympathetic report invite the reader to "take sides" and either promote or reject "queer spectacle." It is much more productive to grasp the "logic" behind the privileging of "spectacle" and to understand that from the practice of "spectacle," other practices follow. The logic of the politics of spectacle is explained by Lauren Berlant and Elizabeth Freeman in their comments on one of Queer Nation's strategies: "Queer Nights Out," they argue, "demonstrates two ominous truths to heterosexual culture: one, that gay sexual identity is no longer a reliable foil for straightness, and, two, that what looked like bounded gay subcultural activity has itself become restless and improvisatory, taking its pleasures in a theater near you" (207). In the same vein, Eve Sedgwick argues that progressive social change cannot take place "in the absence of a strong, explicit, erotically invested affirmation of some people's felt desire or need that there be gay people in the immediate world" (79). In other words, queer politics amounts to giving the world an "eyeful." Such arguments minimize the ease with which the politics of spectacle collaborates with the processes of consumption. Once the modality of spectacle is privileged as the proper mode for negotiating political issues, other corresponding modalities get privileged on other planes: on the level of reading/writing, particular (non-explanatory) genres—narrative, description, confession, intimate critique, personal criticism—are also privileged and on the level of subjectivity, all persons become ultimately "voyeurs" of other people's practices as of their own. The point, of course, is not to reject narration, description, confession, voyeurism, or even any particular sexual practice as inherently "bad": the point is to ask where various understandings of them ultimately lead. In the end the foregrounding of the reading/writing/understanding of cultural and social practices as "spectacle" is a part of an ideological maneuver aimed at backgrounding analytic and explanatory modes of understanding cultural and social practices, especially in the most rigorous form of Marxist theory which insists on conceptualization, on prioritization (of class relations), on determination and on causality (of the relation of base to superstructure).

It is important to inquire not only into the silent assumptions behind the queer "politics of spectacle" but also into its consequences. Itself a political "construct," the politics of spectacle is premised on the post-al notion that *compulsory heterosexuality* has actually rendered homosexuals "invisible" and that lesbian/gay/queer politics must therefore be a politics of finally rendering visible what was formerly invisible. (Post)structuralist theory—especially as elaborated in Barthes, in Cixous and *écriture feminine*, in Irigaray, in Wittig, in de Lauretis . . .—has mystified the marginal subject by claiming it is the space of the "unreadable," the "unsayable," the "unknowable," the "terra incognita" of "white writing" and "zero degree."[4] Rather than wanting the margins to be in fact "known" and rationally negotiated like the center, however, (post)structuralism promotes the strategy of undermining conceptuality/knowability itself across the entire field of the social. Against such mystification, materialism argues that marginal subject positions are positions that have been "recognized," "known," and rejected (marginalized) *for cause* using particular arguments and concepts in support of a particular historically determined, oppressive and exploitative regime of truth. It is therefore that regime of truth, its attendant structures and enabling concepts that have to be changed. The (post)structuralist-inspired politics of spectacle—rendering the "invisible" "visible"—moves far away from anything so "determinate" as "concept" and appeals instead to "sensation"—consumption by the eye and other senses.

Social Text's ludic celebration of sensation actually points to its own naturalism. The valorization of sensation, as in S/M, is a crucial element in that systematic shift of economic/social/political/cultural . . . practices needed under the regime of late multinational capitalism which—as I have already argued—aims, at the ideological level, to interpellate the subject as compulsory consumer unable to distinguish between use value and exchange value. In "harder" versions of S/M, the pursuit of unfamiliar sensations in the practice of fist-fucking involves not only "a whole new dimension of pain threshold" but also a whole new level of physical risk ("potentially internally ruptur[ing] the slave or ultimately kill[ing] him") (Edwards

82]). What Queer Theory manages to do is take the local pursuit of unfamiliar sensations in S/M practices and elevate the emphasis on sensation to a theoretical principle for the interpretation of all social practices. As a part of these complex shifts of the 1990's, the old gay/lesbian liberationist theory must be repudiated because it was based on an "intense critique of gender" (Adam 97), which is to say, on *conceptual distinctions* along the axis of gender difference. Since the conceptualizing subject, which is capable of distinguishing between use value and exchange value, is the one most threatening to compulsive consumption, it must be undermined and attacked. Therefore, following the imperatives of the (post)structuralist subversion of "conceptuality" by "textuality," Queer Theorists have worked feverishly to displace the category "gender" (a too "conceptual" and not sufficiently "bodily" notion) with the category "sexuality" (more "concrete," "specific," "corporeal," and less "abstract") as the focus of inquiry. As one critic has recently put it, Queer Theory has been constructed "as a vanguard position emphasizing sexuality that announces its newness and advance over against an apparently superseded and now anachronistic feminism with its emphasis on gender" (Martin 104). Because it is a set of cultural practices that to many transcends gender distinctions, sado-masochism has taken a central place in the new queer "logic."

While many feminist commentators have read S/M along the axis of gender and emphasized the "importance of masculinity in structuring sado-masochistic activities" (the dominant as male, the submissive as female), others have argued that "master and slave are not necessarily male and female and may operate according to male or female same-sex sexuality or in heterosexual reverse" (Edwards 83). In her contribution to *Leather-Folk* anthropologist and self-styled sex radical Gayle Rubin offers an ethnographic description of a favorite S/M institution, the Catacombs, which not only hints at S/M's "transcendence" of gender (she calls the Catacombs a "temple of the butthole," thus distancing while not wholly separating the practices pursued there from any form of phallocentrism) but also identifies it as a site "thoughtfully constructed to enhance the ability to focus on *intense physical sensation*" (126, emphasis added). Rubin thus places "thought" (the conceptual) at the service of S/M (intense physical sensation). In the same volume, John Preston vividly underscores Rubin's points when he remarks about his own practices that although he could "have had an intelligent discussion with one of these young men" (that is, could engage with them "conceptually") such discussions "shouldn't be necessary": "The simple pleasure of watching a well-rounded rump turn pink and then red under my ministrations has its own aesthetics and its own justification" (217). What neither Preston nor Rubin is willing to say is that compulsory consumption requires that such conceptual conversations be rendered unnecessary.

As a one-time defender of the kind of structural analysis Rich once offered, Rubin has played a pivotal role in the queer shift of inquiry from the category gender to the category sexuality: since it calls for moving beyond both feminism and Marxism for explaining sexual oppression, her essay, "Thinking Sex: Notes for a Radical Theory of the Politics of Sexuality," is appropriately the lead essay of Routledge's "state-of-the-queer-art" anthology, *The Lesbian and Gay Studies Reader* (1993). Whereas in an earlier essay, "The Traffic in Women," Rubin had analyzed oppression (in this case of women under the gender system) in conceptual and structural terms, in "Thinking Sex" she argues "for theoretical as well as sexual pluralism." In her narrative of changing theoretical patterns, she argues that Marxism, although a "powerful" tool for understanding "those issues of gender most closely related to issues of class and the organization of labor," had to be supplemented with feminism to "detect and analyze gender-based hierarchies." But in order to understand sexual power, she proposes that "an autonomous theory and politics . . . must be developed" (34). What this comes down to in the end—and what makes her essay so crucial for celebrators of Queer Theory—is a declaration that desire is autonomous from need. The basic contradiction of Rubin's position is revealed by the fact that she says, on the one hand, that investigations of the domain of sexuality will require "their own conceptual implements" (34), while on the other she treats sexuality in just the same way Queer Theory has come to treat it—as a matter of the "pleasures" of the senses ("taste"): "A person is not considered immoral, is not sent to prison, and is not expelled from her or his family, for enjoying spicy cuisine. But an individual may go through all this and more for enjoying shoe leather" (35).

Once sado-masochism is situated in *Social Text* as receivable by the senses (nature), one consequence is that the kinds of texts it therefore includes are "speculary" texts of personal narrative, description, confession: indeed the cover announces that inside "sex workers 'Barbara' and 'Jasmin' chronicle their experiences"; "Candida Royale talks about directing erotic films"; "'Mistress Vena' [and] Robert/'Stella' . . . inquire into female domination and commercial fetishism." Alongside these, we also get a set of "analytical" texts which either confirm outright the priority of the category of spectacle or only weakly resist such premises. In the latter category is Nancy Fraser's essay which on the one hand questions the adequacy "of the master/subject model . . . for analyzing gender inequality in contemporary late capitalist societies" (174) while, on the other hand, agreeing with the view that dominates the collection that prostitution should be understood as a *"staged representation"* of *"'male sex right'"* that involves a "performative contradiction" by which "The fantasy of mastery that is sold through prostitution is undermined even as it is enacted" (179). On these terms, prostitution is "playful"—not the enactment of "actual" male power but a performance of its "fragility" (179). In the former is Linda Williams' essay on Annie Sprinkle's incipient career shift from porn-star to sex-educator-as-performance-artist: Williams identifies Sprinkle as a "sex educator" who in her teaching "flex[es] her orgasmic muscles" [129]. By reading Sprinkle's performance art as an instantiation of Judith Butler's theory of gender and sexual performativity in which pedagogy and erotic pleasure inevitably converge, Williams indicates the links between today's porn and post-al theory: both rely on an understanding of politics as a politics of representations and of representation—whether of the educational or the erotic sort doesn't finally matter—basically as "playful" "spectacle" and thus interpellate the subject as voyeur (either of her/his own or of other people's "acts"). Again, the subject is not a conceiving but above all pre-eminently a sensing/consuming subject.

It is clear that from the perspective of bourgeois theory, *Social Text* is supposed to mark a significant advance over *Leather-Folk* in the understanding of sado-masochism. Relying as it does on a patently essentialist, empiricist, experientialist, pro-Enlightenment conceptual substructure, *Leather-Folk* openly celebrates the sado-masochist's pursuit of unfamiliar sensations as an encounter with "nature." However, while at one level, the (post)modern *Social Text* collection supposedly de-naturalizes the inquiry into S/M by rendering those practices as highly mediated (performative, representational, textuo- and techno-cultural, Enlightenment-problematizing), *Social Text* creates, on another level, its own more sophisticated "nature-ism" by situating the issues in terms of a "spectacle" for compulsory consumption. What the dominant reading of the two books along the "nature/anti-nature" axis does is create a distinction-without-a-difference: it obscures the fact that throughout history all sexual practices have been socially constructed. (It was, for example, his conviction that all sexual practices have a social rather than natural character, that made Engels express doubt in *Origin of the Family* [61] that there ever has been such a thing as "promiscuity," while acknowledging that there has been such a thing as "group marriage.") Indeed under different modes of production and their corresponding regimes of "truth," different sexual practices get constructed as "natural." Because any form of naturalization serves hegemonic class interests by obscuring the manner in which social practices are constructed by changes in the mode of production, both these texts—whatever their differences—ultimately serve bourgeois class interests. By representing S/M as "theater," *Social Text* provides a more "sophisticated" naturalization of those practices and hides their historicity, that is, obscures their connection to other social practices. By contrast, in the comparatively "naive" *Leather-Folk* (which is less effective in hiding connections) there is at least a hint of the systematic link between the formation of the S/M margin and other historical and material events: "Immediately after World War II," editor Mark Thompson writes, "a loose-knit fraternity of men who recognized themselves as social outcasts began to organize. Some were emotionally wounded veterans, others deeply felt the rejections of a homophobic society . . . these queer and flagrant loners took to the road together" (xv). *Leather-Folk*'s "hint" at historicization has to be expanded by pointing out the significant shift adumbrated in these two books at the level of history: while the first book points to the pre-post-al moment when the "organized outcasts" of the social margins of "a homophobic society" exploded with the justifiable political anger in the Stonewall riots, the second book points to the post-al moment when in the face of continuing injustices of "a [still] homophobic society" the riots of Stonewall have been assimilated and representationally transformed and tamed as the "spectacle" of the annual Gay Pride Marches. In other words, the first points to the potential energies of revolutionary transformation and the second, to the complacency of reform.

In terms of political economy, *Leather-Folk* constitutes sado-masochism—no matter how "seriously" pursued—as largely a leisure-time activity, an "off-hours" avocation devoted to the formation of a counter-cultural *subject of sensations*, while in *Social Text* it has become a commercial/professional practice (anyone who can afford it can pay money to engage in) devoted to the formation of the *subject of*—more and more "overt," "public," and "legitimate"—*commodified sensations*. In *Leather-Folk*'s modernist political economy, sado-masochism is a practice "by amateurs" "for amateurs" who draw a firm distinction between the "work world" and the "play world" and who unequivocally situate S/M in the latter: "Leather," Scott Tucker writes, "has no workaday utility for me: It's one more sensual skin" (3). *Leather-Folk* associates S/M with the "gay" community whose search for unfamiliar sensations is undertaken "privately" as a set of marginal social practices involving only an "initiated" sub-subgroup ("an odd tribe within a tribe that arouses feelings both hostile and seductive," xi; the "queer among queers," 179ff) who accept their "doubled" social marginality as a determinate matter. In this "modernist" political economy, the S/M amateur is therefore an unpaid participant in a set of "private" sensual games. The *Social Text* collection—situated in a (post)modernist political economy—represents a historical moment when two significant shifts have taken place. At the economic level, S/M practices have increasingly become a "public" market for paid professionals: thus the shift from S/M amateurs to S/M professionals marks the moment when sado-masochism moves from being a form of non-productive labor and exchange to becoming productive labor and exchange. Such a change at the level of mode of production, however, requires a corresponding change at the level of relations of production. Hence the old relations of production will have to be abandoned and new ones produced. This will mean that not only those citizens constructed to occupy "centrist" positions but also those citizens constructed to occupy "marginal" positions along the axis of sexual practices will have to undergo ideological re-training into the new social relations of production. The new post-al view of sado-masochism which turns it into a "queer playground" for both those at the center and those at the margins is the medium for this re-training. Both centrist and marginal citizens must become the new consumer-subjects of a commodified sado-masochism. Post-al culture situates all subjects as "consumer"-subjects so as to block the recognition that "producer"-subjects (the proletariat) still exist: to achieve this end it subsumes "work" (production) into "play" (consumption) so as to deflect attention away from the prevailing global conditions of labor in today's society and away from the class relations that govern those labor relations.

Commonsensically it seems patently absurd to suggest that McClintock's collection deflects attention away from the prevailing conditions of labor in today's society and from the class relations that govern those labor relations. After all, isn't her text devoted precisely to a sympathetic investigation into "Sex Workers and Sex Work"? In the end, I would argue, the title marks nothing more than the guilty embarrassment of the bourgeois academic who, unwilling to undertake a rigorous examination of the causes of social injustice, nevertheless knows it would be "unethical" to ignore entirely questions of labor and class. But "class" gets lost in what McClintock calls "the politics of alliance across social imbalances of power" (2). By "alliance," McClintock seems to mean that we are all "involved" in the commodification of sexuality, that the space of "sex work" crosses all boundaries. As one prostitute reports, she has clients of *all kinds*—"businessmen," "married men," "virgins," . . . (11-12). With "all involved," such a presentation of sex work doesn't so much *expose*, as it *occludes*, the fact that society is "hierarchical" (anyone, from any class or group, can buy these services, the unspoken assumption being that she/he has the money). In this queered post-al space of the politics of spectacle all persons can assert their "power" and their "agency." Just how "far" the "liberating agency" of the sex-worker takes us is illustrated by the prostitute "Barbara," who reports that one of her "good group of regular clients" once asked for and acted on her advice to buy a BMW rather than a Jaguar (16). "Barbara" even reports that she is sometimes "disturbed" that she has "that much power" over her clients (17). A more sustained illustration of Barbara's kind of "liberation" through "surprising" "discursive" "power" reversals is offered in Gail Pheterson's essay, "The Whore Stigma: Female Dishonor and Male Unworthiness." In a "deconstructive" reading of "dishonor" and "unworthiness," Pheterson proposes that social change can be produced merely by the re-valencing of "words" and argues that the situation of prostitutes will be improved by a discursive shift, that is, by "re-defining" "whore neutrally as sex worker" so as to allow for "honorable women and worthy men . . . in the realm of sexual transaction" (60). In other words, to make the commodification of sexuality even more secure in late capitalism, paying for sexual services has to be rendered "honorable" and "worthy" and "legitimate." What we are to conclude from this is finally that the problem of the sex-worker is not at all a matter of "exploitation" (the extraction of surplus value from the labor of workers) but merely a matter of "social stigma" and lack of confidence in her/his own ability to "grasp" and "reverse" "power"—which is to say, make capitalism work for her/him. The notion of progress here is not to fight the exploitation under capitalism of all workers (including those in sex work), but to "improve" the "moral" standing of entrepreneurial sex workers relative to other workers so that all can compete for wages on the same ground.

While the overall effect of post-al theory is to show—as in the instance of "Barbara"—that sex work relations are merely relations of "power" (not "exploitation") and are therefore post-ally "reversible," there still creep into the *Social Text* accounts symptomatic instances of shifts in work practices caused by shifts in exchange values. One example of what post-al "sex radicalism" and post-al "sexual liberation" mean is the "experience" of Candida Royale, the one-time porn star in a male-dominated business producing mainly fantasies for middle-class, white male autoeroticism, who has recently become herself the producer/director of the new genre of "couples porn." Like any "good" post-al theorist Royale offers an "ethical" rationale for starting Femme Productions: to "produce explicit porn that had integrity," was "nonsexist," and "life-enriching" (23). Unlike a good post-al theorist, however, she is more direct in recognizing the ultimate ground for her "success," the profit motive: "I knew that a new market had opened up that no one was addressing. I knew that, financially, it could be a very good business venture" (21). Once again post-al "empowerment" amounts to nothing more than a "local" reversal demonstrating the fact that capitalism is ultimately a mode of equal opportunity exploitation: the woman who once worked for male porn entrepreneurs has now herself become a female porn entrepreneur. In other words, while the overall structure of exploitation remains safely in place, some specific positions within it have been shifted.

Three

Just how difficult it is to sustain an oppositional and socially transformative use of historical materialist knowledges against hegemonic understandings of sexuality is shown by what version of historical materialism is today being circulated and recirculated in the publications of the dominant academy. Perhaps the best known and most readily available Marxist analysis of homosexuality is John D'Emilio's essay, "Capitalism and Gay Identity." First delivered as a lecture "for gay audiences during 1979 and 1980" (3) and first published in 1983 the anthology, *Powers of Desire: The Politics of Sexuality* edited by Ann Snitow, the essay has been reprinted in D'Emilio's own collection of essays, *Making Trouble* (1992), and was recently canonized in the queer anthology *The Lesbian and Gay Studies Reader* (1993). The text is comprised of two basic movements corresponding roughly to the two concepts of the title, the one explaining the operations of capitalism and its impact on sexual practices and the family as ideological site for sexual training, the other drawing out from this explanation "lessons" about identity for his gay audience.

D'Emilio begins the first movement by critiquing two particular "myths" circulating in the gay community, both produced by an ignorance of history: the one myth greatly fore-shortened history and gave the impression that there were no homosexuals before Stonewall (a notion fed by reliance on the template of very localized personal experience of coming out that says recent history is all the history there is) and the opposite myth universalized history and proposed the existence of the "eternal homosexual," that "Gay men and lesbians always were and always will be" (5). D'Emilio argues that gay identity did not always exist but is part of new relations of production brought into being by changes in the mode of production, a thesis he follows along both objective and subjective lines of historical change. He traces the effects of changes in mode of production in the Northeastern US from the seventeenth-century when "white colonists . . . established villages structured around a household economy composed of family units that were basically self-sufficient, independent, and patriarchal" (6) to a nineteenth- and twentieth-century capitalist "wage-labor" system, which took production out of the family which then was shifted from being a productive economic unit to "an affective unit" providing "not goods but emotional satisfaction and happiness" (7). There was thus a corresponding ideological and subjective shift in the meaning of heterosexuality itself: rather than being the means to provide children as the laborers needed within the family as a productive economic unit, heterosexuality "came to be a means of establishing intimacy, promoting happiness, and experiencing pleasure" (7). With these and other lines of development (the separation of sexuality from procreation, the geographical mobility of workers under a wage-labor system, and continued growth of large urban centers), "capitalism . . . created the conditions that allow some men and women to organize a personal life around their erotic/emotional attraction to their own sex" (7). Capitalism thus produces contradictory and destabilizing pressures on the family: on the one hand, capitalism renders the family ideologically "necessary" for citizens since it meets their subjective, affective needs; on the other hand, through the spread of wage labor capitalism materially weakened the bonds of a mutual productivity "that once kept families together" (12).

When in the second movement D'Emilio shifts from explaining the operations of capitalism to the discussion of gay identity, the essay becomes confused and loses its materialist coherence and rigor. Instead of drawing the conclusions that everyone must acquire the knowledges of this mode of materialist explanation and join the fight against capitalism, in other words instead of continuing to pressure his gay audience through critique, D'Emilio turns to flattering that audience by proposing the thesis (already there in Rich's text) that lesbians and gay men are the prototypes of "personal autonomy" (13) for a new society. In other words, the problem with D'Emilio's thesis is that it assumes that—against its own Marxist intentions—ideology/identity (that is, consciousness) makes the material world (future society) and not the other way around. This collapse of materialist coherence is especially notable at that point two-thirds of the way through the essay when D'Emilio poses what is an "odd" question from the materialist perspective: "How is it," he asks, "that capitalism, whose structure made possible the emergence of a gay identity and the creation of urban gay communities, appears unable to accept gay men and lesbians in its midst?" (11). Such a question only confuses the connections between mode of production and relations of production. Social contradictions result from the gaps and strains created when the mode of production has moved to a new stage of development while the relations of production have lagged behind. Far from being unable to accept gay men and lesbians, the late capitalist mode of production (which has reached the stage of increasingly commodifying sexual practices of all sorts) finds the homosexual-as-queer subject the "good" consuming subject; the backlash against the queer is not an opposition from capitalism itself but from the older social relations (now defended by the conservative New Right) that had once fit capitalism's earlier stages. This in fact is why new conservatives like Newt Gingrich are attempting to argue (against the Dick Armeys, William Bennetts and Bob Doles) for a futuristic Third Wave capitalism (drawing on the Tofflers) and for some degree of "tolerance" (though not endorsement) of gays in the Republican Party. In other words, the historical mission of Gingrich's cyber-conservatism is to shorten the lag.

In other words, having begun by attacking unproductive "myths," D'Emilio creates a new "myth" of his own. By proposing that capitalism is actually "against" gays and lesbians when it is not, he in effect re-naturalizes the position of lesbians and gay men: if capitalism is already by definition against them, they don't need to do anything but "be themselves" in order to be in effective "opposition" to capitalism. D'Emilio confirms this conclusion at the end of the essay when he encourages his gay audience to believe that social change will be significantly effected if they build their own kinds of "'affectional community'" (14) from the position they have been assigned to occupy outside the heterosexual family. Having begun the essay critique-ally by pressuring his gay audience to thoughtful examination of their own social production under capitalism, D'Emilio ends the essay by romanticizing their "outsider" status and flattering them as models of "autonomy." Thus beginning in the mode of critique, he ends in the mode of self-affirmation. By failing to keep up the critique-al pressure on his lesbian/gay audience, D'Emilio invites them to merely confirm their present identities, a possibility which opens a dangerous logic that runs contrary to D'Emilio's own stated intentions: if capitalism has opened a new space for homosexual social relations ("gay identity"), then to affirm that identity may be—again as Warner's model of the urban gay male suggests—to affirm capitalism by association. The politics of affirmation leads to a wholly unproductive renaturalization of identity. Such a renaturalization is at the core of today's ongoing struggles over sexualities. The Associated Press recently reported that "[a] day after his lesbian sister lobbied Capitol Hill on gay rights, House Speaker Newt Gingrich" again raised the specter of "recruitment" and stated his opposition to "school programs" that try to "counter discrimination" by giving "homosexuals a forum for promoting their way of life" (*Gingrich* A-6). What Gingrich's rhetoric manages to do, of course, is what the Republican Party managed to do in the 1994 elections: rally and consolidate the reactionary rage of white, middle-class heterosexual males who feel threatened by changes in social relations and who are thus marshaling their political forces under the banner "Save Our (Hetero)Sexuality!" All the queer politics of affirmation permits is a mirroring slogan: "Save Our Other Other) Sexualities!" The ready recuperation of D'Emilio's essay within the Routledge queer anthology may be explained in part as an effect of the fact that the editors are employing Derridean supplementary logic and, on that model, need not exclude anything. Nevertheless the essay actually invites such recuperation because of the collapse of the critique-al pressure and the final naturalizing move of stressing the "affective" and thus of producing a "variant" on the desire-affirming and desire-promoting moves of Queer Theory.

This reading is further reinforced when one examines the headnote D'Emilio added to the essay when it was reprinted as the lead text in his *Making Trouble: Essays on Gay History, Politics, and the University*. Again there is evident confusion when he declares that in his essay he was "not trying to claim that capitalism causes homosexuality nor that it *determines* the form that homosexual desire takes," when in fact the essay is a defense of constructionist theory and shows that capitalism shapes both homosexuality and heterosexuality. Such a statement can easily be taken as a "softening" of the essay's determinist claims under the pressure of the ludic logic of indeterminacy. Similarly, his remark in the same headnote that Foucault's *History of Sexuality* does not "convincingly specify" how the homosexual was "the creation of the nineteenth century" (3) will look rather naive to knowledgeable readers who know that Foucault was one of the strongest proponents of the "specificity" of cultural phenomena among (post)modern theorists. Both the tone and content of that headnote, in which he tries to address questions about the effects of contemporary theory on his own materialist analysis reveal that by that 1992 ludic (post)modern and queer theorists had managed to put D'Emilio on the defensive. Rather than historicizing, reunderstanding, and extending his own theory to supersede ludic idealist theories of sexuality, D'Emilio simply reprints the original essay and goes into retreat in the face of Queer Theory, glad to be included in its embrace.

Further development of historical materialist analysis requires ongoing critique of the dominant starting from the premise that, as I have argued all along, the structure of exploitation itself changes as the mode of production changes and these changes find their correlates in changes in the relations of production, which is to say in social practices. Under the intense performance pressures created in late multinational capitalism (including the pressure for city companies to go regional and regional companies to go national and national companies to go multinational) new business practices have developed along with new instruments for amassing capital: the increasing pressure creates a tolerance for increasing risk. In a recent article on such changes on Wall Street, a reporter investigated one of the new and complex forms—called "derivatives"—in which capital is being deployed today (see Skow). It was the failure of investments centered around derivatives that caused both the 1994 financial collapse of Orange County, California, and the 1995 collapse of the Barings Bank, a stable capitalist institution in business since the 18th century. Reports about the latter in the *New York Times* attributed the collapse to "playing fast and loose" with derivatives—a complex form of "trading" that "can be accomplished much more quickly, and with much less cash" that is part of today's high-finance "risk-taking culture"—by a single bank official in Singapore (Hansell D9). While today's high-risk, venture capitalism—now known as "casino capitalism" (see Friedman)—is popularly associated as a 1980's phenomena, with such figures as Michael Milken and the slogan (from the film, *Wall Street*) that "Greed Is good," it continues in the 1990's as a drive for a pure "de-regulation," as a go-for-broke gambling with capital barely constrained, if at all, by "rational calculation" about "risk." In his article, Skow indicated that the introduction of "derivatives" has produced new laborers (called "quants" for "quantitative analysts") who have the high-level computer skills for dealing with the complexities of these new "risky" financial instruments, and links the production of these new workers even to changes in socio-sexual practices. When the writer notes that the "quants" "mate, if that's the word, mostly in one-night stands" (Skow 35), he is drawing out a contrast of consciousness and ideology between the new defenders of capital (the "quants") and the "old-style" defenders who still—nominally at least—adhere to monogamous marriage. In other words, he is pointing to changes in the relations of production brought about by changes in the mode of production.

No doubt the reporter is drawing these connections from an idealist not a materialist perspective, but my point in this essay is to indicate the systematic material connections between the economic drive for "risk" and the ideological glamorization of "risk" in sexual practices such as "sado-masochism." In the dominant sexual ideology symptomatized in the emergence of post-al queerity, politics is rendered as the politics of "spectacle," the subject is thus constituted basically as a "subject of sensation" not of concept, and the very need for "rational" calculation—while not completely "rejected" since post-al theory rejects nothing—is problematized (rendered "questionable"). In other words, on the cultural plane the politics of the spectacle and the speculary (which minimizes the importance of "calculation" and thus maximizes the conditions for "risk") is the ideological correlate to late capitalist financial speculation which has grown risky indeed.

At a time when the AIDS epidemic has suddenly escalated "risk" enormously and dramatically increased the importance of rational calculation, it is not just disturbing but outrageous to find that critics and theorists committed to intellectual inquiry into (homo)sexual practices are promoting sexual politics as the politics of spectacle and immediacy. It doesn't take much imagination to understand the consequences for the lives of homosexuals (and others) if the principle of undecidability and the logic of "spectacle" are extended to the area of health care and AIDS. In a recent article titled "Unsafe: Why Gay Men Are Having Risky Sex," Michael Warner, drawing on his own experience, ponders "why I wanted risky sex, knowing that the danger was part of the attraction" (33). Quoting Douglas Crimp's critique of "12-step programs," Warner complains—seemingly unaware of the risk-orientation of today's capitalist finance—that one safe-sex campaign urges "men to treat sex the way you might buy municipal bonds: 'Playing it safe, making a plan, and sticking to it'" (35). On his view, to think so calculatingly about sex is to fail to "acknowledge that you have an unconscious" (35). Warner concludes—repeating the basic move of the ludic logic of the supplement—that having risky sex "may mean not so much a gamble with the banalities of infection and disease as a way of trying on the cultural identity of the HIV-positive" (35). Recoiling a bit from his own conclusion, Warner then notes that it will be "crippling" if gay men's "erotic practice of risk supplants thinking about their way of life" (35-36). However, Warner nowhere acknowledges that the very Queer Theory his work helps to support has been both a sustained attack on and subversion of conceptual thinking and an alibi (the "unconscious") for compulsory consumption (impulse buying). It is through Queer Theory, which constructs the subject as living "from moment to moment," that the necessity of risk in late capitalist economic ventures is glamorized at the level of social practices. How very "queer" indeed that risk itself should now become the mark and criterion of political solidarity. And how "logical" that a critic calling for "queering the planet" should have become a mini-celebrity spokesperson in the culture industry for the late capitalist ideology of "risk."

Notes

1. For her hostile remarks on Marxism, see for example, her *Of Woman Born*, 110-12.

2. See Morton, "The Politics of Queer Theory"; Morton, "Birth of the Cyberqueer"; and Morton, introduction to *Queer Theory*.

3. Martin Duberman's recently published account of Stonewall, following the lives of six people in those times, supports this view (see Duberman).

4. In fact, in the discussions of the meaning of "queer," sexual politics tends to break down into arguments over whose desire is more "fluid," "deregulated," indeterminate," and "transgressive." For example, in recent discussions about bisexuality on the Internet's Queer Studies Mailing List discussion group, bisexuals on the one hand celebrate their subjectivities as exemplary of a Utopian idea of sexual deregulation while some (of the more sexually "limited") gay contributors express impatience over this celebration of "transgression." Such celebration, the latter argued, sets up a competition within the sexual margins for the prize of "most-deregulated" desire rather than providing a basis for solidarity against the regime that makes them marginal in the first place.

5. See especially the texts by Stimpson and de Lauretis.

Works Cited

Abel, Elizabeth, ed. *Writing and Sexual Difference*. Chicago: University of Chicago Press, 1982.

Abelove, Henry, Michèle Aina Barale, and David M. Halperin, eds.*The Lesbian and Gay Studies Reader*. New York: Routledge, 1993.

Adam, Barry D. *The Rise of a Gay and Lesbian Movement*. Boston: Twayne, 1987.

Berlant, Lauren, and Elizabeth Freeman. "Queer Nationality."*Boundary 2* 19.1 (1992): 149-80.

Bredbeck, Gregory W. "The Postmodernist and the Homosexual." Readings and Schaber 254-59.

Browning, Frank. *The Culture of Desire: Paradox and Perversity in Gay Lives Today*. New York: Crown, 1993.

Case, Sue-Ellen, ed. *Performing Feminisms: Feminist Critical Theory and Theatre*. Baltimore: Johns Hopkins University Press, 1990.

Chancer, Lynn S. *Sadomasochism in Everyday Life: The Dynamics of Power and Powerlessness*. New Brunswick, NJ: Rutgers University Press, 1992.

Clark, Danae. "Commodity Lesbianism."*camera obscura* 25/26 (Jan./May, 1991): 181-201.

de Lauretis, Teresa. "Sexual Indifference and Lesbian Representation." Case 17-39.

D'Emilio, John. *Making Trouble: Essays on Gay History, Politics, and the University*. New York & London: Routledge, 1992.

Doan, Laura, ed. *The Lesbian Postmodern*. Between Women—Between Men: Lesbian and Gay Studies. New York: Columbia, 1994.

Duberman, Martin. *Stonewall*. New York: Plume, 1993.

Edwards, Tim. *Erotics & Politics: Gay Male Sexuality, Masculinity and Feminism*. Critical Studies on Men and Masculinities, 5. London: Routledge, 1994.

Engels, Friedrich. *The Origin of the Family, Private Property, and the State*. Trans. A. West. New York: Penguin, 1986.

Friedman, Thomas. "The Global Casino."*New York Times* March 1, 1995: A19.

"Gingrich Raises Flag over Homosexuality." *The [Syracuse] Post- Standard.* March 8, 1995: A-6.

Hansell, Saul. "For Rogue Traders, Yet Another Victim." *New York Times,* Feb. 28, 1995: D1, D9.

Hart, Lynda. *Fatal Women: Lesbian Sexuality and the Mark of Aggression.* Princeton, NJ: Princeton University Press, 1994.

Hill, Richard E., Jr. "'Queer' Activism Promoted at Gay Studies Conference."*Campus Report.* Vol. X, no.1 (January 1995): 1, 10-12.

Kruger, Barbara. "No Progress in Pleasure." In Vance, ed.*Pleasure and Danger,* pp. 210-216.

Martin, Biddy. "Sexualities Without Genders and Other Queer Utopias."*diacritics* 24.2/3 (summer-fall 1994): 104-21.

Marx, Karl. *Grundrisse: Foundations of the Critique of Political Economy.* Trans. Martin Nicolaus. New York: Random House, 1973.

Morton, Donald. "Birth of the Cyberqueer."*PMLA* 110.3 (May 1995): 369-81.

_____. *Queer Theory: A Lesbian and Gay Cultural Studies Reader.* Boulder, CO: Westview Press, forthcoming.

_____. "The Politics of Queer Theory in the (Post)Modern Moment."*Genders* 17 (Fall 1993): 121-150.

Readings, Bill, and Bennett Schaber, eds. *Postmodernism across the Ages: Essays for a Postmodernity That Wasn't Born Yesterday.* Syracuse: Syracuse University Press, 1993.

Reiter, Rayna, ed. *Toward an Anthropology of Women.* New York: Monthly Review Press, 1975.

Rich, Adrienne. "Compulsory Heterosexuality and Lesbian Existence." Abelove, Barale, and Halperin. 227-54.

_____. *Of Woman Born.* New York: W. W. Norton, 1976.

Rubin, Gayle. "Thinking Sex: Notes for a Radical Theory of the Politics of Sex." Abelove, Barale, and Halperin. 3-44.

_____. "The Traffic in Women: Notes on the 'Political Economy' of Sex." Reiter 157-216.

Sedgwick, Eve Kosofsky. "How To Bring Your Kids Gay." Warner 69-81.

"Sex Workers and Sex Work." Special issue of *Social Text,* ed. by Anne McClintock, 37 (Winter 1993).

Skow, Joh. "Attack of the Data Miners." *Time Magazine* April 11, 1994: 34-35.

Stimpson, Catherine R. "Zero Degree Deviancy: The Lesbian Novel in English." Abel 243-59.

Thompson, Mark, ed. *Leather-Folk: Radical Sex, People, Politics, and Practice.* Boston: Alyson Publications, 1991.

Vance, Carole S., ed. *Pleasure and Danger: Exploring Female Sexuality.* New York: Pandora, 1992.

Warner, Michael, ed. *Fear of a Queer Planet: Queer Politics and Social Theory.* Minneapolis: University of Minnesota Press, 1993.

_____. "Unsafe: Why Gay Men Are Having Risky Sex."*Village Voice,* January 31, 1995: 32-36.

Weeks, Jeffrey. *Sexuality.* London: Routledge, 1989.

Wiegman, Robin. "Introduction: Mapping the Lesbian Postmodern." Doan 1-20.

Alan Sears and Colin Mooers

The Politics of Hegemony: Democracy, Class, and Social Movements

I. Introduction

A large amount of work concerned with theoretical approaches to social movements has been produced in the past decade. Much of this work is frankly hostile to marxism, arguing that completely new theories are required to account for contemporary movements. This article contends that marxism has a great deal to contribute to the theory and practice of movements struggling against racism, for women's liberation, against war, for the environment and for lesbian and gay liberation.

Marxism has a great deal to learn from the wave of social movements which emerged in the 1960s and 1970s. At the same time, the fundamental precepts of marxism can provide a theoretical basis for building powerful and effective movements. Much of the current work deals with marxism as yesterday's error. We argue here that it has a crucial place in tomorrow's struggles.

The analysis of social movements and social change is dominated at the present time by the perspectives of "movementism." This term is used here to group together those theories which argue that the struggle for liberation requires a coalescing of autonomous movements, each with its own political terrain and governed by specific dynamics. Feminism is undoubtedly the most prominent of these movementist theories, though complementary perspectives have been associated with movements ranging from anti-racism to environmentalism.

Those who employ movementist perspectives clearly see them as an advance beyond Marxism. Indeed, Marxism forms a recurring point of reference for these perspectives, as a kind of negative model seen as outdated (at best) or wrong-headed (at worst). The most common element in this rejection of Marxism is the idea that it is a theory of the "white male working class." It is portrayed as doubly reductionist, understanding society as a system of class relations (economic reductionism) and politics as a matter of class struggles (class reductionism). Movementist perspectives have tended to emphasize culture as an antidote to economic reductionism while countering class reductionism with what is seen as a broader approach to domination encompassing class, gender, race and sexuality.

Marxism is often set up as a straw figure in the movementist literature. Many critics engage in what Fisk (7) describes as a "careless rejection of marxism." This casual dismissal has allowed critics to elide the real losses in the shift from Marxism to movementism. In particular we wish to stress the loss of a conception of totality linked to a comprehensive strategy for emancipation.

The alternatives to Marxism on offer have various strengths and weaknesses, but tend to share one fundamental flaw. In their commitment to rejecting the reductionism they see in Marxist theory, critics have opted for a kind of indeterminacy, a view that contemporary social life is made up of numerous discrete elements which cannot be understood in terms of a single totality or hierarchy. This is most obvious in the case of the new social movement theorists who argue that civil society has fragmented to such an extent that it cannot be understood in terms of any "essential" relationships.[1] The idea of an overall social transformation grounded in overturning "essential" relationships such as class is replaced by the idea of local and limited changes.[2] An indeterminate picture of social relations leads to a partial conception of social change. Social relations cannot be mapped, fundamental connections cannot be specified, priorities cannot be enumerated without totalizing or essentializing.

A similar problem confronts theorists who seek to overcome what they see as marxist reductionism by analyzing class, gender, race/ethnicity and sexuality as separate but related and intersecting systems. This easily slides over into indeterminacy since the precise relationship between these elements remains vague. We are repeatedly offered, in the words of Armstrong and Connelly (6), "clues for a more systematic understanding of how gender, class, race ethnicity, region/nation and ideology intersect." The difficulty is that we are offered only "clues" and seldom more than that. We do not deny the difficulty of the task, or the value of exploratory work. However, such work will not produce systematic answers if it is founded on theoretical premises which reject conceptions of totality and a structured relationship between various aspects of social life. That is precisely the legacy that the wholesale rejection of Marxism has left in many of these theories.[3]

Albert (44) speaks for many when he argues that Marxism has marginalized "women, blacks and others, as well as their interests and agendas." This problem is apparently so fundamental that it cannot be corrected within the boundaries of Marxist theory.

> Only a systematically post-marxist theory, grounded in the rhythm and flow of modern social movements, can stimulate a full reconceptualization of the revolutionary process. (Boggs 9)

In contrast, we wish argue that it is possible within the parameters of Marxism to account for the relationships between culture and political economy on the one hand and class, gender, race/ethnicity and sexuality on the other. In constructing what we hope is a non-reductionist defense of marxism, we also wish to insist on the "fundamental" importance of human productive relations in structuring social and political life. Issues such as social inequality, war and environmental degradation can be understood in terms of the way societies are organized around the process of production. This does not mean the "economy" in any narrow sense, but rather the multiplicity of processes through which people organize socially to transform nature to meet human needs.

This argument is conducted at a broad theoretical level and by no means represents a full treatment of the many difficult issues involved. While much more empirical work on contemporary social movements is required to flesh out this argument, we believe that theoretical clarity is an essential component in any such research agenda.

II. The Myth of the White Male Working Class

A. Exclusive and Inclusive Conceptions of Class

Movementist critics often present Marxism as a partial and inadequate theory of emancipation, concerned with the freedom of only one relatively privileged stratum in society, the "white male working class." This view is based on the claim that Marxism is fundamentally reductionist, subordinating all aspects of social life to economic class relations and political class struggle. This criticism is grounded in a view of class politics that can be labeled an "exclusive conception of class." While this exclusive conception of class is certainly present in some versions of Marxist theory, the most powerful versions are those grounded in an inclusive conception of class.

The exclusive conception of class criticized by movementist critics of Marxism has two aspects. First, the working class is narrowly defined in empirical terms to include only certain forms of industrial labor which are still largely male.

> Not only are working-class women largely forgotten (an error corrected by marxist feminists, and then frequently re-forgotten by male marxists and socialists), but the whole conceptualization and understanding of the proletariat is male . . . (Hearn 76)

Secondly, the purview of class politics is narrowly confined to economistic issues in the workplace. Thus, class struggle is reduced to the efforts of a small segment of the population to improve their immediate economic conditions. Epstein (60) argues that one reason many on the left are uncomfortable with class politics is that "`the working class' conjures up organized labor and the white men who are its largest constituency."[4]

This exclusive conception of class has its roots in specific versions of Marxist theory. It is based first on a concept of productive labor, which as Lebowitz (100) points out "has been the subject of endless (and singularly unproductive) discussion among Marxists." This concept is rooted in Marx (152-7), who distinguished between productive labor which created surplus-value for capital and unproductive labor which who did not. A working class comprised only of those engaged in productive labor would exclude all those who do not directly produce surplus value.

> If we accept productive labor as defining the working class, then only wage-laborers in extractive, manufacturing, and freight industries would form the proletariat. On such a view, the working class would be narrowed down to its nineteenth century stereotype of male manual workers (Callinicos 19).

Such influential writers as Althusser (171) and Poulantzas took this narrow view of the working class, excluding for example state employees. Even Epstein (60), who is critical of this narrow conception of class, sees it as perhaps the only tenable Marxist position.

> Expanding this definition to include the vast majority of the population leaves one without a clear definition of working-class boundaries. It also involves losing some of the power of traditional class analysis, which claimed a revolutionary role for the working class on the basis of its relationship to surplus value.

The exclusive conception of class combines this narrow conception of class boundaries with an economistic understanding of class struggles. The domain of class struggles is reduced to the narrow question of wages paid to productive laborers. The result is a view of class politics which excludes women laboring in the household, the unemployed, people working on the margins of the economy, and workers in certain sectors (such as the state and social services) which include a high proportion of women workers. The working class is then seen as a privileged core, distinguished from a periphery or underclass which is more exploited and more vulnerable. (see Sivanandan 8,17,24; Atkinson and Gregory).

This view of the working class has achieved particular currency in the post-fordist argument that the contemporary workforce has been reshaped by the requirements of "flexible specialization." The working class is depicted as a shrinking core of well paid full-time workers being forced to learn new and varied skills and an adaptable and participatory work style, while a growing low-paid portion of the labor force (including disproportionate numbers of women and people of color) become "flexible" in the sense that they are employed on a part-time or temporary basis at the convenience of employers.[5]

This exclusive conception of the working class is often marshaled as part of a critique of unions which are depicted as bargaining to defend white male privilege against the claims of a more exploited and oppressed periphery comprised largely of women, people of color and immigrants.

> The traditional priorities of union bargaining—focusing on the wage and on the maintenance of differentials—have not helped lift women out of low paid ghettos, or to alleviate their domestic responsibilities. On the contrary, the process we know as "free collective bargaining" is primarily a defense of the interests of male workers (Coote and Campbell 166).

Lebowitz (103) argues persuasively that this exclusive conception of the working class does not flow from the logic of Marxism, but rather from the logic of capitalism. It is, after all, capital that would define "productive" labor as that which produces surplus-value and it is capital that tries to limit the purview of legitimate class politics to narrow collective bargaining issues. A Marxism rooted in this narrow conception of class will "not only be found wanting by feminists and others but it also cannot challenge capital" (Lebowitz 103).

Critics who attack Marxism as a theory of the "white male working class" are responding to this narrow definition of class developed within Marxist theory. Their strategy has generally been to supplement a narrow vision of class politics with separate perspectives covering gender, race/ethnicity and/or sexuality. There is, however, another alternative and that is to develop a broader, <u>inclusive</u> conception of social class. An inclusive conception must begin with a broader definition of the boundaries of class. Wright (49), for example, argues that there is no basis for excluding unproductive workers from the working class.

> both productive and unproductive workers are exploited; both have unpaid labor extorted from them . . . .In both cases, the capitalist will try to keep the wage bill as low as possible; in both cases the capitalist will try to increase the productivity by getting workers to work harder; in both cases, workers will be dispossessed of control over the labor process.

Therefore, the boundaries of the working class can be drawn widely to encompass productive and unproductive, full-time and part-time, employed and unemployed. It includes all those who are dependent on the sale of labor-power (whether or not they directly produce surplus value or are employed at a given moment) and who do not own or control their workplace.[6] The point of production constitutes the single greatest source of power for those dependent on the sale of labor-power, but neither limits class membership to those employed at a given moment nor class politics to narrow workplace concerns.

Resnick and Wolff usefully distinguish between fundamental classes, those which directly produce surplus value for capital, and subsumed classes, those who are employed as wage-laborers but whose labor does not directly contribute to surplus value (such as state employees). In this way, they are able to point to the central place of surplus production to capitalism without losing sight of the fact that subsumed workers are still part of the working class. In this regard, subsumed workers such as state employees have as much potential to engage in class struggle as industrial workers.[7]

The working class can be defined in this way without sacrificing specificity, as Epstein (60) feared above. Carchedi argues that it is possible to analyze any workplace in terms of the dynamics of control and location in the process of production.

> A commercial enterprise—as with an industrial one—is organized in such a way that there are those who perform the functions of capital (control and surveillance) on the one side, and those who perform the function of the collective worker on the other, and those whose function has a double nature. . . . (Carchedi 67)

Workers, then, are those who rely on a wage and produce (things, ideas, services) under the control of others (Miliband 23). The middle class is comprised of those who combine productive activity with a degree of control and/or ownership. The line between these classes is not static and requires further elaboration of the kind developed by Wright (44-58, 61-4). This provides a rough outline of how inclusive boundaries might be drawn around the working class. This broader conception defines a class that is growing around the world, north and south, east and west (see Kellogg 1987). It is also a class that is changing, and it is certainly important to understand the rapid development of an industrial working class in places like South Korea and Brazil as well as the shift from industrial labor to service and state employment in the more developed capitalist countries. These are, however, changes in the character of the working class and not movements out of that class (see Callinicos 23).

Drawing broader boundaries around the working class is only the first, and perhaps the easiest, step in elaborating an inclusive conception of class. More important, in light of current debates, is the challenge to the view that class politics is narrowly restricted to economic workplace issues leaving "non-class" issues such as gender, race/ethnicity and sexuality in the realm of autonomous (non-class) movements. It is to this conception of class politics as narrowly economistic and exclusive of "non-class" concerns that we now turn.

B. Class, Culture and Political Economy

The charge that Marxism is narrowly economistic derives from the idea that Marxism is rooted in a deterministic political economy. Political economy is seen as separate from the realm of culture.

> But Marxism leads one to look towards the working class as the dominant influence within social movements, and to look at the formation of a working-class party oriented towards seizing power and establishing socialism; the transformation of culture has played little role in its vision. (Epstein 38)

It is certainly true that one of the legacies of stalinism was a mechanistic vision of Marxism founded on economic and indeed technological determinism (see Clarke 83; Sayer 83-6). The critique of mechanical determinism has been one of the hallmarks of contemporary marxist thought. E. P. Thompson has been one of the most influential Marxist critics of mechanical determinism. He argued that Marx's work was impoverished by his engagement with political economy. Marx's critique, in his view, ended up reproducing the limits of political economy.

> He entered within it in order to overthrow it. But, once inside, however many of its categories he fractured (and how many times), the structure remained. (Thompson 60)

Specifically, Marx was caught within the category of the "economy" as the determining element which shaped the rest of human social life (Thompson, 60-1). Culture was reduced to a mere reflection of the economy in post-Capital Marxism just as it was in classical political economy. Dorothy Smith (54-5) presents a similar critique of political economy:

> As political economic discourse participates in and is structured by the relations of ruling, it participates in this ground and walks the same circumference. So do our feminist riders to the theorems of political economy.

The argument that there is a fatal flaw in political economy, infecting its classical, Marxist and Feminist variants, has been broadly influential. The logic of this argument has tended to lead its adherents in the direction of what Palmer (210) describes as an "emerging orthodoxy" which:

> closed its nose to the foul smell of economism without reflecting on the extent to which it was also, simultaneously, shutting its eyes to materialism. The cultural because the material; the ideological became the real (see also Clarke 152-4; Lebowitz 8-11).

Even those who have resisted this slide toward idealism have tended to see political economy and culture as distinct, externally related, realms of social life. A deterministic theory of political economy is often wedded to a voluntaristic view of culture. This is true, for example, of the post-fordists who tend to combine an extreme pessimism about the possibility of changes in political economy due to globalization and the apparently irreversible victory of the market with the voluntaristic assertion of identities in the realm of culture (see Mooers and Sears 1992).

Weir argues that a dichotomous approach to political economy and culture is present in the theory and practice of many socialist feminists. At the level of practice, this has produced a tension between (economic) labor activism and (cultural) sexual politics. At the level of theory, it has led to a conflict between economism and culturalism. Weir described economism as "a view that the working class alone will lead anti-capitalist struggle, and that this class is politicized only on the basis of workers direct experience of exploitation at the site of production"(Wier 73).

In contrast, the perspective of culturalism (or cultural deviationism) is that "cultural struggles external to class organizing provide the cutting edge of emancipatory politics" (Wier 73). This tension between culturalism and economism parallels a division of labor in the women's movement between those focusing on the labor movement or coalitions (largely socialist feminists) and those concentrating on sexual politics (predominantly radical feminists).

This dichotomous approach is not limited to socialist feminism alone. Indeed, it can be identified within the left or socialist current of the social movement theories. Across the range of social movements, a distinction can be made between "cultural nationalist" and "socialist" currents (Adam). The focus of cultural nationalism, from radical feminism through black nationalism to aboriginal traditionalism and lesbian/gay separatism is the assertion of identities through the formation of communities. The socialist current of movementism, in contrast, aims for a broader social transformation which is only possible through some combination of culture and political economy. This is most often conceived in terms of a division of labor between a range of autonomous movements (culture) and the labor movement (political economy). These distinct elements are combined in a politics of alliance, to be discussed below. This is often rooted in an analysis which separates production (political economy) from reproduction (culture).

The rejection of economic determinism has led socialist movementists to reject the Marxist method. The further development of Marxism is seen as a dead end. Marxism has to be corrected from the outside by adding on complementary elements (a theory of culture or patriarchy or sexuality or racism). The result has been to produce a not-Marxism, what Lebowitz (2) describes as "Something Else."

> Marxism is not advanced by grafting alien elements onto it in some eclectic effort to salvage it ; in such a case we have a syncretic operation which produces not an improved Marxism—but Something Else.

Of course, most socialist movementists are aware that they have produced Something Else—that is precisely their intent. The problem is that in rejecting Marxism and its concept of totality, these theorists have launched themselves onto a theoretical trajectory which leads towards indeterminacy. The most important indicator of this is a chronic inability to specify the process of social transformation that will lead to emancipation.

At the heart of the Marxist method is an insistence on conceiving the capitalist mode of production as a totality (Lebowitz 2). As Georg Lukács insisted, the concept of totality is vital to making sense of the complexities of the historical process:

> Only in this context which sees the isolated facts of social life as aspects of the historical process and integrates them in a totality, can knowledge of the facts hope to become knowledge of reality (Lukács 8).

Marxism locates the aspects of social life in a contradictory totality and identifies within that totality its potential negation (the working class). The rejection of totalistic thinking carries with it the loss of that potential for overcoming. The problem with not-Marxism is, in the words of Lukács (9) "that it obscures the historical, transitory nature of capitalist society."

> The dialectical method was overthrown and with it the methodological supremacy of the totality over the individual aspects; the parts were prevented from finding their definition within the whole and, instead, the whole was dismissed as unscientific or else it degenerated into the mere 'idea' or 'sum' of the parts.

The alternative to totality is indeterminacy. The whole becomes the product of an intersection of systems each with its own set of dynamics. This leads to a view that society and history can only be understood in fragmentary, partial terms. One example of this is the failure by some feminist writers to produce a theory of the state grounded in a conception of society as a whole. MacKinnon (157-9), for example, argues that "[f]eminism has no theory of the state."

Insofar as feminist state theory has been structural, understanding the non-neutrality of the state in terms of the dynamics of the social system, it has tended to rely on Marxist theory. But feminist theory has also tended to incorporate elements of liberal pluralist state theory. The tension between the two is evident in much socialist feminist work on the state. Findlay (32), for example, holds that structural accounts of state power provide some assistance in understanding state power. However, due to their "implicit determinism" they leave "little incentive to explore the relationship between the state, the women's movement and the latter's potential to struggle effectively at the political level to transform the relations of power."

The problem is that once the "implicit determinism" is dropped, the structural analysis is reduced to an elaborate backdrop for liberal pluralist state theory. Findlay (48) offers the useful insight that there are moments "when the state is more vulnerable to women's demands." She does not, however, devote much attention to theorizing the factors which create this vulnerability, though that would be a fruitful area for further work. However, she does go on to argue that success in these moments of vulnerability "depends on the extent to which feminists inside the state have been able to maintain their relations with the women's movement and to use their position to advocate reforms. . . . "

Here the influence of liberal pluralism is obvious. The state is conceived as a neutral terrain. Portions of this terrain can be captured and used for feminist purposes. Certainly, placing demands on the state is a crucial element in movements for social change. But there is an important distinction to be drawn between gains which have been won largely against the state and those which have been granted in order to pacify or co-opt social movements. Movements against the state cannot, by definition, be conducted from inside the state.

The theoretical basis for this slippage into liberal state theory is a failure to locate the state within a structured totality. Marxist theory sees the state as a form of class rule. Capitalist class rule has necessarily relied heavily on various forms of oppression, and the state is certainly not neutral in the dynamics of gender, race/ethnicity or sexuality. The problem is that once these dynamics are conceived as separate from class rule, state theory loses its anchor in a conception of totality.[8] The drift towards liberal pluralism is very strong once that anchor is lost. Indeed, the drift often goes beyond liberal pluralism to a kind of indeterminacy in which the state is deprived of any specificity.[9]

C. Class, Gender, Race/Ethnicity and Sexuality

Perhaps the strongest argument used against the Marxist conception of totality today is that reduces a diversity of experiences to a unitary system and subordinates a range of struggles to a single dynamic. Churchill (199) wrote, for example, that Marxism could not hope to relate to native struggles without a rich appreciation of native perspectives: "Only through learning the specifics of the local struggle can one hope to 'fit it into the broader picture' without intellectually forcing it, a priori, into the constraints of preconception and stereotype."

Lenin himself would have endorsed this statement, arguing the need for detailed knowledge of the concrete situation. However, opponents of Marxism use the argument for detailed local knowledge as the basis for a rejection of Marxism tout court. Any attempt to "fit it into the broader picture" is likely to be accused of "forcing it." It is common sense among many on the left that Marxism is a "male-stream," "eurocentric" (and undoubtedly straight) theory (see for example Burstyn 81 and Churchill 200). This kind of reasoning is used to disqualify Marxism in advance as an answer to pressing social questions. The alternative to Marxism is generally some variant of multiple systems theory linked to the politics of alliance and the abandonment of any conception of totality. If Marxism is to be a credible alternative it must be able to show the possibility and efficacy of an inclusive class politics.

Lebowitz (1992) provides an important theoretical starting point for this kind of politics with his critique of the "one-sidedness of capital." Marx's *Capital* presented the dynamics of capitalism and class struggle from the perspective of capital only. The other side of the capital relation, namely the working class, was held constant in *Capital* to permit an elaboration of the laws of development of capitalism (31-4). This, Lebowitz argues, must be complemented with an account of "class struggle from the side of the wage-laborer" to give an inclusive picture of class conflict (56). Looked at from this perspective, workers encounter capital as a barrier to meeting the rich and diverse needs that they develop in particular historical circumstances. These include not only a wage required to secure the goods that workers need or want, but also the time required for the self-reproduction of the worker. More than this, such a perspective must encompass the myriad of conditions required for social life itself and the realization of the full creative potential of the worker as an individual (see 56-7,96-100).

This broader conception of class struggle, which encompasses the rich world of workers' needs provides the basis for an inclusive politics capable of embracing issues around gender, race/ethnicity, sexuality, and other special needs. Creese (193-4) pointed out the need to overcome the inadequacy of dealing with issues such as gender and race as "add-ons" to class analysis:

> Ethnic/racial and gender relations of power and domination are embedded within capitalist practices. The class relations that are thereby generated are not gender and ethnically/racially neutral in form; rather, classes are gendered and racialized (Creese 193).

An inclusive conception of class struggle allows us to understand classes as gendered, racialized and sexualized while connecting the diverse needs and capacities of workers to a common struggle. Lebowitz (123) argues that workers approach capital "already divided by (among aspects) sex, age, race and nationality." This division is fostered due to "the inherent tendency in capital itself to foster competition among workers. . . ."

These divisions need not be unbridgeable. The demands of lesbians and gay men, people of color, women, people with physical or mental special needs and others are class demands against capital and its dominance over society. HIV infected people, for example, may require a more flexible working day due to the need for rest, or ways to meet their needs and wants without engaging in wage-labor if unable to work (see Sears and Adam 1992). Women may have particular needs in the configuration of wage and domestic labor (see Vogel 1990 and Luxton 1987). These issues may or may not manifest themselves directly in the workplace. That is not the central point. Class struggles include more than struggles around wages or conflicts in individual workplaces.

Rather than directed against particular capitalists, they are struggles against the power of capital as a whole. And, insofar as they are directed against capital's position as the owner of the products of social labor, they have the potential of unifying (rather than maintaining the separation of) all those who have nothing to sell but their labor power (Lebowitz 147).

This unity has an objective basis: it is founded on the fact that forms of exploitation and oppression are related <u>internally</u> to the extent that they are located in the same totality—one which is defined and governed by capitalist social relations. Each of these struggles has the potential of strengthening the others. Conversely, the failure to connect these struggles weakens each of them. This is precisely what Marx (118) referred to when he wrote "A people that subjugates another people forges its own chains."

The myth of the "white male working class" presents class struggle as one in which a gain for some workers means a loss for others. This is based on a static picture of a relatively constant wage packet which gets divided between sections of the class on the basis of power and privilege. Thus, the "white male working class" is presented as the beneficiary of lower wages paid women, people of color and immigrants. By this logic, gains for women, people of color and immigrants are necessarily losses for white men (e.g. Coote and Campbell 247).

The overall size of the wage packet, the length of the working day, the comprehensiveness of social programs and indeed the amount of direct management control is not fixed, but varies with the strength and tactics of each side in the class struggle. Workers who attempt to defend relative privileges through exclusionary and sectional strategies weaken their own position. The failure, for example, to campaign vigorously against racist privilege in the American South not only weakened the position of southern workers but indeed that of the whole American labor movement. The downward pressure of a non-unionized low wage sector historically divided by racism is one of the tools American employers have used in their anti-union offensive in the recent past (see Davis).

This does not mean that workers will automatically recognize their broader class interests or that sectionalism will be easily overcome. This requires a political struggle. However, there is an objective basis for building solidarity. It is when workers enter into struggle that the opportunities are greatest for the subjective recognition of this objective basis (see Lebowitz 163). McCaskell (249) showed just one example of these possibilities when he described the development of a general strike in an area of the Basque country following the shooting of a transvestite by the Spanish National Police:

the industrial suburb closed down in a general strike protesting the killing. Sexual liberation was a focus of discussion in dozens of workplaces. Two thousand people marched through San Sebastian under the banners of EHGAM [the Basque gay liberation front]. . . .

This was a mobilization on a class basis which connected national liberation and sexual politics. This kind of political generalization is not inevitable in large-scale workers struggles; politics are required to make these links. There is, however, a very real basis for such generalization. Indeed, this should not be surprising. At the level of daily experience, there is an obviousness to the connections between different aspects of exploitation and oppression.

> The divisions between gender, class and race don't exist at the level of the everyday/everynight world of people's actual lives; to be black, a woman and working class are not three different and distinctive experiences. (D. Smith 54)

We would argue that these are not separate experiences precisely because they are grounded in a single social totality. There is a connection within this totality between, for example, economic crisis and the rise of the racist right (see Sivanandan v-vi). The relations within this totality have a specifically capitalist character even where they are not directly economic (see Wood). This is the basis for an inclusive class politics.

Albert has attacked this inclusive conception of class struggle, which he labels as "Marxist monism" (44).

> The absurdity of this view that women and blacks, for instance, can only be critical social agents as representatives of some class, and that hey cannot be agents of history simply by virtue of their position as women oppressed by gender relations and blacks oppressed by racist community relations fortunately has struck more than a few activists.

This is a caricature. The argument is not that class is the only subject position in society, but that it is a unique one in the process of emancipation. There are two reasons for this uniqueness. First, as Marx (58) argued, the working class is a class with "radical chains" which to free itself must break the all the chains which bind society. Secondly, the working class is the only force which can break through the limits of the capitalist totality to forge a new society (see Lukács 28).

III. Two Concepts of Hegemony

The politics of alliances which lies at the heart of movementism is fundamentally at odds with the strategic claims of Marxism. Marxist politics is not about simply adding on to the struggles of the working class other "non-class" struggles of the oppressed. Rather, an inclusive conception of class politics challenges the idea of separating class from non-class struggles. All struggles take place on a terrain defined by capitalist social relations and have specific class dynamics. Marxism is not about externally related struggles but ones which are internally related as part of a broad social totality.

At the heart of the strategic debate between Marxism and much new social movement theory are competing conceptions of the meaning of hegemony. Central to this debate is the claim that Marxism sees all struggles other than those of the working class as somehow of secondary importance. This myopic focus on the working class, it is claimed, fails to take account of other "non-class" identities not captured by the concepts of class and class struggle. The struggle against capital is only one locus of struggle among others; the attempt to fit the new social movements into the preconceived mold of "the struggle for socialism" is deadening and must be rejected (Magnusson and Walker 59).

Therefore, critics of Marxism argue, a new and broader concept political mobilization is required which dispenses once and for all with narrow notions of class interest and struggle. As Smardon (143) has written: "What is required at the present time is a hegemonic strategy against global capital that builds on the existing foundation developed by the social movements and by labor activists in various countries, rather than a strategy which systematically alienates large segments of potential support by insisting on the primacy of the working class in any process of transformation."

Gramsci's concept of hegemony is invoked here to argue for a politics in which working class struggle becomes at best one among many different forms of struggle. Since this is now a taken as more or less axiomatic on the left (so much so that few feel compelled to justify such assertions), it is worthwhile briefly considering Gramsci's concept of hegemony before returning to the question of the relationship between working class struggles and those of the new social movements.

A. Gramsci's Concept of Hegemony

Gramsci's concept of hegemony grew out of his general assessment of capitalist society, in particular his recognition that capitalist class rule rested on both consent and coercion. In modern capitalism consent on the part of the ruled was essential to the maintenance of capitalist social relations. Hegemony, therefore, was defined as "the entire complex of practical and theoretical activities with which the ruling class not only justifies and maintains it dominance, but manages to win the active consent of those over whom it rules . . ." (Gramsci 244).

In Western capitalism, Gramsci argued, direct coercive force by the state was less important than the network of institutions in civil society—political parties, trade unions, educational institutions, and the mass media—which secure the ideological consent of the masses. Gramsci's emphasis on the complexities of the ideological forms of capitalist domination marked his work off from determinist trends in Marxist thought which tended to see a more or less automatic relationship between class position and the development of revolutionary consciousness among the working class. Moreover, his emphasis on the central role of human agency and consciousness places a premium on practical activity and politics in forging the kind of anti-hegemonic struggles necessary to overcome the structures of capitalism.

The strategic importance of ideological struggle in the battle between the classes for hegemony was illustrated by Gramsci through his distinction between the war of position and the war of maneuver. A war of maneuver involved the rapid and sudden military assault on a rival army. The insurrectionary assault on the capitalist state during a revolutionary upheaval like that which occurred during the Russian Revolution epitomized the political equivalent of the war of maneuver. The war of position, on the other hand, was more like trench warfare. A war of position involved a longer term battle for ideological hegemony on the part of the working class and its allies. In the advanced states of the West, the war of position took precedence because "'civil society' has become a very complex structure and one which is resistant to the catastrophic 'incursions' of the immediate economic elements (crises, depressions, etc.)" (Gramsci 235).

It is important to emphasize that for Gramsci it was precisely because he saw capitalist social relations as resting on both consent and coercion that he also saw the necessity of combining the war of position and the war of maneuver. The historical context in which Gramsci discusses the war of position is important. He was writing in the context of a fascist reaction which had helped defeat a massive wave of working class struggle in Italy in the early 1920s. He was trying to chart the strategic tasks for socialists under such harsh conditions. But, even in conditions where the war of position dominates Gramsci still talks of a "'partial' element of movement." A war of position was still, after all, a war (Harman 18). Moreover, nowhere does he suggest that the struggle for hegemony can by itself resolve the problem of state power. Gramsci continued to believe that an insurrectionary war of maneuver on the capitalist state "capable of wounding and inflicting grave blows on it at the decisive moment of struggle" remained essential.[10]

B. Stuart Hall: Ideology and Hegemony

It is necessary to make these points not as an appeal to the holy texts but because so many of those who have sought to justify either a partial or complete jettisoning of class politics have done so by appeal to Gramsci's thought. The result has too often been a highly one-sided and undialectical rendering of some of Gramsci's key ideas. This in turn has blurred the divide between Marxist and movementist conceptions of hegemony.

Stuart Hall's work is representative of this trend. The concept of ideology adopted by Hall has had important implications for the way he has conceived the politics of hegemony. His initial assessment of Thatcherism emphasized the combination of coercive state power and the ideological attack on welfare collectivism (Hall et al. 1978). The main success of Thatcherism was ideological: it had "shifted the parameters of common sense" by pioneering a new and reactionary "authoritarian populism " (Hall 188). The Right, unlike the Left, have taken the struggle for ideas seriously:

> To this struggle the radical right have devoted themselves with conspicuous success. In the categories of common sense, 'freedom' has not only been separated from, but has effectively displaced 'equality.' The state, as representative of the 'caring society' and the 'national interest,' has attracted to it all the negative connotations of the spendthrift, bureaucratic totalitarian machine. In its place there flames once more that spark of hope, freedom and individual choice: free enterprise (Hall 189).

But if Hall's initial assessment of Thatcherism rested on the idea that a strong state and a concerted ideological assault was necessary to shift the balance of class power in Britain, the state took a back seat to Hall's increasing "ideologism" (Jessop et al. 35-37). No serious attempt was undertaken by Hall to assess the contradictions of the Thatcherite state. For example, Thatcher's assault on trade unions in Britain was not completely successful, leading McBride (145) to describe it as "authoritarianism without hegemony." Nor does Hall seem troubled by the fact that throughout the Thatcher years public opinion polls indicated strong majority support for maintaining spending on health and education, state intervention in the economy, government job creation, and fighting unemployment rather than inflation (Callinicos 151). All of these commitments were supposedly no longer part of the new "common sense" of Thatcherism.

Hall's prescriptions for the left are merely the flip side of his assessment of Thatcherism: the right has understood the value of ideological struggle, the left has not. The revival of the left is conceived as an almost exclusively ideological project. Renewal "has to be made, constructed and struggled over. Socialist ideas win only because they displace other not so good, not so powerful ideas. They only command because they grip people's imagination" (Hall 184).

Both Hall's analysis of Thatcherism and his prescriptions for the renewal of the left are justified by reference to Gramsci. Gramsci, we are told, inaugurated a conception of politics "which is fundamentally contingent, fundamentally open-ended" (Hall 10). Moreover, Hall claims Gramsci rejected the necessity of the revolutionary overthrow of capitalism. Gramsci's politics "draw the decisive line between the formula of "Permanent Revolution" and the formula of civil hegemony. It is the cutting-edge between the "war of movement" and the "war of position": the point where Gramsci's world meets ours" (Hall 168-69; see also Cunningham 287).

Yet this is a profoundly one-sided reading of Gramsci. Hall's gradual decoupling of consent and coercion, signaled by his growing "ideologism," and his insistence on drawing a "decisive line" between war of maneuver and war of position, are symptomatic of a larger drift in his strategic political thinking. Although Hall and some of his associates, such as Eric Hobsbawm, have not explicitly broken from class-based politics, they have increasingly advocated a political strategy based on the assumption that working class struggle is of declining importance. The emergence of "post-Fordist" capitalism and Thatcherite restructuring "have decomposed and fragmented class as a unified political force, fracturing any so-called automatic linkages between economics and politics: if, indeed, any such "unity" or "automatic linkage" ever existed (which I beg leave to doubt)" (Hall 281).

Gramsci (184) recognized that there was no automatic reflex between changes in the economy and changes in ideology, but he never severed the connection between the two and the ultimately determining role of the economy. Indeed his whole conception of "organic crises" rested on the exploring the relationship between crises in the economic terrain where classes acquire their basic identity and interests and the "conjunctural" field where political and ideological forces fight out the underlying conflicts in the relations of production (Callinicos 153). Indeed, Gramsci could have had Stuart Hall in mind when he wrote:

> A common error in historic-political analysis consists in an inability to find the correct relation between what is organic and what is conjunctural. This leads to presenting causes as immediately effective which only oper-

ate indirectly, or to assert that the immediate causes are the only effective ones. In the first case there is an excess of "economism," of doctrinaire pedantry; in the second, an excess of "ideologism." In the first case there is an overestimation of mechanical causes, in the second an exaggeration of the voluntarist and individual element (Gramsci 177-78).

In an effort to escape the "doctrinaire pedantry" of crude economism, Hall has committed the opposite error of elevating ideology to the status of an independent variable of history. He believes that a new politics of hegemony will have to be constructed at the level of ideology since there exists no necessary relationship between the class position of the working class and human emancipation. Hall (275) calls for a new "hegemonic political project" through which the left will reposition itself both ideologically (by contesting the major claims of the new right) and strategically (by fostering new forms of alliance).

The ideological aspect of Hall's new politics of hegemony is grounded in a pessimistic overestimation of the right's ability to reconfigure politics through the 1980s. Hall (10) and Hobsbawm (206) both described Thatcherism as virtually unstoppable, discounting the important waves of opposition to the Tory project in Britain. As a result, he concedes in advance much of the ideological terrain. He claims that the left must decide "on the underlying issue of strategic principle— that of "market or state.'" It must accept that the fiscal crisis of the state is set by real limits to economic growth. The left must "elaborate a strategy for an expanding economy" (Hall 277-78). The possibility of an overall ideological challenge to capitalism as a crisis-prone and fundamentally inequitable system unable to deliver on its material or moral promises in any sustained manner is written out of Hall's hegemonic project.

This ideological bent also underpins Hall's conception of strategic alliances. It is necessary to begin to construct alliances across classes around the "new social identities." It will be "a politics which is at last face to face with, and knows how to address, the great diversity of contemporary society." It must be capable of addressing "the subjective moment in politics because unless people identify with and become the subjects of a new conception of society, it cannot materialize" (Hall 279-82; see also Simon 25). The problem is that this subjective politics is not accompanied by an analysis of the objective bases for social power, and thus offers no overall strategy for emancipation.

Ironically, therefore, in his effort to define a new and expansive hegemonic project for the left Hall has narrowed its political options to those achievable within the existing structures of capitalism. He seeks to conduct an ideological battle on terms largely defined by the right. He wants to base alliances on the fragmentation of experience rather than the overarching power structures shaping society as a whole. The possibility of overturning capitalism, so central to Gramsci's conception of hegemony, is simply written out of Hall's.

C. Hegemony and the Post-Marxists

If Hall's work remains somewhat ambiguous on the relationship between class, ideology and the politics of hegemony others have been less so. Laclau and Mouffe (85), for example, argue that it is precisely because there is no relationship between class and ideology that a new hegemony which takes account of the "radical contingency of the social" will have to be constructed. Although they claim Gramsci as their inspiration, they explicitly reject his "essentialism," i.e., his insistence on the centrality of the working class. Nevertheless, they claim that Gramsci's theory of hegemony "sets the basis of a democratic practice of politics, compatible with a plurality of historical subjects" (Laclau and Mouffe 171).

The concept of hegemony is thus recast to fit in to a project of "radical democracy," which "will combine private and public ownership of the means of production" and "institutional mechanisms . . . that enable the different sectors of the population to participate in the economic decisions of society as a whole" (Laclau 239).

But, the appeal of radical democracy and its variants does not rest in its economic and institutional prescriptions.[11] Its main appeal rests in its confirmation of what is taken to be a self-evident truth: the new social movements are now the main vehicles of social transformation and the labor movement is at best one among many. Smardon (142), for example, feels confident to simply assert that the "growth of the social movements and the dramatic failures in Eastern Europe have changed the context of struggle in a way that undermines the tenability of traditional Marxist arguments concerning the leadership of the working class."

Freed of the straightjacket of class and capitalism, politics can now be freely defined any which way. Now "self-transformation" becomes as significant a part of politics as confronting the structures of capitalism (Magnusson and Walker 63). Socialist demands, at any rate, "must simply take their place alongside other democratic demands . . ." (Laclau 229). Hegemony now depends on the ability of any discourse—socialism included—to "extend its argumentative fabric in a number of directions, all of which converge in a hegemonic configuration" (Laclau 244).

The flight into indeterminacy has resulted in an equally vague and indeterminate politics of alliances. Any theoretical basis for solidarity or coordinated action is left unspecified. It hardly seems an advance to argue that socialists should simply "allow the movements to be our teachers . . . without prejudging them in terms of bourgeois/socialist categories" (Magnusson and Walker 61). This is version of movementism is surely represents an abdication of political responsibility especially when it is admitted that many social movements "react to immediate conditions, lack any grand strategies, celebrate small victories, fail to reconcile their objectives, and have no clear revolutionary potential" (Magnusson and Walker 67).

D. Hegemony, the Working Class, and Socialism

Movementist critics of Marxism have reconceived hegemony in such a way as to emphasize ideological struggle within the limits and around the margins of dominant power relations. In contrast, we believe that a genuinely Marxist politics of hegemony can connect diverse struggles to an overall strategy for emancipation. These politics must be founded on what we have called the "inclusive conception of class" which makes it possible to locate what are often termed "non-class" issues within the ambit of capitalist social relations. This does not mean engaging in the reductionist exercise of collapsing forms of oppression into class relations. It simply means that we need to take seriously the specific ways in which capitalist social relations have shaped and configured various forms of oppression. It is no disservice to those who suffer from racism, gender oppression or homophobia to attempt to uncover the underlying dynamics of that oppression.

Certain strategic conclusions follow from these claims. If it is true that those who suffer specific forms of oppression are represented in the working class and, secondly, that these forms of oppression are linked to capitalist social relations, then it should follow that the working class has a pressing need and interest in ridding itself not just of the exploitive relations of production but also of those other forms of oppression which capitalism perpetuates.

The movementist claim that the working class must forge alliances with "non-class" actors in the new social movements misses the extent to which capitalism itself has "unified" forms of oppression and exploitation. As Michael Lebowitz argues:

> A strategy calling for 'external alliances' between workers and new social actors takes as its starting point the theoretical reduction of workers to

> one-dimensional products of capital. Rather than an inherent opposition between 'new social movements' and the struggle of workers as a class against capital, the former should be seen as expressing <u>other</u> needs of workers and as the development of <u>new</u> organizing centers of the working class, functioning "in the broad interest of its <u>complete emancipation</u>. (Lebowitz 147)

In its hegemonic struggle for socialism Gramsci believed that the working class would undoubtedly have to make certain sacrifices to in order to win the support of other classes and popular forces.

> But there is also no doubt that such sacrifices and such a compromise cannot touch the essential; for though hegemony is ethical-political, it must also be economic, must necessarily be based on the decisive function exercised by the leading group [the working class] in the decisive nucleus of economic activity. (Gramsci 161)

The working class, then, has a unique position in the struggle for liberation based on a specific capacity for self-emancipation rooted in the workplace. This brings us back to the issue noted at the beginning of this section. Movementist critics of Marxism often argue that assigning a leading role in the struggle for socialism to the working class means relegating all other struggles to secondary importance. But this is to confuse two separate issues. To say that the working class has a central strategic role in the struggle against capitalism is not to say that its moral claims are any greater than other struggles against oppression.

Many vitally important struggles take place today which do not fundamentally challenge capitalist social relations. There is vital qualitative difference between the struggles of workers and other social actors:

> only the struggle of workers as wage-laborers directly poses the alternative of workers as their own mediator; only this provides workers with a sense of themselves as the producers of social wealth. In this respect, the new social movements do not in themselves contain the basis of a new form of social production subordinated to the association of free and associated producers. (Lebowitz 149)

Recognition of this fact does not to diminish the importance of struggles against oppression. Rather, it provides a basis for connecting diverse and partial movements to an overall strategy for emancipation. The main political weakness of the new social movements is connected with a general feature of capitalism: its ability to keep political and economic struggles separate. Capitalism has a remarkable ability to "disorganize" struggles in such a way that democratic politics is kept at a safe distance from the real sources of social power. It is not a strength but a weakness of movementism that it attempts to make into a political virtue the fragmentation and sectionalism of many contemporary social struggles.

The advance of capitalism has both widened and vastly narrowed the "extra-economic" domain. It has opened up areas of social life in "civil society" which appear to be free of the constraints of economic life. This is realm of "new political spaces" so much celebrated by new social movement theorists. And yet today there is hardly an area of social life which is free from "the commodification of extra-economic goods" and the logic of the market (Wood 18).

The concomitant of this process has been the centralization of ideological power in advanced capitalism. Contrary to many social movement theorists who see an expansion of civil society in relation to the state, the number of institutions between the individual and the state has declined. Increasingly the only institution mediating between citizens and the state is the media. And the only forms of organization in civil society which have not been subjected to fragmentation and atomization are workplace based trade unions (Harman 24).

In these circumstances the "defensive network of trenches" available for the maintenance of ruling class hegemony in a period of crisis can become very weak, especially when confronted by mass working class action. Apathy can turn to anger very rapidly. This is a point which has been ill appreciated by those on the left who have succumbed to the argument that working class politics are no longer viable.

The problems facing the left internationally are both theoretical and practical. The ascendancy of movementism over Marxism has played a significant role in disorganizing and disorienting the left in general. The absence of any concept of social totality has led these theorists to make a virtue of the fractured and fragmented character of many social struggles today. This has led them to construct political strategies based on only the vaguest notions of solidarity and united action. It has led to a retreat not only from the possibility of socialism but also from the eradication of the root causes of the oppression which they seek to address.

Notes

1. We discussed these theories in detail in Mooers and Sears (1992). This view of the plurality of the social can be found in Laclau and Mouffe (139), Keane (19) and Hall (28), among others.

2. Melucci (168) makes the case in his particular terms when he argues that contemporary society has reached a level of complexity which defies simple analysis or revolu-

tionary illusions. "Changes within complex systems are always changes of an adaptive type; while they may also entail ruptures, these changes always pertain to overall systemic balance."

3. Michele Barrett's trajectory from "Marxist Feminism" to an encounter with postmodernism provides a clear example of the slippage from a position of multiple determination (viewing gender, race/ethnicity and class as separate forces which intersect) to one of indeterminacy (rejecting any specific relationship between such forces in social life). Barrett argues that the overtaxed Marxist/Feminist dichotomy could not accommodate an additional axis of race/ethnicity. In contrast, the more flexible perspectives of postmodernism allow for the exploration of "these issues without being constrained by the need to assign rank in what is effectively a zero-sum game of structural determination" (Barrett x). However, the theoretical premises Barrett adopts to attain flexibility and inclusiveness concede in advance the impossibility of developing a clear picture of social power as a guide to social change (see Palmer 1990a: 126-8).

4. This is particularly true in the United States where organized labor has lost considerable ground and represents only a relatively small minority of the working population.

5. See critical assessments of this argument in Clarke, MacDonald, and Pollert.

6. This pulls together aspects of Marx (1977: 270-80); Callinicos (1987:6,20-21); Mandel (1977: 47-54); and Miliband (1991: 23).

7. In our view, however, Resnick and Wolff's conception of "class process" suffers from an artificial distinction between classes as agents and classes as structures. They write, "Classes, then, do not struggle or do anything else for that matter (Resnick and Wolff 161)." We would argue that the working class can and does act as a conscious agent of social change.

8. We can see this in Burstyn's (1985) influential piece on state theory. Her account offered a useful development of Marxist state theory, showing how nation-building in the context of a class society has included a definite gender dimension often under-theorized in Marxist works. This, however, was overlaid with an attempt to offer a separate explanation of the dynamics of masculine dominance in terms of "gender-class" which dislocates the theory of the state in terms of totality. Burstyn (79-80) ended up offering a complexity sliding towards determinacy, when she argued that economic and gender class relations "cut across one another, but this makes them no less real, just more complicated." The result is a more "complex" vision of overcoming, when she argued that gender-class relations "cannot be "smashed'-they must gradually be dismantled and wither away."

Marxists have never argued that the moment of smashing the state is the one in which all previously existing relationships are suddenly and irrevocably dissolved. Rather, the argument is that a workers' state created through a revolutionary process is a crucial condition for the formation of new relations. Once we move into the realm of "displacing" rather than "smashing," we have lost totalistic thinking and the conception of overturning a system. Of course, this does not negate the struggle for reforms, but rather argues that these struggles will only be successful if they include a conception of the whole system and the possibility of transcending it.

9. We have argued that this is the general direction of much social movements theory (Mooers and Sears 1992, Sears 1992). This seems to be the direction of D. Smith (1990: 83-106) and G. Smith (1990) who replace the state with a broader regime of "relations of ruling" which is rich in its ability to capture the diversity of forms of power but impover-

ished in its ability to identify their central dynamics.

    10. Gramsci, quoted in Harman, p. 10.

    11. For related discussions of radical democracy, see Bowles and Gintis, Cunningham, Melucci, Magnussen and Walker, and Golding.

Works Cited

Adam, Barry. "(Post?) Marxism and New Social Movements." *Canadian Review of Sociology and Anthropology* 29.1 (1992).

Albert, Michael. "Why Marxism Isn't the Activists' Answer." *Monthly Review* 39.7 (1987).

Althusser, Louis. *Reading Capital*. London: New Left Books, 1976.

Armstrong, Patricia and Patricia Connelly. "Feminism and Political Economy: An Introduction." *Studies in Political Economy* 30 (1989).

Atkinson, J. and Gregory, D. "A Flexible Future: Britain's Dual Labour Force." *Marxism Today* (April 1986).

Barrett, Michele. *Women's Oppression Today: The Marxist Feminist Encounter* (revised edition). London: Verso, 1988.

Boggs, Carl. *Social Movements and Social Power*. Philadelphia: Temple University Press, 1986.

Bowles, Samuel and Herb Gintis. *Democracy and Capitalism*. New York: Basic Books, 1986.

Burstyn, Valda. "Masculine Dominance and the State." *Women, Class, Family and the State*. Ed. Valda Burstyn and Dorothy Smith. Toronto: Garamond, 1985.

Callinicos, Alex. "The Politics of Marxism Today." *International Socialism* 29 (1985).

_____. "The New Middle Class and Socialist Politics." *The Changing Working Class*. London: Bookmarks, 1987.

_____. *The Revenge of History*. London: Polity, 1991.

Carchedi, G. *On The Identification of Social Classes*. London: Routledge and Kegan Paul, 1977.

Carroll, William K. "Restructuring Capital, Reorganizing Consent: Gramsci, Political Economy and Canada." *Canadian Review of Sociology and Anthropology* 27.3 (1990).

Churchill, Ward. *Marxism and the Native American*. Boston: South End Press, 1983.

Clarke, Simon. "The Crisis of Fordism or the Crisis of Social Democracy?" *Telos* 83 (1990).

_____. "Althusserian Marxism." *One-Dimensional Marxism*. Ed. Simon Clarke. London: Alison and Busby, 1980.

_____. "Socialist Humanism and the Critique of Economism." *History Workshop Journal* 8 (1979).

Coote, Anne and Beatrice Campbell. *Sweet Freedom: The Struggle for Women's Liberation*. Oxford: Blackwell, 1982.

Creese, Gillian. "The British Columbia Working Class: New Perspectives on Ethnicity/Race and Gender." *Labour/Le Travail* 27 (1991).

Cunningham, Frank. *Democratic Theory and Socialism*. Cambridge: Cambridge University Press, 1987.

Davis, Mike. *Prisoners of the American Dream*. London: Verso, 1986.

Epstein, Barbara. "Rethinking Social Movements Theory." *Socialist Review* 20.1 (1990).
Findlay, Sue. "Facing the State: The Politics of the Women's Movement Reconsidered." *Feminism and Political Economy*. Ed. H. J. Maroney and M. Luxton. Toronto: Methuen, 1987.
Fisk, Milton. "Why the Anti-Marxists are Wrong." *Monthly Review* 38.10 (1987).
Golding, Sue. *Gramsci's Democratic Theory*. Toronto: University of Toronto Press, 1992.
Gramsci, Antonio. *The Prison Notebooks*. New York: International Publishers, 1971.
Harman, Chris. *Gramsci vs. Reformism*. London: Bookmarks, 1983.
_____. *The Fire Last Time*. London: Bookmarks, 1988.
Hall, Stuart. "The Great Moving Right Show." *The Politics of Thatcherism*. London: Lawrence and Wishart, 1983.
_____. *The Hard Road to Renewal*. London: Verso, 1988.
_____. "And Not a Shot Fired." *Marxism Today*. (December 1991-January 1992).
_____, Chas Critcher, Tony Jefferson, John Clarke and Brian Roberts. *Policing the Crisis*. London: MacMillan, 1978.
Hearn, Jeffrey. *The Gender of Oppression: Men, Masculinity and the Critique of Marxism*. Brighton: Wheatsheaf, 1987.
Hobsbawm, Eric. *Politics for a Rational Left*. London: Verso, 1989.
Keane, John. *Civil Society and the State*. London: Verso, 1988.
Kellogg, Paul. "Goodbye to the Working Class?" *International Socialism* 51 (1987).
_____. *Downturn*. Toronto: IS Publishing, 1988.
Lebowitz, Michael. *Beyond Capital*. New York: St. Martin's Press, 1992.
Laclau, Ernesto. *New Reflections on the Revolution of Our Time*. London: Verso, 1990.
_____ and Chantal Mouffe. *Hegemony and Socialist Strategy*. London: Verso, 1985.
Lukács, Georg. *History and Class Consciousness*. London: Merlin, 1971.
Luxton, Meg. "Time For Myself: Women's Work and the 'Fight for a Shorter Week.'" *Feminism and Political Economy*. Toronto: Methuen, 1987.
MacDonald, Marcia. "Post-Fordism and the Flexibility Debate." *Studies in Political Economy* 36 (1991).
MacKinnon, Catherine. *Towards a Feminist Theory of the State*. Cambridge: Harvard University Press, 1989.
Mandel, Ernest. "Introduction." *Karl Marx, Capital*, Vol. 1. New York, Vintage Books, 1976.
Marx, Karl. *Theories of Surplus Value*. Moscow: Progress Publishers, 1963.
_____. "Contribution to the Critique of Hegel's Philosophy of Right," in T. Bottomore, ed. New York: McGraw-Hill, 1964.
_____. *The First International and After*. New York: Vintage, 1974.
_____. *Capital*. Vol. 1. Trans. Ben Fowkes. New York: Vintage Books, 1977.
Magnusson, Warren and Rob Walker. "De-centering the State. Political Theory and Canadian Political Economy," *Studies in Political Economy* 26, 1988.
McCaskell, Tim. "Out in the Basque Country," *Flaunting It*. Eds. Ed Jackson and Stan Persky. Vancouver: New Star Press and Toronto: Pink Triangle Press, 1982.
Miliband, Ralph. *Divided Societies*. Oxford: Oxford University Press, 1991.
Mooers, Colin. and Sears, Alan. "The New Social Movements and the Withering Away of State Theory," in *Organizing Dissent: Theory and Practice of the New Social Movements*. Eds. W. K. Carroll and R. S. Ratner. Toronto: Garamond Press, 1992.

McBride, Steven. "Authoritarianism without Hegemony? The Politics of Industrial Relations in Britain." *Regulating Labour*. Eds. Larry Haiven, Steven McBride and John Shields. Toronto: Garamond Press, 1991.
Melucci, Alberto. *Nomads of the Present*. Philadelphia: Temple University Press, 1989.
Palmer, Brian. "The Eclipse of Materialism: Marxism and the writing of Social History in the 1980s," *Socialist Register*, 1990.
_____. *Descent into Discourse*. Philadelphia: Temple University Press, 1990.
Pollert, A. "Dismantling Flexibility," *Capital and Class* 34, 1988.
Poulantzas, Nicos. *Classes in Contemporary Capitalism*. London: New Left Books, 1975.
Russell, Bob. *Back to Work*. Toronto: Nelson, 1990.
Sayer, Derek. *Marx's Method*. Brighton: Wheatsheaf, 1979.
Sears, Alan. "'To Teach Them How to Live': The Politics of Public Health from Tuberculosis to AIDS," *Journal of Historical Sociology*. 5.1 (1992).
_____ and Barry Adam. "AIDS and Work: PWH Experiences," presentation at the Canadian Sociology and Anthropology Association, 1992.
Shields, John. "The New Industrial Relations: A Hegemonic Project?" Unpublished, 1990.
Simon, R. *Gramsci's Political Thought*. London: Lawrence and Wishart, 1991.
Sivanadan, A. "All that Melts into Air is Solid: The Hokum of New Times,"*Race and Class* 31.3 (1990).
Smardon, Barry. "Liberalism, Marxism and the Class Character of Radical Democratic Change," *Studies in Political Economy* 37, 1992.
Smith, Dorothy. "Feminist Reflections on Political Economy,'*Studies in Political Economy* 30 (1989).
_____. *The Conceptual Practices of Power*. Toronto: University of Toronto Press, 1990.
Smith, George. "Political Activist as Ethnographer," *Social Problems* 37.4 (1990).
Thompson, E. P. *The Poverty of Theory and Other Essays*. New York: Monthly Review Press, 1990.
Vogel, Lise. "Debating Difference: Feminism, Pregnancy and the Workplace,"*Feminist Studies* 16.1 (1990).
Weir, Lorna. "Socialist Feminism and the Politics of Sexuality," in Heather J. Maroney and Meg Luxton, eds. *Feminism and Political Economy*. Toronto: Methuen, 1987.
White, Jerry. "The State and Industrial Relations in a Neo-Conservative Era," in Larry Haiven *et al.*, eds. *Regulating Labour*. Toronto: Garamond Press, 1991.
Wood, Ellen. *The Retreat From Class*. London: Verso, 1986.
_____. "Capitalism and Human Emancipation," *New Left Review* 167 (1988).

Colin Hay

Narrative as Meta-Narrative: Post-Modern Tension and the Effacement of the Political

1. Begging to Differ

> "Playing with the pieces—that is postmodernism"
> —Jean Baudrillard, 1984

My aim in this paper is to consider what is sacrificed on the altar of post-modernism in the name of transcending the tyranny of enlightenment thought: namely the *political*. This effacement of the political has it origins in the performative contradiction, or "post-modern tension" that has characterized post-enlightenment philosophy.

Such an aporia is most clearly and self-consciously expressed in the work of Michel Foucault yet it characterizes post-enlightenment philosophy more generally. It can be summarized in terms of the contradiction between,

1. the position such thinkers are *philosophically* drawn towards—a profound skepticism towards claims to objectivity and privileged access to knowledge, and a rejection of metanarratives; and

2. the position many of them remain *politically* sympathetic to—an engaged and 'emancipatory' politics premised upon critique and motivated by the desire to undermine and transform the repressive institutional contours of contemporary society.

In Foucault this tension remains largely unresolved (cf. Habermas 1981). The result is an alternation, which becomes increasingly frequent in his later work, between a politically and normatively informed critique (reliant, albeit implicitly, upon some conception of emancipation), and an anti-foundationalist deconstruction of the very notion of "progress" on which such a politics might be premised (Best & Kellner 1991: 36, 72-3; Habermas 1989: 173-9; Larrain 1994; compare Foucault 1977: 151 and 1988: 156, 1982: 216). As such, it is perhaps inappropriate to regard Foucault as a post-modernist (cf. Best & Kellner 1991: 36; Larrain 1994: 290-1).

In sharp contrast, post-modernist philosophers (most notably Lyotard and Baudrillard) have consistently resolved this tension (which they have scarcely if ever explicitly acknowledged) in favor of the former position, thereby subordinating their political concerns to a philosophically-inspired rejection of meta-narratives. Not surprisingly this assertion of the primacy of the philosophical has proved profoundly politically debilitating. The characteristic post-modernist revulsion towards meta-narratives and the violence of in-*difference* they impose has resulted in a re-specification and restriction of the "political" to an individuated ethics and a multitude of disaggregated and decentered struggles which reflect the *singularity* of spatial-temporal contexts. Post-modern "politics," then, concerns the *appropriation*, as opposed to the *transformation*, of the contexts in which relations of domination are sustained and reproduced. This is, in turn, premised upon an ontology of singularity in which the radical heterogeneity of contexts, actions, discourses, utterances and effects is asserted and their broader embeddedness, inter-relatedness, articulation and reproduction are systematically ignored. In a sense this consistent oversight is convenient since postmodern theory effectively precludes the possibility of identifying the processes which link contexts, and hence the voice to express such connections.[1] An emphasis on individuated ethics and (con)textual appropriation thus makes a dubious political virtue out of a philosophical necessity (born of epistemological skepticism). The cost is the effacement of the political. As David Harvey has noted,

> the mere pursuit of identity politics as an end in itself . . . may serve to perpetuate rather than to challenge the persistence of those processes which gave rise to those identities in the first place. (1994: 118)

Ironically then, and despite pretensions to the contrary, it would appear that post-modernism ultimately fails to extricate itself from the chilling embrace of the "dialectic of enlightenment." For, far from rejecting the *question* of the epistemological foundations for knowledge and critique which characterizes the Enlightenment, post-modern theory continues to privilege the epistemological. Indeed, the effacement of the political and the unwillingness to contemplate progressive or emancipatory social transformation derives directly from the abortive attempt to find rational/objective grounds for critical theory. Post-modernism thus inherits from the Enlightenment the need for an objective or rational foundation for critical theory, but denies that such a basis exists. Having hastily erected this somewhat shaky foundation of anti-foundationalism it then proceeds to effectively abandon the political as a distorting and disciplining Enlightenment project that simply cannot be defended. Once again the primacy of the philosophical is asserted. No consideration is given to the possibility of alternative *ethical* or *normative* foundations for critical theory and projects of political transformation.

Adorno's desire to "maintain the freedom to think that things might be different" is thus sacrificed on the basis of the less than startling observation that politics might not be objective. If "enlightenment is mythic fear turned radical" (Adorno & Horkheimer 1944/72: 16), then post-modernism is fear of enlightenment turned reactionary.

2. The Meta-Narrative to End All Meta-Narratives?

Despite is post-Enlightenment pretensions, then, post-modernist thought is characterized by its ultimate failure to overturn the dialectic of enlightenment. Yet this is not its only contradiction. Indeed, much more frequently challenged is the status of the postmodernist proclamation of the end of metanarratives; its disavowal of the hopes of enlightenment, progress, and emancipation; and its rejection of totalizing social theories. Stated most bluntly: how can such a position be articulated? Is the claim of the end of metanarratives not silenced by the very voice that expresses it? Is this not the meta-narrative to end all meta-narratives?

Ironically, Lyotard himself comes very close at times to admitting as much. For in his role as educator and legislator (as opposed to, say, interpreter)[2] in *Le Postmoderne expliqué aux enfants* (1986/1992), Lyotard concedes,

> one is tempted to give credence to a grand narrative of the decline of the grand narrative. (1992: 40)

The rhetorical strategy deployed here invites a rejection of meta-narratives on the basis that this might elevate us to a more "enlightened" state, a reading which does not sit uncomfortably with Lyotard's self-styled role as educator. We are lured into a temporary suspension of our "incredulity towards meta-narratives" so that we might "learn" from this particular mega-narrative, ironically in order to further fuel our suspicion of *other* meta-narratives. Yet this is no modernist *faux pas*, no one-off lapse into the totalitarian discourses of enlightenment rationalism.

Indeed, in the passage that immediately precedes this extract, Lyotard engages in a classic exercise in "enlightened" Popperian refutation by dismissing a catalogue of meta-narratives on the basis of a list of "invalidating" events:

> In the course of the last fifty years, each grand narrative of emancipation—regardless of the genre it privileges—has, as it were, had its principle invalidated. *All that is real is rational, all that is rational is real:* 'Auschwitz' refutes the speculative doctrine. At least this crime, which is real, is not rational. *All that is proletarian is communist, all that is communist is proletarian:* 'Berlin 1953,' 'Budapest 1956,' 'Czechoslovakia 1968,' 'Poland 1980' (to name but a few) refute the doctrine of historical materialism: the workers rise up against the Party. *All that is democratic is by the people and for the people, and vice versa:* 'May 1968' refutes the doctrine of parliamentary liberalism. Everyday society brings the representative institution to a halt. *Everything that promotes the free flow of supply and demand is good for general prosperity, and vice versa:* the 'crisis of 1911 and 1929' refute the doctrine of economic liberalism, and the 'crisis of 1974-79' refuted the post-Keynesian modification of that doctrine' (1992: 40; cf. Douzinas, Warrington and McVeigh 1991: 111-2).

The rhetorical style is distinctively rationalist, even empiricist, although the supporting "evidence" is so scarcely plausible that it is dubious as to whether Popper would recognize this as refutation (as distinct from, say, mere conjecture). Nonetheless, the performative contradiction at the heart of Lyotard's work is here starkly exposed, as he slips into the refutation of meta-narratives *by assertion* and engages in precisely the sort of distorting and totalizing symbolic violence of which he accuses them.

Similarly, in one of the most telling interchanges in post-modern philosophy in *Just Gaming*, Lyotard is backed into something of a corner by his *interlocutor*, Jean-Loup Thébaud. In defending his conception of a multiplicity of justices reflecting the singularity of specific language games, Lyotard concedes that

> the justice of multiplicity . . . is assured, paradoxically enough by a prescriptive of universal value. It prescribes the observance of the singular justice of each [language] game such as it has just been situated. (Lyotard & Thébaud 1985: 100)

Thébaud notes the paradox in this, tellingly observing that Lyotard is here "talking like the great prescriber himself" (Thébaud, 100). The conversation ends in (embarrassed? ironic?) laughter. This reveals an important aspect of the performative contradiction in Lyotard's work. For Lyotard here adopts an albeit weak procedural notion of justice[3] in which

> doing justice in a field of language games consists of resisting the pretensions of certain language games to provide the rules for other games, to become metalanguages.... [I]n each language game we must try to judge without importing criteria from other games, such as that of theory (which claims to give criteria to all games). The language game, in Lyotard's reading, thus demands an indeterminate judgment, without criteria, on a case-by-case basis. (Readings 1991: 107)

In as much as such procedural prescription inevitably involves the suppression of alternative conceptions of justice, Lyotard is once more engaged in the formulation of a meta-narrative to end all meta-narratives. As Best and Kellner note,

> Lyotard is inconsistent in calling for a plurality and heterogeneity of language games, and then excluding from his kingdom of discourse those grand narratives which he suggests have illicitly monopolized the discussion and presented illegitimate claims in favor of their privilege. (1991: 172)

The outcome of this characteristic inconsistency is what might be termed a "hollowing-out" of meta-narratives. Lyotard's "kingdom of discourse" is cleared of enlightenment meta-narratives of progress and emancipation. These are replaced by a profusion of *micro*-narratives which are constrained within a procedurally prescriptive *mega*-narrative. The full extent of the performative contradiction is revealed in the subject-positions adopted by Lyotard in the titles to his major works. For the somewhat immodest subtitle of *The Postmodern Condition: A Report on Knowledge*, and the patronizing and condescending attitude displayed towards his correspondents in *Le Postmoderne expliqué aux enfants* and his readers in *Instructions païennes*, sit somewhat uneasily alongside his central claim, that

> the task of art and politics is to evoke or testify to differends, to exacerbate them so as to resist the injustice which silences those who cannot speak *the language of the master*. (Readings 1991: xxx, emphasis added).

3. Politics as (Meta)-Narrative

If post-modernism is the meta-narrative to end all meta-narratives, supposedly clearing the decks of homogenizing and distorting discourses which efface *différence* and deny the *singularity* of language games, then it is crucial that we reflect on the nature of *meta*-narrativity. For clearly much hinges on how the apparently somewhat arbitrary distinction between narrative and meta-narrative is drawn. Yet, as Larrain notes, despite their almost evangelical fervor to acknowledge the specificity, singularity and difference of language games,

> in their onslaught against metanarratives and theories of universal application, poststructuralists and postmodernists feel nonetheless perfectly able to discriminate between the theories which fall under such labels and those which can be saved. (1994: 303)

So, when is a meta-narrative not a meta-narrative? Presumably *either* when it is "the meta-narrative to end all meta-narratives" which after all is the very condition of post-modernism, *or*, more importantly when it sustains a micro-politics. Yet this preference for micro-narratives, micro-practices, and micro-politics is not unproblematic. It would appear that both Foucault and Lyotard reject totalizing meta-narratives merely to formulate equally totalizing narratives in localized contexts: preferring meta-narratives in smaller ponds. The implication presumably being that provided the context is sufficiently parochial (and hence the political practice it might give rise to sufficiently revisionist not to cause effrontery), the "meta" prefix can be conveniently overlooked.

This raises a second and more important question on which the whole fragile post-modern edifice hangs: *when is a narrative not a meta-narrative?* If we are to view meta-narratives as stories which distort language games and efface difference then it is not difficult to see that all narratives are meta-narrative in some sense. Narration involves abstraction. Abstraction involves distortion and simplification. Hence narration necessarily entails the occlusion of, and thus the doing of violence to, certain singularities, certain differences. A narrative is always a meta-narrative. Indeed, were we to be able to identify a narrative which did not do some violence to difference it would be a less than gripping story, and of epic proportions. Nonetheless clearly some narratives are more "meta" than others,[4] and clearly we can choose to emphasize different aspects of discourses and language games: their narrative and meta-narrative qualities. Yet this merely demonstrates the need to transcend the artificial and unhelpful dualism of narrative and meta-narrative. To recognize both the narrative and meta-narrative dimensions of *any* discourse or language game is ultimately far more useful, and potentially emancipating, than the *ad hoc* and dualistic policing of discourses with which postmodern theory has become associated.

We are, then, inescapably condemned to narrative as a condition of all strategy, action, intervention and hence politics. Not only is all narrative political, all politics is narrative. Politics is necessarily concerned with the simplification of "reality," making it amenable to political intervention through abstraction. For it is only through abstraction that responsibility and causality are attributed; it is only through abstraction that we can grasp "the lost unity of social life, and demonstrate that widely distant elements of the social totality are ultimately part of the same global historical process" (Jameson 1981: 226). Hence abstraction is the condition of political mobilization and intervention: the very condition of making a difference. Yet abstraction is inherently and necessarily distorting. Our vantage point and hence the subject positions from which we narrate (which are in turn reflective of the material contexts we inhabit and the experiences to which they give rise) determine the range of differences and singularities we identify, and those we overlook and thereby marginalize.

Thus, it is through abstraction and, inescapably, through distortion, through simplification, and through violence to other "others," that we act. A perfect reflection of the social cannot guide political action. Furthermore, a pure description is uninteresting, providing no basis (objective or otherwise) for political action *prior to its interpretation*. That interpretation necessarily entails the subsumption of description to narrative (and hence meta-narrative) and the effacement of (certain) difference(s). Politics is narrative, politics is meta-narrative, politics is violence. . . . The implications of this are clearly profound. Firstly, it suggests that even postmodern political discourses, in as much as they take narrative form, necessarily impose their own violence of in-*difference*. This merely reiterates the need to take ethical responsibility for the *others* who necessarily remain marginalized from the narratives (however little) which inform political strategy and intervention.

Yet this ethical responsibility also extends to those who remain trapped within the disciplining *macro*-structures whose reproduction we remain complicit with if we seek a politics founded on micro-narratives and the imperative to uncover *différence*. As Lovibond perceptively notes,

> if there can be no systematic political approach to the questions of wealth, power and labor, how can there be any effective challenge to a social order which distributes its benefits and burdens in a systematically unequal way? (1989: 32)

There is, then, a constant, and within postmodern theory, largely unacknowledged trade-off between the respect for difference and singularity on the one hand, and the political potential to challenge the broader processes and mechanisms which sustain specific and singular relations of domination in particular contexts on the other hand. The respect for difference if taken to its logical extreme is profoundly politically debilitating, proffering an anti-politics of abstention and asceticism. As Larrain observes, by suspecting those who suspect the established system, postmodernism explains away the problem of, and hence cannot but implicitly support, the status quo. (1994: 313)

4. Accounting for Différence

How then can we reflect theoretically the uniqueness and singularity of specific relations of domination, whilst sustaining a politics of resistance and structural transformation?

The identification of *différence* need not result in the fallacy of theoretical and political singularity: the view that the singularity of effects, events and utterances dictates a parochialism of both theory and practice. For, it is one thing to reject totalizing modes of thought which are incapable of recognizing and accounting for the apparent singularity of particular social relations in particular contexts; it is another thing altogether to abandon attempts to identify broader *processes* which impinge upon a variety of contexts in different ways to produce disparate effects.

If each singularity is seen as requiring its own narrative, then the possibility of any political intervention transcending the limits (however drawn) of context is denied. The casualty is politics itself which is tragically and ironically sacrificed in the name of the other. Yet there is an alternative: the identification of generic processes which interact in different ways in different contexts to produce specific, even singular effects. Within such a dialectical ontology, the singularity of contexts, effects and utterances derives from the interlocking of processes that are not themselves singular and which necessarily transcend context.

There are, then, different strategies of accounting for singularity, leading to different political consequences. Within postmodernist theory the recognition of the singular nature of spatial-temporal contexts, utterances and effects is reflected in a politics of micro-contexts, strategies and practices. Within a dialectical ontology, by contrast, the articulation of generic processes gives rise to specific outcomes enabling a politics that transforms the *processes* which sustain relations of domination across contexts, not mediate their (singular) effects in specific settings. The politics of structural change replaces that of parochial revisionism.

If we are to recognize our ethical responsibility to those who remain trapped within the disciplining structures of our profoundly capitalist, patriarchal and racist societies, then we must retain the possibility of systematic and "progressive" political change. Tempting as it might be, we cannot afford to sacrifice the political in the name of the other whose difference we must respect.

Notes

1. For a discourse which identifies processes linking contexts, utterances or effects must necessarily abstract from their specificity and singularity, thereby engaging in a distorting effacement of difference through the formulation of an inherently repressive meta-narrative.

2. On the transformation of the role of the intellectual from modern legislator to post-modern interpreter see Bauman 1987: esp. 1-8; 1992: 1-26; cf. Lyotard 1989: 153.

3. In many respects not that dissimilar from Habermas' procedural conception of truth (realized through communicative action).

4. None more so, perhaps, than the postmodernist "meta-narrative to end all meta-narratives."

Works Cited

Adorno, Theodor and Max Horkheimer. 1944. *Dialectic of Enlightenment*. London: New Left Books, 1972.
Baudrillard, Jean. "Games with Vestiges," *On the Beach* 5 (1984): 19-25.
Bauman, Zygmunt. *Legislators and Interpreters*. Cambridge: Polity, 1987.
_____. *Intimations of Postmodernity*. London: Routledge, 1992.
Best, Stephen and Douglas Kellner. *Postmodern Theory*. New York: Guilford Press, 1991
Douzinas, Costas and Ronnie Warrington with Shaun McVeigh. *Postmodern Jurisprudence*. London: Routledge, 1991.
Foucault, Michel. *Language, Counter-Memory, Practice*. Ithaca: Cornell University Press, 1977.
_____. "The Subject and Power" in H. L. Dreyfus and P. Rabinow, eds. *Michel Foucault: Beyond Structuralism and Hermeneutics*. Chicago: University of Chicago Press, 1982.
_____. *The Care of the Self*. New York: Vintage Books, 1988.
Habermas, Jürgen. "Modernity versus Post-Modernity," *New German Critique* 22 (1981). 2-14.
_____. *The New Conservatism*. Boston: MIT Press, 1989.
Harvey, David. "Class Relations, Social Justice and the Politics of Difference" in Judith Squires, ed. *Principled Positions*. London: Lawrence & Wishart, 1994.
Jameson, Fredric. *The Political Unconscious*. London: Routledge, 1981.
Larrain, Jorge. "The Postmodern Critique of Ideology," *Sociological Review* 42.2 (1994): 289-314.
Lovibond, Sabina. "Feminism and Postmodernism," *New Left Review* 178 (1991): 5-28.
Lyotard, Jean-François. *The Lyotard Reader*. Andrew Benjamin, ed. Oxford: Blackwell, 1989.
_____. *The Postmodern Explained to Children*. 1986. London: Turnaround, 1992.
_____ and Jean-Loup Thébaud. *Just Gaming*. Manchester: Manchester University Press, 1985.
Readings, Bill. *Introducing Lyotard: Art and Politics*. London: Routledge, 1991.

Bob Hodge

Labor Theory of Language: Postmodernism and a Marxist Science of Language

Lyotard's influential *The Postmodern Condition* announced the death of all Grand Narratives, and he included Marxism and Science amongst the corpses. Language and discourse have the biggest role to play in his new "postmodern" condition. Mainly seen as superstructural forms in classic Marxism, and a transparent medium of communication in modernist science, they now form the new master discipline and object in his postmodern "report" on the postmodern world.

I want to suggest that these death certificates may have been issued somewhat prematurely, but that paradoxically not all forms of Postmodernism are as opposed to Marxism as Lyotard's polemic suggests. Language is undoubtedly an important object of study for Marxism, and Postmodernism has in some respects established new more favorable conditions for the establishment of a Marxist science of language, a materialist linguistics. The dominant linguistic theory in the West, the structuralist linguistics of Chomsky and others, was based on premises that were hostile to the basic assumptions of Marxism. Its scientism established an idealized view of language split off from social forces and conditions, in which categories like historical materialism, labor, dialectic, class and ideology were difficult to apply. "Modernist" linguistics was not well adapted for Marxists to use as a critical tool for the analysis of social meaning.

Lyotard's rhetoric makes it seem as though Science has shrunk to become a province in the study of language, and the study of language has expanded to be a new all-competent meta-discipline. In this vein he writes:

> Scientific knowledge is a kind of discourse. And it is fair to say that for the last 40 years the 'leading' sciences and technologies have had to do with

language: phonology and theories of linguistics, problems of communication and cybernetics, modern theories of algebra and informatics, computers and their languages . . . paradoxology. (3)

What is startling about this passage is not the careless over-statement of the first sentence, so much as the level of ignorance and complacency displayed in the second. On the one hand he seems to accept uncritically that modernist linguistics (phonology etc.) has achieved major advances at the "leading" edge of scientific thought. This is one Grand Narrative that he chooses not to deconstruct. On the other hand his list does not mention any of the recent developments in Science that can be grouped under the term Post-modern Science: Catastrophe theory in the 1960s, Chaos theory, Complexity Science. For a theorist who privileges language so much he has an inadequate theory of language, and as a theorist of post-modernity his information about science is seriously out of date.

However, Lyotard's list includes developments that are indeed new and important, which in practice are culpably not addressed by modernist linguistics: informatics, computer languages, cybernetics, developments in communications technologies which are playing an increasingly significant role. In classic Marxist terms, these phenomena are among the forces of production which make up the material base. As Marx predicted in the 19th century, Capitalism is committed to renewing its technological base in order to maintain itself, and "Postmodernism" is a convenient short-hand for all the stratagems that late Capitalism has come up with to perpetuate its existence. Lyotard's term "Postmodernism" points to new, emerging phenomena which a dynamic and evolving Marxism will keep track of (as this prophet of post-modernism should have done himself).

It is as well at this point to warn that I will be using the term "Postmodern" loosely, because any other approach is made untenable by the nature of the term itself. As Harvey and Frow argue, the term is "logically incoherent" (Frow 9) and has come to mean so many things to so many different theorists that it is now impossible to give it anything like a single meaning. However, both write from a broadly Marxist point of view, and like them both, I see the term as still having an indicative, heuristic value.

Given that the meaning of the word is incoherent, indeterminate and irretrievably dispersed, I will isolate three distinct strands of meaning, all of which have some currency among different groups. None of these versions of the word is the "real" meaning. Nor do I see the "real" meaning of the word as made up of these two added together. "Postmodernism" is a contested semantic field so thoroughly trampled on that all its boundaries have become obscured.

The first meaning is the sense given the term by a group of theorists who include most notably Lyotard and Baudrillard. For this group "Postmodernism" is primarily a *rhetorical tactic*, a device to assert without need of proof that all previous forms of thought (including Marxism and Science) are obsolete and need not be taken seriously. This tactic is irritating, especially because it seems to give high value to sloppy and uncritical thinking (as in the text we have just looked at). It is also militantly anti-materialist, with a basic premise that nothing is knowable and/or exists outside of discourse. Following Teresa Ebert's work, I will call this form of Postmodernism *Ludic Postmodernism*.

However, postmodernism is also potentially a form of scientific theory, or more precisely a project for scientific theory that aims to produce a *materialist* theory capable of systematic understanding of dramatic (systemic, revolutionary) change. In this aspect its orientation has much in common with Marxism. Marx's theory of history was concerned to understand where society had come from, where it was going and what forces were driving it there. The term "Postmodern world" points forward more urgently than "late Capitalism," which tends to foreground the determination of the phenomena it describes by the (late, decaying) stage of capitalist production it is embedded in, at the cost of recognizing the presence of the new forms that may have begun to emerge vigorously.

"Postmodern science" is a powerful set of conceptual tools to address some of the problems that Lyotard's Postmodernism solves merely rhetorically, by turning them into discourse and celebrating them. Marxism as a scientific theory of society has always made discriminating use of the best available knowledge it can glean, and "postmodern science" is a resource it can now draw on. In practice, I want to argue, this is not a new role for Marxism. Marxism has always been a revolutionary science, a postmodern science, whose claims to scientific status have been fiercely repudiated by guardians of the dominant definitions of what science is.

I believe that there is merit in making a stronger claim for this form of postmodernism: that it is necessarily both revolutionary (as against the ultimately reactionary politics of ludic postmodernism) and scientific (as against merely rhetorical): revolutionary because it is scientific, although the form of science it requires is necessarily itself revolutionary. For this reason I will call it scientific postmodernism, with the understanding that scientific postmodernism is necessarily a revolutionary science.

Ludic postmodernism has its uses in this project, since it has opened up a space in which it is easier now to explore the relations of Marxism and science than has been the case for most of this century. That of course is the direct opposite of the intentions of postmodern theorists like Lyotard. However, it is no surprise within Marxism to find people's actions producing results that are in direct contradiction to their stated aims.

My specific concern in the rest of this article is to develop an argument for a "postmodern" Marxist science of language. In doing so I believe that the annoying defects of Postmodernism in its first guise, as a rhetorical tactic, should not distract us from the positive value of scientific Postmodernism. It has not been easy in the past to develop a Marxist science of language. The work of Voloshinov is a notable exception. Pecheux in France and the body of work known as Critical Linguistics (see e.g., Fowler, Hodge and Kress) attempted to apply basic Marxist categories to the study of language, but the hold of modernist science has in general proved a powerful impediment to the development of a Marxist linguistics. Scientific Postmodernism offers an opportunity to put this project onto a new footing.

The Place of Language in Marxism

There is no major body of work we can easily point to to indicate the nature and scope of a Marxist science of language, whether modernist or post-modernist. This is where ludic Postmodernism has a point in its emphasis on discourse, even though paradoxically its extreme claim that everything is discourse makes discourse itself inexplicable. The central problem in Marxism has been the ongoing dispute about where language is to be situated in terms of the classic division between "base" and "superstructure." In these terms, language as the primary carrier of ideology seems most obviously to be located in the superstructure, a set of shifting and contingent forms that are less suitable objects for a Marxist science than economic or political facts. (For a discussion of the "Base and Superstructure" problem in Marxism see Williams).

Marxism itself, however, was born out of ideological critique, and throughout their career Marx and Engels were superb critics of the ideological assumptions carried by particular turns of phrase. The crucial point about this criticism was that it was always grounded in a historical materialist analysis that made sense of ideological and linguistic forms while not in the least ignoring them or minimizing their importance.

The early *German Ideology* contains a critique of Marx's contemporary

Young Hegelian opponents which could apply without much change to fashionable ludic Postmodernists of the 1990s:

> The Young-Hegelians, in spite of their allegedly 'world-shattering' phrases, are the staunchest conservatives. The most recent of them have found the correct expression for their activity when they declare they are fighting only against 'phrases.' They forget, however, that they themselves are opposing nothing but phrases to these phrases, and that they are in no way combating the real existing world when they are combating solely the phrases of this world. (36)

If "phrases" is replaced by "discourse" the ludic Postmodern project in its most aggressive phase is backdated by more than a century. However, Marx and Engels themselves would be guilty of self-contradiction if they are interpreted as condemning all kinds of criticism of ideology, since that is precisely what they are doing here and throughout the massive German Ideology, using their phrases against the phrases of the Young Hegelians. But their target is not ideological critique as such, but critiques which begin from ideology and never reach the world of practice. The famous image of ideology as a "camera obscura" in which men and their relations appear upside down is not part of a program to ignore ideology, but rather the first premise for a form of ideological critique that at last understands the relationship between ideology and material practices.

In this work, the first major text in which the foundations of the theory of historical materialism were developed, language is given an important role.

> Language is as old as consciousness, language is practical, real consciousness that exists for other men as well, and only therefore does it also exist for me. (49)

Marx and Engels here are insisting that language is embedded in the primary processes through which men (and women) make themselves as social beings. They point out that every "mode of production, or industrial stage, is always combined with a certain mode of co-operation, or social stage, and this mode of co-operation is itself a 'productive force'" (49). The first division of labor is a split within the set of productive forces:

> the *division of labor* implies the possibility, nay the fact, that intellectual and material activity, that enjoyment and labor, production and consumption, devolve on different individuals, and that the only possibility of their not coming into contradiction lies in negating in its turn the division of labor. (51)

That is, the theoretical separation of language and labor, far from being something advocated by Marx and Engels, is precisely what must be overcome in order to achieve Marxism's aims as revolutionary practice.

This sense of the vital connection between language and labor is restated in a late work by Engels, his fragment "The part played by labor in the transition from ape to man" of 1876: "First labor, after it and then with it, speech" (357). This is the first premise of a labor theory of language, in which tools, technology and forces of production are privileged components of an interdependent complex which is as it is because of the co-presence of relations of production, including every transformation and product of speech in the rest of human history. Language is not only ideology (as my own work among others has implied) it is also technology. The study of technology cannot leave out the study of language, and the study of language is part of the study of technology. Lyotard's inclusion of developments in language alongside developments in science and technology implies something like this, though in an undeveloped and untheorized form.

"Language" in this sense has a broader scope than mere "phrases" (or "discourse"). In this work, Marx and Engels use the term *Verkehr* or "intercourse," to cover all the relations between humans that are the conditions in which material production takes place. These include trade and war, systems of exchange and international relationships, all the conditions under which money or goods, spears or bullets or ICBMs are exchanged directly or symbolically in all their significant materiality. This notion of language, then, is minimally materialist and semiotic. It involves the reconstitution of a single scientific enterprise which unites linguistics and ideological critique with political economy, just as classic Marxism insists on the unity between economics and political science that had been lost by "bourgeois" academic disciplines.

The scope of a Marxist linguistics in this account must include at least three components:

> 1. *A theory of the constitutive material processes underlying all forms and processes of communication.* This will be a materialist form of social semiotics. It will include all communications technologies, in all media. It will include all systems of exchange and the rules and conditions for their operation—that is, economic and other forms of transaction, including money and other 'languages' of exchange.
>
> 2. *A theory of ideological processes and forms.* This will be a materialist theory of meaning and the processes through which meaning is constituted: that is, a theory which takes for granted the intrinsic relation be-

tween ideological forms and the material life processes that determine them. It will include the sedimented systems of meaning encoded in cultural forms, religion, law, architecture etc. and reinforced by specific rules for the distribution, consumption and reproduction of these meanings. Concepts of class conflict and the division of labor will be fundamental assumptions, and issues such as alienation, ideology and false consciousness will be examined in these terms.

3. *A theory of transformations.* Marxism is a revolutionary theory, committed to not only interpret the world, but to change it. Historical materialism is a theory that discovers a dialectic movement in history which progresses through crises and revolutions, and only when historical processes are seen in these terms will revolution be thinkable. Thus it identifies the conflicts and contradictions in any one phase that will lead to its negation. It seeks to use this understanding not simply to predict the future or to produce fantastic projections in the form of utopic or dystopic visions, but to change it.

Marxism and Science

Marx and Engels normally described their theory as *Scientific* Socialism, to distinguish it from other forms of socialism which they called Utopian, and from other forms of bourgeois knowledge that they saw as ideological (although they did not see all bourgeois economists, historians etc. as equally or invariably ideological or incapable of producing valid knowledge, and they made discriminating use of a wide range of works from the academic establishment of their day). They respected the achievements of the natural Sciences, and accepted in general the importance of the scientific method as a means of understanding the world. As materialists it would have been inconsistent for them to have excluded the natural sciences from their field of thought, and it was important to them to ally their own form of intellectual production to the methods and assumptions that underpinned the natural sciences.

However, in later polemics about the status of Marxism as a science there has been a tendency to identify Science with certainty of knowledge, as though Science's defining quality is its possession of truth. But Marx and Engels were not so uncritical of science as to have such a view. Engel's *Dialectics of Nature* of 1875-76 is the most substantial statement of their views about Science, but the complete text was not published till 1925, in German and Russian, and it became implicated in the Stalinist project of the 1930s to establish a purely Marxist form of Science.

Engels began the introduction to this work with a celebration of "Modern natural science, which alone has achieved a scientific, systematic, all-round development" (338). However, his account of the development of this tradition is similar in broad outline to the later account popularized by T. S. Kuhn in his *Structure of Scientific Revolutions*. Engels distinguishes between an initial heroic age of science which was part of 'the greatest progressive revolution that mankind had so far experienced' (339) and a later period of stultification, an account which corresponds to Kuhn's distinction between "revolutionary science" and "normal science." However, in spite of the title of his well-known work, Kuhn, himself, was symptomatically unable to describe or account for scientific revolutions or revolutionary science, which in his account was an inexplicable interruption between periods of "normal" science, mythologized to later generations as the heroic achievement of a few great men.

For Engels the nature of revolutions, in science as in society, was by no means inexplicable. In the revolutionary phase, according to him, science was revolutionary ("moving in the midst of the general revolution and . . . itself thoroughly revolutionary" (339)). During this time the leading figures were "giants" who consistently spanned different fields of learning, all of them achieving distinction in the arts as well as the sciences. "or the heroes of that time had not yet come under the servitude of the division of labor, the restricting effects of which, with their production of one-sidedness, we so often notice in their successors" (339). He notes, speculatively, a phenomenon of exponential progress in this initial phase: "Thenceforward, however, the development of the sciences proceeded with giant strides, and, it might be said, gained in force in proportion to the square of the distance (in time) from its point of departure" (340). Kuhn also notes a spectacular initial flowering in the wake of a successful scientific revolution.

This revolutionary phase of modern science, however, comes to an end which Engels associates with the achievements of Newton (who for Kuhn was the archetypal Revolutionary Scientist as paradigm-founder). There are two major factors that Engels emphasizes. One is the effect of the division of labor in the construction of disciplinary knowledges. The other is a conservative premise which is imposed on nature and then becomes the justification for a conservative Science, a "peculiar general outlook" whose central point is "the view of the absolute *immobility of nature*" (341). As he puts it:

> All change, all development in nature, was negated. Natural science, so revolutionary at the outset, suddenly found itself confronted by an out-and-out conservative nature, in which even today everything was as it had been at the beginning and in which—to the end of the world or for all eternity—everything was to remain as it had been since the beginning. (341)

For Engels, of course, this contradiction was not forced on the scientific establishment by the nature of Nature, but by social conditions under which scientific knowledge was produced. "Normal" science was the product of a non-revolutionary (anti-revolutionary) stage of society. In contrast, the only community Kuhn investigates is the scientific community, a classless, genderless and raceless society that is nearly autonomous from its surrounding society.

Engels writing in 1875 believed that this phase of science had been definitively superseded by a new revolutionary phase of science, marked not only by the work of Darwin but also others in fields such as astronomy and microbiology. This new phase had two main characteristics. It was radically interdisciplinary, "reducing the gulf between inorganic and organic nature to a minimum," and it emphasized dynamism, change and process:

> The new conception of nature was complete in its main features: all rigidity was dissolved, all fixity dissipated, all particularity that had been regarded as eternal became transient, the whole of nature shown as moving in eternal flux and cycles. (346)

This description was programmatic, capturing his conviction that the theory of dialectic that he had worked with in other fields was being vindicated by work in the natural sciences. However, in spite of the advances that he pointed to, and others that he did not live to see which conformed to his account of the "new conception of nature," modernist (non-revolutionary, "normal") science did not disappear but continued to provide the dominant definition of the nature of science and the physical universe. In the so-called "social sciences" such as psychology, sociology and linguistics it was positivistic ("normal," "modernist") science that was invoked to legitimate the authority of those disciplines as they "reached maturity," that is, became autonomous components of the curriculum at schools and universities.

Since for Engels the previous phase was "modern science" he might have characterized the next phase as "post modern science" if the term had had currency then. Certainly his description of the "new conception of nature" has much in common with the characteristics of what I call "postmodern science," although Engels' prophetic description shows how unhistorical is this term. Post-modern science of today is perhaps best seen as yet another reappearance of revolutionary science, which may eventually like all earlier forms be frozen and parceled off into various discrete and inaccessible disciplines of a new "normal" (modern) science. Even if this proves the case with "postmodern science" of the 1990s, it remains important for Marxists to note the difference between the two kinds of Science, and to recognize that as a revolutionary scientific theory Marxism is incompatible at many points with any "normal" science.

From this proposition there are a number of important consequence. One is that a revolutionary view of history and society and a revolutionary view of the natural world have many points in common, so that the relationship between the two is not one of fanciful analogy but rather a recognition of fundamental principles in common, which can and should be examined rigorously within a comparative framework. This means that discoveries in natural sciences or in social sciences should be applied systematically to different fields and the abstract common principles developed in this way. In fact, far from it being an intellectual virtue to keep the two areas apart, and to sustain this basic division of intellectual labor, major advances in science only happen when the two are brought into the closest contact. A Marxist linguistics will find much of value in Scientific postmodernism, specifically in post-modern science and its concepts, methods and models. The converse also applies. Postmodern science would do well to look closely at the theories of Marxism as the longest established continuous tradition of scientific postmodernism.

Postmodern Science

I have introduced the term "Postmodern science" to refer to a specific contemporary movement in science. However, it is still too new and disparate and undeveloped, as well as too complex, for its characteristics to be easily summarized. For present purposes it will be sufficient to indicate some tendencies and concepts that may be most useful in the development of a Marxist science of language.

"Chaos theory" as one major strand has been popularized in the work of Gleick and Hall. This popularization shows one of its qualities, its popular appeal, an appeal that crosses the boundaries of the distinction between science and arts, experts and members of the general public. Chaos theory touches on "soft" sciences as well as "hard," linking biology and physics, economics and history and poetry, pointing out the similarities between snowflakes and computer-generated art. These are characteristics of "heroic" (revolutionary) science according to Engels.

In the scenario that I have in mind, a revolutionary (postmodern) Marxist theory of language will be explosively productive. For some time at least, it may, as Engels suggests, produce an exponential series of new insights and discoveries. If it does, this will be due in part to the homologies that exist between postmodern science and Marxism—in spite of the best efforts of ludic Postmodernism to refuse to acknowledge the existence of serious postmodern science or the continuing viability of Marxism.

Towards a Postmodern Marxist Science of Language

In proposing a postmodern Marxist science of language, I am aware that for many (postmodernists, Marxists, scientists and theorists of language alike) this project is impossible or undesirable, an attempt to yoke together things that are incompatible. My case is that on the contrary these tendencies or traditions of thought urgently need to be brought together in order to understand the interdependent aspects of a single common object that they all in different ways address. Specifically, a Marxist science of language will be more genuinely postmodern (that is, using new tools of thought to make sense of new emerging phenomena) than ludic postmodernism, at the same time as it is more scientific than modernist science, providing a more powerful and comprehensive understanding of language than any other kind of linguistic theory past or present: and it will be no less strongly Marxist for doing all this.

In saying this I am not proposing a vague and abstract form of these various traditions, one so imprecise that all differences cease to be discernible in an overall conceptual blob. A science of language must be systematic and rigorous, and if the synthesis is properly to be called Marxist then basic propositions of Marxism must be foundational in it. That of course is not to say that these propositions, in a canonical form, should be treated as dogma to be accepted without question. Marxism itself will become dead when it ceases to participate in the flux and development that Engels saw as the necessary condition of every revolutionary science.

The following observations are offered as suggestions toward this project, rather than as a systematic treatment of a branch of Marxism which has yet to be fully developed. I will take some basic terms from classic Marxism and suggest some fruitful connections with postmodern science, looking particularly at how they might be applied to topics in the area of language.

(i) Historical Materialism

> Marx reflected on this principle in *Preface to a Critique of Political Economy*:
>
> Just as our opinion of an individual is not based on what he thinks of himself, so can we not judge of such a period of transformation by its own consciousness; on the contrary, this consciousness must be explained rather from the contradictions of material life, from the existing conflict between the social productive forces and the relations of production. (182)

This formulation does not disvalue consciousness as an object of analysis. The premise of materialism simply insists that *explanations* must be grounded in an account of material circumstances which condition the objects and processes of consciousness. But the study of language is not confined to a study of consciousness. It is the medium of consciousness and therefore a medium for both ideology and understanding. It is also a component of socially productive forces, and the medium through which relations of production are negotiated.

This proposed three-fold location of language is very different from the proposition that is commonly found in ludic postmodernism, that "everything is discourse." On the contrary, though discourse is indeed everywhere, it is always everywhere a product of material forces, always with human agency. It is not confined to the "superstructure" as in some forms of Marxism, but nor is it ever the whole of reality, or explicable solely in its own terms. Its three functions normally overlap in practice: ideological (to transform material reality in the interests of specific material groups and purposes); technological (to achieve specific purposes as part of work); and social (to organize the political and social relationships of all members of a given society).

(ii) Contradiction, Conflict and Unpredictability

In Marxism revolutions, major transformational processes are intrinsic to the system, not inexplicable interruptions to the normal state of a given system as in modernist forms of knowledge. The dynamic that drives this process is the existence of contradictions and conflicts: conflicts within the relations of production (class antagonisms, exploitation etc.) and contradictions between the state of the forces of production and the relations of production. A development in the forces of production taken to its logical (linear) conclusion turns the relations of production that initially were most compatible with it into its opposite, into fetters, impediments to its very existence. This contradiction impacts in turn on the conflictual relations of production that were always there and produces the conditions for a social revolution.

Marx's form of materialism, then, describes a shifting relationship between forces and relations of production, leading to periodic crises or catastrophes. This indeed was one of the most marked differences between Marxism and the dominant forms of neo-classical economics. But one consequence of this form of materialism is that material conditions can never in principle produce, deterministically, a one-to-one form of consciousness. Ideology itself is necessarily plural, a set of forms of consciousness through which humans "become conscious of this conflict and fight it out" (182).

Modernist science operates with a model of linear causality, attempting to identify and isolate causes and effects which are conceptually distinct, so that ultimately events can be understood as the totally predictable product of a set of causes. The distinctive property of so-called "Chaos theory" is to include non-linear forms of causality which produce behaviors that are unpredictable except in broad principles. As Gleick puts it:

> Where chaos begins, classical science stops. . . . The irregular side of nature, the discontinuous and erratic side—these have been puzzles to science, or worse, monstrosities. (3)

However, for chaos theorists unlike ludic postmodernists, this chaos and unpredictability is a challenge to develop an appropriate and non-simplistic explanation, not a reason to congratulate oneself for not trying to explain anything. For 150 years Marxism has been theorizing chaos, discontinuity and unpredictability, aspiring also, as a scientific not an ideological practice, to understand such phenomena as systematically as possible.

Chaos theory recognizes that science must be concerned with what is inherently unpredictable as well as what is predictable. Weather is a case in point. At a certain level it is not predictable. It is part of a chaotic system, in which there are identified forces at play, and patterns and regularities that arise, but not absolute predictability.

Marx's thinking allowed for the place of accidents in processes that were nonetheless also subject to regular laws. In a letter to Kugelman, he wrote:

> World history would indeed be very easy to make if the struggle were

taken up only on condition of infallibly favorable chances. It would on the other hand be of a very mystical nature, if 'accidents' played no part. These 'accidents' naturally form part of the general course of development and are compensated by other accidents. But acceleration and delay are very much dependent on such 'accidents,' including the 'accident' of the character of the people who first head the movement.

Marx's point here is similar to the so-called "Butterfly effect" in Chaos theory, the recognition that in some systems there is a "Sensitivity to Initial Conditions" that can lead to inherently unpredictable outcomes. Why for instance do revolutions take a specific form in different places, which increasingly diverges from the common base (e.g., the Russian revolution versus the Chinese or Cuban revolutions)? What is it about phase transitional systems that makes them so critical? Marx was aware of these factors, but it was not easy when he was writing to see them as fundamental to a scientific understanding, rather than as exceptions to take into account.

At the core of Marx's theory of historical materialism is the recognition of the presence of non-linear causality and chaotic systems. Marxism could not specify the year or place of the next crisis for capitalism, but it did describe the kinds of crisis that capitalism was liable to. Neo-classical economics was a typical form of modernist science in that it rigorously and incorrectly predicted that there would be no crises at all. Even neo-Keynsian economics could recognize crises only because the scale of the crisis of capitalism in the 1930s was too great to ignore.

In these terms, a condition of language is like a day's weather: not immediately predictable from an inventory of the material conditions, while still fully a product of those conditions. If a system (weather, Capitalism, the mass media) can produce both A and not-A (and innumerable other combinations) then linear (Aristotelian, Modernist) logic will not work. Contradictions within the relations and forces of production produce unpredictable outcomes, so that forms of language cannot be simply deduced from a stage of development of society. This is a kind of "indeterminacy" but its role in developments of theory is very different to what is proclaimed by ludic Postmodernists. The fact that a specific phenomenon cannot be deduced unequivocally from previous conditions as far as these are understood does not mean that it cannot be explained, specifically in relation to material forces. On the contrary, precisely because the relationship between textual forms and material reality for instance is intrinsically variable and unpredictable at the level of detail, explanation must refer to the specific forces and relations of production, relating the complexity and indeterminacy to contradictions and conflicts within and between forces and relations of production.

Marxist Linguistics and Critical Practice

Marxism insists on the unity of theory and practice. A Marxist linguistics is necessary precisely for this reason: Marxists need to analyze language wherever it is a factor in social and political processes.

The form of Marxist linguistics I propose draws on theories of language as technology and ideology to contribute illuminating readings of events and their textualization to an overall materialist Marxist interpretation. To illustrate what is at issue I will use the Gulf War as a reference point, along with a reading of a specific text.

Undoubtedly, new media and military technologies were show-cased in the conduct of this war, and there were predictably inflated ludic Postmodernist claims about the over-riding importance and novelty of these developments. In a good example of this kind of criticism, Wark analyzed the war as an "event" constructed by the media, which operated a 'feedback loop' into the 'real' actions and forces at work" (7). In this analysis, media technologies play a decisive role, complemented by military technology such as the revolutionary "Missile-cam," and CNN's successes become more significant than any battle fought by Stormin' Norman.

But Wark's account misses out on some important aspects of this war. One is the predictability of much that he celebrates as new. He quotes Pilger's trenchant criticism: "The true nature of the Gulf is civilian slaughter" (18) but this comment by a radical investigative journalist is untouched by postmodern sophistication. The ideological process Pilger exposes is much older than the technology that it employs.

In Wark's narrative the triumph of the new technologies is foreordained if lamentable. But with hindsight it becomes easier to see contradictions he ignores, which made any specific outcome more unpredictable than he assumes. For instance, the 90% support President Bush enjoyed at the climax of the war had eroded into defeat by the next election. The Falklands war, seemingly comparable to the Gulf War but with less advanced media technology, translated into a landslide win for Thatcher.

Specific forms of textuality are no more predictable than outcomes of events, and their interpretation raises precisely the same issues for a Marxist linguistics. To illustrate I will look at the following text, which appeared in the *Australian Sydney Morning Herald* during the Gulf War (25-2-91).

cing the beginning of the ground offensive to eject the Iraqi Army from Kuwait. Full text, Page 23

STORM IN

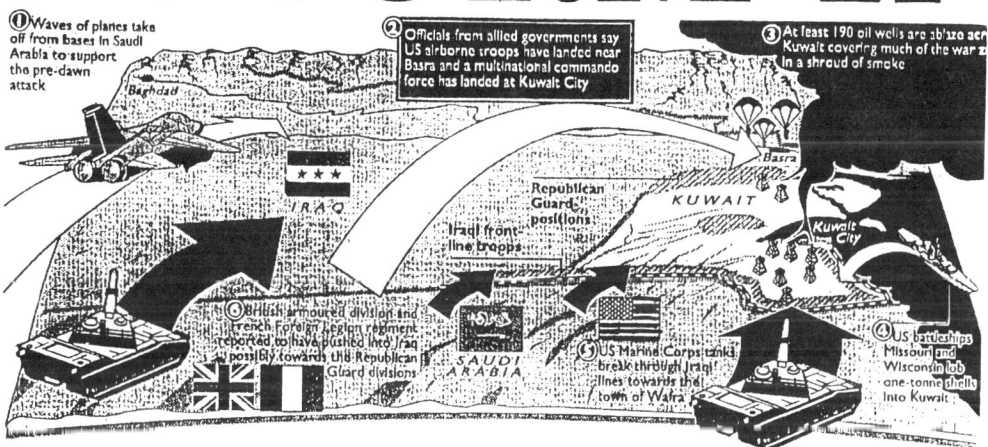

① Waves of planes take off from bases in Saudi Arabia to support the pre-dawn attack

② Officials from allied governments say US airborne troops have landed near Basra and a multinational commando force has landed at Kuwait City

③ At least 190 oil wells are ablaze ac Kuwait covering much of the war z in a shroud of smoke

④ US battleships Missouri and Wisconsin lob one-tonne shells into Kuwait

⑤ US Marine Corps tanks break through Iraqi lines towards the town of Wafra

⑥ British armoured division and French Foreign Legion regiment reported to have pushed into Iraq possibly towards the Republican Guard divisions

At first sight this text seems to illustrate the claim that this was a thoroughly postmodern war in which high-tech systems of representation produce persuasive images of a war like a computer game played on a global scale. The image was clearly produced by computer graphics from American sources, reproduced by the Australian newspaper with the instantaneity that modern communications technologies make possible.

But there is more that can be said about this image, using the simple but open categories "forces and relations of production" as a guide to explanations that are capable of recognizing the constant presence of conflict and contradiction as constitutive features. For instance, the computer graphics produce an image whose "reality" is significantly variable but not predictable. The map has been swung around so that it recedes into the image of a three-dimensional space that exists only as a construct of a computer. Inserted onto it are three dimensional images of planes, ships etc. that do potentially exist in the material world, though here they are dislocated from that world, entirely under the control of the graphic artist who can put any image anywhere in the picture, whatever "reality" is like.

This technology allows an image to be effortlessly constructed in which different kinds of reality are equally easy to produce alongside each other, with no markers to identify the difference. This is the "postmodern condition" identified by Baudrillard who claims that under postmodernism it is no longer possible to distinguish the real from the simulacrum: though this difficulty only exists for theorists who refuse to study the material processes used to construct this illusionism.

There is more ideological work being done in this text. The three-dimensionality positions the reader of the image below Kuwait, with Iraq opposite stretching into the distance. This is not the world as seen from Kuwait either, but Kuwait is closer to "us."

The computer graphics insert verbal text as easily as images, thus incorporating all the devices of verbal language. For instance, the entire population of Iraq is compressed into a single word, "Iraq," plus a flag. The old technologies of verbal language produce the same effects as the new technologies, mutually reinforcing each other. The resources of verbal language transform a complex socio-political situation into a simplistic ideological form, perhaps more effectively than the newer technologies because it is so simple and taken for granted. In understanding what is going on we should not ignore the role of the new, but equally we should not underestimate the continuing importance of the old.

There are different kinds of verbal text in this text, which are as different as the kinds of visual image but work along the same lines. As well as single-word labels ("Baghdad," "Kuwait") there are full sentences ("Waves of planes take off from bases in Saudi Arabia to support the pre-dawn attack"). Sentences have direct modalities (simple present tense, no qualifications) when they are talking about American activities, indicating no doubts at all about the truth of what "we" (Americans) do and know, but complex tenses and modalities when talking about others than Americans (Americans "attack," whereas British are "reported to have pushed"). Truth, that is, is only a property of reports about Americans (and, interestingly, the Iraqis). Regarding the British and others we have to rely on reports which may be wrong or out of date. A side-effect of this is that Australian consumers of this text are constructed as honorary Americans, only able to be directly certain about what Americans (and Iraqis) are doing.

There is much more to say about the ideological stratagems of this text, but from the point of view of a Marxist linguistics what needs to be insisted on is the difference between explications and explanations. Explanations require us to know who did what to whom, with what resources; Pilger's kind of realism is old-fashioned Marxism that is just as much needed in the "post-modern age."

Again, behind the unpredictability is contradiction. Computer technology, for instance, underpins both media and military technologies. The media technology implied by the text is advanced (though no more advanced than the simplest of computer games) but the military technology represented is simple—no images of "smart bombs" or communication systems. The meaning of this split is the conflictual relations in the production of the image—between producers and consumers, rulers and ruled in a political order where the consent of the governed has to be managed. The idea is to look smart (smarter than Saddam) but not too smart, for a public that is suspicious of too much technology used against them.

What we have is a text which in its details is as complex, indeterminate and unpredictable as any ludic Postmodernist could want, yet those qualities are not self evidently beyond explanation. On the contrary, a materialist Marxism draws attention to precisely the qualities in the conditions of production which account for the novelty that can be attributed to this text. But where ludic Postmodernism can only notice and be overwhelmed by novelty, Marxism traces the effects of all linguistic processes, old and new. It is hard to see how Marxist accounts have been rendered redundant by ludic Postmodernism, so long as the Marxist account does indeed recognize genuine novelty, and attempts to account for the intricacy that is characteristic of this and so many other examples of language at work.

Works Cited

Baudrillard, Jean. *Simulations*. P. Foss, trans. New York: Semiotext(e), 1983.
Ebert, Teresa. "Ludic feminism" *Critical Survey*, 1991.
Engels, Frederick. "Introduction to Dialectics of Nature" 1975-6. In Marx and Engels, *Selected Works* .
_____. "The part played by labor in the transition from ape to man'. In Marx and Engels, *Selected Works*.
Frow, John. *What was Postmodernism?* Sydney: Local Consumption Publications, 1991.
Fowler, Roger, Bob Hodge, Gunther Kress, and Tony Trew. *Language and Control*. London: Routledge and Kegan Paul, 1979.
Gleick, James. *Chaos*. London: Cardinal Books, 1988.
Hall, N., ed. *The New Scientist Guide to Chaos*. Harmondsworth: Penguin, 1992.
Harvey, David. *The Condition of Postmodernity*. Oxford: Blackwells, 1989
Hodge, Robert and Gunther Kress. *Language as Ideology*. 2nd edition. London: Routledge, 1993.
Lyotard, Jean-François. *The Post-Modern Condition: a Report on Knowledge*. G. Bennington and B. Massumi, trans. Minneapolis: University of Minnesota Press, 1984.
Kuhn, Thomas S. *The Structure of Scientific Revolutions*. Chicago: Chicago University Press, 1962.
Marx, Karl, and Frederick Engels. *The German Ideology*. Moscow: Progress Publishers, 1976.
_____. *Selected Works*. London: Lawrence and Wishart, 1968.

_____. "Preface to A Contribution to the Critique of Political Economy (1859)." In *Marx and Engels, Selected Works.*
_____. "Letter to L. Kugelmann, April 17, 1871." In *Marx and Engels, Selected Works.*
Pecheux, Michel. 1982. *Language, Semantics, Ideology.* London: Macmillan.
Voloshinov, V. *Marxism and the Philosophy of Language.* New York: Seminar Press, 1973.
Wark, Mackenzie. "News Bites: War TV in the Gulf." *Meanjin* 50.1 (1991): 5-18.
Williams, Raymond. *Marxism and Literature.* Oxford: Blackwell, 1977.

Jorge Larrain

Identity, the Other and Postmodernism

Introduction

The difficulty of accurately defining postmodernism is well known and, to a certain extent, understandable since it seems to refer to a variety of phennomena belonging to disparate fields and areas of activity. In effect, postmodernity claims to exist no only in art, architecture, literature, theology, philosophy and social science but also as a new structure of feelings that pervades common people, as a particular way of experiencing, interpreting and being in the world which has undermined modernist sentiments (Harvey 53). If this is so, it is then a good idea to introduce a distinction between the theoretical or academic discourse of postmodernity which constitutes a social imaginary from which new meanings and significations are drawn, and the more concrete feelings, orientations and social practices of people which could be more or less postmodern if one compare them with the discursive claims.

It is my contention that between the postmodern discourse and the newly emerging feelings about the world there is an important distance in the sense that although the new ways of experiencing the world have undoubtedly prompted the emergence of a postmodern discourse which seeks to explain them, this is by no means the only plausible explanation. Moreover, sometimes one can distinctly detect in the postmodern discourse a tendency to exaggerate the emergence of feelings of disunity, fragmentation, contingency, chaos, division, difference, discontinuity, meaninglessness and purposelessness as if they all were prevalent and widespread throughout society.

In dealing with the issues related to personal identity I intend to use this distinction as an important tool of analysis. Let us state first what the problem is.

There seem to be two ways in which the postmodern discourse relates itself to the issue of identity: on the one hand there is an approach which focuses on the discovery of "otherness" and the right of the "other" to speak for itself. On the other hand, there is an approach which focuses on the decentering of the subject and the loss of its identity. I shall explore the way in which the postmodern discourse arrives at these two opposite results and shall examine critically their coherence and tenability.

Modernity and the Constitution of the Other

In the first place, the idea of and concern for the "other" does not arise with postmodernism. In the formation or construction of any cultural identity the idea of the "other" is crucial and this had been noticed long before the postmodern discourse made its appearance, for instance in the work of William James and George Mead. The construction of the self necessarily involves the existence of others against which the self acquires its distinctiveness and specificity. The self is not given but develops in an individual as a result of his/her social experiences, it presupposes the prior existence of the group. Even a national or collective kind of identity presupposes the existence of others who have different modes of life, different values, customs and ideas. In order to define the self the differences with others are accentuated. The other can be defined in at least three dimensions: time, space and essential characteristics. By means of the temporal dimension the other is located in the past; it is the antithesis of a new project. This is the way in which most theories typical of modernity understood modern society, in opposition to traditional society. The other of modernity is the old or obsolete, the primitive and backward.

But the other can also be defined in terms of those who lack a fundamental characteristic. Most discourses of modernity, for instance, find in reason and civilization, and those who represent them, the most important source of cultural identity. This is why there are subordinate social categories and groups within modernity itself which assume the role of the other insofar as they represent the lack of reason and civilization. Wagner has identified the working classes, women and mentally ill people as the three main categories of "others" of early modernity, identified as such because of their lack of reason (Wagner 39). The working classes were at the beginning considered as dangerous classes with far too many boundless aspirations which introduced disorder in society. Women, in their turn, were systematically excluded from public and political life throughout the 19th century and a good part of the 20th, because of their supposed "emotiveness," "lack of control" and lack of rationality. Finally, mad and insane people represented as well those irrational "others" which have no control over themselves.

In the third place, by means of the spatial dimension, the other is defined as that who lives outside or beyond the boundaries of a particular society, the barbarian or backward primitive who has still to be civilized. It is very important to understand that in the construction of the European cultural identities from the 16th century onwards, the presence of the non-European other was always crucial. The discovery and conquest of America in particular played a very important role because it coincided with the beginning of modernity, the beginning of capitalism and the formation of the European nation-states. Therefore, the formation of the European cultural identities at the beginning of modernity was carried out in opposition to some "others," who were provided not just by their own feudal past, not only by their own "non-rational" social sectors, but also by the contemporary but spatially different reality of America, Africa and Asia. In all these cases the opposition to the "other" seems to be determined by rationality criteria. Thus, a more or less complete picture of the "others" of early modernity and their specific lack of reason might be like this:

wildness	>	black people, savages, non-civilized peoples
tradition	>	nobility, priests
disorder	>	working classes, masses
emotiveness	>	women
insanity	>	mad people

Of course, some of these social sectors later ceased to play the fundamental role of "other" and little by little were incorporated into the mainstream society. This is especially true of the working classes and women, the two sectors closer to society itself and numerically very important. Their incorporation was partly the result of their own successful struggles and partly the consequence of social pacts which gave them citizenship in exchange for moderation and order. The more advanced modernity becomes, the more "otherness" becomes concentrated in the spatial dimension, including those who live outside or come from abroad. This is the reason why ethnic factors have acquired preponderance in the contemporary definition of otherness.

Nevertheless, the other internal factors have never ceased to have some presence as "others," even if marginally. A notable example is the neo-conservative crusade of Mrs. Thatcher in Great Britain which made a serious attempt to renovate the old military values of English identity by adding to the external enemy, Argentina, an "internal enemy," the trade-unions, which had to be defeated in order to revert the country's declining economic trends. Something similar was attempted by general Pinochet's government in Chile, where workers and shanty town dwellers were reconstituted anew as dangerous classes for national security.

Postmodernity, the Other and the Self

The postmodern discourse no longer considers reason as the basis for the construction of identities and their others. For postmodernism one cannot aspire to any unified representation of the world, or picture it as a totality full of connections and differentiation. What one has is a conjunction of perpetually shifting fragments. There is no single history, only images of the past projected from different points of view. It is illusory to think that there exists a supreme or comprehensive viewpoint capable of unifying all others. Hence the postmodernist emphasis in discontinuity and fragmentation. Neither philosophers nor social scientists can find a global sense in the world.

This is connected with the fact that we live in a society of generalized communication and mass media. Contemporary culture has become increasingly affected by them to the point that some authors speak of the "mediazation" of modern culture: "the general process by which the transmission of symbolic forms becomes increasingly mediated by the technical and institutional apparatuses of the media industries" (Thompson 4). Radio, television and newspapers have become the agents of a general explosion and proliferation of images and world views. This is what makes society more complex and chaotic. The increase in information and images about the many forms of reality makes it increasingly difficult to conceive of a single reality. According to Vattimo in the world of the mass media Nietzsche's prophecy is fulfilled: in the end the true world becomes a fable. We can no longer arrive at reality itself. Reality is no longer something simple concealed behind images, reality is rather the intersection of a multiplicity of images (Vattimo 7-8).

This is the reason why postmodernism believes in ephemerality, fragmentation, discontinuity, and the chaotic. In spite of the fact that the postmodern discourse is very critical of the modern discourses of emancipation, Vattimo has argued that this very erosion of the principle of a meaningful reality is connected with a new sense of liberation and emancipation:

Emancipation here consists in disorientation, which is at the same time also the liberation of differences, of local elements, of what could generally be called dialect. With the demise of the idea of a central rationality in history, the world of generalized communication explodes like a multiplicity of 'local' rationalities—ethnic, sexual, religious, cultural or aesthetic minorities—that finally speak up for themselves. They are no longer repressed into silence by the idea of a single true form of humanity (Vattimo 8-9).

Thus postmodernism allows "otherness" to emerge not just as the mere antagonist of well defined rational identities, but as the new protagonist of a plurality of discourses. Modernity with its totalizing discourses of emancipation "presumed to speak for others (colonized peoples, blacks, minorities, religious groups, women, the working class) with a unified voice" (Harvey 47-48) and a unified discourse. Postmodernism rejects these totalizing discourses, be them religious, Liberal or Marxist. All groups have the right to speak for themselves, in their own voice or dialect, and this would show the pluralistic stance of postmodernism. But there is also another side to this approach.

According to the postmodern discourse discontinuity, fragmentation and incoherence affect not just the real world but also individual themselves and their personalities. For modernity the subject was thought to be well integrated, a coherent and centered self, the origin and cause of actions, ideas and texts. For postmodernity, on the contrary, the subject is essentially fragmented and decentered in his/her inner being, internally divided, unable to unify his/her experiences. It is not the pre-given origin of meaning but rather is itself constituted in language or discourse. The idea of a well integrated and causal subject is an invention of modernity, especially of the rationalism of the Enlightenment. Hence to the destruction of a single reality and the lack of meaning of history corresponds a decentered subject which has lost its identity.

As the self is not coherent but fragmented, cannot unify the past, present and future of its own biographical experience or psychic life. The project of modernity with its rationalism, determinism and sense of historical progress, required subjects with a sense of personal identity and coherence which allow them to project themselves in time. The very critique of alienation (religious, political and economic), so important for modern authors, presupposed a centered subject which somehow could be alienated by external factors which could be changed. Hence, emancipation.

For postmodernity, on the contrary, the subject is constructed in internal conflict, it exists in a radical incoherence of his/her personal identity and cannot therefore even picture or devise strategies to produce a radically different future. There is no sense in the question about a better future, about emancipation. The subject only lives in the present, surrounded by the spectacle of signifiers which have lost all connection with the signified. Hence the loss of identity means that the subject cannot coherently act in the world nor can it engage in a global project.

Stuart Hall has proposed a sort of historical progression by distinguishing three very different conceptions of identity which correspond to three different types of subject: the Enlightenment subject, the sociological subject and the postmodern subject. The Enlightenment subject was based on a conception of the human person as a fully centered, unified individual, endowed with the capacities of reason, consciousness and action. The self or human center was an inner core which came with the individual as s/he was born and remained basically the same throughout life. The sociological subject goes beyond an individualistic conception of the subject to emphasize the fact that the inner core of the subject is not autonomous and self-sufficient but is formed in relation to significant others. The self could only be the result of the symbolic interaction between the subject and the others, the self is not given but develops in an individual as a result of his/her social experiences. Finally, the postmodern subject is conceptualized as not having a fixed and permanent identity, the subject has become fragmented and composed of a variety of identities which are contradictory or unresolved. Those identities are not unified around a coherent self. In fact the coherent self is just a story, a fantasy we tell ourselves (Hall, Held & McGrew 275-277).

Here is then the paradox: the postmodern discourse seems to sanction the emergence of the other, of a different identity, but also seems to sanction the dislocation of the self. The "other" can now speak for him/herself but the self seems to be unable to speak for itself with a unified voice. The other appears to be integrated around a coherent, if local or different, identity but the self seems to be fragmented in a variety of contradictory identities. The obvious crucial questions to postmodern discourse are then these: is not the other, which speaks for her/himself with a unified voice, a coherent kind of identity? Why would be any self so dislocated if the others are not? Is there not a contradiction between this so-called discovery of the other and the announcement of the end of the coherent self? Before trying to see whether there are adequate answers to these questions within the postmodern perspective let us examine in greater detail each separate claim.

The Other in the Modern and Postmodern Conceptions

What can be said about the discovery of otherness by postmodernism? A first reaction tends naturally to be positive. If postmodernism propounds concern for the other, and opposition to total visions which reduce difference to uniformity, it must play a positive role. Modern totalizing theories are always in danger of believing that the particular, the local and the historically specific, acquire meaning only insofar as they are instances of the general. The belief in a general historical rationality may easily conceal the difference and autonomy of local rationalities. Postmodernism, on the contrary, seems to allow the cultural other a voice of its own, the right to be different and not to be subsumed by a general logic which eliminates its specificity. It is ironic that in the case of Third World others these rights appear to be defended not by their own self-affirmation but, yet again, by a theory constructed in Europe. Still, one cannot begrudge a helping hand. However, a closer look at this problem and a comparison with theories of modernity may show that not all is so clear-cut.

It is certainly true that modern theories and postmodern discourses have a different approach to the cultural "other." But this does not mean that the latter are necessarily better than the former. In fact both have problems of a different order. While modern universalistic theories have difficulties in understanding otherness and difference and see history as a series of stages through which everybody has to go, postmodernism has difficulties in understanding the elements of shared humanity which underlie all cultures. Like all forms of historicism, postmodern discourses conceive of history as a segmented process or, as Foucault would put it, as "the space of a dispersion" (Foucault 10). There is no single center, principle or meaning but a variety of different cultural essences which each nation develops and whose understanding requires a kind of empathy.

Universalistic theories tend to look at the "other" from the point of view of the European rational subject; they tend to apply a total pattern which postulates its own absolute truth and the backwardness of the rest. Hence all cultural differences are explained in relation to its own unity and therefore they tend to be reduced to a moment or stage which will be historically overcome. Postmodern discourses look at the "other" from the perspective of its unique and specific cultural set-up, thus emphasizing cultural difference and historical discontinuity. There are dangers implicit in both positions. While the emphasis on absolute truth and historical continuity may lead to reductionism and neglect of the other's specificity, the emphasis on difference and discontinuity may lead to the construction of the other as less than human or inferior.

This is why the idea that modern theories tend to be intolerant and racist whereas postmodern theories tend to be pluralistic and tolerant is simplistic if not misleading. It is true that there is a form of racism which stems from universalistic theories which do not recognize and accept the other as different. But there is also another form of racism which stems from postmodern discourses which although allowing the other to speak for itself, do not want anything to do with it because it is constructed as totally different, as belonging to an alien world. The other may be acknowledged in its right to exist but it is suspected as culturally invasive and so different as to be inferior or unacceptable according to the main cultural standards.

Modern and postmodern discourses have therefore different conceptions of history and cultural identity. But this does not make the latter superior to the former. Modern discourses tend to conceive of history as universal, unilinear and teleological progress, whereas postmodern theories conceive of history as a discontinuous, segmented and purposeless process which has no universal direction. Paradoxically, the emphasis on historical discontinuity leads postmodern theories to conceive of cultural identity in a non-historical way, as an essence, as an immutable spirit which marks an unbridgeable difference between peoples and nations. The emphasis on history as unilinear progress, on the contrary, may disregard historical discontinuities and specificities, but usually accepts a notion of cultural identity as a process of construction and reconstruction which cannot be reduced to an essence.

An unchecked emphasis on difference may easily transform itself into a judgment of purity and a wish to exclude and keep separate: different cultures are accepted as long as they remain home and do not come to encroach on the cultures of the center. Postmodern positions fail to appreciate the existence of the common ground, of hybridity. To them one can exactly ask what Said asked "Orientalism":

> Can one divide human reality, as indeed human reality seems to be genuinely divided, into clearly different cultures, histories, traditions, societies, even races, and survive the consequences humanly? By surviving the consequences humanly, I mean to ask whether there is any way of avoiding the hostility expressed by the division, say, of men into 'us' (Westerners) and 'they' (Orientals). For such divisions are generalities whose use historically and actually has been to press the importance of the distinction between some men and some other men, usually towards not especially admirably ends. (Said 45)

Decentered Subject and Contradictory Identities

If one takes Hall's distinction between the Enlightenment subject, the sociological subject and the postmodern subject in a historical sense there would have been a progression from the subject as an immutable essence to the subject as a social construction and from this to the subject as divided, as a collection of disparate tendencies. If we take the point of view of identity the progression would have been from identity as a fixed and given essence to identity as social construction and from this to the disappearance of a single integrated identity altogether. If one surveys the history of modern philosophy one can find many elements which seem to confirm this evolution.

It is very clear that modernity, especially as represented by the Enlightenment, put the human being at the center of the world and made it the measure of all things. The human being was "the subject," which by means of reason became the basis of all knowledge, the master of all things, the necessary point of reference for all that goes on. But originally, this conception of the subject was abstract and individualistic, separated from history and social relations, that is to say, deprived of a sense of change and of its social dimension. It was conceived as an inherent essence. This is why the modern philosophical conception of identity was based on the belief in the existence of a self or inner core which emerges at birth, like a soul or essence, and which, in spite of being able to develop different potentialities in time, remains basically the same throughout life, thus providing a sense of continuity and self-recognition.

Locke and the French philosophers of the Enlightenment wanted to leave metaphysics behind and conceived of personal identity as depending on memory, on the material continuity of consciousness over time. Even Leibniz, who still regarded an identity of metaphysical substance to be necessary, agreed on the importance of memory. Whatever their differences, from Descartes to Leibniz most philosophers developed a conception of an individual and isolated subject with its own identity. With Kant, the subject assumed an even more abstract and transcendental character insofar as he took away the notion of identity from the field of sensuous experience (phenomena) and put it back into the sphere of metaphysics (noumena). So Kant confirmed an abstract, supra-temporal and non-historical notion of the subject. Hegel added to it the historical dimension and the dialectical reference to the other, but maintained its abstractness as the idea substituted for real human beings.

Marx was one of the first authors within modernity to attack the individualistic conception of the subject as an illusion derived from the "Robinsonades" of "eighteenth century prophets" (*Grundrisse* 83). He criticized Feuerbach for abstracting from the historical process and presupposing "an abstract—isolated—human individual." If there is a human essence this is in its reality "the ensemble of the social relations" and not an "abstraction inherent in each single individual" (*Theses* 29). Marx detects the paradox that "the epoch which produces this standpoint, that of the isolated individual, is also precisely that of hitherto most developed social relations" (*Grundrisse* 84). Human beings can individuate themselves only in the midst of society (84); they "become individuals only through the process of history" (*Grundrisse* 496). This means that subjects do not act entirely according to their free will, they are conditioned by the objectified products of their own practice, they are socially determined. However, although circumstances condition human beings, human beings can change circumstances. In a way it could be said that Marx started or anticipated the emergence of Hall's "sociological subject."

The "sociological" conception of the subject as produced in interaction with a variety of social relations became crucial for philosophers, sociologists and social psychologists. Thus for instance William James identified three constituent elements of the self of a human being. Apart from a spiritual element comprising the capabilities and psychic and mental functions, a material element is described in terms of the possession of material objects and the acquisition of wealth and a social element is defined as the recognition which each individual obtains from other human beings. Mead, a distinguished social psychologist, argued that the conception of the self as a soul with which the individual was born had to be abandoned in order to study the "self in its dependence upon the social group to which it belongs" (Mead 1). The self is not given but develops in an individual as a result of his/her social experiences through language and communication. This is why the formation of the self presupposes the prior existence of the group.

Most sociological and social-psychological conceptions recognize the social character of individual identities, as they are shaped and formed in interaction with a variety of social relations. Identity, in a personal sense, is something which an individual presents to the "others" and which the others present to him. The meaning of identity responds not so much to the question "who am I?" as to the question "who am I in the eyes of the others?" (De Levita 7).

In the terms of Gerth and Mills, the subject is composed of the combination of roles that he or she enacts and "our total self-image involves our relations to other persons and their appraisal of us" (Gerth & Mills 80). This is the result of the fact that roles are not just patterns of conduct, but expected patterns of conduct, that is to say, in internalizing a series of roles the subject internalizes the others' expectations of him/her, and these expectations of others become his/her self-expectations. However, only the appraisals of those others who are in some way significant to the person count for much of the building and maintenance of his/her self-image. Parents are the most significant others at the beginning but later a variety of other significant others begin to operate.

Mead accepts that because the self arises in the context of a variety of social experiences it is very complex, full of aspects or parts which make reference to certain social relations and not to others. That is why it is even possible to speak of a variety of selves or elementary selves. However, there is also a complete self, a socially constructed inner core, which responds to the community as a whole or, at least to the conjunction of significant others (Mead 142 & 144). In other words, the complete self responds to a "generalized other," which is composed of an integration of the appraisals and values of the significant others of the person. It is assumed that the socially constructed self more or less successfully integrates the various aspects of its immense complexity and thus is coherent and consistent in its tendencies and activities. This is precisely the assumption which postmodernism puts into question giving rise to Hall's idea of a "postmodern" subject.

Following a line of thought which started with David Hume and Nietzsche, and which received the influence of Freud, structuralism, Althusserianism and poststructuralism, postmodernism is just the last stage in an onslaught against the subject which started much earlier but has become increasingly influential. Foucault is the first author to speak of the "decentering of the subject," an occurrence which for him has been brought about by the researches of psychoanalysis, linguistics and ethnology (Foucault 13). The subject is constituted, not the starting point.

In the work of Laclau and Mouffe the very term subject is replaced by the notion of "subject positions" in order to indicate that a subject can only arise within a discursive structure, and that, consequently, it is eminently dependent, contingent and temporal. Every discourse constitutes its own subject positions (Laclau & Mouffe 115). Similarly, Lyotard argues that "a self does not amount to much . . . a person is always located at 'nodal points' of specific communication circuits" (Lyotard 15). Baudrillard in his turn argues that the position of the subject has become untenable, since it can no longer control the world of objects as it used to. The objects are now in control, and this must be recognized by what he calls "fatal theory" (Baudrillard 198).

This brief analysis of the history of ideas shows that there are some elements which seem to confirm Hall's progression from the Enlightenment subject to the Postmodern subject. There is certainly a crisis of the subject in contemporary social theory and the crisis of the subject is bound to be lived and experienced as a crisis of identity, of the sense of self. To the non-unitary subject corresponds a decentered or fragmented identity. Stuart Hall argues that the postmodern subject has no fixed or permanent identity, that the subject assumes different identities at different times, that there are contradictory identities which cannot be unified (Hall, Held & McGrew 277).

That the subject has no fixed, biologically determined identity and that it may assume different identities at different times is not new and has been recognized since the early twentieth century, for instance in the work of Mead. What may be more authentically new and a product of the postmodern times is the allegation that these various identities lack a coherent or integrated self, lack a unity. What for Mead and others were exceptional cases of dissociated personalities would seem now to be the normal situation. What the new postmodernist positions seem to be saying is that in contemporary times the elementary selves, although still co-existing, have become incompatible and impossible to integrate. The integration of the generalized other would have failed and this is why the self has become dislocated, decentered, incapable of unity.

What would be the cause of such change? It is not simply the emergence of the postmodern discourse, it is the result, we are told, of the new feelings and practices brought about by unintended complex processes of rapid and chaotic change which seem to control individuals. New forms of globalization entail a decline of the nation state and the growing trend towards the internationalization of the economy. Time-space compression has meant that spatial barriers have been drastically reduced and spatial categories have come to dominate over time categories, time has become spatialized (Harvey 240). The explosion of communications, images and signifiers has made it more difficult to detect where or how is reality itself. The acceleration of change increases the obsolescence and ephemerality of products, ideas, labor processes fashions and all sorts of practices. The change towards a Post-Fordist "flexible regime of accumulation" has led to smaller firms and flexible work systems including part-time, temporary and sub-contracted labor (Harvey 147-156).

These changes are at the basis of the crisis which Europe has recently gone through. The crisis manifests itself in the growing urban and racial violence; the semi-permanent high rates of unemployment; the more frequent economic recessions; the weakening of the trade-union movement and the emergence of new social movements and, finally, conducts of personal withdrawal, the loss of interest in politics and public activities. Even in the social sciences the effects of such changes are felt: theories of evolution and teleological conceptions of history have lost their legitimacy, instrumental reason has been subjected to stern critique, knowledge has been systematically related to power, etc.

All these changes, are alleged to be able to dislocate the sense of self, to disintegrate the sense of identity. The question is, do these new feelings and practices brought about by accelerating change amount to a dislocation of identity? Is the postmodern discourse about the decentered subject a good explanation of what is going on? Is the crisis of the subject announced by postmodernism really happening for most people at the level of social reality? Although I am convinced of the importance of all the changes occurring in late modernity and of their far-reaching effects on individuals, I have doubts as to whether they are in any way responsible for a totally decentered and fragmented subject.

Here some lessons from the old social psychology should be heeded. For adults, the image of self, although dependent in varying degrees upon the current appraisal of others, is normally strong enough to exist with some relative autonomy. That is to say, up to a point the adult has already built his or her self-image on the basis of a long sequence of previous appraisals. Indeed if there were not some autonomy of self-image and the adult were totally dependent upon what others think of her/him at any moment, that person would be thought to be inadequate. The self-image which we have at any given time is a reflection of the appraisals of others as modified by our previously developed self (Gerth & Mills 85). This means that it has more stability and resilience than postmodern ideas allow for.

In overemphasizing the dislocation of personal identity postmodernism makes it impossible for the "generalized other" to be integrated and hence everything happens as if the individual were constituted by the internalization of a variety of others which oppose each other and can never be unified. This assumes either that the right conditions for the early formation of an integrated identity do not exist anymore or that already formed identities easily crumble under the impact of new disparate realities. I reject both these assumptions. Young people continue to construct their identity in relation to significant others located in a variety of spheres of society, even if these are no longer the traditional ones, and are still able to integrate their various elementary selves.

Perhaps this is not as easy as it was before, perhaps the number of truly significant others has expanded and become less uniform and youngsters have to choose who to listen to or identify with. Perhaps, as Kellner observes, on the surface identity has ceased to be a serious affair and has become "a freely chosen game," "centered on looks, images and consumption," "a function of leisure" (Kellner 158 & 153). But all the same, I do not see that young people has become a dislocated conjunction of contradictory identities without coherence or sense and, as Wagner has rightly pointed out, a distinction should be kept between wishful self-presentations and the actually ongoing social practices (Wagner 168). Older identities do not easily crumble either. Many people who have gone through very quick and dramatic changes in their ways of life may experience feelings of bewilderment, disorientation and discontinuity, but will not adapt easily to live in contradiction and will try to find some personal coherence.

Postmodern Discourse, Cultural Identities and Ideology

I have tried to show so far that the postmodern claims about the discovery of the other and about the decentering of the subject are problematic when separately considered. When one considers them together further problems appear. Is it not contradictory to celebrate the emergence of the other who can speak for him/herself and at the same time postulate the decentering of the subject? Is it not the case that the emergent "others" are themselves subjects with an apparently well integrated identity? How can some subjects be dislocated and others speak for themselves with such clear sense of identity? The postmodern discourse falls into this contradiction partly because it introduces too wide a gap between the subject and the other. It reduces otherness to pure difference and opposition, it understands otherness as an incommensurable world of its own and fails to recognize it as internalized by the subject. This leads not only to an essentialist conception of cultural identity, but also makes it more difficult to conceive of any socially constructed identity.

In conceiving of the other as pure difference and opposition, it is impossible to understand how can the subject internalize and integrate the expectations of significant others and hence the construction of his/her identity becomes impossible. I do not dispute the existence of feelings of disorientation arising in late modernity, but I argue that the postmodern explanation of them in terms of total fragmentation and dislocation is not adequate.

In fact it is possible to explain the effect of late modernity's rapid changes upon personal identity in a manner very different from the postmodern discourse.

An important clue is provided by Marx and Engels who also faced another period of bewildering change brought about by capitalism in the mid 19th century:

> Constant revolutionizing of production, uninterrupted disturbance of all social conditions, everlasting uncertainty and agitation distinguish the bourgeois epoch from all earlier ones. All fixed, fast-frozen relations, with their train of ancient and venerable prejudices and opinions, are swept away, all new-formed ones become antiquated before they can ossify. All that is solid melts into air, all that is holy is profaned. . . . (Marx & Engels 38).

This often quoted passage, by referring to uncertainty, quick dissolution of relations and rapid change, might justify the idea that the socially dependent self must have also lost the sense of continuity and identity which characterized the traditional society. Very few authors quoting this passage though, remember to add the continuation where Marx and Engels said "and man is at last compelled to face with sober senses, his real conditions of life, and his relations with his kind." This seems to discard the idea of a dislocated identity, rather it forces human beings to face their real conditions of life and their relations to others. It seems to be a moment of discovery of how things and relations work, and hence a discovery of how one's own identity is shaped.

In other words what the modern dramatic changes brought about was greater consciousness about one's own identity, a greater opportunity for self-definition, the idea that identities are constructed and can be modified within the boundaries of certain social relations. Thus for instance old sources of cultural identity may give way to new ones. Religion and tradition, the main sources of identity in the medieval times gave way to nation and class as the new collective sources of identity during modernity. I believe the radicalization of modernity (Giddens 51)[1] which is occurring in recent years produces similar conditions. A new trend is detected whereby people tend less and less to define themselves in terms of nation and class and more and more in terms of sexuality, gender and ethnicity. But this does not mean total dislocation it only means reconstruction and change of the old categories for new ones.

In forming their personal identities most individuals share certain group allegiances or characteristics such as religion, gender, class, ethnicity, sexuality, nationality which contribute to specify the subject and its sense of identity. All personal identities are rooted in collective contexts. This is how the idea of cultural identities emerges. In modern times the cultural identities which have had a most important influence in the formation of subjects are class and national identities.

The changes in late modernity alluded above have not made identities in general impossible but have profoundly affected some of them, especially class and national identities. As Wagner has argued, big social transformations tend to uproot widely shared cultural identities and, as a consequence, also affect personal identities. Processes of disarticulation and dislocation occur whereby many people cease to see themselves in terms of traditional collective contexts which provided a sense of identity (Wagner 56).

Class identity has declined because of a series of factors. First, its power of attraction supposed a well organized and strong class, like the working class, or the bourgeoisie in its beginnings, which struggled in order to be recognized and to have their rights respected in society. The further they managed to get their objectives by becoming dominant (bourgeoisie) or through the welfare state (working class), the more the continuation of their struggle and the opposition to it lost sense. I am not saying that classes can ever entirely lose their importance in a capitalist society. But it is true that by the end of the 20th century, after years of economic development, the situation has considerably changed within advanced capitalist countries: politics has begun to be restructured in a different sense where classes and their traditional parties play a much more restricted role. The crisis of Marxism and the fall of communist regimes has also had an adverse ideological impact on class identity. In addition to all these factors there is the numerical decline of the working class and its increasing atomization which is the result of the new more flexible regimes of accumulation of the Post-Fordist era.

The decline of the nation-state and the processes of globalization have certainly affected national loyalties and identities. But it would be a mistake to believe that its effects are simply a tendency to dissolve nationalisms, localisms and regionalisms. As Hall has argued, the more profound the universalizing tendencies are the more particular peoples, ethnic groups or sections of society seek to reaffirm their difference and the more they become attached to their locality (Hall 33). One has only to look at the dissolution of the Soviet Union and of Yugoslavia to realize that nationalism is not dead in the early nineties. National identities were strengthened as a form of resistance to the monolithic central power which used to rule those countries. Yet from another point of view it is also true that the cultural homogenization implicit in the globalization of culture is eroding national identities and such tendencies can be clearly seen at work in the European community and, to a lesser degree, in Latin America.

Nevertheless, while some social categories decline new social contexts appear or become articulated as the most accepted providers of a sense of identity. It is not the case that individuals are left entirely deprived of collective contexts for identification. Personal identity does not disappear in total fragmentation and dispersion, as postmodernists imagine, it is reconstructed and redefined in other terms (Kellner 157-58). Thus the decline of class and national identities is accompanied by the rise of other relevant collective contexts which are connected with the emergence of new social movements: ethnic identities (anti-racist movements), gender identities (feminist movements), sexual identity (homosexual movements) and many others.

However it is not only the decline of categories such as class and nation, that has affected the sense of identity. It is also true that the quicker the pace of change in all sorts of relations the more difficult it is for the subject to make sense of what is going on, to see the continuity between past and present, and therefore the more difficult it is for the subject to form a unitary view of itself and to know how to act. Furthermore, the general explosion of communications, images and simulacra makes it more difficult to conceive of a single reality both at the social and individual level. But from this to accept the total fragmentation of the subject there is a big jump.

These difficulties produced by rapid change and time-space compression justify the emergence of these new feelings of ephemerality, contingency and lack of unity. But they do not necessarily justify the idea of a totally dislocated subject. In this sense I fully agree with Wagner when he says that the postmodern sweeping statements about the fragmentation of the subject "do not take the situation of actually living human beings really seriously, human beings who define their lives, act and are constrained from acting, in and by very real social contexts" (Wagner 167).

The supposed decentering of the subject corresponds with the supposed triumph of objectivity, the supposed victory of unconscious and chaotic forces which totally destroy the individual's sense of unity. To accept the total decentering of the subject is to accept the final loss of agency and purpose, the inability of the subject to attempt to change the circumstances, its inability to posit any rational alternative future. It is the end of all political practice of transformation. I do not believe that this has irreversibly happened or may ever totally happen, although I accept that it is more difficult than before for individuals to understand all changes and to have a sense of direction.

It is here that one begins to suspect that the postmodern discourse plays an ideological role in the Marxian sense of a theory which conceals the true contradictions of advanced capitalist societies in order to reproduce them in the interest of the ruling class. The effect of concealment is now more subtle than before and takes into account the double face of the market: on the one hand, the fact that from the point of view of individual participants the market works by means of the values of freedom, equality, property and self-interest; and, on the other hand, the fact that, if left alone, the market produces irrational results from the point of view of society. The postmodern discourse does not act like the old liberalism telling people that there is freedom, equality and property for all. It rather tells people that there is chaos in reality (carefully concealing the fact that this is brought about by the same market forces) and dislocation in themselves and that there is nothing they could do about it.

Postmodernist conceptions are therefore ideological in that they contribute to mask the real contradictions of the global capitalist system and objectively seek to deviate the attention of people from them into the rarefied world of simulacra and hyperreality. They are ideological also in the sense that by unilaterally emphasizing discontinuity and difference, they tend to conceal the elements of shared humanity between different cultures and races (Larrain 13-16).[2] In times of accelerated technological change, political and economic crises in the ex-communist world, and deep economic problems in the capitalist west including the third world, no other ideological form seems to be better suited than postmodernism to defend the system as a whole, because it makes of chaos, bewildering change, and endless fragmentation the normal and natural state of society.

I regard this idea of decentering and the announced demise of the subject as being suspiciously close to and corresponding with the conservative neo-liberal emphasis on the supremacy of the blind forces of the market which on no account should be interfered with. Liberal positions have always warned against the idea that human agents can construct the world as they wish and rejected any tampering with the market, but what is new about neo-liberalism is that it counts now on the postmodernist philosophical outlook as a powerful ideological ally which seeks to convince people that it is impossible for human beings to act politically with effect on society as a total entity. The rapidly changing world which has lost a sense of direction, purpose and unity has finally undermined, so we are told, the very ability of the individual to know what he or she wants or how he or she could act. In times of confusion and mind-boggling changes this is a most dangerous and insidious ideology which can only protect the interests of the ruling class.

Notes

1. Here I follow Giddens's idea that "we have not moved beyond modernity but are living precisely through a phase of its radicalization" (Giddens 51).
2. My point here is that a Marxian concept of ideology can be easily extended to cover the concealment of contradictions in the field of race and international relations (Larrain 13-16).

Works Cited

Baudrillard, Jean. "Fatal Strategies," *Selected Writings*. Ed. Mark Poster. Cambridge: Polity Press, 1988.
De Levita, David J. *The Concept of Identity*. Paris: Mouton & Co., 1965.
Foucault, Michel. *The Archeology of Knowledge*. London: Tavistock, 1977.
Gerth, Hans, and C. Wright Mills, *Character and Social Structure*. New York: Harbinger Books, 1964.
Giddens, Anthony. *The Consequences of Modernity*. Cambridge: Polity Press, 1990.
Hall, Stuart. "The Local and the Global: Globalization and Ethnicity." *Culture, Globalization and the World-System*. Ed. Anthony King. London: Macmillan, 1991.
Hall, Held, McGrew, ed. *Modernity and Its Futures*. Cambridge: Polity Press, 1992.
Harvey, David. *The Condition of Postmodernity*. Oxford: Blackwell, 1989.
James, William. *Principles of Psychology*. London: Macmillan, 1890.
Kellner, Douglas. "Popular Culture and the Construction of Postmodern Identities." *Modernity and Identity*. Ed. Scott Lash and J. Friedman. Oxford: Blackwell, 1992.
Laclau, Ernesto, and Chantal Mouffe. *Hegemony and Socialist Strategy*. London: Verso, 1985.
Larrain, Jorge. *Ideology and Cultural Identity: Modernity and the Third World Presence*. Cambridge: Polity Press, 1994.
Lyotard, Jean François. *The Postmodern Condition: A Report on Knowledge*. Manchester: Manchester University Press, 1984.
Marx, Karl. (a) *Grundrisse*. Harmondsworth: Penguin, 1973.
_____. (b) "Theses on Feuerbach", *The German Ideology. Collected Works*. Vol. 5. London: Lawrence & Wishart, 1976.
_____ and Frederick Engels. *Manifesto of the Communist Party. Selected Works* in one volume. London: Lawrence & Wishart, 1970.
Mead, George H. *Mind, Self, & Society*. Chicago: The University of Chicago Press, 1974.
Said, Edward. *Orientalism*. London: Penguin, 1985.
Thompson, John T. *Ideology and Modern Culture*. Cambridge: Polity Press, 1990.
Vattimo, Gianni. *The Transparent Society*. Cambridge: Polity Press, 1990.
Wagner, Peter. *A Sociology of Modernity: Liberty and Discipline*. London: Routledge, 1994.

Paul Le Blanc

Culture, Identity, Class Struggle: Practical Critique of the Discourse on Post-Marxism

One

Common themes in post-Marxist discourse involve a tendency to turn from class struggle to culture critiques, questioning the centrality of class while privileging "identities" relating to race, gender and sexuality, and exchanging the goal of socialism for that of "radical democracy," sometimes with a greenish hue. It is an Hegelian commonplace that there is generally some element of (overextended) truth in an erroneous analysis. So it seems to me that not all elements of the post-Marxists' challenge are without interest, that in fact some of their notions can be engaged/incorporated/transformed/superseded in an historical materialist critique.

What follows constitutes a practical critique of much post-Marxist discourse: it is a non-polemical effort to put forward—in relatively clear language—an analysis which touches on themes that relate both to the post-Marxist debate and to practical problems of the class struggle and socialist political work today.

Two

The concept of "culture" is an essential tool for those who want to apply the historical materialist approach of Marx and Engels to the question of how class consciousness develops among those of us who are part of the working class, that is, those of us who make our living through the sale of labor power, as opposed to making a living through the ownership of businesses. Before discussing culture, we need to look more closely at this working class and its consciousness.

The working class, as defined here, constitutes a majority of the people in U.S. society, but a majority of those who are, in this sense, working class, do not automatically or necessarily have a sense of themselves as being part of something called the working class. They don't necessarily believe that they can best improve their conditions by joining with other workers in a struggle against the big businessmen, the capitalists, who own and run our economy. They don't automatically or necessarily see themselves as having common interests with working-class people of other countries (or even of working-class people of our own country who have different racial or ethnic backgrounds, different occupations and income levels, different sexual identities and orientations, and so on). And they don't automatically conclude that they can and should, as a class, take political power in order to transform our society in a way that gives *them* control of our economic life. These beliefs—(1) that there is something called the working class to which we belong, (2) that our interests are necessarily counterposed to the interests of the capitalists, against whom we must struggle, (3) that we should identify with and have solidarity with *all* members of our class, and (4) that the working class should struggle for political power in order to bring about the socialist transformation of society—these beliefs are traditionally seen by Marxists (in this case Lenin) as constituting the class-consciousness of the proletariat, of the working class (LeBlanc 21-26).

People who are born into the working class are not born with these ideas. *Nor do we get our ideas simply from raw experience.* In our families, among our friends, in school, and in the larger society, we are taught certain beliefs, values, moral codes, ways of understanding things, and forms of behavior. These constitute a framework that helps us make some kind of sense of the world around us, affecting the way we process our experience, and therefore shaping our consciousness. This, according to culture theorists, is what is meant by the theoretical concept known as *culture*. This conception of culture involves: the social habits and learned behavior shaping our lives and consciousness; our beliefs and values and ways of understanding reality; the various activities and institutions which help to transmit these habits, beliefs and values; and the intellectual, technological, artistic and other products of human creation. Included in this, of course, is the realm of art, literature, film, television, music, etc. which is sometimes more narrowly given the label of "culture."[1]

Marxists insist that culture cannot be adequately understood unless we see it dialectically—composed of complex and contradictory elements, dynamic and evolving, which not only shapes people but also is shaped by them as they seek to adjust to and transform the realities of which they are part. Here it may be helpful to emphasize the central importance (in contrast to some "post-Marxist" theorists) of *materialism* and *economics* in this way of seeing culture. Obviously, if I do not physically exist, I cannot engage in any form of activity, cultural or otherwise; a pre-requisite of my existence is the intake of nourishment. Marx and Engels noted, in *The German Ideology*, that "by producing food, man indirectly produces his material life itself." They elaborate:

> The way in which man produces his food depends first of all on the nature of the means of subsistence that he finds and has to reproduce. This mode of production must not be viewed simply as reproduction of the physical existence of individuals. Rather it is a definite form of their activity, a definite way of expressing their life, a definite *mode of life*. As individuals express their life, so they are. What they are, therefore, coincides with what they produce, with *what* they produce, and *how* they produce (Marx, 409).

The way we each make a living, taken together, adds up to our way of life; the activities and relationships which we enter into for the purpose of securing our subsistence is what is meant by an *economy*. As Marx put it in *The Poverty of Philosophy*, "economic categories are only the theoretical expressions, the abstractions, of social relations of production" (Marx, 480).

The concepts of culture, society and economy overlap here. Marx sees economics "anthropologically"—which means that culture is necessarily permeated with the economic realities from which it is inseparable. Of course, not all economies are the same. As historical materialists, Marxists insist that culture must also be comprehended, in capitalist society, as something in which we find reflected the actual, divided class experiences and conflicts existing under capitalism. To the extent that we speak of a so-called national culture in one or another capitalist country, the dominant influence in that culture is enjoyed by the dominant social class: the capitalists, who own and control the economy, and this control shapes the so-called "way of life" of the society.

But there are also elements of popular culture, attitudes, practices, values and viewpoints arising from the other classes, especially the working class, which are different from and sometimes in conflict with the dominant cultural orientation of the capitalist class. This broad working-class culture—sometimes influenced by the dominant bourgeois-national culture, sometimes drawing on deeper pre-industrial or pre-capitalist traditions, sometimes powerfully asserting itself through social struggles against the capitalists—has been the basis for a distinctive radical-democratic and socialist sub-culture arising in various capitalist countries of the past century and a half, including in the United States.

Three

There is, then, the larger culture of capitalist society, in which, under normal circumstances, ethical orientations, ideology, values and social habits consistent with capitalism tend to predominate. But also within this larger culture there is a different cultural orientation which reflects the life-experience of those who are part of the working class—life-experience which is refracted and interpreted, to be sure, through the ideological orientation (ways of seeing things and understanding reality) into which one has been socialized. In fact, there is a considerable amount of cultural variation within this working class, given the ethnic and racial differences, as well as occupation and income differences, differences in gender and sexual orientation, and so on. *There is, nonetheless, a fundamental cultural divide between bourgeois and proletarian social layers.* From television—if we compare the more or less proletarian way of life depicted on "Roseanne" with the more or less bourgeois way of life depicted on "L.A. Law," then we get some sense of the broad cultural difference of class being suggested.

There should be no mystery about the source of this cultural divide. Those who are part of the working class share an intimate knowledge of having no way to make a living except by selling their own labor power, finding someone willing to hire them, and being under the economic domination of a boss who tries to convert that labor power into as much actual labor as possible. It involves a sense of common cause (despite petty aggravations) with one's workmates, a desire to exercise at least some common control over one's work situation, and a shared resentment over the "boss-ism" of management and the owners. It involves a feeling (shaped by one's economic situation) that you earn every penny that you make, and in many cases a vivid sense that your labor enriches others. There is a shared understanding with millions of others that those on top will always have many more advantages, privileges, tax breaks, perks, resources, opportunities, etc., and that the majority of us—looked down upon and taken for granted—pay for that. All of this necessarily and profoundly impacts on one's entire world-view and way of life.

Within that broad working-class culture (which permeates the lives of a majority of the American people), we can sometimes find in history a substantial radical-labor sub-culture, which has involved millions of working-class people. And here we can also find what might be called the "micro-cultures" of specific left-wing groups—whether the Workingmen's Party of the United States, the Socialistic Labor Party, and the International Working Peoples Association of the 1870s and '80s, or the Socialist Party and IWW of the period spanning 1901 through 1919, or the Communist Party of the 1920s and '30s, as well as among Trotskyists and others (Nelson; Buhle, Buhle, and Georgakas).

The micro-culture of a revolutionary organization involves a relatively elaborate set of values and analyses, commitments and relationships, standard activities and rituals, a collective pool of knowledge and experience. It includes an understanding of the past, a critique of the present, a vision of the desired future, and some notion of how to bring about that future. These critiques are, of course, based on a general theory as to how a society works/should work. Also involved is the transmission of certain skills and practical perspectives, which presumably can help to influence and mobilize large numbers of people to bring about social change. If the micro-culture of a left-wing group can connect with a broader labor-radical sub-culture, and if this labor-radical sub-culture is a dynamic element in the larger working-class culture of the country, then the kind of class-consciousness defined earlier will be a powerful and growing force within the working class as a whole.

Four

Throughout the period stretching from the late 1860s through the 1930s, a distinctly working-class culture existed, and within this there was a radical-labor sub-culture. This helps to explain how the organized left-wing workers' parties—whose members taken together never exceeded 200,000 (and who often added up to considerably less)—were able to exercise an influence within the working class far greater than their actual numbers, at certain points having a profound impact on the larger culture and politics of the United States.

At the same time, a number of factors combined to obliterate the labor-radical sub-culture which had existed for about eight decades: the development of a mass consumer culture; the weakening of an independent Left thanks to the absorption of many leftists into the New Deal wing of the Democratic Party; the impact of World War II; the twin poisons of Stalinism and Cold War anti-Communism; and the unprecedented economic prosperity of the 1950s and '60s. The interpenetration of all these factors—which might be variously labeled as economic, political, social, cultural—must be grasped if we hope to analyze U.S. realities leading up to our own time (Lipsitz). While we cannot develop a complete analysis of these factors here, it is possible to elaborate on a few salient developments. Consider the comments of Communist Party organizer Steve Nelson, describing the post-World War II period: "Although I experienced the changes in working-class values and culture in terms of the foreign-born community and their children, I can see now that the entire American working class was undergoing a transformation during and after the war." Noting that this was driven home to him "with a vengeance" during the Cold War anti-Communist hysteria of the 1950s, he reflected: "The Party, which had historically been rooted in a heavily immigrant working-class culture characterized by economic insecurity and political alienation, was unable to adjust to these changes. We could not evaluate the significance of the changing composition of the work force and its new patterns of community life and consumption" (Nelson, Barret, Ruck 285).

    Of central importance were profound developments in the economy. From 1947 until 1972, impressive increases were registered in productivity and real wages, with the rate of profit—despite fluctuations—remaining relatively high through the mid-1960s (Mandel 131,142; Shaikh and Mandel, 24-25). The impact of this on what had been, in the 1930s and '40s, militant sectors of the industrial working class was described in 1952 by the veteran revolutionary socialist James P. Cannon to his fellow Trotskyists in the Socialist Workers Party:

> We have eleven years of unchanged prosperity. . . . [W]e think in historic terms and we know that it is not only an episode but that it is going to change and must change as a result of the contradictions of the capitalist system itself. But how does it impress the ordinary worker? All he knows is that for eleven years he has been working more or less steadily and enjoying better wages and living conditions than he knew before. Do you mean to say that has not had a conservatizing effect on his psychology? I don't think you read it correctly if you say it hasn't. (Cannon 47)

    "The pioneer militants of the CIO," Cannon elaborated, "are sixteen years older than they were in 1937. They are better off than the ragged and hungry sit-down strikers of 1937; and many of them are sixteen times softer and more conservative." Cannon noted that these sectors—"formerly the backbone of the left wing"—provided the main social base for the relatively conservative union leadership of ex-socialist Walter Reuther. "They are convinced far less by Reuther's clever demagogy than by the fact that he really articulates their own conservatized moods and patterns of thought" (Cannon 57).

In his study of Detroit autoworkers, John Leggett wrote that "A new middle class arose which included a large number of young people of working-class background," and noted that many prospering working people had moved out of traditional working-class communities to become homeowners in the suburbs. "The class struggle abated with the end of the post-World War II strikes, although repeated flare-ups between management and workers occurred during and after the Korean War," he added. "At the same time, another trend pointed up this harmony. Governmental boards and labor unions often helped minimize class conflict as unions grew more friendly toward companies which were willing to bargain with, and make major concessions to, labor organizations. Even working-class minority groups [i.e., some African-Americans] improved their standard of living and sent sons and daughters into the middle class" (Leggett 52, 53). The left-wing micro-cultures, to a large degree, became isolated from the working class as such. Class consciousness became minimized, as many relatively well-off working people concluded that—neither rich nor poor—they were part of a growing and hard-working "*middle* class" for whom life would get better and better.

Within this context, when the Left began to grow again in the late 1950s and 1960s, for the most part it did not do so as part of a self-consciously *working-class* movement. Many new-left activists, although coming from families supported by blue collar or white collar employees, saw themselves as "middle class." Masses of people were moved not by notions of *class* oppression, but by important issues having to do with civil liberties and civil rights, war, the environment, race, gender, and so on—having to do with seemingly "non-class" issues and identities. When sectors of the revitalized Left began seeing these issues and identities as being related to class, and as various left-wing organizations began focusing on explicitly working-class organizing in the 1970s and early '80s, it seemed that breakthroughs were about to be made. But then came the so-called "de-industrialization" of America, more accurately a global economic restructuring which brought about the partial decomposition of the traditional industrial working class which had been the base of the labor movement. This was accompanied by the dramatic decline, once again, of the organized Left.

Five

The realities discussed here have lent credence to the post-Marxist stress on *identity politics* as an alternative to working-class politics. In his popularization of

Ernesto Laclau's and Chantal Mouffe's *Hegemony and Socialist Strategy*, Stanley Aronowitz notes that they are actually following Sidney Hook's earlier path away from Marxism in arguing that ideology, politics, culture, economics are relatively autonomous. Aronowitz approvingly concludes: "Thus, if the political level is autonomous, just as the economic and ideological, then the centrality of class and class struggle in the Marxist paradigm must necessarily be denied" (Aronowitz 182). Marxism, to the contrary, because it stresses the interpenetration of these categories and the realities which they reflect—offering a unified analysis of history, economics, politics, culture, society—provides the basis for a compelling revolutionary program centered precisely on the working class. This comes through in a brilliant study of Nicaragua by Roger Lancaster. Far from blurring or subordinating all forms of social identity under the rubric of class, Lancaster offers among the most penetrating analyses available of the relation of race, gender, and sexuality to the Nicaraguan experience. He nonetheless feels compelled to reject the "happy pluralism" of post-Marxist identity politics, which "diminishes the significance of class—with all the political consequences that follow." Lancaster has aptly stressed the fundamental reality:

> The class dimension *is* privileged, if only circumstantially and politically (not analytically), and by this index: class exploitation necessarily produces an exploiting minority, and an exploited majority. The same cannot be said of other dimensions of oppression. Whether one is seeking to reform or to overthrow *any* system of exploitation, the dynamics of class and class resistance remain, in Marx's sense, strategic and paramount (Lancaster 282).

Marx and Engels, unlike the post-Marxists, saw "a necessary connection of materialism with communism and socialism" (Marx 394). The fundamental class relationships arising from the structure of the economy—the basis for human subsistence—do not obliterate, but they *do* permeate and connect all other forms of oppression which exist in capitalist society. *The interpenetration of the various dimensions of human identity and relationships must be grasped in order to achieve a more complete understanding of social dynamics*: an understanding of the distinct dynamics of sexual oppression, of gender oppression, of racial oppression are essential for grasping the social totality, but this must be combined with an understanding of class oppression if we want to illuminate the realities of race, sexuality, gender and class. This will provide keys for achieving "the coincidence of the change of circumstances and of human activity or self-change [which] can be comprehended and rationally understood only as *revolutionary practice*" (Marx 401).

Six

Today there is a process of recomposition of the working class and of the labor movement. After the mid-1960s, thanks to a falling rate of profit, pressures developed for increasingly severe cutbacks in real wages (which were carried out on a wide scale beginning in 1972) and—especially in the 1980s—cuts in employment, combined with a global restructuring of the economy and heightened competition between various industrial capitalist nations (Mandel 132, 142; Shaikh and Mandel; Kolko; Magdoff). The experiences of "de-industrialization," and the assaults on the living standards of the blue-collar and white-collar working class, assaults carried out under both neo-conservative Republican and neo-liberal Democratic Party banners, have generated a heightened sense of class. Unemployment, under-employment, poorer-paying jobs, declining quality of life, economic insecurity, and deteriorating communities—these have been the experience of growing layers of the working class, which has a profound impact on culture and consciousness over the past two decades. The badly battered and shrunken trade union movement has begun to feel among its membership more militant and radical stirrings (Rachleff; Moody; Fantasia; La Botz; Brecher and Costello; Lynd). Many of the social movements (for example, reflected in the composition and positions of the National Association for the Advancement of Colored People, the National Organization for Women, and even some of the environmental groups)—find among many of their white-collar and blue-collar working-class members a similar radical tilt and shift in the direction of class consciousness, often to the dismay of their more "respectable" leaders.

This ferment is taking place on a global scale. If we look at cultural developments in working people's and low-income communities of, on the one hand, newly-industrialized "third world" countries (such as Brazil, Korea, Malaysia) and, on the other hand, of older industrial countries such as Britain and the US, we will find various forms of resistance which reflect and contribute to a radicalization of consciousness in both sectors (Sader and Silverstein; Hart-Landsberg; McAllister 1991; McAllister 1993; Blackwell and Seabrook 1985).

If we look at certain aspects of popular mass culture, we can find music, films, books, television programs which reflect, and respond to, and seek a market in some of these shifts in the more specific culture and consciousness of workers and the oppressed in the United States today. It is not the case, as some radical theorists used to argue, that the minds of working people are simply turned to mush and manipulated by late capitalism's mass consumer culture (Macdonald; Marcuse). The cultural process is more complex, more interesting, more interactive than that. Donald Clark Hodges has noted that the ideological orientation of his industrial co-workers of the 1950s and '60s, far from being that of superficially happy and mindless consumers of "mass culture," reflected a socially-critical cynicism, laced with humor, which had profoundly radical implications—an insight which finds corroboration among other observers as well (Hodges; Terkel; Buhle).

Sometimes the larger culture—seeking to appeal to the radicalizing consciousness of working-class consumers—can be altered in ways that at least partially subvert capitalist ideological domination. On television in recent years, such programs as "Roseanne," "Grace Under Fire," "The Simpsons," "Homefront," "TV Nation" fall into that category. Some examples can also be drawn from rap music, rock music, country and western music, and other forms of popular music. It is also important to include in this framework recent U.S. films, not only the work of Spike Lee and John Sayles, but also such historical epics as "Glory" and "Last of the Mohicans," such melodramas as "Regarding Henry," "The House on Carroll Street," and "Guilty By Suspicion," such comedies as "Raising Arizona" and "Roger and Me," such futuristic productions as "Blade Runner" and "Robocop," etc..

Class-conscious and ideologically radical cultural products which gain mass distribution are hardly generated spontaneously. They reflect contradictory intersections of different cultural currents: the very conscious and sustained intervention on the part of radical artists and media activists; initiative on the part of more or less bold entrepreneurs seeking to profit from a new market; and the "market" itself, which is composed of millions of individuals who happen to be shaped by, reflect and perpetuate, tastes and sensibilities that are part of the broad working-class culture. Often the contradictory intersections are reflected in the cultural products themselves. It certainly cannot be argued that such things render superfluous the development of working class cultural institutions that are independent of capitalist control.

A labor-radical sub-culture on the scale of the 1880s, the early 1900s, or the 1930s cannot be said to exist today—and yet there are elements for the recomposition of such a sub-culture. Aware that the most radical democracy (rule by the people) is at the heart of socialism, the Brazilian theorist Frei Betto writes that "there can be no real democracy without popular participation, and that implies anonymous and tireless self-sacrificing work directed towards those in city and countryside, in the shanty-towns and workers' neighborhoods, who have not yet discovered that workers' unity is like the waters of a dam that has burst." Strikes, demonstrations, development of popular organizations of struggle—all of these contribute to a culture of solidarity without which there can be no working-class consciousness. Essential to such work, Betto concludes, is "popular education that changes all popular values—roots and cultural relations, religion and art, solidarity and fiesta—into an energy that changes history" (Betto 33, 35).

Without such efforts, there will be no socialism.

Notes

1. While this approach is consistent with that of earlier theorists such as Luxemburg, Lenin, Trotsky, Gramsci, it finds even more extensive development in the work of such later analysts as C. L. R. James, E. P. Thompson, Herbert Gutman, Eleanor Leacock, and Raymond Williams.

Works Cited

Aronowitz, Stanley. *The Politics of Identity: Class, Culture, and Social Movements.* New York: Routledge, 1992.

Betto, Frei. "The Socialism Syndrome." *International Viewpoint* 242 (1993): 32-35.

Blackwell, Terry and Jeremy Seabrook. *A World Still to Win: The Reconstruction of the Post-War Working Class.* London: Faber and Faber, 1985.

Brecher, Jeremy and Tim Costello, eds. *Building Bridges: The Emerging Grassroot Coalition of Labor and Community.* New York: Monthly Review Press, 1990.

Buhle, Mari Jo, Paul Buhle, and Dan Georgakas, eds. *Encyclopedia of the American Left.* Urbana: University of Illinois Press, 1992.

Buhle, Paul, ed. *Popular Culture in America.* Minneapolis: University of Minnesota Press, 1987.

Cannon, James P. *Speeches to the Party.* New York: Pathfinder Press, 1973.

Fantasia, Rick. *Cultures of Solidarity: Consciousness, Action, and Contemporary American Workers.* Berkeley: University of California Press, 1988.

Hart-Landsberg, Martin. *The Rush to Development: Economic Change and Political Struggle in South Korea.* New York: Monthly Review Press, 1993.

Hodges, Donald Clark. "Cynicism in the Labor Movement." *American Society, Inc.* Ed. Maurice Zeitlin. Chicago: Markham Publishing Co., 1970.

Kolko, Joyce. *Restructuring the World Economy.* New York: Pantheon Books, 1988.

La Botz, Dan. *The Troublemakers Handbook, How To Fight Back Where You Work—And Win!* Detroit: Labor Notes, 1991.

Lancaster, Roger N. *Life is Hard: Machismo, Danger, and the Intimacy of Power in Nicaragua.* Berkeley, CA: University of California Press, 1992.

LeBlanc, Paul. *Lenin and the Revolutionary Party*. Atlantic Highlands: Humanities Press, 1990.
Leggett, John C. *Class, Race and Labor: Working-Class Consciousness in Detroit*. New York: Oxford University Press, 1968.
Lipsitz, George. *Rainbow at Midnight: Labor and Culture in the 1940s*. Urbana: University of Illinois Press.
Lynd, Staughton. *Solidarity Unionism, Rebuilding the Labor Movement from Below*. Chicago: Charles H. Kerr, 1992.
Macdonald, Dwight. *Masscult and Midcult*. New York: Partisan Review, 1961.
Magdoff, Harry. *Globalization: To What End?* New York: Monthly Review Press, 1992.
Mandel, Ernest. *Late Capitalism*. London: New Left Books, 1975.
Marcuse, Herbert. *One Dimensional Man: Studies in the Ideology of Advanced Industrial Society*. Boston: Beacon Press, 1964.
Marx, Karl. *Writings of the Young Marx on Philosophy and Society*. Ed. Loyd D. Easton and Kurt H. Guddat. Garden City, NY: Anchor Books, 1967.
McAllister, Carol. "Capitalist Development in Malaysia and Prospects for Political Struggle: Women's Work and Resistance." *Against the Current* 46 (1993): 30-38.
McAllister, Carol. "Uneven and Combined Development: Dynamics of Change and Women's Everyday Forms of Resistance in Negeri Sembilan, Malaysia." *Review of Radical Political Economics*. 23.3/4 (1991): 57-98.
Moody, Kim. *An Injury to All, The Decline of American Unionism*. London: Verso, 1988.
Nelson, Bruce. *Beyond the Martyrs, A Social History of Chicago's Anarchists, 1870-1900*. New Brunswick: Rutgers University Press, 1988.
Nelson, Steve, James Barrett, Rob Ruck. *Steve Nelson, American Radical*. Pittsburgh: University of Pittsburgh Press, 1981.
Rachleff, Peter. "Seeds of a Labor Resurgency." *The Nation*, February 21, 1994. 226-229.
Sader, Emir and Ken Silverstein. *Without Fear of Being Happy: Lula, the Workers Party, and Brazil*. London: Verso, 1991.
Shaikh, Anwar and Ernest Mandel. "International Capitalism in Crisis—What Next?" *Bulletin in Defense of Marxism* 100 (1992): 23-29.
Terkel, Studs. *Working*. New York: Avon Books, 1975.

Jennifer M. Cotter

"Left" Journals After the "Post" and the Construction of the Political "Everyday"

In the last twenty-five years the United States and Britain have seen an institutionalization of the "New Left" in the knowledge industry through a revision of disciplinary practices in the social sciences and the humanities and the development of "cultural studies." This institutionalization is in part the effect of the emergence of a series of "post-al" theories from post-Marxism to post-structuralism. At the center of this post-alization of the "left" lies a fundamental shift in "left" practices from politics (the principled understanding of and intervention into existing socio-economic configurations) to "ethics" (the understanding of the "social" as a series of incommensurate, aleatory, "events"—individual instances that have to be approached "care-fully" without the security of any common and underlying principle of judgment). Ethics, of course, has always been in the forefront of social theory. However, there is a radical difference between the traditional "ethics" (of Plato, Rousseau, John Stuart Mill, etc.) and the post-al "ethics." The post-al ethics (which is the consequence of a re-reading of Kant by, most notably, Jean François Lyotard) is an "ethics" without foundation: an ethics in which its evaluation is completely immanent and has no reference to any "outside" principles. "Principles" in the post-al left are regarded to be an act of imposing universality and similarity on irreducible differences. This abandoning of "politics" for "ethics" marks the practices of all "left" journals after the ascent of the "post." Post-al left journals such as *Social Text, Socialist Review, Rethinking Marxism* and others that I will discuss in this text represent themselves as "progressive" but, as I will demonstrate through analysis of their post-al logic, they are in fact most effective collaborators with the dominant regime of capital and wage-labor and its social arrangements.

Their "success" in this collaboration is owing to the fact that they legitimate capitalism and its reforms in an effective postmodern rhetoric that strikes their readers as "fresh," "non-dogmatic," and above all, "non-totalitarian" and "democratic." The "democracy" advocated in post-al left journals is the alibi for the "free market" (i.e., the deregulation of ruling class interests). The "democratic" left, as it will become clear in my text, produces theories and discourses that legitimate the economic hegemony of Euroamerican capitalism in the so called "New World Order." Through legitimating the interests of the North Atlantic ruling class, the post-al journals help to construct the "everyday" political debates and discussions toward these ends and interests. It is through their contribution to these "everyday" debates that concepts and terms such as "class" and "exploitation" are now replaced by such concepts as "individual responsibility," "market socialism," and "desire."

The philosophical impetus for these ethical revisions can be found in the institutionalization of (post)structuralism which has opened up the space to challenge enlightenment notions of "experience," "individuality," "identity," "reality," "knowledge," and "common sense" through re-understanding these as totalizing effects of the closure of meaning production. These totalizing effects, according to post-al left writers, are the product of a suppression of the slippage of the signifier along the chain of signification (which within post-al theories operates along Derrida's notion of *différance*). In short, on the terms of (post)structuralism, because meaning is discursively produced and not inherently given, imposing a definite meaning on "the real" is to instantly reify it. More recently this has involved a move to an increasingly "post-theoretical" phase in knowledge production in which the possibility of conceptuality—of historically produced explanatory concepts—is delegitimated as a totalizing gesture which suppresses differences. This has led to an increasingly localist understanding of "politics" (i.e., "politics" as "ethics" of interpersonal local relations) which draws back into the field of knowledge production the possibility of knowledge based on experience—albeit experiences that are the product of a particular (post-al) subject's slippage along the chain of signification.

The current field of knowledge production in cultural studies, the humanities and the social sciences rests primarily on the abstraction of knowledge production from class antagonisms under capitalism. The impact of such rethinking on cultural studies has led to a revision in "reading practices" which has involved reading texts through the tropes of "race," "gender," "nationality," "the queer," etc. as well as revising the canon itself in order to include texts by women, people of color, gays and lesbians, and people of the "third world." In turn, the content of "politics" that this revision of knowledge practices endorses is one that displaces the proletariat as the agent of revolutionary struggle toward socialism and replaces it, at various levels of knowledge production, with "popular alliances" as the agent(s) of social change toward "radical democracy" or the agents of liberal reform. This acceptance is manifested in various degrees of explicitness from "first order" critiques of orthodox Marxism as manifested in *Capital & Class* (52), to the argument for "radical democracy" advanced by Manning Marable in *Race and Class* (35.1: 113-130) and Stanley Aronowitz in *Socialist Review* (23.3: 5-79), to Terry Eagleton's appraisal of the values of liberalism in *Textual Practice* (8.1: 1-10), to the liberal "grass roots" (i.e., local) politics of green consumerism advocated for in a recent issue of *In These Times* (18.9).

Significantly, this shift away from historical materialism in struggles for social change has occurred at the same time capitalism has entered a period of deep stagnation and decline as manifested in the rapid decrease of full-time, steady employment—even on the campuses in which most of the writers of these journals reside—in the "first world," the increase of unemployment and part-time, contingent labor, and the lowering of rates of profit for capitalists. Because of this stagnation inter-capitalist competition has increased immensely as individual capitalists are compelled to compete more ruthlessly in order to maintain existing levels of profit. This has given rise to a tremendous backlash against the proletariat in which advances made from previous stages of the struggle have been set back and re-privatized in the interests of the ruling class—a backlash primarily enabled by the rapid and voluminous shift of capital from the "first world" to the "third world" where class struggle has been relatively subordinated (in part because many sectors have not yet been proletarianized, or are being proletarianized for the first time) and, as a result, cheaper labor is available. However, at the same time there has been a serious backlash, the forces of production are being increasingly collectivized. That is, the shift to late (transnational) capitalism objectively requires increased co-operation, communication, and collectivization of the forces of production around the globe and therefore opens up the historical necessity for the mobilization of the *transnational* proletariat in their own material interests. The backlash advanced by the ruling class, then, is in part an effort to render impossible the further advancement of class struggle on the side of the proletariat. What is necessary to combat this is the development of class solidarity among the *transnational* proletariat which requires an intervention into the discourses and practices which maintain divisions by naturalizing or reifying social difference within the working class.

An historical materialist analysis, contrary to what many "New Left" inspired post-al journals claim, is not indifferent to the abolition of racism, sexism, heterosexism and other manifestations of social oppression, rather it argues for the transformation of the social structures that give rise to and legitimate such social practices. Part of building class consciousness involves developing the understanding that *all* workers as a collective—regardless of race, gender, sexuality, etc.—are entitled to the fruits of their own labor. All workers must collectively have ownership and control over the means of production and subsequently of their own productive capacities. *For a revolutionary left journal to contribute to this project, it must provide the means for the production and development of class consciousness.* This, in large part, requires the production of knowledges that can explain how social differences (such as class, race, gender, sexuality, and so on) are (re)produced and proliferated under capitalism in order to naturalize economic exploitation. A revolutionary movement needs knowledge that can explain the social inequalities that arise from capitalist exploitation and fracture class solidarity and commitment to revolutionary struggle by pitting members of the working class against one another. Left journals after the "post" however, are aimed at developing an "ethical" consciousness which is opposed to class solidarity on the grounds that it excludes other differences (most notably introduced by the "new social movements" of the New Left). The shift toward what is in actuality merely a superficial appreciation of "differences" at various levels of knowledge production (i.e., both "high theory" and local "reading"/"low theory"), and not a fundamental transformation of the capitalist mode of production (which necessitates social division so that the ruling class can, at various moments, increase its rate of profit by legitimating relatively high rates of exploitation of particular sectors of the global workforce), insofar as it works merely toward the reform of the knowledge industry itself, is actually useful to the ruling class in maintaining political and ideological divisions between sectors of the working class despite the increased collectivization among the forces of production.

Particularly exemplary of "first order" criticisms of orthodox marxism is the journal *Capital & Class* (52). Arguing for "revolutionary reforms" (Burkett 9-16) in the form of a redistribution of resources (particularly the military budget) along the lines of the individual and collective needs of the entire society, *Capital & Class*, while seemingly progressive in relation to other journals, makes its argument for "bringing social production under social control" through a fundamental revision of historical materialism's recognition of the proletariat as the objective agent of social transformation. In other words, while *Capital & Class* may appear relatively progressive (insofar as it still insists on socialism) it must be situated within a history of the post-Marxist revision of class in which it can be seen to be capitulating to the pressure of the ruling-class for further shifts away from the project of socialism.

This shift can be seen most clearly in its Negreist line (which was fully developed in a recent issue of *Polygraph* [6/7] on "Marxism Beyond Marxism?" by contributions from such post-al marxists as Fredric Jameson, Arif Dirlik and Richard Wolff) of replacing the urban proletariat with the "socialized worker" and hence, of replacing exploitation with domination. Nick Witheford, in his essay "Autonomist Marxism and the Information Society" (*Capital and Class* 52: 85-125) also argues for the concept of the "socialized worker" which is the effect of an "information society" in which work has become highly technologized and the forces of production have moved "beyond" exploitation. The crucial point here is that, this theory assumes that because many workers are employed in jobs that do not *directly* produce surplus-value (such as: data processing, telecommunications network systems, etc.) these workers have moved beyond exploitation.

The post-al left writing, in all its forms, is essentially a repetition and reinforcement of this point: we now live in a post-Fordist, post-proletariat, post-work, post-exploitation society, and the evidence offered with numbing predictability is the emergence of an "information society." Another instance of this theme is reiterated in a recent issue of *The Yale Journal of Criticism* (6.2) which endorses this theorization of a new "postmodern worker" through a revival of the writings of the late Vilém Flusser. Flusser, rejecting the labor theory of value, claims that "who works [sic] are machines" (290) and that as a result "the question of who has power and makes decisions has thus shifted . . . it is not the owner of machines but the information-specialist (not the capitalist but the systems-analyst and programmer) who holds the power" (291). Such an argument enables the claim to the primacy of intellectual labor over manual labor (serving to further reify the split between the two) "at this moment in time" and works to support the idea that social transformation is primarily accomplished through cognitive mapping and by ideological means. On these terms, social transformation amounts to the transformation of consciousness.

These arguments for an "information society" or (as Donna Haraway and other post-al feminists have come to call it) an "informatics of domination" deny the fact that while some workers may not be *directly* producing surplus-value they are part of the process which insures its actualization. In other words, what is needed is a higher level of abstraction in which the movement of capital can be accounted for beyond the particular labor divisions which have been created and systematized in order to accelerate this process. Just as in a factory the labor divisions are such that individual workers may not be directly producing a whole commodity (but merely a part) and therefore it is all of the factory workers as a whole (i.e., collectively) that contribute to the production of surplus-value for the individual capitalist, so it is in the "global assembly line" where the working class is *collectively* producing surplus-value for the capitalist class. It is ultimately the *class as a whole* that produces surplus-value and this can be shown through the regime of wage labor in which capital, in order to reproduce itself, compels the working class (with the threat of starvation, homelessness, etc.) to work part of the day to reproduce its own means of subsistence (i.e., necessary labor-time) and the rest of the day to produce surplus-value for the capitalist class (i.e., surplus labor-time). Without conceptualizing class at this level, "information society" theory remains at a local level and ultimately purports that class is largely defined not through exploitation but through individuals and their "occupation."

In "information society" theory, subjects are not determined by their position within the global relations of production: whether they own the means of production or must sell their labor power to survive (and hence are the subjects of the extraction of surplus-value by those who do own the means of production). Instead, workers are capable of maintaining a certain amount of autonomy from the logic of capital. According to this theory, this "autonomy" is evidenced by the fact that while the logic of capital is such that the ruling class will always attempt to raise the rate of exploitation, workers will resist this in their daily practices through their own initiative and desire. Along these lines, Witheford suggests that "[t]he horizon to which they [i.e., workers] point is the separation of labor from capital. Ultimately, capital needs labor, but labor does not need capital. Labor, as the source of production can dispense with the wage relation: it is potentially autonomous" (*Capital and Class* 52: 89). In short, because workers are the "source of production," through their *will* they can separate from capital and maintain control over production and abolish wage labor, without the *material* abolition of private ownership of the means of production, and hence the abolition of capital itself.

This line of argument is further extended in the concept of a "post-work" society which was fully developed in a recent issue of *Social Text* (38) in which María Milagros López, in her essay "Post-Work Selves and Entitlement 'Attitudes' in Peripheral Postindustrial Puerto Rico " argues for the "disassembly of the metaphysics of labor and its tyranny as moral arbiter" (*Social Text* 38: 114). Along these lines, López maintains that in particular social contexts "post-work" subjectivities have emerged which challenge both the right and the left's investment in "work" as a fundamental concept defining human existence. This claim is grounded in the assumption that social oppression is caused by work itself not the social relations of production. From here the struggle for social emancipation is no longer conceived as a struggle over ownership and control of the means of production and the emancipation of work from exploitative conditions rather, it is understood as the freedom of labor *from work.* In short, social emancipation is achieved by workers "refusing to work." On these terms, "the new actors in this 'postmodern' drama are not the working class, but the lumpen proletariat" (*Social Text* 38: 114). According to this logic, the "lumpen proletariat" signifies a "resistance within" capitalist relations of production because, while it is composed of non-working poor, it still necessitates a share of the social wealth through, for instance, demands for increased welfare benefits. In short, a "post-work" subject is one who, with the aid of a highly technologized culture (in which machines have replaced humans on the production line), refuses to work.

On their own terms, the aim of post-al left journals in contributing to this project is to produce knowledges that dismantle the traditional work ethic of "self-sacrifice" (which relies on the possibility of a "self-producing" subject autonomous from the social arrangements in which it is situated) in favor of a "post-work" ethic of care which understands all members of society to be dependent upon, and hence entitled to, equal shares of the social wealth regardless of their contribution to the production of this wealth. However, at the same time a "post-work" ethics purports that the subject is not autonomous from its social arrangements (and therefor cannot "pull itself up by its own bootstraps" as the traditional work ethic would have it), insofar as it grants labor an autonomy from capital (and hence the logic of the capitalist mode of production), it reasserts the autonomous, cognitive subject that can transcend the socio-economic relations in which she is situated through assertion of hers will. López and other "post-work" theorists endorse a redistributionist theory of social emancipation in which the aim of a progressive social movement is to redistribute social wealth *without accounting for the conditions under which this wealth is produced in the first place.* Ultimately, securing the conditions necessary for a "post-work" society ends up being no different from capitalist reform: the call for higher wages, less hours of work, increased social security and welfare benefits, and so on, without the fundamental transformation of capitalist relations of production. While demands for all of these are important in the development of a revolutionary movement, "post-work" ethics understands these demands as ends in and of themselves. In doing so, a "post-work" ethics elides the fact that *class exploitation is not simply a result of the unequal distribution of social wealth but is located in the production process itself, through the extraction of surplus-value.*

This elision is owing to the fact that at the heart of "post-work" and "information society" theory is a rejection of the labor theory of value (which argues that it is only human labor which can produce social wealth—so that even if part or all of the production process is mechanized, the value of the technology used in the production process is no more than the human labor time put into its production). Nothing is more so the case than in *Rethinking Marxism*, a journal dedicated to bringing economic concepts back into political discussion, while articulating them in a "new" and "updated" form (i.e., after a post-al "rethinking" of them) which empties them of all material content and reduces them to the effects of a cognitive process of meaning production. This is evident in, for instance, "Essentialism and the Economy in the Post-Marxist Imaginary: Reopening the Sutures" (*Rethinking Marxism* 6.3: 28-48), in which the authors, Jonathan Diskin and Blair Sandler, in the interest of demonstrating labor's autonomy from the logic of capital, propose a "reworking" of economic concepts within a "post-marxist" framework (a project that they criticize Laclau and Mouffe for failing to do, while still accepting their fundamental rejection of socialism). In doing so, they argue (in contrast to Laclau and Mouffe) that labor-power is a commodity and that as such "once purchased (or contracted for), [it] may change in nature or meaning, thereby changing the nature of production" (37). On the terms of this argument a commodity is defined by the use-value that can be appropriated from it—and what determines this value is the meaning that is attributed to it. In other words, *signification* is the foundation of the production process (or as Stanley Aronowitz claims in an article I will discuss later: "knowledge has become the major productive force" [*Socialist Review* 23.3: 67]). Consequently, "exploitation" itself is understood as an effect of discursive practices and not the material practice of compelling workers to work *for free* beyond the time necessary to produce the value equivalent to their own means of subsistence.

What this does not explain (besides the fact that most wage-workers are paid *after* they have fulfilled the task they were employed for and hence rarely have the flexibility to refuse to work or alter their services and still get paid) is: How, historically and materially, has it been possible for commodities (which are also *exchange*-values) to be exchanged in the first place? This can only be possible if, despite their diverse use-values commodities have something in common which can be measured. What can be measured is the socially necessary labor-time it takes to produce a particular commodity under the historically given social conditions of production. In short, a commodity, insofar as it is not simply a use-value but also an exchange-value, cannot be understood in abstraction from the human labor-time invested in its production (Marx 178-87). To do so would be to understand commodities as transhistorical and self-producing entities. By eliding the conditions under which commodities are produced "post-work" theory is, finally, an alibi for simply giving working and non-working poor a greater share of the results of exploitation without eradicating exploitation itself—that is, it is an alibi for the reform and preservation of capitalist relations of production.

Through the logic of the post-al "left" knowledge industry, the very possibility of a mode of "abstraction" and "conceptuality" capable of *explaining* and effectively opposing global capitalist exploitation is erased from the scene of theory. Insofar as the knowledge industry elevates itself "above" and "beyond" everyday class antagonisms it elevates "knowledges" above these antagonisms as well. Concepts, then, are not understood as historically produced explanations of "reality" (that is, of the status of the relations of production) made possible by the objective historical development of the forces of production. Instead they are understood as "self-producing" entities which shift through a process of "self-differentiation" of the discourse (or textuality of the concept) itself. The philosophical support for this is provided by the development of "cultural materialism" advanced as a "progressive" democratic rewriting of historical materialism in journals such as *Theory, Culture & Society*. Andrew Milner in his essay "Cultural Materialism, Culturalism and Post-Culturalism: The Legacy of Raymond Williams" (*Theory, Culture & Society* 2.1: 43-73) aims at giving "culture" a(n at least) semi-autonomy from economic determinations. In other words, Williams and Milner revise the "base/superstructure" model of social totality in classical Marxism through providing a theory of "the material" in which "culture" is equally determining of human existence. Milner's rereading of Williams is informed by Foucault's post-al understanding of discourse in which discourse forms objects for us. On these terms, because we only have access to "reality" through discourse for all "practical" (pragmatic) purposes discourse constitutes reality. The primary object of critique and transformation in these theories is "discourse" itself. Here we can see that once culture and "discourse" are separated from labor and economics and hence, from class antagonisms, the project of social transformation becomes a project of (as Judith Butler calls it) "re-signification."

At this point "domination" and "power" have been completely severed from economic exploitation and are instead understood as effects of discursive relations so that to "categorize" or "conceptualize" becomes a totalitarian act in itself. Along these lines, the special issue of *diacritics* (23.2) on "histoires coloniales" serves as a text of deconstructive vigilance which argues that postcolonial studies, and the experience of colonialism cannot be equated with British postcolonial studies and the experience of British colonialism. To do so would be to mystify the cultural specificity of French colonialism and the experience of people oppressed by it which "bears a striking resemblance to the colonial crime of universalizing the particular" (*diacritics* 23.3: 3). And, indeed, it is extremely enabling to the capitalist class to have workers within so called "postcolonial" nations to identify themselves along national, rather than class, lines. This is useful for capital which relies on its ability—in the face of workers developing revolutionary consciousness and beginning to advance their interests in the class struggle—to close down production sites in one nation and move to another where working class consciousness and transnational solidarity is at a lower stage of development.

Through the proliferation of an "ethics of difference" the principled action of a collective is rendered totalitarian and hence "political action" becomes an alibi for pragmatism. Such pragmatism is advanced in William Phillips' attempt to resurrect the anti-Marxist writings of pragmatist Sydney Hook in *Partisan Review* (1994: 7-8). While he attributes "The Ideological Blacklist" against Hook's work, in part, to the discourses of postmodern philosophy (as well as what he understands as a "Stalinist consciousness" in the U.S. by which he actually means a revolutionary Marxism—that is, Stalinism becomes a "moral" alibi for the suppression of Marxism) we can see elsewhere that contrary to appearances there is a link between pragmatism and postmodern philosophy. Meili Steele's "How Philosophy of Language Informs Ethics and Politics: Richard Rorty and Contemporary Theory" in *boundary 2* (20.2), his primary aim is to break down the "stalemate" between pragmatism and poststructuralism and, indeed, he finds this bridge in Rorty whose (post)argument works to get rid of the possibility of "conditions of possibility" and therefore enables a conceptualization of politics as "spontaneous" (i.e., without foundation).

Interestingly, such an understanding of politics as spontaneous is also supported by Terry Eagleton in *Textual Practice* in what appears to be a rejection of the post-al conception of politics and the state but is in fact a wholehearted embracement of it (8.1: 1-10). Here Eagleton voids political philosophy and practice from any economic content whatsoever by arguing that, "*obviously . . . [t]he interest of the liberal state is to be . . . genuinely disinterested*" (2). In other words, Eagleton takes the claims of the liberal state to be self-evident (in a post-al mode of re-signification which now merely re-understands "disinterestedness" to, in fact, be an interest), and in doing so obscures the fact that the liberal state, as a capitalist form of the state, serves the material interests of the capitalist class in producing "free market" subjects. This erasure of economics enables Eagleton to claim that "socialism is the consummation of liberalism, not its antithesis" (6). At the core of this claim is the post-al notion that ethics, not economics, is the underpinning of the political organization of the state. The "choice" between socialism (which Eagleton claims is a synthesis of the "best" elements of liberalism and communitarianism), and postmodernism (which he claims is a synthesis of the "worst" elements of liberalism and communitarianism) that Eagleton poses at the end of his essay is then an "ethical" choice on the part of "responsible subjects," not a matter of historical necessity.

This works to support a localist politics, such as the green consumerism which is the recurring "progressive" cause in *In These Times* (18.9), and the focus of its special issue geared toward challenging the E.P.A. policy reforms under the Clinton administration.This localist politics is further manifested in the reform of mental health institutions as a "resolution" to the crisis of homelessness advocated for in a recent issue of *The New York Review of Books* (41.8). Each of these obscures the fact that while the *international* forces of production have reached the productive capacity to fulfill the basic needs of all human beings on the planet (including the needs for shelter, clean air, clean water, etc.) in *less than* a forty-hour work week, the relations of production (i.e., private ownership of the means of production) are such that the forces of production are mobilized primarily to produce profit for the ruling class, not meet human needs. *Until workers gain control over their own productive capacities, through a transformation of ownership of the means of production from private to public, they will remain subordinated to the interests and decision making authority of the capitalist class.*

Not only does an ethics difference work to fracture working class solidarity but it also works to legitimate the voracity of the bourgeois subject of desire. As Steele argues in *boundary 2*: "because a theorist's metaphilosophical commitment is no longer totalizing, his/her selection of a given problematic will depend as much on what he/she wants to recuperate for a given project as it does on the truth of a given linguistic ontology" (172). This understanding of politics, insofar as it does not pressure the class position of the theorist who "decides" what she "wants," enables the bourgeois and petit-bourgeois subject of desire to maintain her interest in "success" and "privilege" at the expense of the working class while meanwhile purporting to work toward "social change." But such a position (again) ultimately implies that "another" class—the "intellectual class"—has a fundamental interest in social transformation. Such a position is ultimately a cynical response to the backlash against the proletariat as it assumes that the proletariat is incapable of producing a revolutionary movement on its own; the proletariat's economic conditions (i.e., exploitation) have not given rise to an appropriate response to capitalism (see Wood's critique of this position in *The Retreat from Chaos*). According to this ideology, the masses of working people are hopelessly "reactionary" on their own and only a cadre of intellectuals are capable of "social change." But such a position obscures the fact that *it is the objective conditions of the forces of production that are the condition of possibility for "conceptuality."* In obscuring this, social transformation is understood as a primarily ideological transformation that occurs "beyond" class antagonisms and exploitation by the "agency" of the liberal consciousness. This severing off of mental labor from manual labor ultimately renders the academy as an autonomous site from the "rest of reality"—and the transformation therein becomes a reformation of the institution itself.

In short, the discourses developed at both "high-tech" and "low-tech" levels in the current field of knowledge production serve the interest of legitimating the retreat from class politics and revolutionary transformation and replacing this with the project of institutional reform of the knowledge industry. That is, the concepts produced in contemporary bourgeois theory are part of an extended mode of self-explanation and self-justification rather than an explanation of objective conditions of existence. What this represents, contrary to Ruth Wilson Gilmore's argument in "Public Enemies and Private Intellectuals: Apartheid USA" (*Race and Class* 35.1: 69-78), is not a "retreat" of social struggles into the academy but an *exclusion* of revolutionary struggles *from* the academy—from an institution that rightfully belongs to the proletariat. While Gilmore insists upon the necessity for the transformation of ownership of the means of production from private to public, and critiques the development of an "intellectual comprador class," the resistance to "private intellectuals" takes the form of compelling intellectuals to engage in local and reformist activism outside the academy without putting pressure on what it is that they do inside the academy—in their *pedagogy*. In other words, the opposition to "private intellectuals" ends up being an opposition to theory as such rather than a critique of the *class content* of particular theories.

Perhaps the most recent, sustained and thorough manifestation of this retreat from class politics can be found in the *Socialist Review* in Stanley Aronowitz's article "The Situation of the Left in the United States" (23.3: 5-79). Aronowitz takes as his point of departure the post-al rejection of class as a material category and the embracement of the notion that we have now embarked upon a new social order—an "informatics of domination" in which "knowledge has become the major productive force" (67)—where the possibility and necessity for the abolition of private property is horribly "outdated" and out of touch with the diverse needs of "the people." Specifically, Aronowitz claims that "socialism as a strategy of economic change . . . can no longer remain a guiding principle for a movement of social emancipation . . . the socialist movement deserves a decent burial . . . [b]ut to attempt to revive socialism *in its present form* would be an exercise in futility, especially after the rise of the social movements" (43, 58-59). As an "alternative" to the struggle for socialism, he endorses a struggle for "radical democracy." This entails, in large part, "decentralization in the control of economic and political institutions, and pluralism in the institutions of everyday life" (65).

Yet, without abolishing private property and ensuring public ownership of the means of production, "decentralizing" the state does not mean the dismantling of it but only its restructuring for accommodation of the historically dominant tendency within capitalism. Since the late 1960s as capital has more fully entered the arena of international competition, this has put tremendous pressure on the national sovereignty of the state. The importance of investing in the "internal" workforce, and the steady increase of the standard of living for workers in the United States that prevailed in the post-World War II era until the late 1960s (in large part resulting from federal regulations and reforms instituted under the "New Deal") has been increasingly cut back and subordinated to the concerns of capitalists in the international market place. Once North Atlantic capital reached a stage of productivity in which it was necessary to compete on the international marketplace in order to maintain existing levels of profit, and once this increased competition made it necessary to also shift production sites to the "third world" where cheaper labor can be extracted, capital's investment in the internal workforce (and hence its "protection" of this workforce through the state's regulation of trade, and national reforms) has waned considerably. What capital now demands is the deregulation of the "free market" and with this it needs a "decentralized" state that will not stand in the way of "free trade." Far from being "radical," Aronowitz's proposal for a "politics of alternatives" (59-75) from the class politics of the "old left," is simply an affirmation of the direction that capital is currently headed.

In order for a revolutionary movement to oppose capital in its historically dominant form (i.e., trans-national capitalism), it is necessary to oppose capital on a transnational level. This is especially the case as while the state is increasingly removing barriers for international business deals such as the North Atlantic Free

Trade Agreement between the United States and Mexico, it increasingly builds restrictions for labor on an international level (by, for instance, building up immigration laws that prevent labor from moving as freely as capital). By opposing working class solidarity on an international level as totalizing (and therefore totalitarian), post-al left writers assist the capitalist class in insuring that the subordination of national labor laws to the "free play" of international capital is made easier.

This is where Aronowitz's essay proves to be most reactionary in its complicity with post-al forms of the deployment of capital. In the guise of advocating for the necessity for a "global" radical organization (by which Aronowitz simply means an "umbrella" organization that gives various *local* groups and individual activists the space to plan for tactical, not principled, "co-operation" in their struggles), Aronowitz in actuality endorses the maintenance of liberal democratic voting procedures among the general populace with merely a change to a more progressive consciousness when exercising their "right to vote." Along these lines, Aronowitz argues that in a radical democracy "proposals such as the public or collective ownership of productive resources would be evaluated on democratic as well as practical criteria, including the degree to which these forms of ownership would best meet human needs under existing conditions" (67). This presupposes however, a central tenant of liberal democracy: that political democracy can be achieved without (and to supplement the lack of) economic equality. Moreover, it also assumes that economic equality can be achieved without public ownership of the means of production—without a transformation of the material conditions under which the majority of the people on the planet live. This point is most explicit in Aronowitz's argument that the goal of a new progressive organization is to institute "a movement of ideas and alternatives" (73). According to Aronowitz "we are hampered by our own prison-houses: the old ideas, the new anti-ideas . . ." (75)—which is to say that the social conditions under which we currently live are adequate in meeting human need and that it is simply a matter of subjects transforming their ideas so that they learn to make use of these structures properly.

Such a retreat from class politics on the part of post-al left journals is a devastating one given the fact that with the internationalization of capital more and more areas of the globe are being proletarianized and therefore inculcated into the logic of capitalist exploitation than ever before. For revolutionary journals to contribute to the collective struggle to emancipate the international proletariat from this exploitation and oppression they must produce knowledges that can explain the world, in its totality, rather than develop means and strategies to deter an explanation of material conditions of existence.

Works Cited

Aronowitz, Stanley. "The Situation of the Left in the United States." *Socialist Review* 23.3 (1994): 5-79.
boundary 2 20.2 (Summer 1993).
Burkett, Paul. "The Strange US Economic Recovery and Clintonomics Historically Considered." *Capital & Class* 52 (Spring 1994): 9-16.
Capital & Class 52 (Spring 1994).
diacritics 23.3 (Fall 1993). (Special Issue: "Histoires Coloniales.")
Diskin, Jonathan and Blair Sandler. "Essentialism and the Economy in the Post-Marxist Imaginary: Reopening the Sutures." *Rethinking Marxism* 6.3 (Fall 1993): 28-48.
Eagleton, Terry. "The Right and the Good: Postmodernism and the Liberal State." *Textual Practice* 8.1 (Spring 1994): 1-10.
Flusser, Vilém. *The Yale Journal of Criticism* 6.2 (Fall 1993): 290.
Gilmore, Ruth Wilson. "Public Enemies and Private Intellectuals: Apartheid USA." *Race and Class* 35.1: 69-78.
In these Times 18.9 (Mar.-Apr. 1994).
Marable, Manning. "Beyond Racial Identity Politics: Towards a Liberation Theory for Multicultural Democracy." *Race and Class* 35.1 (July-Sept. 1993): 113-130.
Marx, Karl. *Capital. Volume 1*. Ben Fowkes, trans. London: Penguin Books, 1976.
López, María Milagros. "Post-Work Selves and Entitlement 'Attitudes' in Peripheral Postindustrial Puerto Rico." *Social Text* 38 (Spring 1994): 111-133.
Milner, Andrew. "Cultural Materialism, Culturalism and Post-Culturalism: The Legacy of Raymond Williams." *Theory, Culture, and Society* 2.1 (Feb. 1994): 43-73.
New York Review of Books 41.8.
Partisan Review 61.1 (1994).
Phillips, William. "The Ideological Blacklist." *Partisan Review* 61.1 (1994): 7-8.
Polygraph 6/7 (1994). (Special issue: "Marxism Beyond Marxism?")
Race and Class 35.1 (July-Sept. 1993). (Special Issue: "Black America the Street and the Campus.")
Rethinking Marxism 6.3 (Fall 1993).
Socialist Review 23.3 (1994).
Social Text 38 (Spring 1994).
Steele, Meili. "How Philosophy of Language Informs Ethics and Politics: Richard Rorty and Contemporary Theory." *boundary 2* 20.2 (Summer 1993).
Theory, Culture & Society 2.1 (Feb. 1994).
Textual Practice 8.4 (Spring 1994).
Witheford, Nick. "Autonomist Marxism and the Information Society." *Capital & Class* 52 (Spring 1994): 85-125.
Wood, Ellen Meiksins. *The Retreat from Class: A New 'True' Socialism*. New York and London: Verso, 1986.
The Yale Journal of Criticism 6.2 (Fall 1993).

Books and Periodicals Received

Books

Aronowitz, Stanley and William DiFazio. *The Jobless Future*. Minneapolis: University of Minnesota Press.
Behdad, Ali. *Belated Travelers*. Durham: Duke University Press.
Bloom, Harold. *The Western Canon*. New York: Harcourt Brace & Co.
Chomsky, Noam. *Keeping the Rabble in Line: Interviews with David Barsamian*. Monroe, ME: Common Courage P.
Cunningham, Frank. *The Real World of Democracy Revisited*. Atlantic Highlands, NJ: Humanities Press.
Deleuze, Gilles and Felix Guattari. *What is Philosophy?* New York: Columbia University Press
Derrida, Jacques. *The Other Heading*. Bloomington: Indiana University Press.
Derrida, Jacques. *Specters of Marx*. New York: Routledge.
Fish, Stanley. *There's No Such Thing as Free Speech . . . and it's a good thing too*. New York: Oxford University Press.
Gross, Paul R. and Norman Levitt. *Higher Superstition: The Academic Left and its Quarrels with Science*. Baltimore: The Johns Hopkins University Press.
Jameson, Fredric. *The Seeds of Time*. New York: Columbia University Press.
Klein, Richard. *Cigarettes are Sublime* Durham: Duke University Press.
Magnus, Bernd & Stephen Cullenberg, ed. *Whither Marxism?* New York: Routledge.
Mandel, Ernest. *The Place of Marxism in History*. Atlantic Highlands, NJ: Humanities Press.
Mandel, Ernest. *Revolutionary Marxism and Social Reality in the 20th Century: Collected Essays*. Atlantic Highlands, NJ: Humanities Press.
Taylor, Mark C. & Esa Saarinen. *IMAGOLOGIES: Media Philosophy*. New York: Routledge.
Traverso, Enzo. *The Marxists: The History of a Debate 1843-1943*. Atlantic Highlands, NJ: Humanities Press.
Wark, McKenzie. *Virtual Geography: Living with Global Media Events*. Bloomington: Indiana University Press.
Wartenberg, Thomas E., ed. *Rethinking Power*. Albany, NY: SUNY Press.
Wright, E. O. *Interrogating Inequality: Essays on Class Analysis, Socialism and Marxism*. New York: Verso.
Wolfreys, Julian. *Being English*. Albany, NY: SUNY Press.
Zavarzadeh, Mas'ud & Donald Morton. *Theory as Resistance: Politics and Culture After (Post)structuralism*. New York: Guilford Press.

Periodicals

Alternative Orange, Vol. 4, No. 1.
Black History and the Class Struggle, No. 12 "South Africa Power Keg."
Border/Lines, Nos. 34-35.
Capital and Class, No. 55.
Cultural Critique, No. 29.
Diacritics, Vol. 24, Nos. 2-3 "Critical Crossings."
In Defense of Marxism, No. 123 "International Women's Day."
International Socialism, No. 65" The Revolutionary Ideas of Frederick Engels."
The Minnesota Review, Nos. 41-42 "states of Theory."
Proletarian Revolution, No. 46.
Public Culture, Vol. 7, No. 2.
Race and Class, Vol. 36, No. 3.
Radical Philosophy ,No. 69.
Socialist Worker, No., 219.
Women and Revolution, No. 44 "Women and the Permanent Revolution in Bangladesh."
Workers Vanguard, No. 610.

The BOOKPRESS
THE NEWSPAPER OF THE LITERARY ARTS

Each month, upstate New York's *only* newspaper of the Literary Arts brings you original articles and provocative, wide-ranging reviews by well-known, as well as first-time, writers

Literary, Scientific, & Cultural Writings by M.H. Abrams, Diane Ackerman, A.R. Ammons, Martin Bernal, Jonathan Culler, Ann Druyan, Thomas Eisner, Gunilla Feigenbaum, Mitchell Feigenbaum, Carey Harrison, Phyllis Janowitz, Biodun Jeyifo, Alfred Kahn, Richard Klein, Theodore Lowi, Alison Lurie, Ali Mazrui, James McConkey, Eleanor Munro, Leslie Silko, Meredith Small, Gary Snyder, John Vernon, Paul West, and Ronald Wright

In-Depth Interviews with Nadine Gordimer, Dan McCall, Lamar Herrin, Jack Delano, Abraham Pais, Charles Bernstein, Benedict Anderson, Robert Morgan, Mark Strand, and Carl Sagan

Subjects Ranging from Literary Theory, Politics, and Fiction, to History, Poetry, Science, the Environment, and more—Children's Books, Painting and Sculpture, Film and Photography, Gardening, Music, the Labor Movement, Theater and Dance, and Education including Black Athena...the Sex Pistols...Jacques Derrida...Salvador Dalí...Sigmund Freud...Dizzy Gillespie...Samuel Beckett...the Haggadah...Edmund Wilson...Thomas Pynchon...Harold Bloom...African conservation...Guatemala...Cuba...Kurt Vonnegut...Allen Ginsberg...Philip Roth...Steven Jay Gould...the Ramayana...Ishmael Reed...Paolo Freire...the Cold War...Native American history...the '60s...Walt Disney...Madonna...Tikkun...language poetry...Henry Moore

"Readers need a literary magazine of discernment, and The Bookpress *is certainly that. It is also approachable, entertaining, and open-minded. No book-lover should be without it."*
—Diane Ackerman

For only $12, the next 8 issues will be delivered directly to your door!

Name _____
Address _____
_____
Phone _____

(Visa / MC / Discover, check, or money order accepted)
Send to: The Bookpress, 215 N Cayuga St., Ithaca, NY 14850

the minnesota review
(a journal of committed writing)

back issues

"PC Wars"
ns 39, Fall / Winter 1992/3

"The Politics of AIDS"
ns 40, Spring / Summer 1993

current issues

"The Institution of Literature"

i. Reconfiguring Fields and Theories c.1994
ns. 41-42, Fall 1993-Spring 1994

ii. Institutional Structures and Stories
ns 43, Fall 1994 (deadline 1 May 1994)

iii. The Politics of Publishing
ns 44, Spring 1995 (deadline 1 Nov. 1994)

with work by Crystal Bartolovich, Michael Berube, Terry Caesar, Don Bialostosky, Ross Chambers, Tom Cohen, Jennifer Cotter, Lennard Davis, Ortwin de Graef, Cora Kaplan, Amitara Kumar, Devoney Looser, Julian Markels, Louise Mowder, Mark Redfield, Bruce Robbins, Veronica Stewart, Paul Trembath, Alan Wald, Evan Watkins, Mas'ud Zavarzadeh, and many others

in planning

"The White Issue"
ns 45, Fall 1995 (deadline 1 May 1995)

Subscriptions are $12 a year (two issues), $24 institutions (+$5 foreign, $10 air) *minnesota review* is published biannually and originates from East Carolina

Please send all queries, comments, submissions, and subscriptions to:
Jeffrey Williams, Editor, *minnesota review*, Department of English,
East Carolina University, Greenville, NC 27858-4353

• "THE OPEN BOAT" • FULL METAL JACKET • MICHAEL WIGGLESWORTH'S DIARY • CALIBAN IN THE CARIBBEAN • HOUSEKEEPING • YUPPIE POSTMODERNISM

–linguae americanae–

ARIZONA QUARTERLY

American literature, culture,
and theory, four times a year

1 year $12
3 years $24

Main Library B 541 • University of Arizona
Tucson, Arizona 85721

–Return this ad for a free sample issue–

• JAMES WELCH • TWAIN'S TWINS • ELIZABETH BISHOP • *BELOVED* • "BENITO CERENO" • *THE GREAT GATSBY* • CHARLES OLSON • ARCHITECTURE IN *SCRIBNER'S*

diacritics
A Review of Contemporary Criticism

Edited by
**Jonathan Culler & Richard Klein,
Cornell University**

Diacritics is the preeminent forum for exchange among literary theorists, literary critics, and philosophers. Each issue features articles in which contributors compare and analyze books on particular theoretical works and develop their own positions on the theses, methods, and theoretical implications of those works. Published quarterly in March, June, September, and December.

Annual Subscriptions:
$23.50 individuals, $59.00 institutions.
Foreign Postage:
$3.50, Canada & Mexico;
$8.40 outside North America.
Send orders with payment to:
The Johns Hopkins University Press,
P.O. Box 19966, Baltimore, Maryland 21211.
MD residents add 5% tax. Orders shipped to Canada add 7% GST (GST #124004946.)

To place an order using Visa or MasterCard, call toll-free 1-800-548-1784, fax us at (410) 516-6968, or send Visa/MasterCard orders to this E-Mail address:
jlorder@jhunix.hcf.jhu.edu

**December 1994
(Vol. 24, No. 4):**

- Towards an Ethics of Decision
- Hallucinogeneric Literature: Avital Ronell's Narcoanalysis
- A Telephone Conversation: Fragments
- Chronic Chronotopicity: Reply to Morson and Emerson

Published by
The Johns Hopkins University Press

EA4

PHILOSOPHY, PSYCHIATRY & PSYCHOLOGY

Editors: K.W.M. FULFORD, D. PHIL. &
JOHN Z. SADLER, M.D.

Sponsored by
The Association for the Advancement of Philosophy and Psychiatry (AAPP), The Royal Institute of Philosophy, *and* The Royal College of Psychiatrists Philosophy Group.

Philosophy, Psychiatry, and Psychology (PPP) publishes philosophical articles pertaining to psychiatry and abnormal psychology, as well as psychiatric and psychological articles relevant to philosophy. This international journal helps psychiatrists, psychologists, and others become more effective practitioners, teachers, and researchers by illuminating philosophical issues in health care. Likewise, *PPP* advances philosophical theory by making the phenomena of psychiatry and abnormal psychology more accessible to philosophers. *Published quarterly in March, June, September, and December.*

SEPTEMBER 1994 (VOL. 1, NO. 3)

The Alzheimer's Disease Sufferer as Semiotic Subject

Mild Mania and Well-Being

Recent Criticism of Psychiatric Nosology: A Review

PPP Concurrent Contents: Recent and Classic References at the Interface of Philosophy, Psychiatry, and Abnormal Psychology

PUBLISHED BY
THE JOHNS HOPKINS UNIVERSITY PRESS

Annual Subscriptions for North American individuals *(includes membership to the American Association for the Advancement of Philosophy & Psychiatry):* $65.00, individuals (£52); $32.00 students (£26). MD residents add 5% sales tax. Canadian residents add 7% GST (#124004946). For orders shipped to Canada or Mexico, please add $4.50 for foreign postage.

Annual Subscriptions for Individuals outside of North America: $54.00 (£44) *(Includes foreign postage, but does not include membership)*

Send orders to:
The Johns Hopkins University Press,
PO Box 19966,
Baltimore, MD 21211.

To place an order using Visa or MasterCard, call toll-free 1-800-548-1784, FAX us at (410) 516-6968, or send Visa/MasterCard orders to this E-mail address:
jlorder@jhunix.hcf.jhu.edu

EA4

PHILOSOPHY AND LITERATURE

DENIS DUTTON, EDITOR • PATRICK HENRY, COEDITOR

In exploring the connections between literary and philosophical studies, *Philosophy and Literature* provides analysis of the philosophical underpinnings of literature and examines the literary dimensions of classical works of philosophy. Written in clear, jargon-free prose by leading scholars from a broad range of disciplines, the journal offers comprehensive coverage of continental, British, and American literature. The best and newest work on the aesthetics of literature, philosophy of language relevant to literature, and theory of criticism is also regularly featured, along with incisive critiques of current books in the field. Sponsored by Whitman College. Published twice a year in April and October.

Subscribe to PHIL-LIT, an electronic forum that directly links contributors, editors, and readers of Philosophy & Literature. To subscribe to the PHIL-LIT Listserve send the e-mail message SUBSCRIBE PHIL-LIT YOUR NAME TO: listserv@tamvmi.tamu.edu For further information, contact the list manager, David Gershom Myers: dgmyers@tamvmi.tamu.edu

Prepayment is required. **Annual subscriptions:** $22.00, individuals; $43.00, institutions. **Foreign postage:** $3.00, Canada & Mexico; $5.50, outside North America. **Single-issue price:** $11.00, individuals; $23.00, institutions. Payment must be drawn on a U.S. bank in U.S. dollars or made by international money order. MD residents add 5% sales tax. For orders shippped to Canada add 7% GST (#124004946).

Send orders to:
The Johns Hopkins University Press, P.O. Box 19966, Baltimore, MD 21211.

To place an order using Visa or MasterCard, call toll-free 1-800-548-1784, FAX us at (410) 516-6968, or send Visa/MasterCard orders to this E-mail address: jlorder@jhunix.hcf.jhu.edu

MLN

MODERN LANGUAGE NOTES

Richard Macksey, Editor
Comparative Literature Issue

MLN pioneered the introduction of contemporary continental criticism into American scholarship. Critical studies in the modern languages—Italian, Hispanic, German, French—and recent work in comparative literature are the basis for the articles and notes in *MLN*. Each of the first four issues of every volume features one language and centers on the critical works of that language. The fifth issue is devoted to comparative literature. Published 5 times a year in January (Italian), March (Hispanic), April (German), September (French), and December (Comparative Literature).

Comparative Literature

(Volume 109, Number 5):
- Re-specting the Face as the Moral (of) Fiction in Mary Shelley's *Frankenstein*
- Afterthoughts on the Animal World
- Other Foods, Other Voices
- Playing Jane Campion's *Piano*: Politically
- Balzac's Art of Excess
- Connecting Pungencies: Borges Conjured and Restored

THE JOHNS HOPKINS UNIVERSITY PRESS

Prepayment is required. Annual subscription (5 issues): $31.00, individuals; $82.00, institutions. Three year subscription to single-language: $30.00, individuals only. Foreign postage: $5.00, Canada & Mexico; $13.50, outside North America. Single-issue price: $9.00, individuals; $18.00, institutions. Payment must be drawn on a U.S. bank in U.S. dollars or made by international money order. MD residents add 5% sales tax. For orders shipped to Canada add 7% GST (#124004946). **Send orders to:** The Johns Hopkins University Press, PO Box 19966, Baltimore, MD 21211.

To place an order using Visa or MasterCard, call toll-free 1-800-548-1784, FAX us at (410) 516-6968, or send Visa/MasterCard order to this E-mail address:
jlorder@jhunix.hcf.jhu.edu

EA4

college
Literature

No longer restricting its focus to pedagogical approaches to particular works of literature . . . College Literature has widened its scope to include important theoretical matters as well. . . . an impressive editorial vision.

CELJ Awards Committee

College Literature has made itself in a short time one of the leading journals in its field, important reading for anyone teaching literature to college students.

J. Hillis Miller

SPECIAL TOPICS FOR 1995-96

February 1995	Third World Women's Inscriptions
June 1995	African American Writing
October 1995	Non-Western Poetics Before European Colonialism
February 1996	General Issue
June 1996	Gay and Lesbian Studies: Politics, Pedagogy, Performance

SUBSCRIPTIONS

Individual: $24 one year, Institution: $48 one year
College Literature, 210 Philips Hall, West Chester University, West Chester, PA 19383. 610-436-2901

MEDIATIONS
Journal of the Marxist Literary Group

ANNOUNCING
THE BIANNUAL JOURNAL OF THE
MARXIST LITERARY GROUP

Mediations has recently been expanded from newsletter to journal format. It now features articles, interviews, exchanges and reviews of interest to left intellectuals in the academy. Recent issues include articles by John Beverley on the discourse of "testimonio" in Latin American political struggles, Douglas Kellner on rap and black radical discourse, Shekhar Deshpande and Andy Kurtz on The Body Shop's "politically correct" advertising strategies, Keya Ganguly on nationalism and diasporic knowledges, Terri Ginsberg on world systems theory, Jane Robson Graham on postmodern cartography, Crystal Bartolovich on cultural studies and multiculturalism, plus an interview with Richard Woolf, co-editor of *Rethinking Marxism* and co-founder of the Association for Economic and Social Analysis.

The Marxist Literary Group is an Allied Organization of the Modern Language Association. In addition to publishing *Mediations*, the MLG sponsors the Institute for Culture and Society, a week-long symposium held annually in June.

Annual subscriptions are $15, student subscriptions are $5.

Submissions and inquiries should be addressed to :

> Mediations
> English Department
> Illinois State University
> Normal, IL 61790-4240

CRITICAL SOCIOLOGY

Announcing

A Special Issue of *Critical Sociology:*

Critical Studies of Lesbian, Gay, and Bisexual Issues
(Volume 20, Number 3)

- Susan Johnston, *Fighting the Anti-Gay Right*
- Barbara Epstein, *Anti-Communism and Homophobia*
- Nicholas Leggett, *The Military's Anti-Gay Policy*
- Mary Beth Krouse, *The AIDS Quilt as Resistance*
- Martha Schmidt, *Jeffrey Dahmer and Gay Identity*
- Amber Ault, *Lesbian Feminism and Bisexuality*
- Cheryl Cole & Harry Denny, *Magic Johnson and AIDS*
- Wendy Chapkis, *Biology and Gay Rights*
- Paula Rust, *Designing a Course on Sexuality*
- Steven Seidman, *Queer Pedagogy*
- Julia Wallace, *Queer-ing Sociology in the Classroom*

Other Special Issues Still Available:
- *German Sociology* (Vol. 17, No. 3)
- *Analyzing Power Structures* (Vol. 16, No. 2-3)
- *Twenty Years of Sociological Liberation* (Vol. 15, No. 2)

Subscription Information: individuals: $20/year (3 issues); students and unemployed: $15/year; institutions: $40/year. Canadian currency add 30 percent. Overseas airmail add $15/year. Back issues: $6/single issue; $12/double issue.

Order from: Critical Sociology, Department of Sociology, University of Oregon, Eugene, OR 97403, U.S.A.

PostModernPositions

Vol. I *Ethics/Aesthetics: Post-Modern Positions*
Robert Merrill, ed.
ISBN 0-944624-00-6 cloth $22.96
ISBN 0-944624-01-4 paper $11.95

Vol. 2 *Open Form and the Feminine Imagination: The Politics of Reading in Twentieth Century Innovative Writing*
Stephen-Paul Martin
ISBN 0-944624-02-2 cloth $22.95
ISBN 0-944624-02-0 paper $11.95

Vol. 3 *Interventions: Displacing the Metaphysical Subject*
Keith C. Pheby
ISBN 0-944624-04-9 cloth $18.95
ISBN 0-944624-05-7 paper $9.95

Vol. 4 *Postmodernism / Jameson / Critique*
Douglas Kellner, ed.
ISBN 0-944624-06-5 cloth $29.95
ISBN 0-944624-07-3 paper $15.95

Vol. 5 *Theory, (Post)Modernity, Opposition: An "Other" Introduction to Contemporary Literary and Cultural Theory*
Mas'ud Zavarzadeh and Donald Morton
ISBN 0-944624-11-1 cloth $29.95
ISBN 0-944624-12-X paper $13.95

Vol. 6 *Crisis Cinema: The Apocalyptic Idea in Postmodern Narrative Cinema*
Christopher Sharrett, ed.
ISBN 0-944624-18-9 cloth $34,95
ISBN 0-944624-19-7 paper $14.95

Vol. 7 *The Myth of the Other. Lacan, Foucault, Deleuze, Bataille*
Frances Dolla, Nelson Moe, trans.
ISBN 0-944624-20-0 cloth $29.95
ISBN 0-944624-21-9 paper- $11.95

Vol. 8 *Positively Postmodern: The Multi-Media Muse in America*
Nicholas Zurburgg, interviewer
ISBN 0-944624-22-7 paper only, $29.95
Interviews with some 40 top American multi-media artists. Includes John Cage, Philip Glass, Laurie Anderson, Nam June Paik, William S. Burroughs, Steve Reich, etc. Many photos from their work.

Vol. 9 *Theory and Its Others: Pun(k)Deconstruction, Posttheory, and Ludic Politics*
Mas'ud Zavarzadeh
ISBN 0-944624-25-1 cloth $36.95
ISBN 0-944624-26-X paper $15.95
A sustained criticism of the manner in which poststructural theory and deconstruction were easily adopted into American universities. Includes commentary on the role of university presses and major refereed journals.

Critical Studies in Community Development and Architecture

Geography and Identity: Exploring and Living Geopolitics of Identity
Dennis Crow, ed.
ISBN 0-944624-23-5 cloth $36.95
ISBN 0-944624-24-3 paper $15.95
Fifteen prominent scholars in architecture, city planning, and cultural studies come together to reflect on the relation of place to personal identity. Essays on Native America, Israel, post-colonial India, New York, Los Angeles, Berlin, the Southwest, and more.

Please request at your local bookstore or order directly from

Maisonneuve Press

P.O. Box 2980
Washington, DC 20013-2980
send check or Visa/MC number and $2.00 postage

NEW LITERARY HISTORY

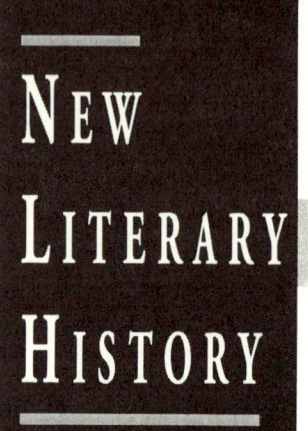

A Journal of Theory and Interpretation

RALPH COHEN, EDITOR

Published by
THE JOHNS HOPKINS UNIVERSITY PRESS

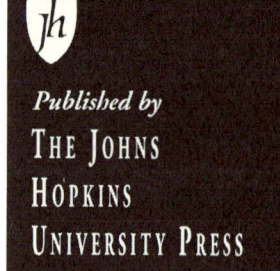

New Literary History focuses on theory and interpretation—the reasons for literary change, the definitions of periods, and the evolution of styles, conventions, and genres. The journal has brought into English many of today's foremost theorists whose works had never before been translated. *Published quarterly in February, May, August, and November.*

This is the second of four issues commemorating NLH's 25th Anniversary

Volume 25, Number 4 includes:
The Ascent of Love: Plato, Spinoza, Proust • The Self and Literary Experience in Late Antiquity and the Middle Ages • The Medieval Travel Narrative • Shrines, Gardens, Utopias • Textual Authority and Performative Agency: The Uses of Disguise in Shakespeare's Theater • Interpretations of Responsibility and Responsibilities of Interpretation • The Experience of Literary History: Vulgar versus Not-Vulgar • Intertextuality vs. Hypertextuality • What Is the Emersonian Event? A Comment on Kateb's Emerson • From Theory to Grammar: Wittgenstein and the Aesthetic of the Ordinary • The School of Criticism and Theory: An Allegorical History • From a Different Perspective • *New Literary History* and European Theory.

Prepayment is required. **Annual subscriptions:** $27.00, individuals; $79.00, institutions. **Foreign postage:** $4.50, Canada & Mexico; $11.30, outside North America. **Single-issue price:** $10.00, individuals; $26.00, institutions. Payment must be drawn on a U.S. bank in U.S. dollars or made by international money order. MD residents add 5% sales tax. For orders shippped to Canada add 7% GST (#124004946). **Send orders to:** The Johns Hopkins University Press, PO Box 19966, Baltimore, MD 21211.
To place an order using Visa or MasterCard, call toll-free 1-800-548-1784, FAX us at (410) 516-6968, or send Visa/MasterCard orders to this E-mail address: jlorder@jhunix.hcf.jhu.edu

Notes to Contributors

Manuscripts should be typed and double-spaced throughout, including "Notes" and "Works Cited," and have one-inch margins on all sides of a page. Explanatory notes should be compiled under the heading "Notes" and placed at the end of the essay (not at the bottom of the page), following the text and before the list of "Works Cited," which make up the final pages of the essay. Do not indent references in the works cited. Italicize book titles if possible; otherwise underlining is acceptable. Please send one hard copy as well as a copy on diskette. IBM compatible word processing software is preferable, but Macintosh programs are also acceptable. Please clearly identify on the diskette the title of your article, the file name(s), and what software was used (i.e., MicroSoft Word 2.0 or WordPerfect 5.1, etc.). Your name and address should appear at the top of the first page of the essay and the pages should be numbered. Please keep formatting (i.e., boldface, different size fonts, etc.) to a minimum; do not use soft-hyphens at the end of lines, or place extra spaces between paragraphs, quotations, or notes—however, you may use extra spaces to indicate section breaks.

Transformation follows the style conventions of *Webster's Third International Dictionary* in such matters as spelling, hyphenation, and the Modern Language Association's recommendations in bibliographical notation and documentation (*MLA Handbook*, 3rd edition). References to works should be included in the text along the lines of the following models:

> She then writes: "I would like nevertheless to suggest that, far from having exhausted itself, the great ideology debate of the 1960s and 1970s was broken off prematurely, before a series of crucial issues could be addressed" (Silverman 15).

> or

> Kaja Silverman writes, "I would like nevertheless to suggest . . ." (15).

The parenthetical documentation (Silverman 15) refers the reader to the "Works Cited," which lists all the texts that are referred to in your essay. If necessary to avoid confusion when two or more works by the same author are under discussion, give a shortened title in the sentence or the parentheses. Do not identify works by the date of publication, as is done in the social sciences. Please notice that there is no "p." or "," after the name of the author.

Sample Works Cited

Silverman, Kaja. *Male Subjectivity at the Margins.* New York: Routledge, 1992.
Marx, Karl. *Capital.* Vol. 1. Trans. Ben Fowkes. New York: Vintage Books, 1976
Deleuze, Gilles and Felix Guattari. *Anti-Oedipus: Capitalism and Schizophrenia.* Trans. Robert Hurley, Mark Seem, and Helen R. Lane. Minneapolis: University of Minnesota Press, 1983.
Peggy Kamuf, ed. *A Derrida Reader.* New York: Columbia University Press, 1991.
Said, Edward. "An Ideology of Difference. *"Race," Writing, and Difference.* Ed. Henry Louis Gages, Jr. Chicago and London: University of Chicago Press, 1986. 38-58.
Barrett, Michele. "Feminism's 'Turn to Culture.'" *Woman: A Cultural Review* 1.1 (1990): 22-24. [note: 1.1 refers to the volume number followed by the issue number.]
Hocquenghem, Guy. *Homosexual Desire.* 1978. Trans. Daniella Dangoor. Durham, NC: Duke University Press, 1994.

Send all editorial inquiries and proposals for essays to

Editors
Transformation
English Department
Syracuse University
Syracuse, NY 13244-1170

Transformation accepts announcements and advertisements for books and other cultural texts. For information on rates and related matters, please write to Robert Merrill, editor, Maisonneuve Press, P.O. Box 2980, Washington, D.C. 20013-2980. Fax 301-277-2467.

Notes on Contributors

Robert Albritton teaches in the political science department and social and political thought program at York University, Toronto. His publications include *A Japanese Reconstruction of Marxist Theory*, *A Japanese Approach to Stages of Capitalist Development*, a collection edited with Thomas Sekine entitled *A Japanese Approach to Political Economy*, and numerous articles on political theory, Marxist theory, and epistemology.

Alex Callinicos is a reader in politics at the University of York, England, and writes a column for *Socialist Worker*. He has written extensively on Marxist theory and on South Africa. Among his most recent books are *The Revenge of History* and *Race and Class*. A new book, *Theories and Narratives: Reflections on the Philosophy of History*, will be published by Duke University in 1995.

Jennifer Cotter is a graduate student in English at Syracuse University. She is currently involved in work covering the development of a Marxist cultural studies, paying particular attention to the development of historical materialist concepts within feminism after (post)structuralism. Her other publications include "On Feminist Pedagogy" (*Minnesota Review*) and a book review of Judith Butler's *Bodies That Matter*.

Greg Dawes teaches Latin American literature and culture at North Carolina State University. He has published articles on literary theory, Latin American poetry, and cultural studies. His first book was titled, *Aesthetics and Revolution: Nicaraguan Poetry, 1979-1990* (University of Minnesota Press). Currently he is working on a manuscript analyzing Pablo Neruda's poetry from 1936 to 1954, as well as his involvement in Popular Front politics.

Teresa L. Ebert's book, *Ludic Feminism and After* will be published by the University of Michigan Press in the Fall of 1995. Her text on Slavoj Zizek will also appear in the Fall issue of *Rethinking Marxism*. Her many essays have appeared in various journals here and abroad, including *Cultural Critique*, *Women's Review of Books*, *Poetics Today*, *Genders*. She has also completed *Patriarchal Narratives* (forthcoming from Michigan) and a collection of essays on ideology.

Colin Hay is Lecturer in Sociology at Lancaster University, UK. He is currently completing a textbook on the state entitled *Re-Stating Social and Political Change* to be published by Open University Press in 1995, as well as a co-edited collection (with Bob Jessup) entitled *Beyond the State? New Directions in State Theory* to be published by Macmillan at about the same time. He is a member of the UK Editorial *Group of Capitalism, Nature, Socialism*.

Bob Hodge has spent many years developing a materialist form of linguistics and cultural critique. Amongst the works he has written are *Language as Ideology* (1993) and *Social Semiotics* (1988), with Gunther Kress, and *Darkside of the Dream* (1991) with Vijay Mishra. He is currently setting up a new School of Humanities at the University of Western Sydney, Hawkesbury, which will initially consist of three programs: Social Analysis, Gender Studies, and Postmodern Studies.

Jorge Larrain is Professor of Social Theory, Department of Cultural Studies, University of Birmingham, UK. He was head of the department from 1988 to 1992. In 1994 he published *Ideology and Cultural Identity: Modernity and the Third World Presence* (Cambridge: Polity Press, 1994)

Paul LeBlanc is adjunct professor of history at Carlow College and author of *Lenin and the Revolutionary Party*. He has co-edited with Scott McLemee *C. L. R. James and Revolutionary Marxism*. He coordinates the "Revolutionary Studies" series for Humanities Press and is on the editorial board of *Bulletin in Defense of Marxism*.

Colin Mooers teaches in the Department of Politics at Ryerson Polytechnic University in Toronto. His published works include *The Making of Bourgeois Europe: Absolutism, Revolution, and the Rise of Capitalism in England, France, and Germany* and with Alan Sears, "'The New Social Movements' and the Withering Away of the State Theory" in *Organizing Dissent*.

Donald Morton writes on critical and cultural theory and the politics of gender and sexuality. Among his writing on contemporary sexualities are "The Politics of Queer Theory in the (Post)Modern Moment" (*Genders*, 1993) and "Birth of the Cyberqueer" (*PMLA*, 1995). His materialist anthology on homosexuality, *Queer Theory: A Lesbian and Gay Cultural Studies Reader* is forthcoming from Westview Press in 1996.

Alan Sears teaches Sociology at the University of Windsor. He has published articles on AIDS, social policy, and Marxist theory in such journals as *Critical Sociology, Journal of Historical Sociology*, and *Studies in Political Economy*.

Mas'ud Zavarzadeh is working on a book on Marxism (without prefix)